Gerhard Uhlhorn

Christian Charity in the Ancient Church

Gerhard Uhlhorn

Christian Charity in the Ancient Church

ISBN/EAN: 9783337003807

Printed in Europe, USA, Canada, Australia, Japan

Cover: Foto ©Lupo / pixelio.de

More available books at **www.hansebooks.com**

CHRISTIAN CHARITY IN THE ANCIENT CHURCH

BY

Dr. GERHARD UHLHORN
ABBOT OF LOCCUM

Translated from the German
WITH THE AUTHOR'S SANCTION

NEW YORK
CHARLES SCRIBNER'S SONS
1883

TABLE OF CONTENTS.

BOOK FIRST.

THE OLD AND THE NEW.

CHAP.		PAGE
I.	A World without Love,	2
II.	Under the Law,	44
III.	The Manifestation of Love in Christ Jesus,	56
IV.	Commencement and Foundations in the Apostolic Age,	73

BOOK SECOND.

THE AGE OF CONFLICT.

I.	Poverty and Distress,	99
II.	First Love,	120
III.	The Means for the Relief of the Poor,	141
IV.	Officials and Offices for Charity,	160
V.	The Work and its Results,	178
VI.	Obscurations,	203

BOOK THIRD.

AFTER THE VICTORY.

CHAP.		PAGE
I.	A Perishing World,	219
II.	Congregational Relief of the Poor,	246
III.	Alms,	274
IV.	Hospitals,	323
V.	Monasteries,	338
VI.	The Church the Refuge of all the Oppressed and Suffering,	361
	Notes to Book I.,	399
	Notes to Book II.,	403
	Notes to Book III.	411
	Index,	421

BOOK FIRST.

THE OLD AND THE NEW.

CHRISTIAN CHARITY IN THE ANCIENT CHURCH.

CHAPTER I.

A WORLD WITHOUT LOVE.

Our Lord calls the commandment of love which He gave to His disciples a new commandment (John xiii. 34). And such indeed it was, for the world before Christ came was a world without love. Lactantius, writing at the time when, after a struggle which had lasted for centuries, Christianity had at length obtained the upper hand, lays great emphasis upon this difference between the Christian and the heathen world, saying: "Compassion and humanity are virtues peculiar to the righteous and to the worshippers of God. Philosophy teaches us nothing of them."[1] And should this witness, as coming from one who was himself a Christian, appear suspicious, there is still quite trustworthy evidence in the astonishment with which the heathen regarded the charitableness of the Christians, which seemed so strange to them; and a still stronger witness may be seen in the endeavour of the Emperor Julian to introduce into heathendom this new thing, which he could not but recognise as a peculiarity of Christianity.

And yet the opinion as to the world before the Christian era, that it was a world without love, requires some explanation, and in a certain sense some modification as well. Of isolated acts springing from natural pity there was never any want. There was at all times a gift ready for the beggar, and that even after the idea that beggars and those in distress were under the special protection of the gods, had long lost its force. In Rome and in the other great towns numerous beggars were to be found sitting at the corners of the streets, on the bridges, before the gates of the temples, and in general wherever the traffic was most lively; and the passers-by readily threw them some small coin, whilst the beggars acknowledged the gift with a blessing in the name of some one or other of the gods. Begging had never been prohibited in the Roman Empire; the first edict against it proceeded from a Christian Emperor. And, indeed, how could men see in begging a punishable offence, so long as they did not see that in work there lay a duty to be performed by all? Towards travellers, those who had been wrecked at sea, and all others in distress, the general attitude was one of generosity; and in great calamities there was never a lack of assistance and relief even from distant quarters. When, in the reign of Nero, the great amphitheatre at Fidenæ fell in and buried beneath its ruins 50,000 men, the wealthy Romans despatched physicians and all kinds of medical appliances to the scene of the disaster, and received the wounded into their houses.[2] At the eruption of Vesuvius, in the year 79 A.D., when Herculaneum and Pompeii were overwhelmed, the readiness to relieve the distress was universal. But it is remarkable that upon the whole we hear of but few similar instances; and still more remarkable are the occasional expressions of opinion on the subject. "Canst thou by any means condescend so far as that the poor shall not appear to thee loathsome?" asks Quinctilian; and in one of the plays of Plautus we meet with the following, which is surely the expression of the general sentiment: "He does the beggar but a bad service who gives him meat and drink; for what he gives is lost, and the life of the poor is but prolonged to their own misery."[3] Moreover, in however great abundance isolated acts of compassion may have been done, the main point is this, that there is no trace whatever of any organized charity. It is not that here and there Christians gave gifts to the poor, or that they here and there assisted those in distress: the new thing, the thing hitherto unknown in the world, was rather that in the Christian communities there was organized a regular system of charity, designed not only to relieve the distress of the poor for the moment, but also to war against poverty itself, and to suffer no one to be oppressed by want. And what in the old world was done with regard to this matter, either by the State or from the resources of individuals, is of quite a different character. A special oversight of the poor, such as we are accustomed to, was at no time and at no place known to the ancient world.

A good deal was indeed done. When Boeckh[4] says: "Compassion is no Hellenic virtue," we assent to what he says, and must even add to his statement this, that it is still less a Roman virtue. But we must not forget that liberality was one of the virtues exercised in the ancient world in the fullest measure. Men gave generously to their friends, to their relatives, and to their guests. The giving of presents was much more customary than it is amongst us. A man displayed his liberality towards his native city, his fellow-citizens, or his fellow-members in the guild or club to which he belonged, or of which he was chosen as patron. To the latter office, indeed, he was elected avowedly with an eye to the liberal donations which were expected from him. What abundance of donations of all kinds is revealed to us by inscriptions! Here one man builds for his native city a new theatre, or a house for gladiatorial shows, rebuilds the ruined walls, or constructs a new road, aqueduct, or fountain. Another makes it his care to see that grain shall always be sold at a low price, or gives corn, wine, and oil to be distributed; provides games and banquets for his fellow-citizens; erects baths where one may bathe for nothing, and in many cases also receive oil for anointing oneself gratis. He founds a library, or whatever else it may be. No man of means, who would worthily fill his position in the State or in his native town, can absolve himself from the duty of voluntarily giving up a share of his wealth for the benefit of his fellow-citizens, or for the public weal. And this spirit of liberality extends even beyond the grave. Legacies and testamentary endowments are frequent, and require special legislation. It is customary to give legacies to one's friends, and to the higher officials. Frequently we read of stipulations in wills, in accordance with which on an appointed day, usually the birthday of the testator, a banquet is partaken of at his grave, and sums of money are distributed amongst those present. The custom amongst the Romans, of honouring the dead by commemorating their acts of generosity in the inscriptions on their tombstones, gives us a glimpse of an abundance of donations and endowments which by no means falls behind anything of the same kind done in our own day. And all this at last found its climax in the liberal gifts of the Emperor and of the State, where it becomes a case of dealing with millions.

No doubt this kind of liberality had in some measure the same effect as that of subsidies for the relief of the poor. It was always of assistance to those of small means, that they should obtain bread at a cheap rate, or grain as a gift, or that they should receive a share in the distribution of gifts of money. But it was, for all that, something quite different from a system of poor relief. Liberality is the heathen virtue which corresponds to the compassionate love, the *caritas* of Christianity; but it is just as different from that love as is heathendom itself from Christianity. The compassionate love of the Christian looks at necessity as the first thing; it cares not to inquire who the needy man may be in other respects, but is rather concerned to know whether he be really in distress. In the case of liberality, necessity falls altogether into the background. Presents are made and given, not with a view to the relief of distress, but rather with an eye to pleasing the recipient; and even in cases where the necessaries of daily life constitute the substance of the gift, no inquiry is made into the needs of individuals. The citizen receives his share, even although he has no need of it; the non-citizen remains shut out, however great his necessities may be. For the most part, the presents are limited to the circle of the citizens; and where they go beyond this limit, where strangers also have a share in the distribution of corn, and a place at the banquets, or where a bath stands free and open for strangers and travellers, this is due not to any regard for their possible wants, but simply to a desire to enhance the splendour of the liberality. It is noteworthy that wherever any proportion in the gifts is mentioned, it is stipulated, either that all shall receive the same amount, or that the higher personages, such as the municipal officers, or the presidents of the guilds, shall receive double or threefold,[5] being thus in the inverse ratio of the necessities of the case; for those obtained the most who should properly have received least, as being the least in need of the gift. It is noteworthy, further, that every one accepts his share without hesitation, even when he does not stand in need of it. Men were then by no means so dubious about accepting gifts as they are now-a-days. Supposing that in our time, at the celebration of the coming of age of some heir, every one present was presented with a small gift of money, we should hesitate within ourselves as to whether we should accept it. In those days every one accepted it. Hence it came to pass that even well-to-do men accepted their share in the distribution of grain, or allowed their freedmen to fetch it away in their stead; indeed, they even took their share of the money distributed to the guests in the more distinguished men's houses. It was never for a moment considered as an alms, and indeed it was not such. The fundamental distinction between the ancient *liberalitas* and the Christian *caritas* lies in this, that the latter always keeps in view the welfare of the poor and needy; to help them is its only object; whereas the Roman, who exercises the virtue of liberality, considers in reality himself alone (I do not mean always in a bad sense), and exercises his liberality as a bribe wherewith to win the favours of the multitude. Nor does he always exercise it in the spirit of common vanity, but in order that it may be the means of displaying and increasing the splendour of his name, of his position, and of his house, or, what he considered of just as much importance, the splendours of his native city, and of the municipal community. Christian charity is self-denying; heathen *liberalitas* is at bottom self-seeking, even although personal selfishness be limited by the interests of the commonwealth, for the sake of which Greek and Roman alike were at all times prepared to make a sacrifice.

That a sense of one's duty to the poor, such as has been introduced by the Christian *caritas*, could not grow up out of the heathen *liberalitas*, is sufficiently clear. One must rather say that we find a number of regulations, not in the least connected with it; but in the development of these we can find traces of a stream as it were flowing out from heathendom over this tract of life, towards the tide of advancing Christianity.

The nearest approach to an actual system of poor relief seems to be what was done in Athens for necessitous citizens. As a rule, the Greek is by natural disposition more inclined to benevolence than the Roman, in whose characteristic traits one finds a certain sort of meanness, not to say avarice; whence he is colder and more selfish than the Greek. At Athens, those who through bodily weakness or infirmity were unable to gain their own livelihood, such as the blind, the lame, and the crippled, received a daily subsidy of two *oboli*. This subsidy was by law restricted to those whose means amounted to less than three *minæ*. The vote for it depended upon the popular will. Inquiry into each individual case rested with the Council of the Five Hundred.[6] The orphans of citizens who had fallen in war were brought up at the expense of the State—in the case of boys till they were eighteen years old, at which age they were dismissed fully equipped. And orphans in general were treated with special leniency, their property not being liable to any property-tax.⁷ All this is peculiar to Athens, and is not found elsewhere. And hence in old times Athens had this to her credit, that no one of her citizens ever lacked the necessities of life, or brought shame upon the State by begging from visitors.⁸ Later on, when Athens sank into a wild democracy, it became the practice of the popular leaders to flatter and cajole the sovereign rabble by distributing amongst it by way of gift the State moneys. Thus Themistocles divided the revenues drawn from working the mines. Next came the moneys for the theatres, the so-called *Theorikai* ⁹—a true curse of Athens. Each citizen received two *oboli* as entrance money to the theatre. For attending the popular assemblies he was paid three *oboli*, and he also received as much, as pay for sitting in the courts of justice; and as every day about one-third of the people sat in the courts, the consequence was that they desisted from work more and more, that they fell lower both in economy and in morals, and thus, when the disastrous issue of the Peloponnesian war put an end to her supremacy, Athens, once so flourishing and prosperous, sank into the lowest poverty.

What was given to the people at Athens at the cost of the State was altogether insignificant compared with what was distributed at Rome. While in the case of the former we have to deal with the comparatively small sums exacted by the Athenians from their allies, in the case of the latter we have to deal with the spoils of a conquered world, their share of which was received by the people in the shape of distributions of money, *Congiaria*, banquets, and theatrical displays.

The providing of the city of Rome with corn, the

Annona, is one of the greatest achievements ever accomplished by statesmanship. The grain was partly collected from the various provinces, partly bought up by the State, and was brought to Rome by a fleet of vessels specially set aside for the purpose; once there, it was stored up in granaries, and afterwards distributed. It was the duty of a whole host of officials to exercise the necessary foresight in providing grain for feeding the metropolis of the world; a famine in Rome would have shattered the whole Empire. In the earlier times it was thought sufficient if the price of grain was maintained at a low rate. Caius Gracchus first of all ordained that the Roman bushel of wheat should be sold to citizens at 5 *as*, which was far under cost price; later on, Clodius procured an enactment whereby a certain quantity was distributed gratis. The consequence was that impoverished citizens flocked to Rome in crowds. Whereas in the year 73 before Christ the price of the grain distributed in Rome amounted to ten million sesterces (£87,700), in the year 46 after Christ it had already amounted to nearly seventy-seven million sesterces (£675,000). Cæsar found that there were 320,000 men who received this grant of corn; he reduced the number to 150,000, and decreed that this should never be exceeded. Only upon the occurrence of vacancies through death could new names be added to the list. Soon afterwards, however, Augustus found that the number on the list had again increased, and he reduced it to 200,000, which appears to have remained the normal number thereafter. The only necessary conditions upon which participation in the distribution rested were Roman citizenship and residence in Rome. In no case was inquiry made into the question of deserving it or not. Nor do the well-to-do appear to have been excluded by law; in order, however, to be put on the list, it was necessary to make application; and the wealthy, at any rate in later times, would not have made this application. On this account those who obtained grants of corn were often known as the poor.[10] Whoever had his name upon the list received a ticket (*tessera*), which entitled him to draw from the granaries five bushels monthly. In addition to this, there were distributions every now and then of oil, salt, meat, and even of clothing. From the time of Septimius Severus oil was regularly given out.[11] Aurelian added pork, and wished to have wine distributed also; but from this latter purpose he desisted on representations being made to him by the *præfectus prætorii* that in that case the people would soon be clamouring for roast fowls.[12] The distribution of grain *in natura* probably came to an end under Alexander Severus. It is not quite clear whether it was at once succeeded by the distribution of bread. It is very possible that during the troublous times the distribution may have ceased altogether for some years. From the time of Aurelian[13] onwards bread was given out instead of corn, each man receiving two pounds of bread a day (*panis gradilis*). This distribution of bread lasted on into the last year of the Empire. Moreover, Trajan had founded in Rome a guild of bakers, who were under the superintendence of the officers of the Annona, and who obtained corn from the public granaries at a very cheap rate, but who were bound in return for this privilege to bake good and cheap bread.[14]

The motives which called into existence this practice of distributing grain were not by any means of a charitable, but, on the contrary, of a purely political nature. Gracchus and Clodius hoped to win over the people by their corn laws. And both Cæsar and Augustus were influenced by political motives when they directed special attention to this branch of the government. Knowing as they did that hunger has at all times been a most powerful agent in promoting revolution, they wished to make the people as content as possible under their loss of liberty. But we must not on that account close our eyes to the fact that such regulations as those for restricting the number of participants, and the confining of them to those citizens who made application, bear somewhat of a different character. It became in the course of the Empire a sort of system of poor relief, though a very undesirable and one-sided one. But it is, for all that, one of those symptoms from which we can learn that something new was beginning to make itself felt even within the confines of heathenism itself.[15]

Nor were the distributions of grain the only way in which the people received their share of the spoils of the conquered world. Of no less importance were the *largesses* of the emperors, the *Congiaria* and the donations. At every accession to the throne, at the celebrations of the fifth or tenth years of a reign, on the occasion of every joyful event in the reigning family, such as a birth, or a triumph, and even from the will of the dead emperor, the people expected and received a *largesse*. This differed both as to the amount and as to the circle of those who received it. Sixty or one hundred denarii (£2 to £3, 10s.) to each was considered little. Hadrian gave 1000 (£35), Septimius Severus 1100 (£38, 10s.), Gallienus 1250 (£43, 15s.). As a rule, the *Congiarium* was given to the recipients of the grain only, but not infrequently the number of those who received it was much greater. A tolerably reliable calculation tells us that from the accession of Nero to the death of Septimius Severus there was distributed annually in this way, on the average, about £300,000.[16] Moreover, there were at the same time public banquets and games. On the occasion of Cæsar's triumph, the people feasted at 22,000 tables; Chian and Falernian ran in rivers, and the people had for once an opportunity of learning the flavour of the much-famed Muranian wine.[17] So also, in connection with the games in the circus, which, under Marcus Aurelius, were provided for the people on 135 days in the year, there were frequently presents made to the spectators. Under the porticos of the theatre was laid out merchandise of all sorts, which at the close of the play was abandoned to be scrambled for by the people. Or money and victuals were thrown amongst the people, or sometimes lottery tickets by which one might win a prize. Thus Nero scattered 1000 lottery tickets, and those who obtained them could win, according to the luck with which they were favoured, corn, money, foreign birds, horses, even ships and landed properties.[18]

The sums which were thus expended were enormous. Even when we appraise the games and the other things in connection with them at a very low rate, we are below the mark rather than above it when we reckon the expenditure at about £1,500,000 annually. So much as this was swallowed up by the one city of Rome, which could not at that time have had more than about one and a half million inhabitants. And what was accomplished by this expenditure? Not even the support of the 200,000 recipients of grain. For five bushels per month were not sufficient for one family. And beyond this nothing was done. There were no poorhouses, no hospitals. Lazarettos in the Roman Empire were curiously enough known as places for soldiers and slaves only. Antoninus Pius indeed tells us that he had built beside the temple of the Epidaurian Æsculapius a building for the reception of the sick. But this was not a hospital. It was rather a kind of hostelry for those who had come to pray to the god on account of their sickness.[19] There was a total want of any care for widows and orphans; and for those who were not citizens there was, as a rule, no help whatever. At the utmost, there fell to them a very little when there happened to be a surplus of grain. The worst feature, however, of this system was its demoralizing influence. A gift springing from true charity elevates him who receives it, such is the power of the love which underlies it. Those fragments of the spoils of the conquered world which were thrown to the people in this way could only corrupt them. The Roman populace became more and more a work-hating, pleasure-seeking crowd, which cheered every new accessor to power in the hopes of new largesse, and which even went out to meet the matricide Nero, when, after that frightful crime, he entered Rome clad in white garments and adorned with wreaths. In no other way than by contemplating the gifts and largesse showered upon the Roman people in such stupendous abundance, can we adequately perceive how that thing was wanting in the old world which alone could lend value to these gifts and make them fruitful. They had not charity.

The provincial towns endeavoured to be in all things copies of Rome. In the liberality which was exercised at Rome they had indeed no share; on the contrary, they were obliged to contribute in order to make that liberality possible. It was only in the case of extraordinary misfortunes that the emperors caused grain to be distributed amongst them also, as, for instance, Tiberius among the Asiatic towns overwhelmed by earthquake, or Marcus Aurelius amongst the Etrurian towns in the time of famine.[20] But as the system of communal government grew up, equal care was taken, although on a smaller scale, to provide abundant and cheap supplies of grain for the provincial towns also. And in consequence of the ever active local patriotism, there were not wanting persons who from their private means gave grain, oil, and even money for distribution. Here, also, it was the custom of the ædiles and prætors, who stood at the head of the State government, for the decemvirs, who occupied in the municipal towns the same position as the Senate at Rome, to give the people banquets and games on the occasion of their election. The president of the *Augustales*, to which guilds the wealthy freedmen had the right of entry—although offices of State were closed against them—were also expected to show their open-handedness; and when a statue was decreed to some prominent man, some wealthy member of the State community, he invariably acknowleged the honour by providing a banquet for the people, or even by giving to each man a money-present.[21] What happened at Rome was repeated in the provinces, only on a smaller scale.

Some, however, while they admit that all this organization was in no true sense of the term charitable, have endeavoured to find a system of poor relief, or, at any rate, something analogous to it, in two other institutions which were an important feature of the social life of the time, the planting of colonies and the system of clientage. The supposition is in both cases without foundation. The colonies were never a charitable institution: they were planted from motives quite apart from any consideration for the welfare of the poor. In the heyday of the Republic they were of use in securing the possession of conquered territory, and later on, after the civil wars, they served to keep in check and to reward the disbanded soldiery. Salla divided amongst his soldiers lands in Italy, the former owners of which had been ejected by force. After the battle of Philippi there were 170,000 men for whom some provision had to be made. In order to accomplish this, possession was taken, under the form of compulsory sale (the purchase money, however, was never paid), of a number of districts, in addition to the properties of proscribed persons. Once driven out of their possessions, the *quondam* owners swelled the numbers of the *proletariat* at Rome; the veterans had no inclination for agriculture, and very soon resold their farms. The consequence was, accordingly, that the possessions of the great landed proprietors, the *Latifundi*, were increased; and the unpropertied classes were increased at the same time. Augustus entertained at one time the idea of transporting into foreign colonies 80,000 poor citizens, but the plan was never carried into effect. So that here also we find that the intention was not really one of providing for the poor, but rather of removing from Rome a restless and hence dangerous class of the population.

Still less was it the intention of the great men of Rome, when they assembled around them crowds of clients, to do anything in the way of relieving necessity; although indeed many a one, who would otherwise have been destitute, might find in the system a chance of some means of subsistence however small. The *clientela*, which was originally a relationship of piety and duty, had already in the days of the Empire sunk into a system of mercenary service. The throng of clients came in the morning to greet the great noble, and accompany him when he went out; in short, they contributed generally to the pomp of the family. In return for this they received the *sportula*. This consisted in earlier times of a banquet; but in later times it took the form of a pecuniary reward, amounting to about fifteen pence per diem. On the occasion of great festivities they were also bidden to a banquet; but in this case they were generally very poorly treated. The food they received was inferior to that served to the other guests; and while the master drank Falernian wine, they had to content themselves with the cheaper brands. On the whole, they eked out but a scanty subsistence. The sum which they received annually was insufficient for their needs, and they had to bestir themselves greatly, in order that by special acts of service they might obtain here and there a supplementary gift. Moreover, there were in Rome many thousands of them. The Roman of that day would much rather busy himself as a beggar and sycophant in the hall of some great man, than stick to any ordinary and regular work.

The case is somewhat different when we come to the so-called *alimentationes*, or endowments for the education of poor children.[22] We find them from the time of Nerva onwards, and Trajan, in particular, took a special interest in them. Antoninus Pius founded such an institution for girls in memory of his wife Faustina (*puellæ Faustinianæ*), Septimius Severus one for boys and girls in memory of Julia Mammæa (*pueri puellæque Mammæani*). The capital devoted to this purpose was invested in landed property at a moderate rate of interest, and with the income derived from this source boys and girls, for the most part free-born alone, were maintained and educated. One of these foundations, that of Beleja in Upper Italy, possessed a capital of 1,044,000 HS. (£9156), which at 5 per cent. interest yielded an income of 52,200 HS. This sum provided for 281 children (245 legitimate boys, 34 legitimate girls, and also two illegitimate children, one boy and one girl). The boys received 16 HS. (3s.) and the girls 12 HS. (2s. 2d.) per month. In the case of the former this subsidy continued till the age of eighteen, in that of the latter to the age of fourteen. In later days similar foundations were scattered over the whole of Italy. They were under their own officers, and their operation was confined to certain districts. They must also have been very numerous, for we find them even outside Italy. Thus there was in Spain the foundation of the *pueri Juncini;*[23] and in the African colony of Cirta Sicca, in the reigns of Antoninus Pius, every one contributed a certain sum. With the proceeds of these contributions 300 boys and 200 girls were educated. There was expended annually for the boys 30 denarii (20s.) and for the girls 24 den. (17s.). The ages of the boys ranged from three to fifteen, and of the girls from three to twelve years. The number was always kept at its highest. The children of Inquilini might be elected as well as the children of citizens.[24]

The motives for making these foundations also were to a large extent of a merely political nature. The overwhelming population of Italy no doubt drew the attention of the Emperor to the rising generation, and the unmistakeable preference given to the boys, as seen from the figures mentioned above, seems to indicate that he had an eye to the provision of recruits for his legions.

But that the endowments were not due to political motives entirely, but sprung in some measure from motives of humanity as well, is shown not only by the fact that girls also had a share in their benefits, but also by the Emperors founding institutions of this sort in honour of their wives, and still more by the fact that a great many of them were the deeds of private individuals. Pliny[25] presents to the town of Comum 500,000 HS. (£4385) as an endowment for free-born boys and girls, and increases the sum by his will by 300,000 HS. (£2630). A wealthy lady, Macrina, bequeathed one million for the same purpose;[26] and even more significant is the already mentioned endowment, of which the inscription found in Spain gives us information. A certain Fabia bequeathed to the *pueri Juncini* and the *puellæ* (the name is wanting in the inscription) 50,000 HS. (£440). The interest at 6 per cent., 3000 HS. (£26), was to be distributed twice a year, on her husband's birthday and on her own. The boys received each 30 HS. (5s. 6d.), the girls each 40 HS. (7s.). If the money was not sufficient for this, the girls were to receive only 30 HS. each; if there was any surplus, it was to be divided in the same proportions. Now in this case, in the fact that the girls were more liberally treated than the boys, we have undoubted evidence of the humane character of the foundation. How very different were the ideas of the ancient world which they put into execution in making foundations of this kind! how meanly were boys and girls alike treated! Here also one seems to perceive that a new influence was making its way. The picture of Trajan which has been preserved to us, of the Emperor in the midst of the children for whom he provided, is an important symptom of that current flowing out from the midst of heathendom towards the advancing flood of Christendom.

We shall notice this current still more distinctly if we turn our attention to the life of the numerous societies (*collegia*) which played so important a part in the whole social life of the imperial age. In these we find for the first time something analogous to Christian charity, or if that is perhaps saying too much, it is in them that the above-mentioned current approaches most nearly to Christianity, and that altogether apart from the importance which the *collegia* also possess in that they laid down the legal form and order for so much in the life of the Christian communities, and in especial for Christian charity.[27]

Even in Greece there were societies of every kind, and with the most diverse objects. If a few young people wished to hold a merry feast, or to celebrate some festivity, or if they designed to accomplish some object through bribery for which a considerable sum of money was requisite, they formed a "society" (*eranos*), and provided the requisite money by contribution. Tradesmen also formed societies; and they were also instituted for purposes of mutual support. If one of their members fell into difficulties, the society made him an advance, which he, when he had retrieved his position, repaid.[28] In Rome, from an early date, we find guilds of tradesmen and societies for other purposes, especially for the common worship of some god or other. The Republic allowed them to do as they pleased, and only restrained them from outrageous excesses. In the eyes of the Emperors the *collegia* were suspicious, since they might so easily become the seats of conspiracies. For this reason the majority of them were suppressed, and the institution of new ones made dependent upon the permission of the Senate. By a decree of the Senate, however, colleges of the humbler classes (*collegia tenuiorum* [29]) were permitted. Their object was, by a monthly subscription of their members (*stips menstrua*), to form a treasury (*arca*), out of which, on the death of a member, the expenses of his burial might be defrayed. Thus they were burial funds. The recognition which was extended to them was united with the condition that they should meet only once a month, and should entertain no other aim than that which had been appointed them. In spite of this strict legislation the *collegia* increased, and the Government allowed them to remain unmolested so long as they appeared harmless. Alexander Severus gave charters to all *collegia* for art or business, and regulated their legal position. From that time onwards they multiplied in the greatest abundance, especially when the reception into the Roman citizenship by Caracalla of all the provincial citizens empowered these also to form themselves into societies. Not only merchants of different branches, artisans of every kind, workers in wool, makers of purple, shoemakers, fishermen, shipbuilders, but even compatriots united as such, the provincials who lived in Rome, and the Romans who lived in the province. The period was one in which there was a great necessity for co-operation; and especially was this felt among the lower classes, for whom the *collegia* were the principal means of bettering their condition and of enabling them to hold up their heads in a society so exclusively aristocratic. In addition to this, there was the necessity for pleasant social intercourse. All *collegia* were at once pleasant meeting-places; indeed, many of them appear to have had no other aim than that of promoting social intercourse. The constitution of the guilds was ordered after the pattern of the constitution of the *municipium*. At the head stood the *magistri* or curators, who were elected annually. From amongst the higher classes the guilds sought to procure patrons, mainly with a view to having the honour thus conferred rewarded by liberal gifts, which constituted one of the chief sources of the society's income. While the poorer societies held their meetings in some tavern or other, the more wealthy possessed their own meeting-house (*schola*), with an assembly and eating-hall, and also with a chapel, or at least an altar. For all had alike some religious background, and worshipped as their protector some one or other of the gods, the special worship of whom constituted one of their objects.

There is nothing in the guilds which reaches to the height of actual charity, and this is a sure sign of how far distant that was from the ideas of the heathen world. Tertullian expressly lays weight on the fact that in Christian communities the collected contributions, which in other respects he treats as parallel to the subscriptions of the guilds, were spent not in gluttony and in drunkenness, but in the relief of the poor.[30] But in many of the guilds mutual support was one of the objects for the promotion of which they had been formed. In the first place, we must remember that, as has been mentioned above, they frequently formed burial funds. Such a guild was, for instance, that of the worshippers of Diana and Antinous (*cultores Dianæ et Antinoi*), with the statutes of which we are familiar through an inscription of the year 136.[31] There belonged to it people of the poorer ranks, freedmen and slaves. Every member paid on entry 100 HS (12s. 6d.), and thereafter as a regular monthly subscription 5 asses (about 20d.). On the death of a member there were paid for the costs of his burial 300 HS. (54s.), whereof 50 HS. (about 9s.) were distributed amongst those members of the guild who were present at the interment. In the event of the dead man having no relatives, the arrangements for the funeral were looked after by the society. Mention is also made of common banquets, at which no doubt the slaves would also be present, and would thus in this circle of friends feel themselves free for at least a few hours at a time. If a slave were manumitted, he was obliged, in accordance with the regulations, to provide an amphora of wine, with which his manumission was celebrated by the others. Mutual funds of other kinds are also to be found. In the Legio III. Aug. there was a schola of 36 persons.[32] The candidate paid on admission 750 den. (£26), and also gave a current subscription. In return he received from the chest, in the event of his requiring to travel over the sea, a contribution towards his travelling expenses of 200 den. (£7); a horseman, of 500 den. (£15), and, if necessary, a contribution of 500 den. towards the expenses of outfit; finally, on his death the costs of his burial were defrayed. Whoever was honourably discharged as a veteran, received on his departure 6000 HS. (£52).

Many of these societies collected in the course of time considerable wealth, especially from the presents or endowments made by their patrons or other leading members. Houses, pieces of land, capital sums were either presented or bequeathed to them, in order that, on appointed days, a *sportula*, a distribution of bread, wine, or money, might be made amongst their members. Especially worthy of notice are the endowments in memory of the dead, as they clearly are the origin of those important kinds of memorials so common in the Church a little later on. It was universally the custom to arrange for one's burial and for one's memory after death. Rich men built mausoleums with chapels, altars, and banqueting-halls, sometimes also with gardens, or even wide-reaching parks. Care was also taken that there should always be those who would think of the dead, and show respect to his memory, especially by bringing wreaths on his birthday, kindling lamps, offering sacrifice, and holding banquets. With this in view capital sums were set aside; and in order to make the endowment more secure, and to obtain the punctual performance of the stipulations in the will, men gladly availed themselves of public bodies, and especially of the guilds. Money and landed property was bequeathed to them, and they were held bound, in accordance with the conditions, to celebrate the anniversaries of the deceased with sacrifices, wreaths, banquets, and distributions of money. In the event of a guild not doing its duty there was a fixed penalty,[33] or it was even stipulated that the money should pass to some other corporation.[34] In the year 149 a certain Sextus Fadius bequeathed to the guild of the *Fabres Narbonenses* 16,000 HS. (£140), in order that the interest might be distributed amongst the visitors and guests on his birthday.[35] Another bequeaths 100,000 HS. (£870), that out of the proceeds there might be provided at his grave each year a banquet for at least twelve men. The duty of seeing to this was confided to the guild of the *Centenarii*.[36] The number of guests is, for the most part, distinctly mentioned, and directions given for the filling up of vacancies caused by death.[37] Moreover, minute directions are frequently laid down.

For instance, one man directs that on his birthday his statue is to be anointed, and crowned with wreaths, and that two wax candles are to be lighted in front of it. Before the pedestal of the statue there was to be, from the third hour onwards, a distribution to the decuriones of a *sportula*.[38] Again, a lady named Valeria bequeaths to the guild of the *Fabres Centenarii* a certain sum, stipulating that out of the proceeds of it there should be held every year on her birthday a banquet to cost 200 den., and that 200 den. should be given away in her memory. Her husband presents to the *Schola Vexillariorum* 30,000 IIS., out of which 250 den. were to be devoted to a banquet, and 250 den. given away as a *sportula* amongst those present.[39] In many cases also the proportions in which the distributions are to be made are fixed, and these are always so arranged that the officials of the society receive more according to their rank. Thus a president of the Augustales bequeaths 100,000 IIS. (£870). The interest is to be divided on his birthday as a *sportula*; the presidents are to receive 4 den. (3s.), the others 3 den. (2s. 3d.), but always only those who are present. If a smaller number should come forward, then those who had appeared were to receive a proportionately larger sum.[40] Salvia Marcellina bequeathed in memory of her husband, who had been overseer of the imperial tablets, the sum of 50,000 IIS. (£438) to the college of Æsculapius and Hygeia. Out of the interest a *sportula* was to be distributed twice a year; the higher officials of the guild were to receive 6 denarii each and 8 jars of wine, the lower officials 4 denarii and 6 jars of wine, and the ordinary members 2 denarii and 3 jars of wine. This was in addition to three loaves to each.[41] In this case again the proportion of the shares shows that we are in no sense dealing with charity. Necessity is not regarded: those who are to all appearances the least necessitous are to receive the most. The object, moreover, of the giver is not to aid the poor, but to honour the memory of herself and her relatives, or at least to procure a gratification for the members of the guild. Still, no doubt, the *sportula* and the banquet, and the distributed bread and wine, might be of service to many a one in distress, and thus although we have no actual charity before us, still we have something analogous to it, something which bears the same relation to Christian charity as does the ancient *liberalitas* to the Christian *caritas*; and in any case, the constitution of these guilds, and the kind of life developed within them, have been of the greatest importance in the history of Christian charity and its development.

Certainly it was the case that these guilds laid down the recognised forms in accordance with which, when once the power of true love began to stir the Christian communities, their charity was to be exercised. Just as in the guilds there was a monthly subscription collected, so also were there subscriptions in the Christian communities: the latter also had an *arca*, and it is remarkable that Tertullian, in speaking of collections for the benefit of the poor, makes use of expressions which had acquired a technical significance in the guilds. Just in the same way as the heathen made endowments in memory of the dead (*ad memoriam*), so do we find hereafter within the Church innumerable memorial-foundations; the only difference is this, that the object of the latter is the relief of the poor. In the former case, and this is important, the guilds cherished the spirit of co operation amongst the lower classes, and the idea of brotherliness. What ties of family and alliances of race were to the higher classes, the guilds were to the lower. Nor must we omit to notice that the members of the guilds called one another brothers and sisters;[42] that their presidents and presidentesses were known as fathers and mothers; and that even in the case of the dead in the inscriptions on the tombs, whilst in earlier times it had been written that they were affectionate towards their friends, it was now recorded that they had proved themselves affectionate towards their guilds.[43] All this is, as it were, a shadow of love and charity; and here again we may recognise traces of that current which flowed out from the midst of heathenism to meet the advancing tide of Christianity. What an elevating thought it must have been to the artisan, excluded from all offices in the State or the municipality, from all priestly guilds and posts of honour, that in his own guild at least he was of some importance, and might there attain to office and honour! And what a boon it must have been to the slave that there at least he was treated as a man! We must try to picture to ourselves the extremely oppressed condition of the lower classes in this aristocratic world, if we would rightly appreciate what the guilds were in their eyes, and understand how it was that they cherished them so zealously.

But we have not yet touched upon the point of chief importance. This lies first of all in the fact that it is in the guilds that we find in heathenism for the first time anything approaching to the life of a Christian community. Indeed, this matter deserves careful consideration. One of the main causes why, in the ancient world, they never arrived at true charity, at true care for the poor, is that the spirit of community, which was its true prop, was wanting. In the course of this sketch we shall have frequent opportunities of observing in how very close dependence upon the rise and fall of the communal life has been the rise and fall of charity. To the ancient world the idea of the community was quite a strange one. Robbertus, in a passage in his treatise on the Roman taxes,⁴⁴ remarks that we can speak first of a community only after Christianity had formed such, and that it is exactly in this that one of the strongest influences of Christianity upon the general social development of mankind lies. In the ancient world there was no political community. Above the family there rises immediately the State, and even the Roman Empire is but a union of States. And just as little do we find in the ancient world religious communities or communities for worship. We are only too apt, when considering the appearance of Christianity, involuntarily to think that there was in the Christian worship something similiar to the heathen, as if there had been in the latter case any community for worship at all. But this is altogether a mistake. The heathen temple is not the place of meeting of any community for worship like the Christian Church: it is the house of the god, which was never entered by the people, but only by the priests. The altar stands in front of the temple, and the assembled people take no share whatever in the worship of the god. They look on at the sacrifice in silence. "*Favete linguis*" was cried out at the beginning of the sacrifice, and a flute-player used to play during the sacred ceremony in order to drown any inopportune word which might, in accordance with the belief of the Romans, be so easily converted into an evil omen. As a rule, the presence of the people at these acts of ceremonial worship was quite a matter of indifference. The State made the prescribed sacrifices by means of the priests in the presence of the officials, who, in conformity with the law, were obliged to stand by during the ceremony. If the people were present, it was only as spectators, just as they were at the games. The utmost that was permitted to them was, as for instance at sacrifices for the Emperor, to make private offerings afterwards, or to throw incense about.

It is abundantly evident from this that the worship afforded no opportunity for or inducement to charity. The giving of alms is no part of it. Certainly it was in several temples the custom to make a present (*stips*) to the god; but this went to the temple, or was in some cases thrown into sacred fountains or lakes. The sin-offerings, *piacula*, required by the indwelling superstition of the Romans were innumerable; as, for instance, at any place which had been struck by lightning, where unlucky birds had been seen passing, or where some bad omen or other had come true. Men made vows to ward off evil, or to secure the good-will of the gods; but the vows had reference to presents, grand sacrifices, games, etc., never to alms.[45] Connected with the worship there were banquets, either recurring regularly or held upon special occasions, and especially for warding off some evil fortune or other, in which case the costs were defrayed by subscriptions; but these were gluttonous banquets of priestly colleges, such as the Salii or the Arvales, which were notorious for their accompanying luxury, or they were the banquets of citizens; poor people were never fed at them. I only find one quite isolated instance of distributing alms in the worship of Ceres, who, moreover, is not one of the old Roman deities, but was introduced first of all in the year 258, in accordance with the requisition of the Sibylline books. The temple of Ceres was under the protection of the Ædiles, and the fines which were recovered by them were given to the temple. Here they were partly expended in offerings and upon statues, but partly also in distributing bread to the poor.[46]

The case of the worship of the *gentes* and the *collegia*, and of the worship of foreign gods, differs from that of the public or State worship. The members of the *gens* or of the *collegium* were bound to be present at the recognised sacrifices of the *gens* or *collegium* on appointed days and at appointed places, and the *schola* of the guild is much more analogous to the Christian Church than the temple of the god. And especially did the societies of foreigners, who united for the worship of some of their native gods in Rome or one of the provincial towns, bear a certain resemblance to the Christian community formed for the worship of God in Christ. To take only one example, there was in Puteoli a society of Syrian merchants who had united for the purpose of worshipping the Jupiter of Heliopolis. While the official temples of the State divinities were richly endowed, societies of this kind must necessarily have of themselves borne the cost of their worship, which must therefore have been defrayed by means of subscriptions amongst their members. Here, then, we have already a kind of community which collected subscriptions for purposes of worship, a thing which was only done in the official worship of Rome in the case of the worship of Apollo, and on a few isolated occasions where we have to do with exceptional ceremonies by way of expiation for sin, such as, for instance, the *Lectisternium*.[47]

Of a *stips* being collected for generous purposes I can

find no instance, but many for the purpose of conferring honours. Thus the people contributed a sextans each to defray the expenses of the funeral of Menenius Agrippa, and on the death of Valerius Poplicola every one threw a quadrans into the house of the consul, in order that his obsequies might be celebrated with greater pomp by means of the money thus collected.[48] Very frequently statues of distinguished men were erected by voluntary subscription. But the man so honoured did not come best off, as he generally displayed his liberality by defraying the cost of it himself.[49] But that a *stips* should be collected to feed the hungry or to clothe the naked was a thing to which their religion did not point, an idea which did not enter into the popular mind. It was only when first the religion of love appeared in Christianity, when first the crowds of men who had believed on Christ formed themselves into real communities, of which the societies of foreigners in the Roman States had been but a shadow, that in their Christian communities a *stips* was collected, just as it had been collected in the societies, but not now to be thrown into sacred wells, no longer to be expended on the erection of statues or on social eating and drinking, but in extending aid to the poor and needy.

Nor did philosophy lead any further towards charity than did religion. Lactantius was right when he said to the heathen: "Of such things your philosophy teaches nothing." The ethics of the Greeks and Romans did not advance beyond a more or less refined eudaimonism. The chief principle of action is always one's own benefit. Even with Plato it is not otherwise, a fact which makes us wonder how it is that in the case of this best representative of the ancient world a naked egoism so frequently comes to the front. According to him the highest idea is that of the good, which, transcending mere existence in strength and value, requires nothing for itself, and the influence of which upon everything else is beneficent.[50] It is the cause of all that is sacred, all that is just and beautiful.[51] Hence the Deity, the prime source of all existence upon the earth, is good, and will reject nothing that is good and well-doing. And to become as like as possible to this God, must be the endeavour of mankind.[52] Hereupon follows the idea of the State, that in the laws enacted by the State there shall be nothing which benefits one class of citizens only, but only that which benefits the whole State; and hence it should strive to bring the citizens into such union with one another, that they shall help one another, each man in such measure as will be to the greatest advantage of the community.[53] To this there are added thoughts which, if carried further into practice, must have led one on to charity as a sharing of the common life. But it is well known how unsatisfactory, confusing, and impossible any extended practical application of Plato's ideas as to the life of a community is. In his ideal State there is no room for the poor. Beggars are simply turned out. They mar the common prosperity. Is a worker ill? There is no obligation binding upon the physician to interest himself in him. If his constitution is not strong enough to enable him to withstand what is hurtful, he must die: the life of such a man has no value beyond his being able to carry on his handiwork. If he is no longer in a position to do this, his life is then no longer worth anything.[54]

We seek in vain for charity amongst the virtues enumerated by Aristotle in his Ethics. We only find a

C

sort of echo of the name in *Generosity*, which, according to Aristotle, is the true mean between extravagance and avarice. But the practice of this is restricted; that is to say, the generous man may give of his wealth when and where and as much as he pleases,[55] so long as these empty rubrics are fulfilled. Moreover, the motive of generosity, with Aristotle, is not benevolence and love: the generous man gives "because it is beautiful to give,"[56] and thus, here again, only for his own sake, only in order to adorn himself with this virtue. However, Aristotle declares, and here he comes nearest to the Christian idea, that the worth of the generosity is not to be measured by the amount of the gift, but by the spirit of the giver. The object, moreover, of this generosity is not to combat distress; its practical proof lies always in the giving of gifts. Aristotle advances a little further when he treats of friendship. Here, also, he discusses benevolence and beneficence. It is a seemly thing to hasten, without being asked, to the assistance of unfortunate friends; for it is a proof of friendship to help the needy without being entreated thereto.[57] In general, with Aristotle, the only incitement towards friendship lies in the virtue of the friend and in the feeling of satisfaction which is experienced in this virtue; but it widens into something very unlike a universal love of mankind. According to the teaching of Aristotle, friendship cannot subsist between such as have nothing in common with one another, for example, between masters and slaves. For, inasmuch as the latter is a slave, he is only an animated machine. But yet friendship with him is possible, inasmuch as he is a man.[58] In connection with this, we may take a saying of Aristotle's, which has been preserved by Diogenes Laertius.[59] When blamed because he had given an alms to a bad man, he is said to have replied: "I pitied not his habits, but the man himself;" or, according to another version: "I did not give to the man himself, but to mankind." Here, indeed, we have arrived at last at the selfish foundation. For all this generosity and benevolence springs not from love, but from the reflection that such conduct is decorous and worthy of a noble man. The generous man does much for his friends and fatherland; he gives treasures, wealth, possessions to attain to the beautiful. For, "of everything praiseworthy, the generous man takes as his own share the best."[60] The best for himself,—how far removed is that from the simple apostolic saying: "Charity seeketh not her own"!

The last quoted version of Aristotle's saying has a strong affinity to Stoicism. The Stoics were the first who broke through the rigid ideas of nationality of the ancient world; they speak of one humanity, in which every one, even the slave, has a share. Here, again, though it is not love which binds together this community of mankind, but nature and our common origin from nature, yet there is an evident advance amongst the Stoics, who have much to say upon beneficence in particular. Thus Seneca has written seven books upon "Good Deeds," in which he discusses from every side the duty of beneficence. He requires not only that we should display kindness towards our fellow-men generally, but also that we shall give willingly and without hesitation; that the gifts which we bestow upon the poor and needy be given quietly, and sometimes even so that the giver shall not be known.[61] He expressly declares that we must not give in the hope of receiving again; that is usury, not beneficence. As true virtue must be exercised for its own sake alone, so also must true beneficence be exercised for its own sake alone.⁶² For in Seneca the thought appears, that by so doing we imitate and secure the favour of the gods, who will reward us.⁶³ This, viewed in itself, seems very like the precepts of the New Testament, and is yet at bottom something very different. It is remarkable how clearly Seneca speaks upon the point of one's duty in choosing very carefully those for whom we are to exercise beneficence. "I would choose out," says he, "a blameless, simple man, one who would be grateful and mindful of the benefit."⁶⁴ For, "it belongs to beneficence to give willingly to any one whom I esteem worthy, and to reap joy as the reward of my good deed."⁶⁵ And it is remarkable that Seneca, while he says so much of beneficence, deals at still greater length with gratitude and the duty of being grateful. He can hardly find words strong enough to characterize the turpitude of ingratitude. He even goes so far as to discuss the question whether the benefactor should not have the right of laying a criminal complaint against the ungrateful man. Seneca himself does not indeed incline to this, but he deduces from it a lesson, that since there is no complaint possible against the ungrateful, for there is no judge who can aid us, we ought on that very account to be more careful in our choice of those to whom we are to do good. He who gives to an ungrateful man acts like him who puts his trust in traitors, or appoints a scoundrel to the guardianship of his children.⁶⁶ This does not exclude us from giving an alms to a chance beggar, or providing an unworthy man with fire and water. For these are not benefits; we do such things instinctively, without considering the individual.⁶⁷ Indeed, Seneca goes even further in such sentences as these: "Kindness persisted in subdues at last even the wicked;" "The ungrateful man only injures himself in the long run;" "I will not therefore weary, but will go on the more diligently, as a good husbandman conquers the barrenness of his land by a double sowing of seed." And he closes with this splendid saying: "It is not the sign of a noble spirit to give and to lose, but it is the sign of a noble spirit to lose and still to give."[68] Thus all that he says of beneficence comes at last to this, though perhaps in a more delicate sense, that what man gives he gives in order that he may receive in return, if not a reward, yet gratitude; if not gratitude, still the consciousness of having a noble spirit. "If you ask me what I receive in return for my benefactions, I reply, a good conscience."[69]

Although it is thus plain that the good deeds, praised by Seneca with so much rhetorical emphasis, are yet something quite different from the simple heartfelt compassion of the Christians, the difference becomes still more distinct when we see that he has no hesitation in considering pity as something morbid and unworthy of a wise man. Just as superstition (*superstitio*) is a morbid perversion of the Roman religion, so is pity a morbid caricature of mercy and kindness. Pity is the fault of a weak spirit, which succumbs at the sight of a stranger in distress. Old women are pitiful, but the wise man is not. He helps the weeping one, but does not weep with him; he gives the poor man a gift, and extends a helping hand to the shipwrecked and dying, but does all this with a quiet unmoved spirit, not from compassion, but from sound judgment, while he gives to man as man of our common possessions, while he says to himself that nature is common to us all.[70]

And now we begin to see how it was that the Roman philosophy, quite apart from the fact that it was never the property of more than the few, could produce no benevolence like the Christian, and how it was that the ancient world, in spite of all its talk of humanity and brotherhood, of kindness and beneficence, was what it was—a world without love. The Stoics, indeed, made a notable advance. The idea of humanity was wanting to the old world; the man was hidden behind the citizen, mankind behind the State. The new idea was indeed promulgated by the Stoics, but in an unsatisfactory fashion. The undying value of the human soul, the eternal significance of every one of these human individualities, remained hidden; for their humanity was nothing but nature, and the dependence upon each other under nature all that unites men. Their view of the world is, like that of all the rest of the ancient world, exclusively one-sided. The other side, eternity and the significance of humanity as regards eternity, is hidden from them. There is an idea, which has been again met with in our own day, that men, when they first clearly came to believe that human life finds its end in this life alone, would be on that account the more ready to help one another, so that at least life here below might be made as pleasant to all as possible, and kept free from evil. But, in truth, the opposite is the case. If the individual man be only a passing shadow, without any everlasting significance, then reflection quickly makes us decide: Since it is of no importance whether he exist or not, why should I deprive myself of anything in order to give it to him? For the rule of life soon becomes this, that every one makes himself as comfortable in this life as possible; and this implies that he need not trouble himself about the poor and needy, whose existence or non-existence is at bottom a matter of no importance. All charity is based upon this, that the man towards whom love is shown is something in himself, and not a mere passing shadow of something eternal, not a mere specimen of a genus, but a personal existence, which as such possesses something possessed by no other person or thing. It was only when through Christianity it was for the first time made known that every human soul possessed an infinite value, that each individual existence is of much more worth than the whole world,—it was only then that room was found for the growth of a genuine charity.

Since the ancient world possessed not this knowledge, the fundamental principle of the ancient life, as well amongst the Stoics as with Seneca, is nothing else than a selfishness or egoism, cramped and confined by the egoism of the State. The State mercilessly makes the other nations bow before her interests. There are no duties towards conquered enemies. They and their property are at the mercy of the conqueror. Mercilessly, again, does the individual make others yield to his interests. Of the duty of love, of compassion, of such a love as denies itself, of such a compassion as is self-sacrificing for the sake of others, we hear nothing. Even in the making of gifts and presents, it is not the individual, but the State, the town, the citizenship that is regarded. There is plenty of liberality, but no compassion; plenty of good deeds, but none of the works of charity. While one furthers the interests of the State, one furthers one's own interests, for one depends upon the State; without it, one is nowhere. Here again we find selfishness at the bottom of all. Each individual is valuable only in so far as he aids in realizing the idea of the State. Therefore the poor are of no account, for they signify nothing to the State; they are but a burden upon its shoulders. If you cannot live, you must perish; as Plautus says: "What is given to the poor is lost." Hence the small interest taken in children. The children of citizens who had fallen in the service of the State were indeed educated at the cost of the State, and guardians were appointed to the children of the noble and wealthy, for it was for the interest of the State that this should be done. Where it was not done, nobody troubled himself about the children. Hence came it that in ancient times there were hospitals for soldiers and slaves only. The State had an interest in the former, the great landowners in the latter. Every possible care was taken of the wealthy in their palaces; about the middle classes and the artisans no one cared. Hence comes the small estimation in which woman was held, her dependent position, her want of all legal rights, which also was a co-ordinate cause why true charity never was attained to, for that only becomes a possibility by the service of that sex specially created and provided for the ministry of the distressed.

This ancient selfishness comes more prominently forward among the Romans than among the Greeks. The only piece of real care for the poor which we meet with is at Athens, not at Rome. The Roman is very avaricious, very careful about the keeping together of his money, very unscrupulous as to the ways in which he obtains it. The well-known saying with which the Emperor Vespasian justified his disgraceful taxes is typical of the Romans. The great men of Rome were not ashamed to gain money even from usury and brothels. The Romans were less influenced by generosity of any kind than the Greeks.

But from the time of the Emperors onwards, as has

been frequently remarked, a new influence begins to make itself felt. We cannot understand the first centuries of the Christian Church, we cannot understand its swift extension and its proportionately swift victory, if we do not notice this influence. And herein the divine wisdom is revealed; it answers to the "fulness of the times" of which St. Paul speaks (Gal. iv. 4). Had the stream of new life flowing forth from Christ encountered the still unbroken ancient life, it would have recoiled from the encounter ineffectually. But now the ancient life had already come amongst the breakers, its strong foundations had begun to be weakened, and the Christian influence meets with a current of heathen opinion already flowing partly in its own direction. In the Roman Empire there had appeared a spirit of universalism unknown to the ancient world. Nationalities had been effaced, and the idea of universal manhood had struggled into the light out of the obscurity of the ideas of nationality. From the Stoics the word had gone forth that all men are equal; they spoke of brotherhood and of the duties of man towards man. The lower classes, up to this time despised, asserted their place. The treatment of slaves becomes more gentle. If Cato likened them to cattle amongst straw, Pliny beholds in them his "serving friends." The position of the artisan is improved; freedmen work their way upwards. The guilds provide them with not only a centre of social life, but also with the means of bettering their social position. The women, hitherto without legal position, receive privileges and rights in increasing fulness. Care is taken of children. The distribution of grain, which was at first a purely political institution, becomes by degrees a sort of system of poor relief. We meet with an ever-increasing number of acts of liberality, presentations, and endowments, which are of a more charitable description. Even the inscriptions give us glimpses of this. Thus a freedman of Hadrian's dedicates his private burying-ground not only to his relations and friends, as in former days, but adds, "and to charity." Thus the foreigner and the stranger may be buried there.[71] Here some one builds baths expressly for foreigners.[72] There a certain Cornelius makes provision for securing a distribution of bread in the surrounding villages.[73] A drug-seller leaves a number of boxes of healing ointment to be given to the sick poor.[74] And a heathen woman is honoured on her tombstone as a "mother to all men;" while a man is commemorated as good, compassionate, and kind to the poor.[75]

This is indeed the turning-point. This heathen influence paving the way for the advancing Christianity must, later on, even after Christianity had completely gained the upper hand, have had the tendency of favouring a combination of heathen and Christian elements. And we shall see hereafter how strongly indeed, more strongly than men are accustomed to suppose, heathen customs and the ancient idea of the world influenced the development of charity; but first of all they paved the way for the reception of Christian ideas, and contributed materially to their spread and victory. How far this current of thought itself was modified by Christian influences it is very difficult to say. At all events, the charity of the Christian made a great impression upon the heathen, and it is hard to believe that this should not have brought forth fruit of some sort or other. But such mutual influences are in their beginnings of inappreciable magnitude. They are first noticed only when the beginnings are things of the past. Therefore, when in the opening of the third century Philostratus makes his Apollonius of Tyana deliver a noble speech to the heathen, in which he remarks upon the sparrows, how they call each other to feed, and share what they have found, and warns his hearers to be of mutual support to one another, and to take care of the poor,[76] these sentiments no doubt flow, not from heathen, but from Christian sources.

But amid all these remains the deep-lying difference between the ancient and the Christian life. Heathendom did not of itself produce a real, organized charity; that is, as it were, something quite new springing from Christianity. The ancient world stretched forth in this respect towards Christianity, but could not of itself produce what Christianity brings. It still is, and remains, a world without love.

CHAPTER II.

UNDER THE LAW.

THE case of Israel, the nation which knew and worshipped the only true God, is different from that of the rest of the heathen world. Of course we do not find even in Israel any completely organized charity, any actual system of poor relief. But there was not, and could not be, a great amount of poverty or any considerable proletariat. The land-laws, in accordance with which the land always returned after appointed intervals of time into the hands of the family, prevented this; and even although these land-laws may never have been put into execution to the fullest extent, yet the character of the people as husbandmen, the want of the greater industries, the simplicity of their whole life, and, above all, that customary respect paid to work as a duty imposed by God upon every man,—a very different view from that taken by the heathen,—all these things prevented any of the more severe kinds of distress. Of course there was not complete freedom from it. There were poor in Israel as well as elsewhere, and a number of the enactments of the law are devoted to the relief of their distress and the softening of their fate. The olive-tree is not to be twice shaken, the vineyard is not to be twice gathered, nor are the sheaves of corn left in the fields to be gleaned; all that belongs to the poor, to the widow and the orphan. It was allowable to pluck with the hand the ears of corn while passing through a neighbour's field (Deut. xxiii. 25), though a sickle might not be used. Whatever crops grow in the seventh year were for the benefit of the poor (Lev. xxiii. 11). They have, so to speak, a share in the land, which belongs to God alone, from whom Israel only holds it in loan. The idea of property in the Old Testament is not the absolute one which appears in the Roman law. All proprietorship is merely relative: there is bound up with it the duty of allowing others also to enjoy a share of it. The Lord over all is God, and He gives it to whom He wills. Every mean advantage over, every act of oppression of the poor, is most strictly forbidden; and in order to give emphasis to this commandment, the people are reminded of the time of their oppression, when they also were strangers in Egypt (Ex. xxii. 21). All usury towards their fellow-countrymen is forbidden (*ibid.* 25). All debts are to be released in the seventh year, and the approach of that seventh year is not to hinder any one from lending to the poor man in distress (Deut. xv. 2 ff.). "The poor shall never cease out of the land: therefore I command thee, saying, Thou shalt open thine hand wide unto thy brother, who is poor and needy." Upon him who does this the blessing of God will descend; to him who does it not, the omission will be reckoned for sin. The poor man is to receive his wage before the sun goes down (Deut. xxiv. 15). The law cares most anxiously for widows and orphans, for "God is a father of the fatherless and a judge of the widows" (Ps. lxviii. 5). A widow's raiment might not be taken in pledge, and both widows and orphans were to be invited to their feasts. An institution specially designed for the protection and relief of the poor was the second tithe, the so-called poor's-tithe. The first tithe belonged to the Levites. What remained over was again tithed, and the produce of this second tithe, devoted in the first two years to a feast in the sanctuary at the offering of the first-fruits, was devoted in the third year to a feast in the dwelling-house, to which the Levites and the strangers, the widows and the orphans, were invited (Deut. xiv. 28, 29, xxvi. 12, 13).

But these legal precepts were in accordance with the ideas of the people, and that the spirit of gentleness which finds expression in them was active in the life of the people, is shown by the Psalms and the Proverbs of the Israelites. Compassion for the poor and distressed is a trait which must not be wanting in the character of a righteous Israelite. "He is ever merciful and lendeth" (Ps. xxxvii. 26); he "considereth the poor" (Ps. xli. 1); "he showeth favour and lendeth gladly" (Ps. cxii. 5). Job, in whom is portrayed the upright man, appears as the father of the poor (xxix. 16). On the other hand, the want of compassion is a distinguishing feature of the ungodly. "The tender mercies of the wicked are cruel" (Prov. xii. 10). For God Himself is compassionate and gentle, He has a father's heart and is full of pity. Therefore "he that hath mercy on the poor honoureth God" (Prov. xiv. 31). Herein lies a deeper reason why that spirit of compassion, for which we seek in vain among the heathen, is to be found in Israel. Israel has a merciful God, who is considerate, who is kindly, merciful, and full of help. Therefore the poor were viewed by the Israelites in quite a different light from that in which they were regarded by the heathen. Here there is no trace of that contempt with which they were treated in the other case. On the contrary, the poor and needy stand nearest to God. He cares for them, He assures their rights, He raises them up out of the dust. And the loving God requires from mankind love in return. "Mercy is better than sacrifice" (1 Sam. xv. 22), and right and beneficent actions are more pleasing to the Lord. "Is not this the fast that I have chosen? to loose the bands of wickedness, to undo the heavy burdens, and to let the oppressed go free, and that ye break every yoke? Is it not to deal thy bread to the hungry, and that thou bring the poor that are cast out to thy house? when thou seest the naked, that thou cover him; and that thou hide not thyself from thine own flesh?" (Isa. lviii. 6, 7). Thus there is a double motive in the commandment to be compassionate; one with reference to God, since mercy is the true way in which to serve Him, and one with reference to the poor, because they are our flesh, and we are thus connected with them. It is the very same idea as that which found its highest expression in the commandment: "Thou shalt love thy neighbour as thyself, for I am the Lord thy God."

We have thus the germ, as it were, of that charitable life which appears in full vigour in the New Testament. And yet compassionate love in the Old Testament is limited in two respects, the national and the legal: there is still wanting that universality and that freedom which is of the essence of true charity. And thus the way of the Old Testament does not of itself and as a natural consequence lead to the charity of the Christian community. It may also lead, and it did lead, to the almsgiving of the Pharisees, that caricature of true love for one's neighbour. Some one was needed to come and sweep away the barriers which in the Old Testament still surrounded it. And thus the charity of the New Testament is something fresh even as compared with that of the Old.

It would indeed be too narrow an interpretation of the Old Testament, if we were to say that by the neighbour, whom the Israelite is commanded to love, is meant his fellow-countryman alone.[1] That would be the Pharisaic interpretation, which extracts from the commandment, "Thou shalt love thy neighbour," its converse, "but hate thine enemy," and at the same time contracts the meaning of the word "neighbour." In opposition to this, let us point to the beautiful precept quoted by the Apostle Paul in the New Testament: "If thine enemy be hungry, give him bread to eat; and if he be thirsty, give him water to drink: for thus shalt thou heap coals of fire upon his head" (Prov. xxv. 21, 22); and to such commands as this, that one must restore to an enemy his lost cattle, even at the expense of one's own time. And since, in reference to this matter, it is of a personal rather than of a national enmity that we are to think, we see that the stranger, the non-Israelite, was by no means regarded simply as an enemy. The foreign settler, "the stranger which is within thy gates," is not without rights. "Ye shall have one ordinance, both for the stranger and for him that is born in the land" (Num. ix. 14). The stranger is to enjoy the rest of the Sabbath, is to be invited to their feasts, and is to be kindly treated (Ex. xxii. 21, xxiii. 9; Lev. xix. 9, xxiii. 22). They are even to treat him as one of themselves: "The stranger that dwelleth with you shall be unto you as one born among you, and thou shalt love him as thyself" (Lev. xix. 34). Moreover, that in this respect the children of Israel were very different from the heathen, is distinctly seen in the humane regulations regarding slaves. How carefully (Ex. xxi. 20 ff.) are they protected against the cruelty and harshness of their masters, and how far beyond the heathen mind is the delicacy displayed in the enactment, that whoever takes to wife a slave from among the captives taken in battle, must first allow her a month in which to bewail father and mother! Of course the stranger has not exactly the same privileges as a native. The usury forbidden in the case of fellow-countrymen is permissible as regards him, his debts are not released in the seventh year like those of the natives, and he cannot inherit land. And the case of the complete stranger differs again from that of the foreign settler, although even in his case also there is often displayed that universalist impulse which is grounded on the Messianic expectations of the Israelites. In the prayer at the dedication of the temple, Solomon prays for those who are not Israelites. Melchizedek, Abimelech, who are set forth as persons worthy of honour, Job, who is the pattern of uprightness—all these are foreigners. Israel is the first-born of God (Ex. iv. 22), and though he therefore has some advantages on that account, yet the other nations are not shut out from God. But all the same, as Ewald says, " The principle of love in the Old Testament is always limited by the idea of the nation." Just as its religion still lay buried in a husk of nationality, so was there wanting to its charity the habit of looking upon men as men, and without reference to nationality. - That universal love which no longer asks, Who is my neighbour? but looks upon every man as a neighbour, is indeed there in the seed-form, but the universalism is still buried in the idea of the nationality. Disinterment is required, and release from its barriers; but all the same it was quite possible to look upon the shell as the principal thing, and thus to pass by the universalism.

In just the same manner as it lacked universality, so also did charity in the Old Testament lack freedom; it is still bound under the law. Let us, in order to make this clear, compare the New Testament with the Old. Nowhere in the New Testament do we find precepts enjoining upon Christians the duty of almsgiving at prescribed times, in prescribed proportions, or in prescribed ways. The feeling of love for one's neighbour is alone enjoined; out of this the deeds of love will quickly come. Charity is quite free to set to herself her own method and measure, to give and to help when and where and in what degree she pleases. "Let every man do according as he is disposed in his own heart, not grudgingly or of necessity, for the Lord loveth a cheerful giver;" such is now the commandment. Nowhere in the New Testament do we find directions given which bear directly upon the clearing away of social difficulties. The removal of these is always expected to proceed from the development of the Christian ideal, to grow from within outwards. It is quite otherwise in the Old Testament. We have already discussed a number of legal regulations bearing directly upon the amelioration or removal of social distress. The fulfilling of these precepts, the giving of tithes, the leaving of fields ungleaned, the releasing of debts, and all such things, constituted in the eyes of the Israelites a religious duty, while in the New Testament almsgiving is nowhere inculcated as such; all that the New Testament requires of Christians in reference to matters of charity, is simply the fulfilment of one's customary duties, which fulfilment grows out of the religious life, but is completely free in its action. We must not, however, conclude that in the Old Testament only the outward performance is required, and not the inner spirit. The passages which have already been quoted from the Psalms and from the prophets would show the opposite; but, as a rule, these exhortations to almsgiving are isolated, and hence the possibility may arise of a man outwardly punctually fulfilling them without possessing the corresponding spirit, just as he would outwardly fulfil the ceremonial law, and then think that he had done enough. This difference between the Old and New Testament is most distinctly shown in the commandment of love for one's neighbour. Now this is indeed found in the Old Testament, but separated from the commandment of love to God. It is something new when our Lord takes the two commandments together, looks upon them as parallel, and combines them in one precept, teaching that true love to God can never exist without love for one's neighbour, nor true love for one's neighbour without love to God, and that the love of God is active in our love for our neighbour, the latter being rooted in the former. Here, in one sense, there was required a limitation of love, and with that limitation it is freed from the fetters of the law, freed from the bonds of national prejudice; and as free love it becomes universal love.

If, then, the love which appeared in Christ Jesus is something new as regards Israel, it is still more so when we consider that our Lord had opposed to Him not the Israel of the Old Testament, but the post-exilian Judaism. In the case of the latter we do not find the seeds of a free and universal exercise of charity sown in the Old Testament grown into the flower; but, on the contrary these seeds which had been provided have been destroyed and in their stead only those things which we have designated as their fetters in the Old Testament have received a one-sided cultivation. There are two characteristics of post-exilian Judaism, national pride and the works of the law. To the commandment, "Thou shalt love thy neighbour," was added the clause, "and hate thine enemy;" and by neighbour was understood exclusively fellow-Jew; every foreigner, every non-Jew being an enemy. Contempt of Gentiles is now a part of piety, and is a sort of proof of zeal for God and for His law. And while this national pride hemmed charity in, its legal aspect must have corrupted, if not altogether destroyed it. The necessary consequences of a legal regulation of charity are of two kinds. In the first place, its activity is at once split up into a number of isolated acts of almsgiving. For, while the truly charitable soul directs his endeavours to the improvement of his neighbour's condition and the prevention of social distress, the legal precept refers only to individual acts, and the accomplishment of these is sufficient. And again, the laying weight upon almsgiving, and upon the making one's alms as large as possible, is always a sign that in that instance the charity is charity enacted by law. So, then, the giving of alms becomes something done for the sake of a reward, for the fulfilling of the law entails a reward.

Both these symptoms of a legal bondage are strongly prominent in the post-exilian Judaism. What a stress the Apocrypha lay upon the giving of alms, how often do they refer to it (Tob. iv. 8, xii. 8; Sir. iii. 3, xxix. 12), how strong a feature it is in the character of the righteous men as presented to us in the portrait of Tobias! Indeed, to so great an extent has the giving of alms come by this time to be considered as a principal part of righteousness, that righteousness and almsgiving have become synonymous. Thus the Septuagint in the passage (Dan. iv. 27): "Break off thy sins by righteousness," translates the word "righteousness" by "almsgiving;" and the later Judaism interprets Ps. xvii. 15: "I will behold Thy face in righteousness," in such a way as to deduce from the passage the duty of giving alms on entering the synagogue. The view of almsgiving as a meritorious action also comes prominently forward. Of course, in the Old Testament the blessing of God is promised to the compassionate and merciful man: "He that hath pity on the poor lendeth to the Lord: and that which he hath given will He pay him again" (Prov. xix. 17); but nowhere is there any expiatory virtue attached to the alms. Even the passage in Dan. iv. 27, when Daniel warns the king: "Break off thy sins by righteousness, and thine iniquities by showing mercy unto the poor," has not this meaning; for here righteousness signifies not the giving of alms, but the whole change to a right moral conduct, in addition to which the second half of the verse names as a generally important part of such conduct, benefactions to the poor. But this (latterly so much abused) passage forms the bridge of communication with those sentences of the Apocrypha which clearly point out alms as having an expiatory effect. The beautiful counsel which Tobias gives to his son (Tob. iv. 5 ff.): "Be merciful after thy power. If thou hast much, give plenteously; if thou hast little, do thy diligence gladly to give of that little," is followed by "for so gatherest thou thyself a good reward in the days of necessity. For thine alms loosen thee from sin, and leave thee not in the fear of death." In another passage almsgiving is joined with prayer and fasting: "Such a prayer with fasting and almsgiving is better than the heaping up of treasures of gold; for alms release from death, atone for sin, and support in life" (Tob. xii. 8). "As water extinguisheth a burning fire, so do alms blot out sin," says Sirach, iii. 33.

These ideas were still more prominent amongst the Pharisees in the time of our Lord and in the Talmud. The Pharisees give alms, but without charity; it is the public performance of a work of the law. It is not the welfare of their neighbour that they bear in mind, but their own glory. When they give alms, they sound a trumpet before them, that they may be seen of men. Thereafter, they set about the robbing of widows' houses. The Talmud calls almsgiving a great commandment. The giving of alms leads to eternal life, and preserves one from untimely death. He who gives them never dies prematurely.[2] Again, the giving of alms is one of those things that prevail to alter the judgment of God upon us, for (Prov. x. 2 and xi. 4) it is written: "Righteousness delivereth from death," and here "righteousness" is considered as synonymous with "almsgiving."[3] The protection of strangers and the visiting of the sick is specially recommended. He who protects a stranger inherits Paradise; he who visits the sick will be saved from hell. There is a characteristic passage in the treatise of Pirke Aboth, which is undoubtedly the finest part of the Talmud. "Four classes of men are there in respect of almsgiving. One gives himself, but will not that another should give. He casts the evil eye upon the other, for he grudges him the blessing of almsgiving, which maketh rich. The second allows others to give, but will not give himself. He casts the evil eye upon himself and his. The third gives himself, and wishes others to give. He is *chasid* (devout). The fourth gives not, nor wills that others should give. He is godless."[4]

Moreover, the Talmud, when it speaks of almsgiving, does so only with reference to giving to one's own fellow-countrymen. Alms should neither be given to nor accepted from the heathen! It is only permitted for the sake of peace. Kindness and compassion is in no sense their due.[5]

Certainly in the time of Jesus there was no lack amongst the Israelites of almsgiving, and of splendid almsgiving too. This is sufficiently clear from the fact that our Lord speaks as of something perfectly well understood, when He says: " When thou givest thine alms." It is also pointed to by the gifts of the wealthy thrown into the treasury, as well as by the alms of Cornelius. The Emperor Julian certifies to the fact that amongst the Jews in his time there were no beggars. And in our own day, what a ready disposition to mutual support has been shown by the Jews, especially the Jews of the dispersion! But although there was plenty of alms, there was but little charity apparent; and in spite of the ostentatious almsgiving of the Pharisees, we must pass upon Israel, even in the time of Jesus, the judgment that it was—a world without love. With regard even to the children of Israel, charity, as it was manifested in Jesus, was something new.

CHAPTER III.

THE MANIFESTATION OF LOVE IN CHRIST JESUS.

THAT which was wanting both in heathenism and in Judaism, is to be found in the Christian community. From the very beginning not only did its members, each in his own sphere, recognise compassion for the distressed as one of the necessary duties of their new life, but the community as such from the very outset accepted as a task laid upon it the practice of charity by means of its different organizations. And although this practice, like the life of the community generally, sank often in the course of time to a very low ebb, it never altogether failed. The Christian Church can never be conceived of as without charity: it was inherent in it from the very beginning. And it was so, not only because its Lord and Head taught love and commanded love, but because He Himself practised it. He was not only a teacher of love, or a lawgiver of love, but His life was also the first example of a life of love. It was not the maxims which He uttered about it, nor the commandments which He gave, but the fact that in Him personally love was manifest, that moved by love He came to us, and lived upon earth a life which from its very first breath to its latest was spent in the service of love, and that He finally, through the greatness of His love, gave Himself for us to the death of the cross; that is the beginning and the never-failing source of charity amid His followers. The beginning and the end of the history which we wish to narrate lies in these words of the Master: "The Son of man came not to be ministered unto, but to minister, and to give His life a ransom for many."[1]

It is not from the idea of the Church that we must set out, but from the idea of the kingdom of God; for Christians exercise charity not in respect of their membership of the Church, but in respect of their membership of the kingdom of God. Only when we have learned that the exercise of charity is a necessary proof of belonging to that kingdom, will we be able to understand why, and with what idea, and in what degree, the Church has been the supporter of this exercise.

The whole work of our Lord may be summed up in this, that He founded upon earth the kingdom of heaven, the kingdom of God. But the kingdom of God is the community of men, in which God is absolute and undisputed Master. God is love, and therefore the kingdom of God is a kingdom of love: and the community of those who have been reconciled to God in Christ must hallow its whole life and conduct by love. The whole duty of members of the kingdom of God is comprehended by our Lord in one word: "Be ye therefore perfect, as your Father which is in heaven is perfect," and again: "Be ye therefore merciful, as your Father also is merciful." The righteousness of the kingdom of God, which our Lord enjoins upon His people, is nothing else than the ordering of their whole life in accordance with the law of love. It is in this very matter that their righteousness approves itself as better than that of the scribes and Pharisees, since these omitted the weightest matters of the law, love and mercy, whilst the members of the kingdom of God practise them. No doubt the commandments of love: "Thou shalt love God above all," and again: "Thou shalt love thy neighbour as thyself," are found in the Old Testament. But our Lord takes the two together, and elevates the commandment of love into the one foundation of the kingdom of God. Love for our neighbours is nothing outside or independent of love to God, but is its active exercise.

Hence all the barriers which restrained love on every side have been broken down. The heathen world could never fully realize that all men without distinction are the proper objects of our love. Polytheism entailed as a necessary consequence divisions among men. Only where the one true God was recognised could the unity of the human race be recognised. The mysterious philosophical recognition of this unity by the Stoics was not sufficient. For philosophy is at all times the privilege of the few only. It was only in religious soil that the universal duty of love could strike root, for only religion is altogether universal. Amongst the Jews the knowledge of the one God was indeed present, but love to God and love to man were torn asunder. The Pharisees, who paid tithe of mint and anise and cumin, and yet devoured widows' houses, considered that they had shown sufficient of their love to God by the punctual observance of the ceremonial law, whilst they omitted that wherein love to God is truly shown, namely, love to men. With them it was: "Corban, it is a gift, by whatsoever thou mightest be profited by me." But so soon as love to one's neighbour is seen to be the exercise of love to God and the necessary sign of belonging to His kingdom, then are all the barriers which surround it broken down. As in respect of the kingdom of God all differences of nationality, of rank, and even of sex are without significance, so also are they in respect of love. It is remarkable that in the parable of the good Samaritan our Lord only says: "A certain man went down from Jerusalem to Jericho and fell among thieves," without particularizing the man in any way, either as to his country, his rank, or his religion. We do not need to know all this; it is a matter of no importance. Enough for us if we know that he is a man, and therefore our neighbour. For all men without distinction are appointed to be members of the kingdom of God, and he to whom the kingdom of God has become the chief object of his life, sees over again in the object of every man's life that of his own, and holds himself pledged to assist every one to attain to it. And all other barriers have also fallen down. As the kingdom of God lays its claims upon all men, so also does love. We cannot in respect of it absolve ourselves by a certain statutory, well-defined quantity of actions: it requires us to place at its service our whole persons, and all that we possess. Love can admit of no other aim but this one, namely, the aiding of our neighbour in his efforts to attain what is the highest aim in life, membership of the kingdom of God: it may not cherish any collateral aims such as honour, advantage, or reward, but must, fully unrestrained in this particular, be a completely self-denying love.

This love to our neighbour embraces more than well-doing, but it includes the whole of that. For, since life here upon earth finds its object in the kingdom of God, so everything that is done to aid the life of our neighbour, and so to order it as to make the attainment of this end most feasible, must work towards that great end. Therefore our Lord includes almsgiving amongst the necessary proofs of love to our neighbour, and in Matt. xxv.

enumerates the works of mercy which must be engaged in by His own people, the "righteous," that is to say, such as belong to the kingdom of God and strive after its righteousness. These are the six recognised works of mercy, "feeding the hungry, giving water to the thirsty, clothing the naked, protecting the stranger, tending the sick, visiting the prisoner;" and to these the Church, in order to complete the sacred number of seven, has added "burying the dead."[2] But all these works possess true worth only in so far as they tend to the higher object than that of helping that distress which is nearest to one, which is ready to hand, namely, the advancement of the kingdom of God. They possess their value in that they are done to Christ in the persons of the distressed. Therein is expressed both their motive and their end. Their motive is love to Christ, and their end is His service, or what is the same thing, what they do they do as members of the kingdom of God, and in order to the advancement of that kingdom.

Hence it becomes clear how very different from that of the heathen world was the treatment of the poor in the Christian world. In the Greco-Roman world the pauper was despised as a cipher, and whatsoever was given him considered as thrown away. And quite naturally so, for the poor man was of no service to the State, and thus there was no object in preserving his life or in maintaining him. The only object which the giving of alms upon grounds of expediency alone can have, namely, that of making the poor happy in this world, is in most cases altogether unattainable. If no aim beyond this life is recognised, there is no higher object to be gained by almsgiving. Christ sees in every man, even in the poorest and most miserable, a human being whose privilege it is to become a member of the kingdom of God.

This end is in all cases attainable, even although we have to allow that it is not in our power to relieve all the distress and misery in the world: for misery and distress are no hindrance to any man's being or becoming a member of the kingdom of God. It is a truly heathen idea to say, as a reason for desisting from works of mercy: "All this is of no use; we can never make all men happy." For that is not the only object of Christian charity. It has a much higher end in view, and all that is done in the way of removing or alleviating misery and distress, is only done as a means towards this higher end, the advancement of the kingdom of God. Accordingly it is a fundamental misconception of the work of Christ and of Christianity to say, speaking from the social point of view, that the work of Christ has failed, and that Christianity has not succeeded in fulfilling the task set before it, since there is at the present time quite as much distress and misery in the world as before. As though Christ had wished to be a social reformer; when what He really did was to proclaim that in comparison with the highest end in life, social position is a matter of absolute unimportance, and to appoint to human life an object, attainable by every one, namely, the kingdom of God, in which every one may have a share, be his outward position what it may, be he rich or poor, high or low, freeman or slave. It was not to take away poverty that Christ appeared; on the contrary, He says: "The poor always ye have with you" (John xii. 8). He came to bring the poor into the kingdom of God. He did not come to put an end to all the distress in the world: on the contrary, He says to His disciples: "In the world ye shall have tribulation" (John xvi. 33). He came to comfort the broken-hearted and sorrowing. Not social reform, but the founding of the kingdom of God was His life's work. And He did found that kingdom which is in Himself, and when this is realized, then are the influences which flow from Christ and play upon the social side of our life found to be sanctifying and healing; but they are only the consequences of the inner change, and hence only indirectly experienced. They are of the things which are "added unto" those who seek first after the kingdom of God. Hence it must appear that it would be imputing an erroneous motive to Christian charity, and adopting a wrong standard whereby to judge of its history, were we to ask how far it has succeeded in doing away with all poverty, and in making all here upon earth outwardly happy.

It will be necessary, however, to define still more clearly the aim and peculiar object of Christian charity. We have already had several opportunities of observing that true Christian charity cannot exist where there is no object beyond this life to be attained. To view the world as being exclusively of this life, is fatal to all charity. The ultimate consequence is always this: He who has not the means of living must die; for him life has no value, and therefore whatever may be done to preserve his life is also valueless. At the same time, however, charity will wither and perish where the world is viewed exclusively from the standpoint of the future life. The Middle Ages afford us a proof of this. The charity itself does not indeed change, but its task, its object, is completely altered. People perform works of mercy not for the sake of helping the poor, but for their own sakes, that they may receive the reward for so doing. If the kingdom of God, which was brought to us by our Lord, had been purely a thing of the future, of the next world, then the gospel of that kingdom could have evoked no charity. For this life would no longer have possessed any worth, and to leave him to die would be doing the poor a better service than to keep him in a life which can only be one of misery and distress. Charity places before herself, on the one hand, a higher aim of life, transcending the limits of this present existence; and, on the other hand, the true value of the earthly existence as a means towards the attainment of that aim. She cannot be properly developed where this life itself is looked upon as the highest and only good, but only where it is considered as but relatively good—as good, that is to say, only inasmuch as it leads to the highest good of all.[3]

Now the kingdom of God, viewed as perfect and complete, is indeed a thing of the next world, a thing of the future; but as growing, it is a thing of this world and of the present time. It is a gift of the grace of God, but at the same time it involves the laying of a task upon us. The importance of the present time is that now, after the Master has gone away, the servants must trade with the talents entrusted to them until He come again. The whole of this earthly life, with all its natural relations of family, state, and society, is the material for the exercise of the righteousness of the kingdom of God. Midst work and sorrow, while fulfilling his earthly calling, and while bearing the sorrows which, under God, overtake him, every man must, in the place appointed him by God, keep himself a member of the kingdom of God, and the peculiar task of charity is to render this a possibility for every one who is willing to try. She strives, therefore, imitating the example of her Master, to save the lives of men wherever she can. For every human life possesses worth, since every one, whoever he may be, is called upon in some way or other, be it through labour or be it through sorrow, to fulfil his task as regards the kingdom of God. It is not a conceivable thing that there can be any human life of no value to this kingdom. Therefore charity strives to put every man in such a position as to make it possible, and so far as practicable, easy for him lightly to perform his life's task. In the natural relations of this life, complicated by sin, lie many hindrances, which make it difficult for men to fulfil their life's task as members of the kingdom of God. Such hindrances are to be found especially in the contrast between rich and poor. Poverty may make it impossible for any one to work, and thus by his work to fulfil his duty as a member of the kingdom. Then it is the task of Charity to give him such assistance as shall put him again in a position to do his work. She strives to make the poor independent again, not only that they may be raised above the need for further assistance,—for that would be a very low view of the case, and would not answer to true love,—but in order that they may again fulfil their calling. Any man may become so poor or be in such distress that it is difficult or well-nigh impossible for him to bear his sorrows with patience, thanking God, as a member of the kingdom should. Then Love steps in and does her duty; she lightens his sorrows, so that he can bear them in patience, and learn even amid his suffering to thank God.

We can now understand how consistent our Lord is, in that while, on the one hand, He simply alludes to property and to the difference between the rich and poor, and declares that this difference is of no importance in respect to the heavenly kingdom, He yet, on the other hand, exhorts His followers to labour with love to remove this difference. It must be removed in so far as it hinders any individual from filling his place in the kingdom.

It has indeed been held that our Lord despised all earthly possessions, and that those only perfectly fulfilled His commandments who renounced all property. Certainly, if we would overcome the world, we must renounce the world; only he who inwardly is free from it, is its master. So is it also with earthly possessions; if our hearts are free from the love of them, then are we no more servants, but lords. This is all that our Lord means when He warns us against the service of mammon, and exhorts us to lay up for ourselves treasures not on earth, but in heaven. This inward renunciation carries with it always readiness to resign outwardly also all earthly possessions, in so far as this is required in the interests of the kingdom. Our Lord requires this of the rich young man (Matt. xix. 17, etc.), not that He may signify thereby a command which is to be binding on all true Christians, nor that He may point out thereby a higher grade of Christianity, a sort of standard of perfection, but because the task which the young man wished to take upon himself, that, namely, of being a disciple and apostle of Jesus, involved, in the circumstances of that time, the surrender of all property; and also because He wished to lead him to recognise the fact that he was not yet free within from the bonds of his wealth. Hence also that lament which our Lord pronounces over the rich, and His saying: "It is easier for a camel to go through the eye of a needle, than for a rich man to enter into the kingdom of God." But these involve no abandonment of wealth as such. For they refer to those selfish men who employ their wealth only for the satisfaction of their personal pleasure, instead of serving others with it. All wealth is property held in trust; we are but tenants of it. Property does not give rights alone; it brings with it duties. He who possesses earthly wealth must make it of service. And this service embraces within it the smoothing away of difference of position in respect of wealth. Our Lord will not remove this distinction. It remains and must remain, for it is part of the divinely ordered creation. To the individuality of a man belong not only those peculiarities which distinguish him from other men, his talents and his inclinations, but also his possessions. But as all these differences are so arranged as to make up a mutual whole, so also must the differences of property be so arranged, through the instrumentality of the work of love, in so far as the objects of the kingdom of God require it. Herein lay the sin of the rich man, in that he did nothing to bridge over the difference between himself and the poor Lazarus whom God had laid before his door. Therefore he receives his punishment; it is that in the next world the difference, which is now a difference the other way, may not be bridged over (Luke xvi. 19–31).

It is as the rendering of a service that almsgiving attains its true worth. The value of it lies not in the associated renunciation of part of our earthly possessions, but in the love manifested in it, the service done by it. Therefore our Lord esteems the farthing of the widow more highly than the large gifts of the wealthy (Mark xii. 41). The story of the widow's mite, however, does not refer directly to this point, since it deals with the casting of money into the treasury, not as alms, but as an offering to the temple; but at the same time it implies a rule which holds good of all voluntary offerings. Therefore our Lord lays down no statutory regulations for almsgiving, either by appointing outward laws for it, or by appointing that it should bear a fixed proportion to one's means. He does not do the one because He requires of us not the outward work, but the inward love, which will itself lead to action; and He does not do the other because He requires of us in asking for our love not a part only, but the whole. Where it is necessary, and when love requires it of them, His people will sell all that they have and give to the poor.

Our Lord therefore appoints the duty of almsgiving without adding conditions or limitations: "Give to him that asketh of thee" (Luke vi. 30; Matt. v. 42). This is no rhetorical hyperbole; our Lord wishes to express in this way the fact that Love finds her only limits within herself. His followers must never place outward limits upon their love by saying: "To so and so will I not give." But Love is not thereby excluded from setting limits to herself. Where Love herself forbids the gift, it is not given; for it may be necessary to withhold the gift for Love's sake. But in other respects she gives to every one. Therefore our Lord expresses the inexhaustible nature of love. It can never be exhausted. The inward bonds of property have all been cast off. Whatever a disciple of Jesus has, he holds for the good of all. But it is only the self-seeking barriers of property that have been removed. Love takes care of her possessions, that she may be able to use them. The same Lord who exhorts His followers that if necessary they must count their possessions as naught, and be ready to sacrifice them all, caused the fragments left after the feeding of the thousands in the wilderness to be taken up.

This affords us an explanation of a passage which is

at the first glance very remarkable, and which requires reference and discussion the more on account of its having been of the highest importance in the history of charity—that, namely, from Luke xi. 41 : "But rather give alms of such things as ye have; and, behold, all things are clean unto you." It might appear as though an expiatory virtue were here assigned to alms ; and in this way the passage was very frequently misinterpreted in the Middle Ages. But it is impossible that our Lord could have meant that, for He would then have been giving utterance to that very error of the Pharisees against which He contends. It is not the property itself that is here stigmatized as unclean, that must first be purified; but the unclean thing is the self-seeking which clings to the property. There is in earthly possessions a wonderful inducement to selfishness. How many does wealth render heartless! Therefore we must purify ourselves from this, and we do so by inwardly releasing ourselves from its power. This inward freedom, however, finds room for exercise in the giving of alms, and first becomes an accomplished fact in the giving of alms. It is a blessing upon almsgiving, and our Lord wishes to point out this blessing in the fact that the man thereby becomes inwardly freed from his worldly possessions, and that thus they lose their power over him.

Neither does the passage assign what some have discovered in it in later days, a standard, that is to say, to tell us what proportion of his income every one must give away in alms. The words which have been translated, " of such things as ye have," have been taken to mean, " of such things as are superfluous to you," and upon this has been based an obligation to give to the poor all that is not absolutely necessary for oneself.[4]

Our Lord has, however, never laid down any such obligation. He has nowhere limited the rights of property to such things as are absolutely necessary for life. On the contrary, at the marriage of Cana He provided wine in abundance, and defended against sordid fault-finders the sacred luxury displayed by Mary in anointing Him.

Our Lord requires of us the giving of alms, without any reference to the receiving of a reward. Of the Pharisees, who stand at the corners of the streets and sound a trumpet before them, He says: "They have their reward." Of His own He requires that they give their alms in secret, nor let their left hand know what the right hand doeth. But, on the other hand, He Himself promises a reward to those who do the works of mercy. Even a cup of cold water, with which one of His people is refreshed, will not pass without reward. But the promised reward is not an outward one, or one connected with the alms; it is one lying within themselves. He who advances the kingdom of God in others, advances it also in himself. He who is merciful wins for himself always more and more of the mercy of God. "Blessed are the merciful, for they shall obtain mercy." Thus we heap up for ourselves abiding treasures in heaven; thus we make friends to ourselves of the mammon of unrighteousness, and find an entrance into the eternal mansions.

Our Lord Himself gave alms, Himself performed works of mercy. Let us remember it well. He is in this respect also the founder of charity within His community. It is no pleasantry, though it may here and there degenerate into such, that leads us to distinguish establishments for Christian charity by Bible names, to call a deaconess-house "Bethany," a hospital for the deaf and dumb "Ephphatha," or a refuge for fallen women "Magdalene." We would imply by so doing that our work is but a continuance of the Master's work. He first took pity upon the sick, the blind, the leprous, and the dumb, brought back the unfortunate to a godly life, gave bread to the hungry in the wilderness; and every one of these works of His has been as it were a seed of corn, which has in the course of centuries brought forth fruit a thousand-fold. He does all this, moreover, so that it may not fail to be observed by them, before the eyes of His disciples, in the midst of the circle of believers which He calls around Him, in order that thus His disciples may themselves take part in His actions. At His orders they give to the poor (John xiii. 29); when He feeds the thousands in the wilderness, they distribute the bread and fishes, and have to serve at tables (Matt. xiv. 19); they lead to Him the blind man who has appealed to His pity. They are in this way led into, educated into a life of charity. Moreover, the employment of women in works of charity, which has been of so much importance in the development of the same in the Christian Church, is anticipated. There is a circle of serving women surrounding our Lord, which is a type of the deaconesses and of all charitable women, in whom the history of the Church is so rich. This circle of men and women disciples which surrounds our Lord is nothing else than the growing Church; and in this growing Church there thus already lie the germs and possibilities of charity. In the Church at Jerusalem is continued what had been already begun: care is taken of the poor and needy, just as they had learned to do from our Lord Himself when in His company. And then, when the Church spread beyond Jerusalem and beyond the Jews, she understood for herself that in every community, just as in the mother-community, care must be taken of the poor, and works of mercy attended to.

And thus charity was implanted in the Christian communities from the very outset: they received it from their Lord Himself. It is not, however, peculiar to them alone. Just as the kingdom of God and His Church are not co-extensive, so also Christian and Church charity are not co-extensive; just as the kingdom of God has a wider embrace than the Church, so also does charity extend beyond the Church. The State, burgh communities, corporations, all take part in the performance of this work. It is owing to a morbid one-sidedness that in the Middle Ages charity becomes exclusively ecclesiastical, and it is the consequence of falsely identifying the Church with the kingdom of God, and placing them in opposition to the State as the kingdom of this world. But we should be one-sided also, only in the opposite direction, were we, as several are inclined to do now-a-days, to contest with the Church its right to the exercise of charity, and especially to the relief of the poor, and to prefer to her, with her vast-reaching embrace, other organizations. If the consequence of the exclusively ecclesiastical character of the charity of the Middle Ages were disastrous to it, they would be not less, but more disastrous to-day if the Church were excluded from it. As there could be no kingdom of God upon earth without the Church, so would charity soon die out in all other spheres if the Church desisted from it; and whatever rendering of assistance and care for the poor there might remain, would be of quite a different character from compassionate love. For all love has its origin in the love of God in Christ Jesus, of which the Church is witness, not only by her words, but also by her deeds, inasmuch as she practises the works of charity. From her is derived the call to, as well as the strength for, charity in all other spheres; she shows to its every form that its highest end lies in the advancement of the kingdom of God; she leads us to love, just as our Lord, while He Himself did works of mercy, taught His disciples to do the same. Just as the idea of the kingdom of God is more comprehensive than that of the Church, while the Church is the central point of the kingdom of God upon earth; so also is Christian charity more comprehensive than that of the Church, but the Church is and remains the central point. Let us remember that there could not be any real charity in the heathen world because there was no community. There is one now; our Lord has founded it. The day of Pentecost was, as it were, the birthday of the Church; and it was also the birthday of that Christian charity which is inseparable from the Church.

CHAPTER IV.

FOUNDATIONS AND BEGINNINGS IN THE APOSTOLIC AGE.

THE church of Jerusalem was at first merely the enlarged circle of disciples. The three thousand baptized at Pentecost were, as St. Luke very significantly says (Acts ii. 41), "added" to the church. The church thoroughly bore the character of the family, and was, even in its manner of life, only the continuation of the family-like circle by which our Lord was surrounded. In this circle community of goods had prevailed. Its members lived upon what was given not merely by those outside, but also by those within it. They contributed according to their means to their common maintenance. And this continued after the Lord's departure, during the days before Pentecost, in the company of the hundred and twenty, and also when this company had been enlarged, by the outpouring of the Holy Spirit and the preaching of St. Peter, into the church first properly so called. Each contributed of that which was his own to what was necessary for the common maintenance, without thereby depriving himself of all property. Still less were any compelled to do this, or to persevere in it, by any decree of the church. The family feeling was, however, so strong, that none of them said "that ought of the things which he possessed was his own, but they had all things in common" (Acts xviii. 32).

This was the so-called community of goods in the church of Jerusalem. There could be no falser representation of it, than to think of it as an institution similar to those prevailing among the Essenes and Therapeutæ. It is far more correct to represent the state of things as an absence of institutions of any kind. We might as well speak of the institution of a community of goods in a family. But as in a family the consciousness of belonging to each other is so strong as entirely to subordinate the individual possessions of each member, so was it in the primitive church. The boundaries of private property were internally abolished, and so far as this was necessary for the service of the community, the individual also gave up his possessions externally, sold his lands and houses, and brought the price to the common treasury presided over by the apostles. No one was, however, obliged to do this. St. Peter emphatically declared to Ananias that he might have kept his land, and also that after he had sold it he might have retained its price (Acts x. 4). Such distribution was an act of perfectly free love, but this was powerful enough to level the existing inequalities of property, so that there were none in the church who lacked anything. Still the fact with which we are dealing is not the institution of community of goods, but noble almsgiving, a free equalization of possessions, carried out in the glow of first love to the largest-hearted and greatest extent, and differing, not in kind, but only in degree and extent, from what we subsequently meet with in the Church at Jerusalem and elsewhere. This explains the reason why we find in the Acts not the slightest hint of the abolition of a previously existing institution, nor any notice of its extension to other churches, a fact which appears a striking proof of the correctness of our view.

As in family life community is especially prominent in the common meals, so also was it in the family of the Jerusalem church. Common meals, with which was combined the celebration of the Lord's Supper, were daily partaken of. These were the so-called *Agapæ* or lovefeasts. And these it was which made a formal institution, an official appointment necessary. Hitherto the entire direction of the church had lain in the hands of the apostles. They had served in "the word," and had also "served tables" (Acts vi. 2). But the two offices could no longer remain united. The chief duty of the apostles could not but suffer amidst the various labours, which "the serving of tables," the equalization of property carried out in perfectly free love in the increasing church, involved; and if the apostles still regarded the ministrations of the word as their first duty, it is not surprising if one thing or another was overlooked in the daily administration of charity. St. Luke, at least, gives no hint that the complaint of the Hellenists, that their widows were neglected, was unreasonable. Hence, on the proposal of the apostles, seven men were chosen "over this business."

It is generally thought that these seven men were the first deacons, and that their selection was the institution of the diaconal office, or to view it more broadly, of an office for the administration of charity, besides that for the ministration of the word.[1] For my part, I think this view a mistaken one. First of all, it is striking that they are never called deacons, but always the seven. Certainly their office is called a "serving of tables," and this expression it is which has chiefly led to their being regarded as the first deacons. But the expressions "to serve" and "service" are used in the New Testament of every kind of ministration existing in the church, and not only of that of the deacons.[2] Still more striking is it, that St. Luke never afterwards mentions the seven in the church of Jerusalem, although he does presbyters (elders) (Acts xi. 30, xv. 6), and that, nevertheless, he nowhere tells us that the former office was abolished and the latter instituted. If this observation borders upon the conjecture, that the seven were not the first deacons, but the first elders, or, to express it more correctly, that their office, at first instituted for a single and quite special need, was afterwards gradually enlarged into the office of elder, the conjecture becomes a certainty by the further consideration, that, according to the express testimony of the Acts, the administration of alms was subsequently in the hands of the elders even in Jerusalem. The relief, which the church at Antioch collected for the poor in Jerusalem at the time of the famine under Claudius, was delivered not to the seven, but to the elders (Acts xi. 30). Of course, the matter may be so represented as to make the office of the seven last only as long as the community of goods existed, to have been done away with at the same time, and elders to have been then appointed for the general direction of the church. But we have already seen that a formal abolition of the community of goods is out of the question. Besides, when the equalization of property in its first and wider extent ceased, it still remained in a more limited measure; for gifts were still given, and almsgiving always practised. There would, therefore, still have been room for the agency of the seven, not to mention the circumstance that it would be strange if St. Luke should give no account at all of such far-reaching alterations in the government of the church, but let the seven disappear and the elders appear upon the scene without a word. We must then picture to ourselves the development in the following manner. The seven were at first chosen to discharge a special present need, that of serving tables, while the management of the church was, in all other respects, left with the apostles who were still in Jerusalem. When the apostles subsequently left Jerusalem, the management also passed into the hands of the seven, whose office was thus gradually enlarged till it reached that of the elders, and was afterwards designated by this name.

It is, moreover, a mistake to represent the diaconate as the "office of mercy," the "office of almonry." The management of works of mercy, of almsgiving, was never conceded to the deacons. It was in the hands of the presbyters and afterwards of the bishops, and the deacons only gave their assistance. And this is, in general, the position of deacons in the organism of the church. The constituting office is that of the elders; it is they who govern and manage the entire church life, and without their office a well-regulated church is inconceivable. To them the deacons, whose office it is to furnish assistance in the most varying respects to the church and the elders, are subordinate. Their office is related to that of the elders as the gift of "helps" is to that of "governments."[3] It is true, that to assist the elders in the care of the poor is so essential a branch of this help, that "*diakonia*" means also almsgiving. The management, however, was always in the hands of the bishops or elders, and a special "office of almoner" never existed as well as the office of elder.

It is striking that deacons are so seldom mentioned in the New Testament. They only occur expressly twice, viz. in Phil. i. 1, where they appear in the salutation, together with the elders, as officers of the church, and in 1 Tim. iii. 8, where the apostle gives directions to them as well as to the elders. They are nowhere else found. Paul and Barnabas ordained elders in the churches they founded (Acts xiv. 23), but nothing is said of deacons. Similarly does St. Paul command Titus to ordain elders in the cities, but never mentions deacons (Tit. i. 5). In the First Epistle also of St. Peter, we meet indeed with elders, but not with deacons. At all events, it is hence evident that they fall far behind the elders. There could not have been a church without elders, there certainly could have been one without deacons. For their services could be very well rendered, at least while a church was still small, by such members as were fit and willing to undertake them, without their assuming any specially official character. This is shown especially by the passage (1 Cor. xvi. 15), so interesting with respect to the origin of the office, where it is said of the household of Stephanas, "it is the first-fruits of Achaia, and they have given themselves to the ministry of the saints."[4] Such voluntary services were, of course, the earliest, and correspond with the origin of offices in the church. Two things appertained to an office, the gift and the calling, *i.e.* the recognition of the gift, the charge to exercise it in a special circle. The order was not, first the appointment of offices by the apostles, but the bestowal of gifts by the Lord,—gifts which were then freely exercised, and not comprised into an office until necessity and order required it. This was especially the case with the diaconate. Those who had the requisite gifts and love rendered of their own accord the service afterwards allotted to the deacons, and it was not till the increase of the church rendered this needful that a regular office grew up out of the free gift and love. The circumstance, that centuries afterwards we find, besides the deacons maintained by the church, others who were not so maintained, but gave their services gratuitously, is a further proof. Nay, in a certain sense this occurrence is ever and again repeated in the sphere of active charity. Where new needs make new work necessary, the Lord endows one and another with the gift and the impulse required for such work. It is at first done freely, and afterwards, when it has proved itself permanently needful and efficacious, it gradually passes into a regular office. The diaconate is moreover, by its very nature, of a more fleeting character than the office of governing. Every Christian is to be a servant with his gift and in his circle (1 Pet. iv. 10). While, then, deacons are but seldom spoken of in the New Testament, serving and service very frequently occur. Besides, if there are persons on whom service is officially incumbent, their official action and their personal service pass into each other. In the office of ruling this is not the case; this was by its nature from the very first more exclusive. Not every Christian is a presbyter; but every one is really and naturally a deacon, a servant of all.

The female diaconate was evidently even more transient, and this is the reason why the notices of it in the ancient church are so difficult to combine into a whole. There undoubtedly were, even in apostolic times, females to whom the diaconate was officially committed. Such a female deacon (the name "deaconess" does not occur in the New Testament) was Phœbe, to whom the apostle delivered the Epistle to the Romans, and whom he designates as a deacon of the church at Cenchrea. Whether the subsequently named Tryphæna and Tryphosa (ver. 12) and Persis, of whom the apostle says "they laboured much in the Lord," were deaconesses, or only women who from love to the Lord freely performed the same services as deaconesses, cannot be determined. Still less probable is it that Euodia and Syntyche, mentioned Phil. iv. 2, were deaconesses. On the other hand, I am convinced that the injunctions given, 1 Tim. iii. 2, do not apply, as is mostly supposed, and as even Luther by inserting the word "*their*" in his translation assumes, to the wives of deacons, but to deaconesses.[5] Of the position of deaconesses and the extent of their services, nothing certain can be learnt from the New Testament. Still the above-mentioned passage borders on the conclusion, that their service was rendered in the houses of members of the church, on which account the apostle requires them not to be slanderers, carrying gossip from one house to another; and also that they had to do with the distribution of alms for the poor, whence he specially enjoins them to be "faithful in all things." Quite different in kind is the institution of widows, mentioned 1 Tim. v. 3 sqq. The deaconesses were in the first place called to render service, and then received, if needful, their maintenance from the church; while in the case of widows, as their age (above sixty years) and the injunction of the apostle, that no widow who could be supported by believing relatives should be admitted on the list, show, maintenance was the main point. Besides this, however, they received, as "widows indeed," who had proved their Christian faith by holy behaviour and active benevolence, an honourable position in the church, and also rendered such services as their age permitted, though the apostle gives more prominence to the obligation of prayer and intercession, of continuing in supplications and prayers night and day.[6] For the rest, we must not imagine that this official organization of charity in the earliest times was as stable as it afterwards became. This would not correspond with the character of the times, in which it was far from the custom to commit exercises of mercy to officially instituted individuals. On the contrary, they then still bore for the most part a private character, each doing willingly and gladly what he could. The Acts speak of a Christian woman, Tabitha of Joppa, whose works of love are, in a certain sense, held up as typical, without saying a word of her occupying any official position, although her care extended to persons who, as widows, were otherwise cared for by the church. There may have been many who, like Tabitha, were "full of good works and alms-deeds," without being deacons or deaconesses. Circumstances, too, were certainly very different in different churches. While Tabitha was voluntarily ministering to the poor in the church at Joppa, the official position was elsewhere predominant. Only the outlines of an organization of charity existed. Besides the voluntary efforts of individual members, churches as such assumed through their organs the care of the needy. The management of this charity also fell to the elders, who were assisted by official but subordinate deacons and deaconesses, or even by widows or other qualified persons.

Let us not forget that it was in this very organization of charity that a novelty existed; but at the same time let us not overlook the fact that this organization itself originated solely in the new spirit by which the church was animated. We recognise this spirit in the apostolical Epistles. We will therefore collect the main features, at least, of what these tell us concerning charity.

F

In Eph. iv. 28, St. Paul says: "Let him that stole steal no more: but rather let him labour, working with his hands the thing that is good, that he may have to give to him that needeth." In these words three points are connected, upon the true moral appreciation and correct combination of which depends the healthiness of moral life, while all its diseases are occasioned by the wrong moral appreciation of these three points, and by their separation from each other. To understand the development and form of charity in the different ages of the Church, we shall have to test each epoch by its position with regard to these three points, by the soundness of its moral judgment with respect to labour, property, and alms, and we shall find that not only does failure in one point involve failure in another, but that the entire charity of the age also correspondingly varies.

In the above-quoted words the apostle already lays down labour as the duty of a Christian; and, indeed, derives the injunction to work from the prohibition to steal. Not to work is also to steal. For he who does not in some manner take an active part in the production of earthly goods, lives in one way or another at the expense of his working fellow-men. Still more decidedly is the command to work brought forward in 1 Thess. iii. 12, where the apostle expressly, in the "name of Jesus," lays down the command "to work with quietness." For a Christian to work, then, is an essential feature in the manifestation of his Christian life, and the apostle, consequently, would exclude from the Christian Church the idlers who walk disorderly, and holds himself up as an example to the Church on this very point. This he does with an unmistakeable touch of pride. He regards it as his glory and honour not to have eaten any man's bread for nought, but to have wrought with labour and travail day and night, that he might be a burden to no one. Labour, in the vocation assigned to each by God, is, however, always meant. A Christian is to work " with quietness ;" he is not to rush from one thing to another, but, constantly aiming at one point, to persevere in doing what God has assigned him in his vocation. It is true that Scripture never speaks of the earthly calling. When a calling is spoken of, as it very often is, the heavenly call, the call to the kingdom of God, is intended. But this calling includes the earthly, for it is in the work of his earthly calling that each is to work out his call to the kingdom of God, to promote the interests of that kingdom, by doing his part towards fulfilling that great task—imposed on man at the creation—of subduing the earth. It is a matter of indifference what the individual calling may be. The relation of the earthly calling is, with respect to the kingdom of God, an entirely neutral one. A man may be bond or free, married or single, and in either condition may equally have part in the kingdom of God. Or, to express it positively, every calling can and may become the material which is to be worked up into and made to manifest the Christian life, adoption of God, and participation in His kingdom. Hence the rule (1 Cor. vii. 20): " Let every one, even the slave, abide in the same calling wherein he was called." For the slave, too, may be, and prove himself, a member of the kingdom of God. It is thus that labour regains its moral dignity, its honour. It is God's, it is the command of Christ, it is the working out of the heavenly calling. The qualitative difference of work is done away with. Simple manual labour,—and it was of this that the apostle was thinking when he spoke of work,—nay, the labour of the slave, is, in a moral point of view, just as valuable as that of the loftiest kind and most comprehensive extent. Everything depends, not on what a man does, but on how he does it, with what motive, and in what spirit.

The result of labour is property. " Study to be quiet and to do your own work," is said 1 Thess. ix. 11, and 2 Thess. iii. 10. "If any will not work, neither let him eat." It is God's moral order, that the possession and enjoyment of earthly goods should be united with labour. Respect for labour involves respect for property. The two are inseparably connected. Respect for property perishes with respect for labour, and *vice versa*. Hence the apostles unreservedly acknowledge the rights of property. Nowhere can we find a trace of wealth being considered sinful, or as springing from sin. It is called uncertain (1 Tim. vi. 17), and a Christian is enjoined not to be proud of nor to trust in his riches; and they that would be rich are warned (1 Tim. vi. 9), because so many temptations accompany wealth, but its possession in itself is recognised. St. Paul can do all things in Christ, can even be rich and have abundance, as well as be poor and suffer need; and St. John does not command the rich to throw away their riches, but to have an open hand for a needy brother. It is not the rights of property—not even the rights of a property exceeding the necessaries of life —that are disowned; it is only the selfishness that accompanies it that is reproved. Against this, too, are directed the striking words in which St. James invokes a woe upon the selfish rich (ver. 1 sq.). The aim of labour is, according to Eph. iv. 18, not selfish acquirement, possession, and enjoyment, but " that he may have to give to him that needeth." The Christian is a steward of earthly goods, and knowing himself to be an incorporated member with others, knows also that it is his duty to minister to them with these gifts of God.

Hence results, on the one hand the duty, and on the other the liberty, of almsgiving. No one ever preached more strikingly the duty of serving one's neighbour in love than St. Paul, the great apostle of faith. In each of his Epistles we find exhortations to this effect. But never did any one also lay such stress upon perfect freedom in giving as he. He reminds us that the Lord gave Himself for us, that for our sakes He became poor (2 Cor. viii. 9). He points to the harvest which is to follow the sowing (2 Cor. ix. 6), and urgently exhorts to a contribution for the poor saints in Jerusalem (2 Cor. viii. 14). But nowhere do we find a word which is even like a law. He exhorts to give liberally, he praises the Christians of Macedonia, who have given almost beyond their power (2 Cor. viii. 2, 3), and strives to excite the Corinthians to imitate them. But nowhere is there even a hint that it is a duty to give a certain proportion, but again and again he insists that it is entirely at the free choice of the individual whether and how much he will give. "Every one according as he purposeth in his heart, not grudgingly or of necessity, for God loveth a cheerful giver" (2 Cor. ix. 7). Such is, so to speak, the Magna Charta of free charity. Everything here depends on readiness, on there being a willing mind (2 Cor. viii. 11), a cheerful giver, on showing mercy with cheerfulness (Rom. xii. 8). To these, and not to the greatness of the gift, is the approbation of God awarded. The Macedonians are praised because they gave simply, and therefore abundantly (1 Cor. viii. 2). Simplicity gives abundantly because it has no secondary motives, but keeps straight in view the work of love and its object. He says of them, that they first gave themselves to the Lord

(2 Cor. viii. 5); and in saying this, tells us what it is that gives its true value to almsgiving, viz. that it should not be a dead offering of money, a merely external renunciation of a portion of property, but a self-devotion, a sacrifice of selfish interest. The object of giving is to level the difference between superfluity and want, and so to produce equality (2 Cor. viii. 14). For if God made an unequal distribution of earthly goods, and allotted to one superfluity, to another want, it was not His purpose that this should continue, but in His plan of the world He calculated on the equalization to be effected by the love which imparts to others, and upon that end prefigured in Scripture by the gathering of the manna being thus attained: "He that gathered much had nothing over, and he that gathered little had no lack." Nor need it be feared that the difference would thus be only, so to speak, shifted, and that want would now arise on the part of the giver. For God, who ministereth seed to the sower, will also minister bread to those who give to others, and cause them to have all sufficiency (2 Cor. ix. 10, 8). The blessing of giving is, that the giver is contented. Contentment is, on the one hand, the presupposition of giving, on the other its moral result. Giving makes a man contented. He who is rich, but discontented, never has enough, and always thinks he neither can nor ought to give. He who has little, but is contented, has always enough, and has something to give, and by giving becomes increasingly contented. Herein lies the secret why the poor so often give more than the rich. The history of charity proves in innumerable instances that the greatest results are accomplished when many small gifts are combined. Hence the Apostle Paul attributes great importance to small gifts. He directs the Church to lay by small gifts on every Sunday, each according

to his income, especially when any one has prospered in business, so that when the apostle comes to fetch the collection, the money may be ready. A large gift is at last the result of many small gifts. Nowhere is the power of the little in this world so evidently seen as in charity. The widows' mites have always effected more than the handfuls of money of the rich. It is not where the rich give with liberal hand, but where many small gifts combine, that Charity has celebrated her greatest triumphs. It is thus chiefly that the blessing is manifested which was expected by the apostle from giving, viz. that it should become a bond to unite hearts, and that God should be glorified by all (2 Cor. ix. 12, 13).

Lastly, the apostle brings forward the carefulness with which the collection is managed. He does not deliver it alone, but associates with himself messengers from the churches, to avoid any blame on account of this abundant collection administered by him, and to ensure all being honestly done, not only in the sight of the Lord, but also in the sight of men (2 Cor. viii. 20, 21). This, too, is connected with perfect freedom of giving. For this freedom presupposes confidence in him who collects and administers the gifts. Where this is wanting, gifts will not come in; nothing but confidence can attract them in rich abundance.

None of the other apostles, indeed, has expressed himself so amply concerning alms and deeds of charity, though all have earnestly exhorted thereto. How does St. James fulminate reproofs against the selfish rich, who nourish their hearts as in a day of slaughter, who keep back the wages of their labourers! How, like a prophet of the Old Testament, does he set before them the approaching judgment! And how, on the other hand, does he insist upon works of love, without which faith is not saving faith! The true worship of God is, to visit the widows and fatherless in their affliction (i. 27). What does it profit, he says, to love in words only? Love must become deed, the deed of giving to one's neighbour what he needs (ii. 14, 15). How often, too, does the exhortation to exercise love recur in the writings of St. Peter, while St. John declares that he who does not love his neighbour does not love God, and exhorts to openhandedness, and to love, not in words and with the tongue, but in deed and in truth.

We do not possess sufficient information to enable us to give a detailed account of charity in the apostolic age. We have, however, enough to show how heartfelt and how abundant was the love that then prevailed. We should, indeed, do well to represent it as simply as possible, and not to conceive of complicated institutions or of anything under rule and regulation. As offices with definite spheres of operation originated in the different gifts with which Christians were endowed, so here, too, did the gift of "helps" still predominate. Voluntary private benevolence, which helps wherever it can, and is combined with no office, was by far the chief point; nay, the smallness of the churches, which assembled in private houses, still caused but little difference to be found between private charity and that of the Church. There certainly was, however, even in small churches, a church treasury, supplied by voluntary gifts, from which was furnished not only what was necessary for the maintenance of church officers, so far as these could not maintain themselves, or of travelling evangelists and apostles, but also means for the relief of the poor. Such means were only supplied when a member of the church was, by reason of age, sickness, or any other misfortune, incapable of earning his bread. Idlers, who walked disorderly, were, according to the direction of the apostle, to be excluded from the church (2 Thess. iii. 6). Such exclusion put an end to all regular support. Individuals might bestow gifts on an excluded person, as also upon a heathen, but they received nothing from the church, which gave no assistance to idlers. It was, moreover, assumed that relatives would do what they could. They were not to abuse the assistance furnished by the church, for the purpose of escaping their own duty. If any provide not for his own, especially them of his own house, he hath denied the faith, and is worse than an infidel (1 Tim. v. 8). It is self-evident that the assistance given was restricted to the necessaries of life. If the apostle requires contentment from all Christians, if they have food and raiment (1 Tim. vi. 8), much more would this be required of the poor.

Assistance was also rendered to the poorer members of the church by means of the *Agapæ*. These were in the church at Jerusalem at first held daily, though afterwards only on appointed days, probably even in early times on the first day of the week, the Sunday. In Troas, at least, we find the church assembled on Sunday for a love-feast, while from 1 Cor. xi. 34 we may at least conclude that the members of the church had their regular daily meals in their own houses. The members of the church brought with them both food and drink for the meal, the rich more, the poor less or nothing. The provisions were then eaten in common; the celebration of the Lord's Supper followed, on which account the apostle (1 Cor. xi. 20) also calls the whole meal the Lord's Supper. In Corinth and, as it appears, in other places also (Jude 12), all kinds of disorders prevailed at the love-feasts. Instead of consuming in common what was provided, each took beforehand what he had himself brought, and made an independent meal instead of the common Lord's Supper. Thus the poor were left with only what they had supplied, and went away "hungry and ashamed." This is severely blamed by the apostle, who enjoins that they should tarry for one another and then partake of a common meal, in which one should not have superfluity and another scarcity, but that the superfluity of one should compensate for what was lacking to another. Thus these love-feasts became a bond uniting the whole church without distinction, and contributing at the same time to the support of the poor, and the more so that the fragments that remained were undoubtedly allotted to them.

Widows and orphans were very specially received among the poor. The Old Testament, in which they so often appear as particularly the objects of the Divine protection, and are commended to the special care of the pious, already pointed to such reception. It was just in this point that the regular care of the church for the poor showed itself most active. That a certain number of widows occupied an honourable position in the church has been already mentioned; but 1 Tim. v. 3 sqq. shows that even those who, because they were too young, or for other reasons, were not admitted to the list of these widows, were supported. Testimony was required concerning those to be admitted to the honourable position of widows, that they had brought up children, meaning certainly not merely their own, but more especially other and orphan children. This shows both that private people received children not their own into their families, for this was required of a widow before she was placed on the list of widows, and also that on the part of the church care was taken for the bringing up of orphans; for the fact that just this good work is brought forward, points out that it belonged to the office of these honoured widows to bring up the orphans provided for by the church. If the Lord Himself had bidden the children to come to Him, taken them up in His arms and blessed them, what could His Church do but interest itself in them? If the Lord Himself had been a child, and as a child lain in a manger, childhood must be a sacred thing to His people.

The entertainment of strangers is very frequently spoken of. It is required of a widow that she have washed the saints' feet (1 Tim. v. 10), and very often do the apostles exhort to hospitality. Be given to hospitality, says St. Paul (Rom. xii. 13). Use hospitality without grudging, says St. Peter (1 Pet. iv. 9); nay, the writer of the Epistle to the Hebrews recalls that great reward of hospitality, that some have entertained angels unawares (xiii. 2). To Gaius it is said with especial praise, in the Third Epistle of St. John, that he dealt faithfully with the brethren and strangers, and set them forward on their journey in a manner worthy before God; while, on the contrary, Diotrephes is spoken of with special reproach, because he neglected these duties. It is quite natural that so much stress was laid upon just this work of love. The church still bore its missionary character; every member regarded it as his duty to propagate the gospel, and to gain more believers for the Lord. All were still under the Lord's command: Go ye into all the world and teach all nations. Hence it cannot astonish us to find a more than usual movement among the Christians of the earliest times. Not only apostles, but other Christians also, went from place to place to labour for the Lord. Thus we meet with Aquila and Priscilla first at Corinth, whither they have come from Rome, then at Ephesus, and then again in Rome. We find Apollos at Ephesus, at Corinth, and then in Crete. There was a continual going and coming of the brethren. If we add to this the sharp severance of the Christians from the heathen who were here and there already of hostile mind, we shall understand why hospitality was so commended, and why it was exercised to so great an extent. The brother who was travelling was not only received into the house and provided for; he was also furnished for his further journey (Tit. iii. 13), accompanied some distance on his road, and then taken leave of with prayer. And not merely did individual Christians exercise this hospitality, but the church too, as such, took care, by means of its rulers, for strangers and guests. Hence, among the qualities required of a bishop is, that he should be given to hospitality (1 Tim. iii. 2); and hence the apostle directs Titus to furnish Zenas and Apollos for their journey, that nothing be wanting to them, for which purpose the members of the church are to render their assistance (Tit. iii. 14). Wherever a Christian came, if he found a church, he found a family, who received him as a member. We learn this from the Acts of the Apostles, and the salutations and thanksgivings of the Epistles furnish a further proof. Indeed, the greatness of the age consisted in this very feature, that Christians of all places knew themselves to be fraternally one, and that in this oneness all differences disappeared.

Even that most deeply rooted social distinction of the ancient world, the distinction between bond and free, disappeared and became unimportant. The relation of the Church and of Christianity to slavery is viewed erroneously, when the former—as is frequently the case—is regarded as labouring from the very first with full consciousness for the abolition of slavery. On the contrary, the position taken up by the church towards slavery was at first an entirely neutral one. In its sphere the contrast between the free man and the slave is, like every other contrast, done away with. Here there is no more master and slave, than there is Greek and barbarian, rich and poor, male and female; all are one in Christ, and bondage is no more a hindrance than freedom is a requisite for admission into the kingdom of God. The slave has just as much a share in it as the free man. If the free man is Christ's bond servant, the slave is the Lord's free man. In the sphere of the external, however, in civil and social life, the church did not think of abolishing these contrasts. The master remained a master, the slave remained a slave. The result of the obliteration of the contrast in the kingdom of God was not the external emancipation of the slaves, but only that the Christian slave served his master more faithfully and conscientiously, and that the Christian master treated his slave with kindness and gentleness as a brother in Christ. There is not in the New Testament a trace of the emancipation of slaves, not even 1 Cor. vii. 21, where the apostle, on the contrary, advises the slave, instead of caring for freedom, rather to make good use of his calling as a slave.[7] Neither can I read in the Epistle to Philemon, that St. Paul entreats for the liberty of Onesimus. Such thoughts were far from the minds of the early Christians, if it were only because they lived in the hope of the Lord's speedy return, which threw quite into the background the span of time still separating them from the longed-for consummation of the kingdom of God. To prepare for and expect that great day of Christ's appearing claimed all their care, and this was as much in the power of the slave as of the free. Of what use then would freedom be to him? Looking to a higher aim, to the freedom which Christ brings, he did better to remain for this short time a slave.

On the whole, this hope of Christ's speedy return, which was the ruling power of the entire sphere of Christian life, was so also of charity. Arrangements were not made in view of a long continuance on earth. The time is short; and if this fact urged on the one hand to employ it profitably in abundant well-doing (Gal. vi. 9), still, not the future, but only the present was its aim. In prospect of the end, when all misery, all need will cease, Christians helped each other as much as they could, shared what they had with each other in brotherly association, and were content and patient in hope of the day which would bring eternal joy. And thus, without many special institutions or need of elaborate arrangements, the end was attained, that in the Christian Church none suffered want. Nay, these poor churches were thus able to stretch out a helping hand beyond their own immediate circle. For when famine was imminent at Jerusalem, the Christians of Antioch sent relief (Acts xi. 29), and St. Paul gathered in the Gentile churches a large collection, whose proceeds exceeded even his expectations, and came with it, in fulfilment of a promise he had made (Gal. ii. 10), for the relief of the poor saints at Jerusalem. Love proved itself to be a powerful bond uniting the Gentile churches with the Jewish mother church at Jerusalem, and with each other. Nay, even the heathen experienced this love. For if it was a rule to do good, specially to fellow-believers (Gal. vi. 10), this love was still large-hearted enough to prove itself to be love to all men, and to show to the heathen what a new spirit—a spirit unknown to the ancient world—here prevailed.

This state of things could not continue. It was the spring-time, which, like every earthly spring, passed away. It was the time of childhood, which with its glow and brightness disappears. It is a mistake to look upon the apostolic age as in such wise a model for after ages, as to make its institutions always a standard. It is only the disposition then prevailing that furnishes a standard. As for institutions, it is only their foundation that was laid, and upon this future ages have to build. The Church has to live its life in the world, to perform its tasks in the world. And this cannot be done without the sin that is in the world working too, and bringing forth its obscuring effects. Even the history of charity exhibits such obscurations. Already in the New Testament itself we hear the reproof: I have this against thee, that thou hast left thy first love (Rev. ii. 4). Still the image of the primitive church, which we take with us, gives us the certainty that there is in it a something new, which the ancient world never knew, that the love of Christ is implanted in His Church; and herein we have a pledge, that although this new life of love may be temporarily obscured, it can yet never disappear. The Church of Christ never can and never will be without the exercise of love and mercy. The sun has risen, and will always triumphantly break through every cloud that obscures it.

BOOK SECOND.

THE AGE OF CONFLICT.

CHAPTER I.

POVERTY AND DISTRESS.

THERE was poverty and distress enough in the mighty Roman Empire. Whether there was more than among ourselves is a question difficult to answer. For, apart from the fact that the information extant does not suffice to furnish even an approximate statistic of poverty, the circumstances of the times were so fundamentally different from those of the present day, that a comparison would only lead to very erroneous results. Thus much may, however, be said, that a pauperism such as we see accompanying our present state of civilisation did not exist, at least in the first centuries of the Church.

In Rome itself, indeed, the Proletariat was more numerous than in any one of our modern cities. If we may regard the 320,000 of the male population of the city (the *plebs urbana*), to whom Augustus presented a bounty of 60 den. each (almost 50s.), as being nearly all persons who could not live without relief, we get—even supposing boys to be included in this number, and therefore adding only a due proportion of females to the plebs—about 580,000 of the class needing support, to 10,000 senators and knights, *i.e.* persons possessed of property. If then we add to these (not reckoning slaves) about 20,000 soldiers, and 60,000 foreigners living by trade and commerce, as persons possessed of a competency, we have

90,000 not needing support to 580,000 Proletarians, *i.e* a proportion of one to six and a half, a proportion very far above that existing in any modern city.¹ In Paris, which may best be compared with Rome, there were in the winter of 1879-80 but 130,000 registered paupers. And this, too, was Rome, the capital of the world, which was privileged to be maintained by the rest of the Empire. We must indeed beware of judging by the utterly exceptional circumstances of Rome those of the whole Empire, a mistake often committed, for the simple reason that we know most about Rome. Things were very different in the provinces; and even large cities like Alexandria and Antioch, much as they strove to be miniature copies of Rome, undoubtedly exhibited more favourable proportions. Chrysostom, at a time when poverty had considerably increased, reckons one-tenth rich and one-tenth poor to eight-tenths between these two classes.² On the whole, the first ages of the imperial epoch, down to the times of the Antonines, under whose government declension was already apparent, are among the most prosperous periods not only of Roman, but of universal history. After the storms of the civil war, the provinces enjoyed a lasting peace. The contests carried on on the borders did not affect the lands of the Mediterranean coasts; the arbitrary government and domestic disorders of the later emperors of the Julian house were felt chiefly at Rome. Many inscriptions testify that the provincials were contented, even under the sway of emperors, whose images, like that of Nero, appear to us in the darkest colours. The government was systematic, the administration of justice in civil cases was uniform, such exhaustion of the provinces as prevailed in the later days of the republic no longer took place, at least not in like proportions. Taxation was moderate, and on the whole justly distributed. The direct taxes were received at the imperial treasury; the indirect taxes were still indeed farmed, and under this system the over-assessment of the taxpayers could not be entirely avoided, though even bad emperors strove to lower it. The rates of taxation were set up for public inspection, and facilities were everywhere afforded to provincials to prosecute legally for any injustice done them in this respect. Trade and commerce flourished. A network of artificial roads, kept in excellent repair, traversed the Empire; the sea was now free from pirates, and the government devoted great attention to harbours, canals, and river navigation. The standard of gold introduced by the emperors failed, indeed, to effect perfect unity of coinage, but it created a coinage willingly accepted throughout the Empire. An intercourse and exchange of produce between the wealthy Mediterranean countries, such as the world had not yet seen, was developed. Besides Alexandria, Antioch and Carthage, Rome was especially the great mart for the wares of both East and West. Enormous treasures flowed into Rome, and the provinces were still taxed in her behalf; but money was always flowing back again from Rome to the provinces, and the luxury practised in the capital, repulsive as may be the form it often assumed, contributed to the promotion of trade and commerce. Even if the industry cannot be compared with that of modern times, it was nevertheless highly developed, skilled handicraft especially having attained a perfection never before witnessed. Agriculture and cattle-rearing were carried on in a rational manner, and their results far surpassed, both in quantity and quality, those of former times. The cultivation of fruit, vegetables and the vine were scarcely behind that of our own days. Pliny's Epistles, which give us a glimpse into life in the country and towns of Upper Italy, exhibit throughout well-ordered conditions, in which poverty, to any large amount, could not occur. This is also the case throughout the whole East, where trade especially flourished, and where the contempt for labour, found in Rome, never prevailed. Even beyond Rome care was taken by the authorities for the regular importation of corn, for the due supply of the markets and the suitableness of the prices charged for provisions. Hardly any other government ever did so much as the Roman for this branch of administration; and whenever a town or district was visited by any special calamity, such as earthquake, conflagration, or temporary famine, even bad emperors showed themselves ready to send relief.

Nor must we lose sight of the fact, that circumstances, in many respects so entirely differing from our own, prevented the occurrence of such distress as we are acquainted with. Even the difference of climate is an important one. The countries lying round the Mediterranean Sea have all a milder climate, in which the struggle for existence is more easy to wage. Whether the necessaries of life were more reasonable in price than at present, is difficult to determine; but at all events, the wants of the inhabitants of the South were less, and this alone would make living cheaper. In Rome everything was of course dearer, especially, as is always the case in large cities, rent. A modest dwelling in the upper stories of one of the large lodging-houses came to about £16.[3] Many possessed only a sleeping-place, or wandered about in the taverns, or in the worst case spent the night in some portico.[4] On the 1st July, the day for change of lodgings, many poor families, driven from their dwelling, might be seen wandering in the streets, because they were unable to pay their rent. Martial describes such a departure.[5] A man, emaciated by hunger and cold, and some women, are dragging a three-legged bedstead, a table with two legs and other old lumber, broken earthenware, a pot smelling of bad fish. This looks like what occurs in our days. In the provinces, however, living was cheaper. The times, indeed, in which, as Polybius relates,[6] a medimnus of wheat (about $1\frac{1}{2}$ bushels) was worth 4 oboli = $6\frac{1}{2}$d., and board could be had in taverns for half an as, *i.e.* a little above half a farthing per day, were indeed past. The imperial epoch exhibits a great rise of prices. But still these bore a not unfavourable proportion to wages. Mommsen reckons the Roman bushel of wheat in the early days of the Empire at 1 denarius; and this was, as the parable of the vineyard labourers also shows, the usual day's wage. Now, the week's ration of an adult would amount to about five bushels, consequently this quantity could be procured for five days' wages. An inscription of the imperial age shows that a traveller paid at a tavern 1 as ($\frac{7}{8}$ of a farthing) for bread, and 2 ases for other food.[7] The two denarii, which the good Samaritan left with the host, were therefore an ample provision. Meat was proportionally dear. According to the famous inscription of Stratonice, Diocletian settled the price of beef and mutton at 1s. $2\frac{2}{5}$d. the kilogram, pork at about 2s. $10\frac{3}{4}$d.; a fowl cost 1s. $2\frac{2}{3}$d. But the lower classes ate little or no meat, which was regarded as a luxury. An edict of Nero expressly forbids the sale of meat in cooks' shops; they are only allowed to offer for sale cabbage and shell-fruits,[8] a restriction which could only be carried out among a southern people.

The inequality of property was indeed considerable, still it was not as great as at present.[9] The largest property mentioned during the imperial epoch does not reach £4,500,000. The augur Cn. Lentulus and Narcissus, the freedman of Nero, are said to have possessed this amount. When it is considered, that such property could in those times be scarcely otherwise invested than in estates, and yielded in this manner at most 4 per cent., the result would be an annual income of £180,000. And what is this compared with property to-day? The property of the Rothschild family amounted in 1875 to £200,000,000, and doubled itself every fifteen years. The consciousness of the equality of all citizens, a survival of the republic still operative, considerably mitigated the inequality of property. Conscious of this equality, the people expected from the rich an equalization of property by means of gifts and the application of wealth to the public good; and such equalization was, as we have seen, extensively practised. "If he has inherited millions of sestertii, he can well spend 400,000!" exclaim the fellow-citizens of Trimalchio in Petronius,[10] and this feature of the satire is certainly taken from life. An industry like ours, now the source of so much distress, was unknown to the ancient world. Equally so was such a system of credit as ours, trade being everywhere carried on for ready money. Property was not so fluctuating, and though it became increasingly so, the fluctuation of the present day was not even approximated. Great possessions for the most part assumed the form of extensive land-owning, and pernicious as was the effect of the *latifundia*, still this form of capital was less oppressive to the classes without property than that which now prevails.

All this considered, we may well declare, that in the earlier ages of the Church, there was no pauperism of the masses except in Rome; and there, imperial liberality took care that every citizen should be fed, however poorly. Independently of great calamities and times of famine, distress was confined to cases of individual poverty. How helpful it was to the Church, that its beginnings and the beginnings of its charity took place at a period so favourable in a financial point of view, need not be further detailed. Its duty was thereby essentially facilitated. In presence of a poverty thus confined to individual cases, its almsgiving could also be of a strongly individual character; while the pauperism of masses always impresses upon almsgiving also a wholesale character, and makes an individual treatment of special cases difficult, if not impossible. The Church had time to strengthen in all directions, that, when the system of the Roman Empire fell into decay, and a hitherto unknown pauperism of the masses was the result, it might prove equal to the greater task imposed on it.

For the Roman Empire was evidently on the road to a universal impoverishment, the first traces of which may be perceived even under the emperors of the Flavian house. Under the Antonines they are still more plainly visible, in connection indeed with the great calamities then experienced by the Empire, the sanguinary wars in East and West, the bad harvests and pestilences. The increasing oppressiveness of taxation, the constant introduction of new objects of taxation, are, as well as the remission of taxes, symptoms that impoverishment was setting in. When, *e.g.*, the Emperor Hadrian remitted £6,750,000 arrears of tribute, which had accumulated during sixteen years, this was a sign of the great difficulty experienced in the collection of taxes. For each year £425,000 had been uncollected. We do not indeed know the amount of this tribute, but the deficiency was in any case disproportionately great. In Prussia, in the year 1863, the deficiency of taxes was only 0·03 per cent. A still more evident symptom is presented in the fact, that estates had now very frequently to be sold to raise money for the arrears of the land-tax. Already, in the reign of Caracalla, a law was enacted to this effect. From a similar law of Aurelian, it appears that such estates often found no purchasers, because none was willing to bear the burdens laid upon them. It was therefore enacted by the emperor, that the Decurions should take the land and pay up the arrears. This, however, not answering, it was appointed that all unsold land should be divided *pro rata* among such neighbouring proprietors as were capable of paying taxes.[11] Another suspicious symptom was the decrease of the population, not only in numbers, but also in physical strength. A great increase of population, such as is now met with, was unknown to the old world. Several causes combined to prevent it. Such were, the want of esteem for infant life, resulting in an entirely disproportionate amount of infant mortality, the exposing of children, which was nowhere regarded as a crime, the widespread and increasingly known hereditary sins. The laws which imposed special taxes on the unmarried and childless, and promised rewards to the married and those who had many children, were of no avail. After the third century, the numbers and strength of the population everywhere decreased. What legions had not Italy formerly sent forth! Pliny already wonders how it could have been possible. All Greece could not supply more soldiers than were furnished by the one city of Platea in the times of its prosperity. Even so early as the reign of Nero, the interior of Sicily was almost depopulated.

The deepest reason for this impoverishment is to be found in the prevailing contempt for labour. No people can attain to lasting prosperity among whom labour is not held in honour. But an Athenian or Roman had a right, and it was even in a certain sense his duty to be idle—a right, for he was a member of the ruling people, and as such had a share of the spoils of war, which in the old world were a special and chief source of the public property—his duty, for the State made claims upon his activity. He had to be present in public assemblies, in the Comitia to vote, and in courts of justice to act as juryman. In Athens a third of the citizens sat daily in court. Hence a trade or business could not be regularly carried on. For such attendance a citizen received in Athens his judicial fee, his theatre-money, in Rome, his corn-money and *congiaria*. Thus the free man grew unaccustomed to work, and let himself be maintained by the State. As for work, there were slaves to do it. It is the curse of slavery that it makes free labour a disgrace. Besides, slave labour is far more costly. It was computed that in Rome a slave performed only half the work of a free man. Nevertheless, free labour cannot hold its own against slave labour. It is supplanted, and the worst injury done by slavery is the ruin of the middle classes. This was the case in Athens, where the once vigorous class of artisans could not compete with the factories in which the work was done by slaves; and in a still higher degree in Rome. The class of small landowners, who formed the strength of Italy in earlier times, gradually disappeared, being supplanted by the large estates of the Roman nobles. In the place of farms and villages appeared the Ergastula, the slave prisons, with their hundreds of slaves. An administrator with slaves divided into decuries and centuries, working by day with fetters on their feet, and sleeping at night huddled together in slave prisons, ruled, where formerly free peasants had tilled their own fields. If the estates were too distant to be safely cultivated by slaves, they were, indeed, let, but under oppressive conditions. The tenant was obliged to deliver up the whole produce, and received only a fifth, or even only a ninth, for himself. Under such circumstances a well-to-do class of tenants would not, of course, arise. It was but natural that, as plantain farming increased, the cultivation of corn should entirely cease on large estates, and be superseded by pasturage. Larger and safer profits were thereby obtained, because fewer slaves were needed; and these, now that the great foreign wars of conquest had come to an end, began to be expensive. Slavery produced similar effects in the sphere of industrial activity. The great estate owners, with their herds of slaves, not only produced the raw material, but also carried on its manufacture by their means. Nay, they even entrusted the sale of, and traffic in these manufactured articles to slaves, who received a certain rate upon them; and thus slaves often acquired property. It not unfrequently happened that slaves carried on some branch of trade at the expense of their masters for a certain share in the profits, or that a master set his slaves at liberty upon condition of their paying him a certain proportion of their gains in business. Thus did Callistus, the subsequent Bishop of Rome, carry on for his master, Carpophorus, a banking business.[12] In the towns there were edifices, etc., for the greater undertakings, and persons who carried these on by means of their slaves, while in the houses of the Roman nobles the productions of handicraft were also the work of slaves; and thus the free artisan could only obtain the custom of those of lower rank. The free workman could not resist such a development of slave labour. He was often worse off than the slave. For the latter was taken care of by his master from selfishness, for the sake of the capital invested in him. "If I were free," says a slave in Plautus to his master, "I should live at my own risk, I now do so at yours."

If the supplanting of the middle class as a result of slavery enlarged the chasm between rich and poor, the perfect economic liberty which existed concurred in producing the same effect. The imperial epoch down to Diocletian was a time of free trade in the widest sense of the word. There were, indeed, customs, excise, harbour rates, but these did not exceed the limits of moderate exchequer dues. There was freedom of transit throughout the Empire, for every freeman could travel and sojourn wherever he would; there was freedom of trade, for every one might seek profit by his own means, where and how he thought he could most advantageously find it. There was no kind of organization of labour. The consequences of this were the same as they are with us. Capital accumulated in ever fewer hands, while great capital in the general struggle outflanked and exhausted small capital. Certain examples of rapid enrichment, met with in the satirists, are characteristic. It must have been Juvenal's own experience, that the barber, "under whose razor his beard had rustled," became the possessor of innumerable estates, and could compete with the aristocracy in luxury;[13] and Martial's, that a manumitted cobbler was rolling in riches upon the estate of his former master, which had now become his own.[14] Under Domitian, a former shoemaker of Bologna, and a fuller of Modena, gave gladiatorial shows.[15] The father of the emperor Pertinax at first carried on a large charcoal, and afterwards a large wood trade. Having grown rich, he traded with his money, especially by the cutting up of peasant farms, lending to small proprietors at high interest, in order afterwards to drive them from their possessions. He thus accumulated large estates. The financial talents of the father were inherited by his son, who had all the paraphernalia of Commodus' extravagance, including hundreds of prostitutes, sold by public auction. That extravagance would thus be dispersed in a larger circle did not trouble him, for it brought in money. Vespasian invested a portion of his capital in a hired-carriage business, on which account the people jocularly called him the hired-coachman. It is quite characteristic of an age of economic freedom to seek gain wherever it is to be found, without much caring how it is acquired.

Capital, thus accumulated in the hands of individuals, took chiefly the form of landed property. As with ourselves large capital swallows up small, and large industrial undertakings lesser enterprises, so too did large landed estates absorb smaller ones. The enormous *latifundia*, the estates of many square miles, which have been already mentioned, arose. Even in Nero's time half the province of Africa belonged to only six owners. Seneca tells us that country-seats were like provinces; and Pliny, in whose days the harm of this system was already very evident, says: "The *latifundia* have ruined Italy."[16]

Times in which capital accumulates on the one side, while means become so much the more straitened and wretched on the other, are exactly fitted to furnish a productive field for usury. All Roman history is interwoven with complaints about usury, and with a fruitless contest against it.[17] In the times of the first emperors the rate of interest in Rome was moderate, viz. 6, and often only 4 per cent., while to take above 12 was reckoned usury. In the provinces much more, 24, nay even 40, was taken, and even respectable people were not ashamed of thus enriching themselves. Seneca, who talks so much of virtue, carried on an extensive traffic in usury. He had invested several millions in Britain, and when he suddenly gave notice that he required higher interest for his capital there, all Britain was disquieted.[18] Countless numbers were ruined by such blood-suckers, and, with increasing impoverishment, the complaints concerning usury and its pernicious consequences also increased.

The result of all these circumstances was not merely a shifting of property, an accumulation of it with the few and the impoverishment of the many, but also the impoverishment of the Empire in general. The unequal distribution of property is in itself no evil, assuming that the money is again circulated with prolific effect by those with whom it has accumulated. The luxury rendered possible by wealth awakens industry, revives trade, and gives employment and food to thousands. And this was the case in Rome. The early imperial epoch everywhere exhibits an enhanced activity running parallel with increasing luxury. The glass manufactories of Phœnicia, the purple dyeries of Tyre, the weaving factories of Alexandria, the whole produce of skilled workmanship then at its perfection, the horticulture, the cultivation of the vine—all these could not have continued unless Rome had been a mart for their different wares, unless the increasing wealth of individuals had made it possible to pay the highest prices for them.[19] But luxury has these results only so long as it remains within certain reasonable limits. There is also a foolish luxury which produces exactly opposite effects, and may, as may generally be said of Roman luxury in the time of the emperors, be certainly carried too far. In fact, it was the luxury now existing in Rome, which could not fail at last to lead to the impoverishment of the whole people. How much fertile land was withdrawn from its proper destination by the country-seats as large as provinces, by the gardens and preserves of the Roman grandees; how much labour power was squandered unproductively in buildings, when lakes were made where land had been, merely to gratify a whim, and a site for a palace produced in the midst of the sea by artificial mounds; what capital was laid out in the silver plate and expensive furniture with which the palaces were filled, silver vases of 500 lbs. weight, triclinia which cost four million sestertii (about £35,000), in ornaments of pearls and precious stones, which were then in fashion; how many strong men, who might by their labour have contributed to the increase of the national wealth, wandered idly about the streets of Rome as clients in the atria of the nobles, as citizens who received largesses of corn. If a great part of the money expended in luxury remained in the Empire, a great part was consumed without results, and no less went abroad. The trade with India and Arabia was almost entirely passive. Some wine and pottery were indeed sent thither, otherwise the silks of China, the precious stones and dyed goods of India, the spices of Arabia, would have had to be paid for in ready money, without any mutual exchange, and Pliny estimates their annual amount at 150,000,000 HS. (about £1,200,000 to £1,250,000).[20]

If such extravagance on the part of private individuals must have been pernicious to the general welfare, how much more so that of the emperors themselves! It was the wasteful profusion of Nero in particular, that laid the foundation of these financial embarrassments of the State, which, notwithstanding the subsequent careful administration of the finances by the emperors of the Flavian house, never ceased and led to a continually heavier burden of taxation. The gifts of Nero to his friends and dependants which can be computed—and how many are there which cannot—amounted to 2200 million HS. (about £19,300,000). After his reign the Pretorians received their corn gratis, and ever increasing largesses in addition. At the commencement of a new reign they received, according to Tacitus, 15,000 HS. (£130), according to Josephus, 20,000 (£175) each, an expenditure of 150 or 200 million HS. (£1,750,000). The government of the State became on the whole increasingly expensive. The army required more, the rising and increasing bureaucracy not less.

Legally regarded, taxation in the Roman State was unlimited. The emperor imposed it arbitrarily. The provinces were a conquered country, which as such was entirely in the hands of the conqueror, and when under Caracalla the provincials collectively received the Roman citizenship, the rule of the emperor was already so absolute, that he could treat the whole Empire as his domain. Augustus, perceiving the importance of a careful administration of finance to the monarchy which was coming into existence, laid a secure foundation for the levying of taxation by instituting an accurate survey of the land. But if the levying became thereby more equitable, the screw was now only the more severely applied. To the original taxes, poll-tax and tribute, were added after Vespasian taxes on trade and commerce. The oppressiveness of taxation was rendered still worse by the manner of levying it. While with us, if an individual is incapable of paying his taxes, his quota gets left out and is paid by no one, the whole body of citizens was, according to Roman fiscal law, answerable for it. The taxes were calculated for the entire community and must be fully paid up, even if ever so many persons were unable to contribute their shares. If even the city could not pay the whole, the deficiency was regarded as a debt due to the State; and thus was formed, it might be said, a negative national debt, of the extent of which we have an example in Hadrian's remission of taxation, and which must have been far more burdensome than modern national debts.

Besides taxes properly so called, a large quantity of natural productions (*munera publica*) had to be delivered. The provinces had to furnish corn, and what was more, to send it where it had to be consumed. Clothing, arms, etc., had to be supplied for the army. There were also endless transports of supplies and soldiers, relays of horses, *ad apparatum annonæ, ad splendorem defensionis publicæ.* When the emperor Probus kept the soldiers to useful labour, *e.g.* to the laying out of vineyards on the Rhine, "that they might not eat their bread for nothing," and, beguiled by the dreams of peace which we often meet with in a world weary of the noise of arms, added, "we shall soon need no more soldiers," his biographer, Vopiscus, breaks out into the sigh: "The blessing is scarcely to be understood! A State at peace far and near! Who in all the world would then need to forge arms, to forward supplies, to give personal or horse service! The ox would again belong to the plough, and the horse to the employments of peace."[21] The supply of post-horses was felt to be a specially burdensome requisition. Augustus had instituted, at the expense of the State, a regular postal service, which was afterwards imposed upon the cities. The use of the post was not open to the public, but the officials all had free travelling. Aurelius Victor shows how severe was this burden, when he calls the post "a very useful institution, which the greed of posterity transformed into a pest to the Roman world."

If we add to this, that with the Antonines the season of peace came to an end, that the whole world was in arms during the third century, that on the boundaries there was the never-ending war with the barbarians, who were already penetrating with desolating results into the Empire, in the interior continual revolutions, no strong government, but a series of conspiracies and assassinations, we shall no longer be surprised at the rapidly increasing impoverishment of the Empire, and shall understand how the emperor Diocletian, with whom a new period begins to dawn, found himself constrained to adopt despotic financial measures, to tax the necessaries of life, etc.,— measures which for a period postponed, but could not entirely prevent, the overthrow of the Empire. From Constantine onwards the Empire already exhibits the appearance of political bankruptcy.

While prosperity was thus everywhere declining, a revolution in political economy was at the same time commencing from very small beginnings. In this sphere, too, the life of the old world was dying out, and gradually giving place to a new; and from the time of Constantine economic relations bear a modern, and no longer the ancient character. And the more powerful the subsequent influence of this revolution upon charity also, the more necessary is it to notice its beginnings.

The entire ancient economy received its impress from slavery. Now, in the imperial epoch the number of slaves began considerably to decrease. There was nothing to compensate for the cessation of the wars of conquest, which had constantly furnished the Empire with fresh hordes of slaves. The Jewish war once more brought a multitude of slaves—for the most part, indeed, tolerably useless—into the market; but from that time the only important supply was from children born in slavery, for the wars with the barbarians yielded but few. Though the marriages of slaves were, consequently, more favoured than formerly, though the attempt was made to preserve the existing races of slaves by better treatment, though they were chastised—we must use the expression, because it answers to the views of the ancients—more rationally, so to speak, all this was insufficient. For the manumissions were now more numerous than the increase. Hence the price of slaves rose considerably. While Cato states the price of an agricultural slave to be £48, 15s., Columella reckons it at £78, 15s. This rise of prices made slave labour so costly, that in the sphere of agriculture, recourse was had to a different system of farming. For this other reasons also existed. The employment of the *latifundia*, especially for pasturage, became increasingly unprofitable, because the impoverishment of the people seriously reduced their ability to purchase the products of pasture farming, meat, wool, skins, etc. Able inspectors for the great estates were, as we perceive from the complaints of Columella and Pliny, difficult to find. Letting was impossible, because a respectable class of tenants did not exist. Thus the farming of large estates gave way again to small farming. The proprietorship of the *latifundia* indeed remained, but the proprietors increasingly gave the farming of portions of their lands to slaves, for the surrender of a portion of the produce. These, indeed, remained slaves, but they already occupied a different position from the former agricultural slaves, who worked divided into decuries, with fetters on their limbs. Slavery was beginning to be transformed into vassalage.

A corresponding change was simultaneously accomplished in trade. Here, too, retail trade was obtaining more room; here, too, the free workman was beginning to supplant the slave. A kind of middle class was being formed out of the numerous freedmen. But the main point is that the period of free trade was ending, and an organization of labour of a peculiar kind beginning. The means were furnished by the *collegia* of artisans, who much resembled the guilds and companies of the middle ages, but nevertheless essentially differed from them in being institutions connected with the State. The State demanded from the *collegia* certain performances, and granted them in exchange certain privileges, especially immunity from other burdens. Their members were a kind of State officials, and the labour thus organized formed a part of the ever increasingly complicated machinery of the State. Something similar had formerly existed. All the officials of the *Annona*, the seamen who carried corn, the storehouse officers who collected, housed, and distributed it, and the bakers who baked the bread, were State *employés*. The State had already a multitude of officials such as the modern State is unacquainted with. The organization of labour was instituted, while this class of officials was increasing; and labour, when organized into *collegia*, was received into the machinery of the State.

The entire development, which commences in the period we are now considering, and comes to maturity in that which follows, was undoubtedly a progress. Labour again began to be appreciated; the thought, that the hitherto despised artisan also served the State, became a customary one. A just moral estimation of free labour was not indeed yet reached. To this the old world never rose. The organization of labour was only a forced organization; and force, as we shall see, became, as the difficulties of the State increased, more and more the impelling and uniting power.

The question, whether Christianity had already had any influence in this change, is an obvious one. It is possible, for it took place at a time when the influence of Christian views in general on heathen views cannot be doubted. On the other hand, Christianity, as then constituted, must be reproached for not making the spirit by which it was ruled more powerfully dominant. If the genuine Christian appreciation of the work of a man's calling had been still active in the Church, and had been carried out to its consequences, the result must have been something very different from this forced organization of labour, which at last transformed all into slaves. But when the Church began to exercise an influence upon public life, the Christian view of labour was already much obscured. This, too, furnishes a proof of the fact, how little Christianity pervaded the ancient world.

Nor could this new organization prevent the financial ruin, being indeed, on the contrary, a symptom of it, and becoming in its turn a co-operative cause; for it made a flourishing state of trade and agriculture impossible. It could only with difficulty postpone it for a period. The characteristic of the age continued to be an increasing impoverishment ever extending to larger numbers. It was in the period next succeeding, that it reached its full development and imposed new tasks and duties on Christian charity. But it was of importance, that the Church was born in a more fortunate age, and its activity begun before it was made difficult by a distress so gigantic in its proportions, that it could gain strength while troubles were increasing, and thus become capable **of greater exertions.**

CHAPTER II.

FIRST LOVE.

THE charity of an age, the proportion of its alms, the motives from which, and the manner in which they are given, the application of its liberality, and the end kept in view therein, are not accidental. For as charity is but one department of Christian life, so too does it receive its impress from the character of Christian life in general during the period in question.

The Christian life of the first centuries still exhibits first of all the character of youthful vigour. Faith developed its full energy in the transformation of the moral life, love was ardent and rendered men willing and capable for any sacrifice, hope for the speedy consummation of the kingdom of God, by the glorious return of Christ, pointed to an aim of the whole life, beside which all others appeared insignificant. The transition to another period is first denoted by the crisis called forth by Montanism. From that time onwards the Church lived, mingled with the world, and itself became different. Its early youth was past. In the time of Cyprian the features may already be recognized—at least as in formation—which give their impress to the Post-Constantinian Church, nay, which in truth characterize the entire mediæval Church down to the Reformation.

Youth does not reflect, it acts from the direct impulses

arising from its present abundant vitality. Youth is willing to make sacrifices, ready in its easily excited enthusiasm to give up anything. Youth is easily moved; the abundance is as yet greater than the form of its vitality. There is as yet nothing of ossification, hence the manifold variety of shape it can assume; it is rather hostile than inclined to uniformity, and its life has a facility for taking new forms. In short, everything is as yet in a state of active fluxion.

So, too, was it with the charity of the period. There was as yet no reflection as to why alms were given and benevolence exercised. For this was self-evident. Still less was consideration exercised as to whom to give and do good to. Where there was distress, relief was given. "We communicate to all, and give to every one who is in need," says Justin; and the older Fathers interpret our Lord's saying, "Give to every one that asketh of thee," to mean quite simply, that every suppliant was to receive without distinction.[1] "Give simply to all," it is said in the Shepherd of Hermas,[2] "without asking doubtfully to whom thou givest, but give to all. For God desires thee. to give to all of that which thou hast. They who receive will give account to God, why and for what they receive. They who take anything under an appearance of pretended need, will have to give account of it to God, but they who give will be blameless." Similarly does Clement of Alexandria[3] warn, not to judge who is deserving and who is undeserving. "For by being fastidious and setting thyself to try who are fit for thy benevolence, and who not, it is possible that thou mayest neglect some who are the friends of God." Still less was it reflected what the giver of alms and kindnesses would obtain for himself. The thought, indeed, that almsgiving and beneficence bring a blessing was not absent, this being already stated in the New Testament. Nay, here and there emerges already that notion, which goes beyond the New Testament, that this blessing consists in the expiation of sin. But all these thoughts are by no means so prominent as they are in Cyprian, and still more so in later writers. Alms were given, not for the sake of the giver getting something, but to relieve the poor and needy, from the direct constraint of sympathizing love, and the consciousness of the love experienced in Christ. How simply does the reference to reward appear in the Epistle of Barnabas, and how does it still keep within the limits of apostolic teaching! "Hesitate not to give, and give without grudging, but consider who will be the good Repayer of the reward."[4]

Great self-sacrifice was found in all the churches. Christians gave willingly, not merely according to their means, but beyond them. They gave not of their superfluity, but of their labour, and shunned no sacrifice. Not till the third century do we hear complaints of the abatement of this readiness for self-sacrifice. Hence there needed as yet no special incentive to arouse it, and still less any constraint, whether direct or indirect. It was the time of perfectly free gifts. "Every man according as he is disposed in his heart!" The apostolic saying was still the rule; and if here and there some teacher of the third century already spoke of the law of tithes and first-fruits, this points, indeed, to the way in which alms would subsequently be given, but in presence of the gladness with which they were then bestowed, it sounds almost like a discord. Nay, there was as yet no need of urgent exhortations to almsgiving. The preachers of the Post-Constantinian age, a Chrysostom, a Basil, an Ambrose, an

Augustine, use every inducement to move their hearers to liberal alms. Of this we find nothing in this period. It is remarked, that it is the command of Christ, love is praised, the love of Christ to us extolled, the congregation are reminded, that they are common sharers in things spiritual, and that it should therefore be their custom to be such in things earthly,[5] but all this so simply and plainly, that we directly feel there was as yet no need of oratorical arts to arouse to activity the love which everywhere existed. Cyprian is in this respect also the first who strikes a different note. His work on alms is the first that was written on the subject. The fact that it should be necessary to write upon it, already shows that the times were beginning to change and first love to abate.

Appointed forms for the practice of charity in the churches existed indeed from the first, appointed rules, appointed persons, on whom the relief of the poor was officially incumbent; but all these were more or less fluctuating. And this is why it is now so difficult to obtain a correct view of them. Undoubtedly there were different arrangements in different places. It was not till church government in general acquired a more stable form, that these rules also took a firmer and more uniform shape. As yet institutions did not exist. There was no need of houses of hospitality, houses for foreigners, orphanages, hospitals, so long as every Christian house was an asylum for travelling brothers, and every Christian man and woman was ready to receive the indigent. There was indeed an official diaconate, but this did not exclude any from freely exercising in their measure and in their own manner the works officially incumbent upon it. Together with the regular charity of the Church, was developed a rich abundance of private beneficence, and the two frequently run into each other without observing any strict limits.

Besides, this period was the time of conflict with the prevailing heathenism, the time of persecution. This not only imposed new tasks on Christian charity—care for those who were the objects of persecution, for confessors in prison, for those who had suffered the loss of property and were in poverty through their faith, for those also whose entrance into the Church caused them to give up their former trade, and so deprived them of the necessaries of life,—it also impressed upon all other exercises of charity a character quite peculiar. Even if persecutions came only by fits and starts and lasted in their violence but a short time, the opposition to the surrounding heathen world, the internal struggle against it, and the consequent tension were lasting. Christian life during this period acquired thereby great energy, deep earnestness, genuine simplicity. Christians, as Tertullian says, are always standing on guard against the dark demoniac powers which rule around them: a " race ready for death," they know what they are about, and what pertains to winning the victor's crown; all their efforts are concentrated on this one point. The task of fleeing from the world was in the front rank of the Christian's duties, that of penetrating the world with the new life only gradually dawned upon him. The Church had as yet no abiding place in the world; it was more like a camp in presence of the enemy than a peaceful city. It had not yet developed the ornamental, the luxuries of life were still far off; no splendid churches, no proud priesthood, no lands, no possession of money or property. Till the turn of the second and third century it was scarcely imagined, that the Church could ever become a ruling power, could ever occupy the same position in respect to the State that heathenism now did. On the contrary, thought was turned to quite another victory, to the Lord's return and to the victory which He would introduce. Hence the future was not yet cared for, the present conflict demanding all the Christian's efforts and strength. In conformity with this state of things, charity, too, was never directed towards the future. The Church as yet made no collections for the benefit of posterity, nor do we meet with institutions calculated to be a benefit to future generations. Such means as it had were devoted to the exigencies of the moment, and men did not shrink, especially in times of persecution, from giving all that they possessed to contribute to the distress of the hour. With respect to this, however, the greatest energy was displayed. The object aimed at and actually attained, was, that no member of the Church should suffer want. But all was plain and simple. Just as there were no large churches, so there were no large buildings and institutions for the relief of the poor. As it was required of every Christian that he should labour with all diligence for his own maintenance and then be satisfied with bare necessaries, so also was this required of the poor. Almsgiving had then nothing of that weak humanity so often apparent in later times, and nothing was more remote from the practice of Christians, than the encouragement of mendicancy and the preparation of a comfortable living for idlers and vagrants at the expense of the Church. " For those able to work, work, for those unable to work, compassion," is a saying which, though found in a heretical work,[6] was the motto of the whole Church.

Work, property, alms—these three are closely united.

A healthy charity is only possible where healthy moral views of work and property prevail, as inversely, a false moral appreciation of labour and property inevitably produces morbid phenomena in the sphere of charity. A healthy charity can neither be attained to, where there is an over-estimation of property, where wealth is regarded as the supreme good, poverty as the greatest evil, nor where property is undervalued and wealth looked upon as no real good, poverty as no real evil. For in the former case no one can feel bound to sacrifice his earthly good, for the sake of a higher good, for the service of his neighbour, and gifts and alms will fail. In the latter these will not indeed be wanting; on the contrary, alms-giving will be enormous, but its right application will fail. For if to be poor is no evil, if, on the contrary, it denotes a higher moral condition than to be rich, the task of charity cannot consist in opposing and alleviating poverty. Almsgiving then becomes a good work in itself, a good work complete in the act of giving and the renunciation of property therein involved, without regard to the application of the gift and the end attained thereby.

A rejection of property on principle is only met with in schismatic circles. The Gnostics, in whose eyes this world was the production of an inferior, and not of the supreme God, could not but consistently reject all possessions and enjoyment of earthly property; and such notions were also so much the more natural to the Judæo-Christians with their legal and ascetic tendency, in that they had in the Essenes[7] the model of a communistically constituted society before their eyes.[8] When, on the other hand, it is said in the Epistle of Barnabas:[9] "Thou must in all things be in partnership with thy neighbours, and not say: That belongs to me! for if we share in imperishable things, how much more in perishable;" or when Tertullian[10] boasts: "We Christians have all things in common except wives," these sayings are but stray expressions for the duty of the equalization of property in love, and do not designedly go beyond the appreciation of property laid down in the New Testament.

It is certain, however, that we do really encounter a strong indifference to earthly possessions. The more heartily the heavenly blessings of the kingdom of God were embraced, the more must earthly goods have lost their value. The more intently the eye was directed to another world and to a speedy termination of this dispensation, the more must earth have appeared a foreign country, and earthly property an uncertain possession. To this was added the fact, that in times of persecution the temptation connected with wealth was stronger than usual, while experience showed, that the rich renounced their faith more readily than the poor. "You are dwelling here in a foreign city," says Hermas to Christians.[11] " Would any one dwelling in a foreign city provide himself with fields and expensive accommodations?" Christians should consider, that in such a case the lord of the city will require of them also, obedience to the laws therein enforced. Then they must obey and thus apostatize from Christ, or lose their possessions and be driven out. Hermas had himself experienced the dangers of riches, and was reminded by the Angel of Repentance: "When thou wast rich thou wast useless, now (after Hermas had lost his property) art thou useful and skilful in thy calling."[12] But such thoughts also have indeed their points of contact in the New Testament, and even if individuals have exceeded in this respect, like the ascetics met with in many churches, *e.g.* the confessor Alcibiades in Lyons, who lived on bread and water only, but was afterwards persuaded by his fellow-confessor Attalus, that it was not wrong to enjoy what God had made,[13] or liket he Christians in Carthage whom Tertullian praises[14] for abstaining from the use of wine and meat, the Church on the whole held firmly to the rule, that it is not sinful to acquire and possess earthly goods and to enjoy in moderation what God bestows. Hermas[15] somewhere compares the rich to round stones, who must be hewn before they can fit into the building of the Church, that is to say, must be deprived of their wealth if they are to be genuine members of the Church. He is, however, by no means of opinion, that their whole property should be taken from them, but only so much, that they may not succumb to the temptations of riches. This happens to them because they are good, and God would have them remain good. Even Tertullian, with his strong tendency to despise the world, and greatly as he delights in certain individual ascetics, like those who took neither wine nor meat, when speaking less from such individual inclinations than from the common consciousness of the Church, describes Christians as taking part in the intercourse and trade of the world and possessing and enjoying the good things of earth: " We are no Brahmans or Indian gymnosophists, no wild men of the woods, and separatists from life. We are mindful of the gratitude which we owe to the Lord our God, and do not despise the enjoyment of His works. We only so moderate it as to avoid excess and abuse. Hence, like yourselves, we do not dwell in the world without markets, baths, hotels, workshops, fairs, and everything pertaining to the intercourse of life. Like yourselves, we practise navigation, agriculture, commerce ; we take part in your trades, we let you make use of our labour for the common profit."[16]

Clement of Alexandria expresses himself the most fully concerning earthly possessions in his work: "*What rich man is saved?*" He first rebukes the fear, that a rich man cannot generally speaking be saved, as unfounded. He can, if he lives rightly. He then shows, in an exposition of the history of the rich young man, how he must live to be saved. "The Lord commanded the rich young man to sell all that he had. But what does this mean? He does not command him, as some too hastily conclude, to throw away his present property, to separate himself from his possessions, but to get rid of false opinions concerning wealth, the desire and pursuit of it, the cares of life, the 'thorns which choke the good seed.' For it is not great and a matter worthy of emulation to suffer want of property. Else indeed, he who is stripped of everything and begs for the barest necessaries, would be happiest and most pleasing to God, and would alone possess eternal life. This too would be nothing new, for even before Christ there have been those who have renounced property, one to have leisure for science, another for the sake of dead wisdom, a third for vain praise and honour. The Son of God does not demand that which is an object of sense. He demands something greater, more divine, more perfect, the cleansing of the soul, the disposition from all that proceeds from passion. This is a learning peculiar to a believer and a teaching worthy of the Redeemer. They who renounce property still retain passion in the soul. They walk in pride and vanity and in contempt for other men, as though they were themselves something supernatural."[17] Clement then expressly acknowledges that wealth is a benefit. It too

I

has its advantages, for it enables us to help others. If the Lord had taught us to cast away our possessions, His teaching would be in opposition to the command to love our neighbour as ourselves. Hence we are not to cast away our property. It is the material, the instrument subjected to the right use of those who know how to make a right use of it. If any one makes a wrong use of a tool, the tool is blameless. And this is the case with wealth wrongly applied, as it is by many. Its nature is to be useful, and everything depends upon how it is applied. Nay, salvation in general depends on nothing external. It is not the question whether a man is high or low, rich or poor, but whether he has faith, amendment, love.[18]

These are thoroughly sound views of earthly possessions; the kingdom of God here occupies a neutral position with respect to riches and poverty. The rich man may obtain salvation as well as the poor, if only he uses his wealth aright. It is true that Clement sees the right use of wealth chiefly in almsgiving, but how healthy the moral views still were is shown by the fact, that while he urgently exhorts to make friends of the poor by means of wealth, he also reminds that this is not done by isolated gifts, but by active association in giving. The right use of property is not wholesale almsgiving, but the application of a man's own property to the care of the community.[19]

It is then upon the community that Clement lays the greatest weight. "God led the race of man to brotherly community by giving up His Son and bestowing the Logos as a common benefit on all, by granting all to all." Hence everything ought to be common, and the rich should desire to have no more than the poor. The saying, "I possess it, why should I not enjoy it?" is therefore not humane nor brotherly. "I possess it, why should I not impart it?" sounds more like Christian love. He who so speaks and acts is perfect, and fulfils the command: "Thou shalt love thy neighbour as thyself." "I know that God has given us the right of enjoying, but only to the limits of the necessary, and according to His will enjoyment must be common. It is not right that one should live in superfluity, while many are in want. And how much better is it to be a benefactor to many, than to possess a splendid house; how much wiser to spend one's wealth on men than on jewels!" [20]

Only the necessary! This is everywhere accounted a principle in the use of earthly possessions. Simplicity, contentment, moderation, are required of every Christian. All luxury, all wantonness met with the more disfavour, the more the surrounding heathen world had at that time sunk into an immoderate voluptuousness, a frequently senseless luxury. The first particular by which a woman who had become a Christian was distinguished from her former female friends, was her simple life and renunciation of luxurious dress. The Christian family was distinguished from the heathen by the great simplicity which prevailed in furniture, in domestics, in eating and drinking. This corresponded with the earnestness of Christian life. How often do Clement and Tertullian insist that luxury enervates, that it is womanly and not manly! "On the road to heaven," says the former, "the best provision is frugality, moderation is the shoe, and beneficence the staff." [21] In his *Pædagogus* he gives numerous injunctions of the kind respecting even the smallest details, and they all amount to this, that a Christian must be moderate in eating and drinking, in clothing and furniture. He pities the insatiable, who collect their dainties from all parts of the world, with whom "the basting ladles and the kitchen form the central point of existence,"[22] who "emasculate" the simplest aliments by the over-refinement of their cookery, and eat cakes and pastry instead of nutritious bread. He does not, indeed, desire to condemn variety of dishes, but says that no special eagerness should be shown for any of them. So, too, he regards it as no sin to drink wine, but reproves the luxury which is practised about different kinds of wine. No one should be eager about Chian wine just when it is scarce, or about Syracusan just when it is difficult to procure. One single kind of wine, the gift of the one God, will satisfy a prudent drinker. So, too, should moderation be observed in house-gear. All such things as polished glass vessels, which cannot be drunk out of without fear of breaking them, silver plates and dishes, and all things made of ivory, must be far removed from our well-ordered life. The Lord also ate out of an ordinary dish, and made His disciples sit down on the grass. He, the humble Lord of the universe, washed their feet, girded with a towel. He brought no silver basin from heaven. He asked drink of the Samaritan woman, who came to draw water in an earthen pitcher, and desired no royal gold.[23] We cannot escape the admission that these details are affected with a certain amount of one-sidedness. The propensity to the renunciation of the world is far stronger than that to the appropriation of it. Here and there we find a certain quaintness in this zeal against luxury, as when Tertullian can suffer no wreaths, because God made flowers grow, but not wreaths, and does not allow dyed wool, because if purple wool had been pleasing to God, He would have made purple-coloured sheep;[24] or when Clement goes on to say, that God openly supplies all that is necessary for life, but, on the contrary, conceals things unnecessary, such as gold and pearls with earth and sea.[25] Clement also rejects wreaths because they are unnatural, we can neither see nor smell the flowers. When the Lord wore a crown of thorns, it does not become His people to crown their heads with wreaths. They know of a better crown, an eternal wreath. At the most, he allows ornaments of flowers on the table.[26] All this sounds somewhat strange to us, though we cannot fail to admire the earnestness by which it is pervaded, its healthy natural contrast to the luxury of the age, a luxury which had degenerated into something contrary to nature, its manly opposition to the prevailing effeminacy, and can understand how, in churches which were on the average but poor, there was never a lack of means when the assistance of oppressed brethren was in question. Simplicity and contentment were, to quote another saying of Clement's, "always full arsenals."[27] "The love which imparts to others is like a spring, which is always furnishing a draught to the thirsty, and yet always fills again."[28]

Very specially does Clement disapprove of the keeping of a large establishment of servants. He describes in one place, and not without biting sarcasm, the life of the aristocratic ladies of the day. There is no spinning or weaving room, no work-room for women; they are surrounded by men, who chatter to them all day long all manner of gossip, and relate to them the scandals of the town. They trifle away their time with deformed slaves, with lap-dogs, peacocks, and parrots. But they care not for the poor widow, who is surely worth more than a

Maltese puppy; they have no eyes for the pious old man, who is certainly of greater value than those caricatures of men; they give themselves no trouble about little children, but feed parrots and plovers. "They turn out their own children and take young birds into their houses."[29] It is very characteristic, that the want of deeds of charity is here placed in connection with the dislike of work, and with a vain and empty life, as on the other hand, that we always find, both in Clement and Tertullian, when describing the Christian woman, the combination of the three features of diligence, simplicity, and beneficence. She works at home, she clothes herself, her husband, and her children in garments made by herself; she works in the kitchen to prepare a treat for her husband; she is not ashamed to stand herself at the hand-mill; and then she stretches out her hand to the poor, bestows upon the beggar the fruit of her labour, and, emulating Sarah, feels no shame in ministering to the traveller. "There is something beautiful," cries Clement, "in a diligent housewife. There is joy all around her. The children rejoice in their mother, the husband in his wife, she herself in both, and all together in God." She is, on the other hand, far removed from a vain love of finery. "The handmaids of Christ should love simplicity. Simplicity is the forerunner of holiness. It smooths out the inequalities of property. A holy ornament should surround your wrists, the joy of giving and the diligence of the housewife. On your feet should glitter untiring zeal in well-doing, and walking in the ways of righteousness. Your necklaces and chains are modesty and simplicity. Such jewellery comes from God's workshop."[30]

Of work we find but little, nay, strikingly little, in the

Fathers. Even when Clement of Rome and Barnabas state in detail what appertains to a truly Christian life, work is omitted. When, however, it is spoken of, we directly feel that it is quite differently estimated from what it was in the heathen world. It is no longer looked on as a disgrace. Clement of Alexandria represents labour, even hard labour with the spade,[31] as something which is an honour to man. That on the part of the Church there was earnest exhortation to labour, is shown by the Apostolical Constitutions. These make the apostles themselves exhort young men: "Work with self-restraint at your handiwork, that you may always have enough for yourselves and for the poor, and may not be a burden to the Church of God. Idleness is a disgrace, and he who will not work among us must not eat, for the Lord our God hates idlers, and none must be idle who honours God."[32] It is characteristic that the apostles therein bring themselves forward as examples of labour, a sign that the remembrance of the apostles, the remembrance that the founders of the Church had themselves been working men, was a strong motive to industry. It was just this side of apostolic life that tradition had carried out still further. We possess an old catalogue of the apostles, in which some trade or occupation is ascribed to each of them. Peter, Andrew and the sons of Zebedee are fishermen, Philip an ass-driver, Bartholomew a vegetable gardener, James the son of Alphæus a mason.[33] It is a sign of the high respect entertained for labour, that the Church should depict these features, or, if we have in them the remains of a true tradition, should maintain them. It also testifies to the high estimation of labour, that many ecclesiastics then carried on, besides their ministrations in the Church, some trade or handiwork, and supported themselves by it. This was not considered as dishonouring nor inconsistent with their clerical calling. Even after the time of Constantine the occupations of clerics were so extended, that the exemption from the trade tax granted them by Constantine was revoked by subsequent emperors, because the loss of revenue was too great. The Apostolic Constitutions also enjoin the bishop to take care that orphans should learn a craft, " for happy is he who can help himself, that he may not take the place of the orphan, the stranger, and the widow.[34] Every kind of work was considered honourable, except such as ministered to heathen worship, and all connected therewith—the theatre, the circus, etc. He, who as a heathen had carried on such an occupation, had to give it up when he became a Christian. But trade, and even stockjobbing, were not excluded. Callistus, afterwards a bishop, formerly kept a money-changer's stall.[35]

It is true that the deeper moral appreciation of work, the idea of the vocation, the connection of the earthly with the heavenly calling, had not yet risen upon the Church. The motive to work still continues to be only, that a man may thereby support himself and give alms, may help others. At most is it hinted, as in Clement of Alexandria, that it is manly and a part of self-discipline to work. The universal duty of work, the importance of the work of any calling, as a test of our Christian life and as promoting the kingdom of God, is nowhere expressed. Hence the Apostolic Constitutions, after having said that no Christian should wander about idly, but should apply himself to his work, can only say of the rich, that they ought to visit believers and hold pious conversation with them.[36] Nevertheless, work and benevolence are, in conformity with New Testament thoughts, most intimately connected, nay, it may be said they were never so intimately connected as then. There were not many of the rich who could give of their superfluity in the churches. The largest quantity of alms and contributions to the Church's labour of love, came from those who had to earn their daily bread by the sweat of their brow. This is undoubtedly one of the reasons why charity was then so greatly blessed. What is easily parted with from superfluity and given without sacrifice, is also easily taken and easily lavished. But where what has been given has been laboured for, care that the gift is rightly applied accompanies it, and a blessing rests upon it. This is among the traits, which bestow upon the charity of the period its peculiar character.

Finally, and this feature of the Christian life should be specially noted, since, more than anything as yet remarked upon, it is specially distinctive of the charity of this age, Christian life is as yet thoroughly congregational. The connection of the Christian community was closer and more intimate than ever again. The individual Christian lived entirely in and for the Church. The churches were still small and like a family; each Christian knew all others. Even Cyprian in a town like Carthage knew all the members of the church.[37] When Marcia, the mistress of Commodus, was about to apply to him for the Romish Christians imprisoned in the mines, she asked, and Victor the bishop told her, all their names.[38] The churches still consisted in an overwhelming majority of living members, of those who, with full conviction and free choice, had taken the step of uniting themselves to the Church, and who were thoroughly in earnest in their Christianity. They were as yet unencumbered by the dead weight of an indifferent multitude. Nor had the notion as yet obtained, that a perfect Christian life could only be led in separation from the ordinary congregation, that this contained only imperfect Christians, while the perfect led their separate lives apart in monasteries or in the desert. The more abrupt the external severance from all non-Christians, the closer was the connection of those who knew themselves to be united by faith to the one Lord. Discipline was strict, but it verified the saying: That which excludes also the more energetically includes. The distress of the times, the common suffering, bound them only the more closely together. How must these churches have kept together in the conflict, how must each persecution have contributed to weld them into a solid whole! If Christians called themselves brothers and sisters, they were so indeed, and the kiss of peace, which was given before the celebration of the Holy Supper, was no empty symbol. Correspondingly with this, charity also was congregational. The individual gave to the Church what love impelled him to bestow; gifts were collected for the poor in the meetings of the Church, at public worship and at the Lord's Supper; the officers of the Church dispensed them. The relief of the poor by the Church is the special characteristic of the charity of this age.

This did not exclude a liberal abundance of private benevolence. "Our compassion gives more in the streets than your religion does in the temples," says Tertullian;[39] and we only need to read the description which he gives of the charity of a Christian woman, as she goes from street to street, even into the poorest hovels, how she receives the stranger brother into her house, and opens kitchen and cellar to provide for him, to be convinced, that there was certainly no lack of such private charity, of personal almsgiving and the rendering of personal service. Nor was there yet any kind of effort to narrow this private benevolence, and to place all charity, in a onesided manner, under the immediate direction of the Church and its officers. The first traces of this are not apparent till the end of this period. According to the Apostolic Constitutions, the individual member of the Church, who desires to relieve the poor, is to apply in the first place to the deacons, for they know the poor; the deacons are also to be the managers when any one proposes to prepare a love-feast for the poor.[40] Nay, they even express the notion, that the bishop is the mediator between God and the poor. "It is fit that thou (the member of the Church) shouldst give, and that he (the bishop) should dispense."[41] But even when such restriction and guardianship of private benevolence was not yet thought of, charity nevertheless found its centre of gravity not in the latter, but in the relief administered by the Church. This is the special characteristic of the times. It certainly continued also, nay, was still more conspicuously developed, during the period next ensuing, the times after the triumph of Christianity. It was then, however, already accompanied by another element, viz. the institutional. For, while the churches had hitherto been entirely relegated to their own resources, the now Christian State asserted itself as a joint factor in deciding; and both these circumstances contributed to alter and to deteriorate the character of Church aid to the poor. In the Middle Ages it entirely disappears, and in its place we find, on the one side, private benevolence broken into endless fragments, a wholesale almsgiving, which properly scarcely deserves the name of relief of the poor; on the other, the agency of the orders in hospitals, monasteries, till at last, in the times of the Reformation, the notion of the relief of the poor by the Church was again brought efficiently forward, and its restoration was striven for under entirely different circumstances.

It is this care of the poor by the Church that we shall specially have to discuss, for private benevolence withdraws by its very nature from observation and exhibition. It is a picture full of light that we have to sketch. It is like a sunny morning, on which indeed the clouds that will afterwards obscure the sun are already appearing on the horizon. It is the time of first love, which passes away, and must do so. Youth cannot last for ever, either in the Church or in an individual. If the charity of this heroic age of the Church, as well as Christian life in general, is comparatively purest and fairest, the germs and beginnings of the subsequent corruption are also latent in this same age.

CHAPTER III.

THE MEANS FOR THE RELIEF OF THE POOR.

EVEN the collection of alms for the relief of the poor is in closest connection with Church life, is an act of this Church life itself. It takes place in the assemblies of the Church, and it is in his contribution to these collections that the individual testifies his membership therein. There were, however, in such collections, gifts of two kinds, the one of which answers rather to Church life on its legal side, the other to its public worship of God. This distinction has hitherto been not, or at least not sufficiently, regarded, a circumstance evidently connected with the fact, that only very recently has the relation of the Christian churches to the Romish *collegia* been clearly perceived.[1] According to its legal form, the Church appears as a *collegium*, very much resembling the legally allowed *collegia* of the poor (*collegia tenuiorum*), and Christians had undoubtedly cause for giving prominence to, nay, insisting on, this similarity, because it afforded them, at least in the more peaceful times, and before systematic persecutions began, a certain legal protection. Now, as we before saw, these *collegia* were allowed to collect contributions for their social purposes, though with this limitation, that only one collection per month was allowed. Thus, too, did the members of the Christian churches give in every month their contributions to the church chest; and Tertullian designates these contributions *stips*, the very same name which they bore in the *collegia*, and the church chest *arca*, as was then also customary. There was indeed this essential distinction, that the members of the *collegia* were obliged to pay a certain sum, while Christians were quite free to choose whether and how much they would put into the *arca*. "Every one deposits a moderate contribution monthly, if he chooses and if he can, for no one is forced, but each contributes voluntarily," says Tertullian, and adds concerning the application of the contributions: "It is, so to speak, a depositum of piety. For it is not applied to feasts and drinking bouts (as was the custom with the *collegia*), but to the support or the interment of the poor, the bringing up of boys and girls who have neither property nor parents, the relief of the aged, the shipwrecked, and those who are in mines, in prisons, or in exile."[2] Similarly Justin Martyr: "Those who are able, and desire to do so, give of their free will as much as they choose. What is collected is deposited with the president, and with it he supports the widows and orphans, and those who through sickness or any other cause are in want, assists prisoners and strangers, and provides for the needy in general." He is not here speaking of the gifts offered at the Lord's Supper, the oblations, but of the voluntary contributions of the Church,[3] which Cyprian also decidedly distinguishes from the oblations.[4] The two were originally offered in quite different assemblies, the oblations at the celebration of the Lord's Supper, the *stips* at morning worship. In Cyprian the church chest is not called *arca*, as in Tertullian, but *corbona*. It is also thus designated in the Apostolical Constitutions.[5] And this is not without significance. The name *corbona* is derived from the Jewish worship (comp. Mark vii. 11), and its employment is a sign, that the likeness between the assemblies of the Christian Church and the *collegia* was already beginning to be lost sight of, and giving way to Old Testament Jewish models. The analogy with the meetings of the *collegia* recedes also in the circumstance, that contributions were afterwards made, not monthly, but on the first day of every week. Cyprian reproves those who, when they attend public worship, disregard the *corban*, with desecrating the Sunday. Similarly do the Apostolic Constitutions regard it as among the duties of a Christian to put something into the *corban* every Sunday.[6] It seems, however, that only smaller sums were at that time put into the *corban*, and that larger gifts had assumed another form. The *corban* had then already forfeited the character of church chest. This latter had become the fund of the poor, and as such remained in the Church, to give every one who entered the house of God the opportunity of also thinking of the poor.

More important than the deposits in the *corban*, at least more significant with respect to the development of charity, are the gifts of natural produce, the so-called oblations, connected with the celebration of the Lord's Supper. If the contributions hitherto discussed manifested that the giver was a member of the flock, the custom of oblations most closely connected the giving of alms with the highest act of worship, brought forward gratitude to God as the motive of giving, and, which is specially important, gave prominence to the sacrificial character of the gift.

The custom of offering gifts at the celebration of the Lord's Supper is evidently connected with the original form of this solemnity. This formed no part of morning worship, but was joined to an evening meal partaken of in common. It is thus that we meet with it in the days of the apostles, and this seems to have remained the general custom down to the beginning of the second century. Then, however, the celebration of the Lord's Supper was separated from the common meal, and transferred to the morning service,[7] while the evening meals continued at first still as love-feasts (*Agapæ*) of the whole Church, and afterwards as meals prepared for its poorer members. To these meals every member of the Church contributed according to his ability, and this custom continued even when the celebration of the Lord's Supper was transferred to the morning service. At its commencement the members of the Church brought natural productions, which were collected by the deacons. Of these, what was required for the Holy Supper was placed upon the altar, the rest was applied partly to the maintenance of church officers, partly to the relief of the poor. A thanksgiving, expressing gratitude for the gifts of the first as well as of the second creation, was then pronounced over the gifts. For believers offered these gifts to God as the first-fruits of the creatures (*primitiæ creaturum*), and at the celebration a portion of these gifts were to be the vehicles of the gifts of the second creation.[8] At the same time, those who had presented the oblations were mentioned by name in the prayer. The prayer in question, which we find in almost the same form in all the older liturgies,[9] and which may therefore be regarded as a component part of the liturgy of this period, runs thus: "And, O Lord, accept also the offerings of those who to-day bring an offering, as Thou didst accept the offering of righteous Abel, the offering of our father Abraham, the incense of Zachariah, the alms of Cornelius, and the two mites of the widow; accept also their thank-offering, and give them back the eternal for the temporal, the heavenly for the earthly." Then followed the prayer of consecration and the distribution of the holy bread and wine.

The gifts offered, at first by no means consisted merely of the bread and wine needed for the Lord's Supper, but of natural products of every kind. This may be inferred from the fact that, at the beginning of the fourth century, a series of resolutions was passed in Councils to restrict the oblations to bread and wine. Milk, honey and oil, which were also required in worship, were only allowable on certain days.[10] Gifts of natural products of another kind did not, however, therefore cease; they were only no longer treated as oblations properly so called, no longer laid upon the altar and blessed, but brought without benediction into the bishop's house, or if church-buildings already existed, into the place appointed for their reception, one of the cells at the east end of the church, the so-called Pastophorium or Gazophylacium.[11]

These oblations then, in the narrower and wider sense, formed during this period the special and chief means for the relief of the poor. They were supplemented by other gifts and collections when a special need made special efforts requisite. This is highly significant with respect to the whole charity of this period, nay, it may be said that herein is its character most strikingly manifested. Herein is disclosed to us its full beauty and purity, but herein too we have already occasion to observe the points on which the subsequent, but now already commencing corruption fastened.

There is significance even in the fact, that almsgiving took place in public worship, nay itself formed a part of

K

worship. The Church moved quite on New Testament lines, and verified the saying of St. James: "Pure and undefiled worship is to visit the fatherless and widows in their affliction" (i. 27), and that of the Epistle to the Hebrews: "To do good and to communicate forget not, for with such sacrifices God is well pleased." Where the Church learnt of the highest love, the love of Christ, who died for His people and feeds them with His body and blood, there love was not merely preached about, extolled and inculcated, but also practised, and there too it was not merely symbolically represented, but an act of love was actually performed, the act of giving to the poor and needy. The Christian, too, did not approach without a gift the altar, where he was to partake of the results of Christ's sacrifice. He showed his gratitude for all God's gifts in creation and redemption by offering a portion of these gifts for the good of the poor. It was just at the altar, where all the members of the Church, both rich and poor, know themselves to be one in the one Lord, that the equalization of property between rich and poor by giving and receiving also took place in love.

Hereby were rich and poor in the first place brought into the right position towards each other. The rich gave what he gave to God, and the poor received what he received from God. Thus the temptation of the rich to exalt themselves above the poor, and the humiliation of the poor at being obliged to receive assistance from others, were removed, while at the same time discontent and murmuring, as well as insolent demands and presumptuous requests, were done away with. The rich became conscious that he only gave back to God what he had first received. The poor became conscious, that the same God, who had imparted to himself a smaller measure of earthly goods, yet took care that he should not suffer want. It was no longer a disgrace to be poor and to receive assistance from the Church. The poor, like the officers of the Church, lived of the altar; nay, to apply to the poor in general a much used expression in the Epistle of Polycarp, with respect to widows, they were themselves "the altar of the Church"[12] on which it deposits its offerings. Such gifts had not the effect, so often occurring in other instances, of separating between rich and poor by increasing and rendering still more prominent the chasm existing between them, but were a bond which united them in God, by making them conscious of their oneness in the one Lord. And the more so that the gifts were accompanied by prayer. From the very first the Church has specially remembered the poor in prayer, the whole congregation praying for its needy and suffering members. Even in the oldest form of Church prayer, as found in the Epistle of Clement of Rome,[13] we meet with intercessions for the poor, the hungry, the distressed, and subsequently widows and orphans are in the Church prayers placed next after Church officers.[14] On the other side the poor pray also for the rich, for, as above remarked, those who brought gifts were remembered in the prayers of the Church. It is a beautiful trait, too, that they also are remembered who would give but cannot, in whom therefore the disposition of love exists, but who lack the means of changing the disposition into the act. In the eyes of the Church they are of equal value with those who actually give, for she prays "for those who give secretly and those who give openly, for those who give much and those who give little, and also for those who would give and cannot."[15] The poor is not even to have the annoyance of feeling, that the rich surpass him at least in being able to give, and that they only are remembered in prayer. If the poor has but his heart full of love, he too is remembered in prayer among the givers.

Thus was perfect liberty of giving inculcated, and the purity of the gift at the same time secured and maintained. No one was in any way constrained to give, and this principle was still most emphatically insisted on. As each participated without compulsion in the Lord's Supper, so too did he without compulsion offer his gifts. The freedom of the gifts cannot be made more strongly apparent than by the fact, that it is made where fullest liberty prevails, viz. at the altar. Thus too it is precisely in the oblations that Irenaeus [16] perceives this freedom. He goes on to say that sacrifices are not absolutely abolished in the New Testament though their form is indeed altered, because they are no longer offered by slaves but by freemen, of which just the oblations are the proof. The Jews gave tithes; Christians, as those who have obtained freedom, "gladly and freely give all that they have for the Lord's service." [17] The Church indeed exhorts to giving, warns also and rebukes the sluggish, but she receives only perfectly free gifts. She takes only such as can be given with a good conscience. No unclean gift may be laid upon the Lord's altar. Profit made from sinful occupations was not accepted as an oblation, neither were the oblations of impenitent sinners. The right of presenting oblations was a direct expression for being in the communion of the Church. Heretics and excommunicated persons could bring no oblation.[18] "It is better to die of want, than to receive gifts from the ungodly and the wicked," say the Apostlic Constitutions. If such gifts are received ignorantly and unintentionally, they should be used for fuel, for it is fitting that fire should consume the gifts of the ungodly.[19] When Marcion, the well-known Gnostic, seceded from the Church, the 200 HS. which he had presented were returned to him.[20] The concern of the Church was not for the amount of the gifts, but for the love shown thereby, for she knew that love is truly a vital force, and that much love with even small gifts can effect more than great gifts without love. This was the reason she watched with such jealousy over the purity of the gifts, and of this jealousy even the above-mentioned unusual decision of the Apostolical Constitutions is a proof.

But above all is it significant that alms should be viewed as sacrifices and given as sacrifices. Herein too does the ancient Church directly follow the New Testament. This thought is excellently developed in Justin Martyr.[21] To the heathen the Christians, who had neither temples nor images, and offered no sacrifices, appeared to be godless. Justin is defending the Christians against such a supposition. He shows that they worship the true and living God and serve Him. It is true, that they bring Him no such sacrifices as the heathen, who burn in the fire what God has appointed for food, but they are taught to regard as sacrifices whatever they partake of with thanks or bestow upon the needy. We meet with exactly the same thoughts in Irenæus. According to Irenæus, God did not prescribe sacrifices to the Jews for His own sake, because He stood in need of them, but for their sakes for pædagogic ends. So too has God enjoined on us Christians the sacrifice of oblations, not because He needs them, but that we may not be unfruitful and unthankful. And the thought that these sacrifices are thankofferings[22] is again and again brought into the foreground in Irenæus. Clement of Alexandria [23] also moves in the same circle of thought. The whole life of a Christian is a festival, a continuous sacrifice, and this sacrifice consists on the one side in prayer and thanksgiving, on the other in imparting of his substance to the needy.

In Tertullian, however, a suspicious change is already apparent in this ancient Christian circle of ideas. He still adheres indeed to the ancient view, in not yet applying the notion of sacrifice to the body and blood of Christ; these are partaken of, not offered. The gifts presented are the only sacrifice.[24] But the character of this sacrifice as a thankoffering is obscured, it becomes instead a matter of works, and acquires thereby a meritorious character. It is a plain sign of this, that oblations were now brought also for the dead. The husband offered yearly for his departed wife, the wife for her husband.[25] In Cyprian, "offering for every one" is already the general custom, and it was a part of Church discipline to refuse permission to make offerings for a person deceased. Thus Cyprian forbids offerings being brought for a late member of the Church, because the deceased had, contrary to the order of the Church, chosen an ecclesiastic as guardian.[26] It is true that this custom of offering oblations for the dead grew out of the thought of communion in love and prayer with the departed. Death does not separate the departed from the Church, they still belong to it, for it is the one Church of both perfected and still militant Christians. Cyprian plainly expresses this thought: "We think of each other, and even with respect to the departed, our love for them in the Lord still continues."[27] "Not merely the high priest, but also the souls of the departed pray with us," says

Origen, and refers to the love which unites the departed and the living. But another thought is soon mingled with this, and then becomes the chief notion. While the offering of the oblation had been hitherto an act of thanksgiving, followed quite simply by the mention of those members of the Church who offered it, with the intention that the offerers should be named before God, this mention in the intercessory prayer at the Lord's Supper next became the special end of the oblation. It was brought for the purpose of obtaining the intercession to which, as made in this place and at this transaction, special efficacy was attributed. For this reason too it was brought for the dead, that the intercession might apply to them also. The husband offered for his deceased wife on the anniversary of her departure, says Tertullian, "to procure for her eternal repose and a share in the first resurrection."[28] These are the first beginnings of a custom, which was subsequently much further developed by the doctrine of purgatory, and which became in the Middle Ages a main lever of charity, nay in a certain sense the centre round which it revolved. Even the other custom mentioned by Tertullian, that custom so excellent in itself, for the newly married to offer a common oblation on the succeeding Sunday, partakes of this notion.[29] The oblation was to procure the intercession of the Church for the newly married pair. From a thankoffering, the oblation had become a work performed for the obtaining of grace.

But the thoughts originally connected with the oblations were also obscured in another aspect. While Tertullian still entirely adheres to the old view, that the presentation of the oblations is itself the thankoffering of the Church, the presentation of the body and blood of

Christ by means of the priest becomes after Cyprian the proper offering. Of course this could not but react upon the manner in which the oblations were regarded. If these had formerly been the common thankoffering of the Church, the symbolical expression of the offering of the heart accompanying prayer, they now became an offering of alms. This change of import is plainly testified by the position taken in the liturgy by the brotherly kiss. This was formerly given before the oblations, these being the proper offering. Now it was given after the oblation, for not these but the priestly presentation of the body and blood of Christ, had become the offering proper.[30]

As the original view of the oblations as a thankoffering more and more recedes, the offering of alms becomes increasingly looked upon as a meritorious act. It is especially Origen who thus regards it. The first forgiveness of sins is obtained by baptism, the second by martyrdom, the third is that which is procured by almsgiving. For the Saviour says: "Give alms, and all things are clean unto you."[31] Similarly does Cyprian regard the offering of alms as the means given to man for obtaining the remission of even post-baptismal sins.[32] The relation too of alms to prayer now becomes changed. Prayer and alms from the beginning always accompanied each other; as Scripture had already combined them. They form together the outward expression of the inward sacrifice of the heart. Now, however, alms are regarded as giving efficacy to prayer. Without alms prayer is unfruitful, it is alms that make it bear fruit, because they dispose God to kindness and indulgence. "For," explains Cyprian, "He who will at the day of judgment reward alms and good works, listens more graciously even to-day to a prayer, if it is accompanied by alms."[33] "A prayer is good when accompanied by fasting and alms." [34] We have here then already the three good works, which henceforth are more and more regarded as properly speaking good and meritorious: prayer, fasting, and almsgiving. The original thought, so well brought out by Irenæus and Justin, that the oblations and other alms are a thankoffering, is choked, and alms have already become a propitiatory and meritorious work.

The proceeds of the fund for the poor and of the oblations formed at this time the chief, and as a rule the sufficient means for relieving the poor, for Church property with any considerable returns did not as yet exist. The accumulation of permanent Church property, at least the acquisition of estates, begins to occur indeed in the last times of the conflict, but the possessions of the Church were still at any rate very inconsiderable. If the ordinary means did not suffice, or if some special need required special resources, these were obtained by a collection, a way of gathering money not unknown to the heathen, who very often obtained funds for a statue, a monument, the building of a bridge or the restoration of a temple, by collecting contributions.[35] Tertullian [36] mentions such collections, and the Apostolic Constitutions enjoin them on the bishop. "If the gifts (the oblations) are not sufficient, tell the brethren so, and appoint a collection and succour therewith the widows and orphans." [37] From a letter of Cyprian,[38] we learn particulars of such a collection. Many Christians having been made prisoners of war in Numidia, the bishops of that country applied for help to Cyprian, who appointed a collection from both clerics and laics, which yielded 100,000 HS. (£877). Cyprian accompanied its consignment with a special list of the givers, "that you may remember the brethren and sisters who willingly and speedily helped in so necessary a work, in your prayers, and give them a compensation for their good work in the offerings and prayers." It is evident that prayer at the celebration of the Lord's Supper in the Numidian churches is intended.

The extraordinary gifts bestowed upon the Church by certain affluent individuals, when they joined it, formed another source. Thus Cyprian at his conversion sold lands and gardens, to give the price to the Church and to the poor.[39] He also subsequently assigned to it part of his private property, when the fund for the poor was during the distress caused by persecution insufficient.[40] That similar acts often took place is expressly mentioned by Eusebius,[41] but they did not furnish considerable sums, because the great body of Christians still belonged to the poorer classes. By far the greater part was given not by persons of property, but was on the contrary the result of the small gifts of people of low condition, who, as the Apostolical Constitutions say, gave of their labour and of the sweat of their brow.[42] It was just this which gave special value to the gifts. In those days it was not a proportionate though still a trifling gift that was given out of superfluity, but they who had little gave much because they loved much. Nay, they who could not give of their earnings imposed privations on themselves, that they might be able to give as alms what they had spared by fasting. Already in the Pastor of Hermas, the shepherd teaches Hermas how he ought to fast. He is to abstain from drink and food, and, after calculating by the expenditure of other days what he has saved, to put it aside and to give it to the widows and orphans and the poor. Thus will fasting be an offering acceptable to God.[43] Similarly

Origen.[44] To abstain from evil, he says, is the true fast, but to abstain from meats which God has created to be received with thanksgiving by believers, is not true fasting. This is not however to be said, to loosen the bridle upon the flesh, for we have the forty days' fast, and the fourth and sixth days of the week on which we fast. The Christian is also at liberty to fast every day, not in the superstition of an observance, but in the power of abstinence. Origen then adds: "There is also another kind of pious fasting, whose praise is expressed in the writings of some of the apostles." For we read in a certain book the judgment of the apostles: "Happy is he who fasts for the purpose of feeding the poor." "Such fasting is acceptable to God and truly worthy. For it imitates Him who laid down His life for His brethren." The Apostolic Constitutions also give the express injunction:[45] "If any one has nothing to give, let him fast and apply the day's share to the saints," which in this place certainly means the Christians condemned to the mines. Besides, it was not merely individuals who employed this means of procuring themselves the power of giving alms, it sometimes also happened, that the bishop would prescribe a fast to the whole Church for the purpose of applying what was thus spared to the wants of the needy. However admirable may be the strength of the love which thus imposed sacrifices on itself, that it might be able to give to others, we must not on the other hand ignore the fact, that this combination of almsgiving and fasting already announced a corruption of almsgiving by secondary motives of an ascetic character. Emphasis was at least laid on the renunciation therein shown, *as well as* on the love of the brethren, and it was just this notion, that there was some independent moral value in self-deprivation of a portion of earthly possessions, which became, as we shall see, extremely dangerous to charity, nay destroyed its inmost core.

Thoughts already emerge fitted to obscure the freedom of giving which was at first so firmly adhered to. The effort may be perceived, though as yet only in its beginnings, to convert freely offered, into legally prescribed gifts. Two things conduced to this. First the inclination, by reason of viewing of Christianity as a new law, to apply to Christians the appointments of the Old Testament law. And this not merely by seeing in Christianity a spiritual fulfilment of Old Testament precepts, as *e.g.* of circumcision in baptism, but also by transferring the appointments of the ceremonial law directly to the Church.[46] Now the Old Testament enjoined the children of Israel to give first-fruits and tithes. The question then, whether Christians were not also obliged to do the same, was an obvious one. Irenæus[47] indeed sees the advance of the New Testament beyond the Old Testament in the fact, that the former contains no external command, but that Christians gave freely more than the Jews gave legally. So long as this was actually the fact, there was certainly no necessity to recur to the Old Testament law. But when love began evidently to wax cold, when Christians no longer gave so much, the thought must have the more impressed itself, that Christians were at least bound to do so as much as Jews. This is shown by the circumstance, that it was none other than Cyprian, the first in whom we encounter complaints of the decrease of free gifts, who was also the first in the West to refer to the tithes, and that just in connection with such a complaint. He recalls the fact, that the primitive Christians sold their possessions and gave the price to the poor. "We on the contrary now give not even the tenth of ours, and while the Lord commands us to sell, we rather buy, and increase our estates."[48] Though we perceive from this, that the tenth was not then the law, also that it was not as subsequently regarded as an apostolic institution, yet there is a ring in the words indicating that Cyprian was well inclined to make it a law.

It is in the East that we already meet with the first attempts to raise it into one. Origen directly declares the Old Testament law to be on this point binding. "The law commands the priests to sacrifice the firstlings of all fruits and cattle. I hold it needful to observe this law, as well as certain others, literally (therefore not merely spiritually as in the oblations, which were often looked upon as the first-fruits). For there are some laws of the Old Testament, which the disciples of the New must of necessity keep."[49] Origen himself evidently gives his view as only a private opinion. It was in the nature of the case, that it soon became something more. The various writings in which the ordinances and rules of Christian and ecclesiastical life were in the end of the third and beginning of the fourth century deposited, and whose latest edition the Apostolical Constitutions appear to have been, all contain the command of the first-fruits and the tenth. In the book of Clement it is required that a believer who tills a field should bring the first-fruits to the bishop.[50] In the canons attributed to Hippolytus, the command is still further enlarged.[51] Not only the first-fruits of the barn-floor and the wine-press, of oil, honey, milk and wool, but also the first-fruits of the profits of handicraft are to be brought to the bishop who then pronounces a blessing upon them, that they may serve for the feeding of the poor. Lastly, the Apostolic Constitutions expressly declare Christians, on the ground of the Old Testament law, to be bound to give first-fruits and tithes. This is in the second book, which is præ-Constantinian, restricted to corn, wine, oil and field-fruits, while in the seventh, which certainly belongs to the times after Constantine, the tenth of everything is required.[52] Of course all this does not show that the tenth was as yet law. The works quoted desired to make it such, and the ample proof adduced for the law of tithes in the Apostolic Constitutions just serves to show, that the command made its appearance as a new one which still stood in need of this. In reality the duty of giving tithes was not yet carried out, although individuals might personally fulfil it. It is well seen, however, which way the current was tending, and how far, even so early as the turn of the third and fourth centuries, that liberty of giving was departed from, which St. Paul makes so prominent in his Epistle to the Corinthians, and which found in Irenæus its enthusiastic eulogist.

The needful data to answer one obvious question, viz. what the means for the relief of the poor in a church might at this period amount to, are wanting. The only two numbers which, so far as I can see, are extant, show however, that the sums must have been, not merely in proportion to the size and means of the church, but also in themselves, very considerable. Cyprian collected in his church 100,000 HS., *i.e.* above £850, for the Numidian prisoners. The Carthaginian church cannot have been large. Cyprian makes the passing remark, that he knew every member. This points to at most from 3000 to 4000 persons. If such a church, in which there were certainly many poor, made in a short time a collection of over £850 for one single definite object, and that moreover for members of foreign churches, this testifies to a great readiness in giving. According to a note in Eusebius, 1500 widows and indigent persons were supported in Rome by the Church. Reckoning then for an adult a month's rations of five Roman bushels, which according to their average value in the imperial era were worth about 4s. 5d., a year's ration would amount to about £2, 12s. Hence, if we reckon only £2, 10s. per head, we have for the 1500, £3750.[53] Here, then, we come upon a considerable sum for even the Roman church. In later times far larger sums were given, but no period gave with a liberality proportioned to this. This indeed, considering the smallness of the churches and the scanty possessions of their members, was only made possible by the fact that all gave and gave liberally. It is just this which distinguishes this period above others.

CHAPTER IV.

OFFICIALS AND OFFICES FOR CHARITY.

It is not in its resources but in individual energy, that charity has its centre of gravity. Considerable as were the sums distributed during this period by the members of the Church, later ages furnished incomparably greater and yet attained incomparably smaller results. What distinguished this period above all others, and produced results never again attained in like proportion, was on the one hand the personal energy which was exerted in the Church, and next the regulations by which and the offices in which this energy and by it the existing means were employed.

The congregational character borne, as we have seen, by the charity of this period, naturally involves the fact, that its conduct lay where the conduct of the Church in general lay, i.e. in the hands of the presbytery, and subsequently in that of the bishop. The few documents which we possess of the same date as the origin of the episcopate, exhibit the deacons in a position equally dependent upon the presbyters, as afterwards upon the bishop. They never independently managed the relief of the poor, not even when indications are here and there found which lead us to conclude, that they disposed with somewhat greater freedom of the contributions for the needy.[1] In the Epistle of Polycarp,[2] and also in the

Shepherd of Hermas,[3] the care of widows and orphans is not designated as the duty of the deacons, but of the presbyters. Here, too, it is seen, that there never was an independent office for the relief of the poor besides that for the government of the Church. When, then, the bishop was .raised above the college of presbyters, and the constitution of the Church became monarchical, the increasing authority of the bishop must naturally have made the position of the deacons still more dependent, whether in the care of the poor or in other duties. The relief of the poor, like the entire conduct of the Church, was more and more concentrated in the person of the bishop, and this concentration rather increased than decreased during the course of the third century. From the Epistles of Cyprian we perceive, that the bishop exclusively administered the means for the poor, and that the deacons merely occupied a position of service, inquiring by order of the bishop into the circumstances of the poor, and then conveying to them what the bishop, with whom alone the decision rested, appointed.[4] Only in the time of persecution, when Cyprian was obliged to retire from Carthage for a period, did he divide the existing resources among the deacons, and commission them to deal with them according to their judgment, "that several may have wherewith to alleviate their affliction and distress."[5] Still Cyprian did not hereby give this branch of his office entirely out of his hands, for even from his place of exile he still communicated injunctions with respect to it, and had even left a larger sum with the presbyter Rogatianus, who evidently exercised, in the place of the bishop, some kind of oversight of the deacons.[6] The same kind of thing took place in Rome. At the time of the Decian persecution, Fabian

L

the bishop[7] divided the Church funds among the seven deacons. It was also during a persecution, that the deacon Laurentius gave away all the existing means to the poor, and then presented the poor to the town-prefect as the treasures of the Church. But these were extraordinary circumstances, from which no general conclusions can be drawn. In quieter times, when all went on in the usual order, the whole care of the poor was concentrated in the hands of the bishop.[8] This too we find in the Apostolical Constitutions. They compare the bishop to a father, the deacon to a son. As a son does nothing without his father, so is the deacon to do nothing without the bishop. He is to give nothing to a poor person without the previous knowledge of the bishop. By so doing he would slander the bishop, as though he did not care for the poor.[9] The bishop himself is responsible to God alone for the management of the alms for the poor. No one must interfere with or control him. It is, however, expressly enjoined as a sacred duty upon the bishop to be faithful and conscientious in the relief of the poor. He is to be compassionate, zealous in love, liberal, one who loves widows and strangers, ready to do service, himself a good deacon, and then he is reminded of the account which God will one day demand of him.[10]

Such a concentration of charity in one hand could be salutary only on the supposition, that sufficient and able assistance was at his command. This he received from the deacons, whom we find in post-apostolic times in all churches. We need but glance at the Epistles of Polycarp and Ignatius to see, the very different appearance they make in these, and in the apostolic epistles. Presbyters and deacons, and afterwards bishop priests and deacons now form the regular official staff of every church. Their numbers vary. In many places the number of seven was felt binding after the analogy of the seven at Jerusalem. It was thus in Rome, where two of the fourteen districts of the town were apportioned to each deacon.[11] The Council too of Neo-Cæsarea, said to have been held in 314, determined the number of the deacons at seven.[12] Elsewhere the number of deacons was regulated by the size of the church. A resolution corresponding herewith is contained in the Apostolical Constitutions.[13] Even so early as the third century, we meet with sub-deacons, evidently because the deacons did not suffice. They relieved the deacons of the inferior duties. There were in Rome seven sub-deacons corresponding to the number of deacons, as we find stated in a letter of the Bishop Cornelius to Bishop Fabius of Antioch.[14] The first mention of them in Spain is in the Synod of Elvira (305). In the East they were of still later appearance, not occurring during our present period.[15] For the rest, the sub-deacons do not seem to have been employed in the care of the poor, but to have relieved the deacons of all kinds of subordinate employments, especially the service at the church door, the maintenance of order in the church, the deliverance of messages, etc., by which arrangement not only was the position of the deacons raised, but their attention was more entirely given to the relief of the poor.

According to the Apostolic Constitutions, the deacons were to be the eye and ear of the bishop, through them he was to learn what was going on in the church, they were at the same time to be the right hand by which he acted.[16] And especially so in the care of the poor. The bishop made use of them both in the collection and distribution of funds. They made exceptions to gifts and gathered contributions, while on the other hand they conveyed to the poor what the bishop appointed for them. Above all, they had to investigate strictly and in detail the circumstances of the poor. They went about into houses, and when they found cases of distress they notified them to the bishop, that he might make the necessary arrangements.[17] They were not to act behind the bishop's back, though a certain amount of freedom was left them; at least the Apostolical Constitutions enjoin the deacons to dispose of the smaller affairs themselves, that the bishop may not be overburdened, and allude on the occasion to the advice given by Jethro to Moses.[18] Probably a list of those relieved by reason of the information obtained by the deacons was now already made, the so-called *matricula* in which were entered the names of all relieved, with a statement of their circumstances and of what they were to receive.[19] The services of the deacon are the most fully described in the book of Clement,[20] which indeed in its present state is perhaps post-Constantinian. He is to minister to the infirm, to strangers and widows, to be a father to orphans, to go about into the houses of the poor to see if there is any one in need, sickness, or any other adversity; he is to care for and give information to strangers; he is to wash the paralytic and infirm, that they may have refreshment in their pains. Every one is to have what he is in need of with respect to the Church. He is also to visit inns, to see if any poor or sick have entered, or any dead are in them; if he finds anything of the kind, he is to notify it, that what is needful may be provided for every one. If he lives in a seaside town, he is to look about on the shore to discover if a body has been washed ashore, and if he finds one to clothe and bury it. He is not to burden the bishop with too many requests, but to make him acquainted with all on Sundays. It is very significant that the deacons have a kind of patronage of the poor. If the deacons are on the one hand enjoined carefully to assist the poor in every respect, the latter have to render obedience and respect to the deacons.[21] This was of special importance, when the question was, to enable the poor to resume work, and to induce them to earn their own living.

There was a female as well as a male diaconate. I say designedly a female diaconate—not deaconesses. For there were not always during this period, nor everywhere in the Church, deaconesses, though there was always and everywhere somewhat of female ministration (*diakonia*), though not by any means in the proportion or development usually supposed. The history of female ministrations in the ancient Church has caused great confusion of two kinds. First, distinction has not been made between widows and deaconesses, but the former have without further ceremony been regarded as deaconesses, *e.g.*, by Bingham in former, and Neander in more recent times. Secondly, the inclination has been fostered to transfer many features taken from the idea of the modern deaconesses to the first centuries, because the desire to find there the deaconesses of to-day[22] caused their presence to be believed. The development of female ministrations was in its larger features probably as follows: that of the two institutions existing in the Apostolic Age, viz. those of widows and deaconesses, the latter for a long period entirely disappeared. In both East and West only widows are met with. Then at the end of the third century the institution of deaconesses again emerges in the East, and attains a maturity and dissemination which it never before possessed, while the Western Church, in which the need of a female diaconate was not nearly so great as in the Eastern, did not accept the institution of deaconesses, at least not as a generally diffused one, but kept to that of widows, which certainly was soon afterwards vitiated, and was never of much importance in the matter of charity. During the whole period terminating about the end of the third century, deaconesses are mentioned but once, and that in the well-known letter of Pliny to the Emperor Trajan.[23] Neither in the writings of the apostolic Fathers, nor in Tertullian or Cyprian, do we meet with them, and Origen's exposition of Rom. xvi. 1 shows, that this teacher no longer knew of deaconesses, whom he also omits in his enumeration of Church dignitaries.[24] Deaconesses have disappeared, though we everywhere meet with widows, who, supported by the Church, occupy a position of honour therein, and at the same time render it their services. This is evidently the same institution with which 1 Tim. v. makes us acquainted. Ignatius frequently sends greeting to the widows, they always follow immediately after the deacons and evidently belong to the clerical body. They are mentioned by Polycarp.[25] In the Shepherd of Hermas, Grapte occupies a position of honour at the head of the widows.[26] In the homilies of Clement, the regulation of the institution of widows forms part of the complete ordering of offices in a Church.[27] Clement of Alexandria reckons widows among Church dignitaries.[28] Origen knows of them,[29] and so does Tertullian. The institution is evidently one spread over the whole Church. We best learn the position of these widows from the writings of Tertullian.[30] They are older widows, who have resolved to remain unmarried. Being chosen for the purpose on account of their exemplary Christian life and other qualities, they occupy an honourable position in the Church, and are at the same time maintained thereby. They are at the head of the women in the Church, and have to speak at marriages.³¹ Although they are reckoned among the clergy, and occupy a seat of honour in the assemblies of the Church, they are not allowed to speak publicly in the Church, though they do instruct the women and children, especially those being prepared for baptism.³² There is certainly no distinct intimation, that they also performed such offices as belonged to the diaconate, though it may be inferred, that in the Western Church the institution continued to exist, when in the Eastern much that was allotted to widows was transferred to deaconesses, and certain intimations which at least tend to this are met with. Lucian, in his satire of the death of Peregrinus,³³ relates that when Peregrinus was cast into prison, the Christians ministered to him with great zeal. Certain aged widows, accompanied by orphan children, were seen waiting at the prison early in the morning. This leads us to assume, that it was among the services allotted to widows, to care for those imprisoned for conscience' sake, to provide them with food and other necessaries, and that for this purpose they employed the assistance of the orphan children. This notice, as well as the circumstance that widows and orphans are always named together, also places widows in relation to orphans. It was, moreover, natural· to entrust the bringing up of orphans to the widows.³⁴ Nor would that care of the poor and sick, which we at present regard as the chief point in the office of deaconesses, be entirely absent from that of widows, though it cannot be denied that it was strikingly in the background. If it had been of greater importance, more would certainly have been said of it by Cyprian, Origen, and Tertullian. The main point certainly was the honourable position occupied by the widows, their belonging to the clerical order, presiding over and instructing the other women of the Church. A passage of Origen is in this respect decisive, for he interprets 1 Tim. v. 10, where it is said of widows, that they wash the saints' feet, figuratively of doctrine. And if the entertainment of strangers had then belonged to the duties of widows, such an exposition would hardly have been possible.

During the last decades of the third and first of the fourth century, a change was effected in the Eastern Church, but certainly only in this. There arose beside the institution of widows an order of deaconesses, to whom the former surrendered both their office and their post of honour, so that they were now only maintained by the Church, and in return prayed for it, while in other respects they fell behind the deaconesses—nay, were under their supervision. It is thus that we find matters in the Apostolical Constitutions [35] in the canons ascribed to Hippolytus,[36] and in the epistles of the pseudo-Ignatius.[37] We are certainly without the documents which might enable us accurately to follow up this change to its motives, but their main features may nevertheless be perceived. It is evident that several motives co-operated, the advancing high estimation of celibacy and depreciation of the married state, the need that various offices should be performed for the female portion of the flock and the development of worship, especially the *Arcani Disciplina*. Already in Tertullian we find traces of a disorganization of the institution of widows. What he characterizes as a monstrosity, viz. that a virgin not yet twenty years of age was received into the viduage,[38] shows, that the thought had already receded which had called the order of widows into existence, viz. that the widow who had behind her an unspotted married life was the worthiest representative of the female sex, and the fittest to assist other women with her advice and comfort, and to set before them an example worthy of imitation, and that, on the contrary, unmarried virginity was beginning to be more highly esteemed. From Tertullian even it may be inferred, that the occurrence which excited his wrath was not an isolated one, and when Clement of Alexandria says of a widow, who was leading a truly Christian widowhood, that she was "a virgin again,"[39] it is a sign that there was already an inclination to value the present unmarried condition of the widow above her former married life. This must certainly have lowered the position of widows and exalted that of virgins; and in fact, though subsequently the admission among the deaconesses of a widow, supposing her to have been but once married, was not excluded, it formed the exception, the rule being that virgins were taken for this office.[40] It is thus evident that the widow, hitherto so highly esteemed, now took a position inferior to virgin-deaconesses. This is plainly shown in the revision of the Ignatian Epistles, which is about contemporaneous with the Apostolical Constitutions. While in the genuine Epistles, the widows immediately succeed the deacons, the order in the revised Epistles is, that the deacons are followed first by the subordinate clergy, then by the deaconesses, the virgins (living an ascetic life), and last of all by the widows. It is the same in the Apostolical Constitutions, in which widows in general occupy a very subordinate position, and scarcely a trace of their former high estimation is to be found.[41]

The higher view of the clerical office co-operated in

lowering the position of widows, and making it untenable. Their position and sphere of action at first corresponded more with the office of the presbyter than with that of the deacon. They were in a certain sense the presbyters of the women. So leading a position as that of instructing the women, however, was no longer in accordance with the notions of office entertained in the third century. The presbyter had become a priest, the climax of his office now lay in the offering. This a widow could not present. Nor could her position with respect to the women be maintained. A woman could only be placed on a level with a deacon, who likewise could not offer, and the whole development may be expressed by saying, that the official position of the woman in the Church fell from the level of the presbyterate to that of the diaconate. Now to provide for the female circle in the Church just those services which the deacon performed for the men, was, with the increase of the churches, at all events in the East, a necessity. The service rendered at baptism, the anointing after baptism, could not be transferred to men. The case too of sick, and the relief of poor females, was not suitable for men, and when, through the enhanced dignity of the priestly office, the pastoral care of women also came into the hands of the priests, there was needed, by reason of the customs of the East, which forbade the intercourse of men and women, some one to be the medium of such intercourse. It is true that many of these needs were also formerly in existence, but when the churches were small, there was found, independently of that rendered by the widows, a sufficiency of voluntary female assistance. And here too it must not be forgotten, that the diaconate, and especially the female diaconate, was of a transient character, and that much of what belonged to the vocation of a deaconess also fell to all women. This is very plainly shown in the Church rules ascribed to Clement. After settling what were to be the services of the deaconesses, it is there added: "But if another woman of the Church is desirous to do good works, let her do so according to her inclination."[42] There is here evidently a glance of the former state of things, which the institution of deaconesses was not intended entirely to do away with. Voluntary services, however, were no longer sufficient to meet the increased claims for them, and as there was in those days a tendency to give official stability to all services, even in the civil sphere, so here too it was no less apparent.

In the book just quoted, there is found a passage, transferred also to the Apostolical Constitutions, as used in the Church in Egypt,[43] plainly showing that the motives stated above, were actually those then active. It is a conversation of the apostles concerning female ministrations.[44] Andrew says: "It is fitting, my brethren, for women also to exercise a ministration." Peter replies: "That has been already done, but that some appointment must be made concerning the dispensing of the body and blood of Christ;" and John then reminds them, "that the Lord had not let women share in the institution of the Lord's Supper." Martha then interposes with the words: "Because of Mary, for He saw her smile." Mary: "I did not smile, but the Lord said beforehand: 'The weak is saved by the strong.'" This sets a limit to the office of the woman, she is not a priestess, she cannot bring the offering, may not dispense the sacrament; the man does this, and through his instrumentality the woman also receives the benefit. But she is to serve. As there is a ministry for men, so is there also a ministry "for women."

Similarly is the bishop enjoined in the Apostolical Constitutions: "Choose a deaconess for the service of the women." Epiphanius too makes a regard for decorum a reason for the establishment of a female diaconate.[45]

To this was added another need, that experienced at public worship. We must not overlook the fact, that public worship was beginning to assume a far more elaborate form than it had hitherto done, that its already often splendid appearance necessitated the performance of a variety of services, that the *Arcani Disciplina* especially, which was now introduced, required an oversight of the worship and its frequenters, quite unknown at a former period. Many persons were required to take care, by strict oversight, and especially by careful watch at the church doors, that no uninitiated persons should take part in the service. The same times in which the inferior male church-officers were increased, created also a corresponding female office, that of the deaconesses. For it is in fact here, viz. in the service of the Church, that we find the centre of gravity of this office, and not, where we are inclined to seek it, in the care of the sick and poor. The deaconesses were above all "the guardians of the sacred doors." This duty stands in the first rank, when they are greeted by the pseudo-Ignatius; and the prayer of consecration for deaconesses in the Apostolical Constitutions does not see the model of the deaconesses in such women as Tabitha, but in Anna and Huldah, who served in the temple, and in the portresses in the Old Testament.

The supposed work of Clement already so often quoted, gives us a glimpse into the transition from the institute of widows to that of deaconesses. Deaconesses properly so called, it is as yet unacquainted with, but it appoints, that there should be three widows in every church, two of whom engage to pray, while the third undertakes the care of the sick and needy. She is to be willing to give her services and temperate, she is to announce the names of the needy to the elders, she is not to be greedy of gain, not given to wine, that she may be able to watch at night services.[46] It is true that the book, from which this notice is taken, does not represent the common faith of the Catholic Church. It is nevertheless likely that a genuine historical feature is here preserved. The attempt was obviously made to supply a prevailing necessity, at first by transferring to a single widow, the services of deaconesses until the further step was taken of instituting actual deaconesses. Perhaps it is in connection with the first step, that only one deaconess is spoken of in the Canons of Hippolytus. The older portions too of the Constitutions have almost always but one deaconess —a number, *i.e.* an order of deaconesses first appearing in the later books.[47]

We must not, moreover, conceive of the matter as though the deaconesses had suddenly everywhere superseded the widows. The institution of deaconesses seems indeed to have spread rapidly. The 19th Canon of Nicea treats it as already generally existing even among the sects,[48] but it was not till the Council of Laodicea that the fall of the ancient institution of widows was sealed by the general prohibition (by Canon 11) of the future appointment of presiding widows. Finally, the West did not agree in making this entire change. The widows here remained in their ancient position. At least, they were not superseded by deaconesses proper. There never were in the Western Church deaconesses like those in the Eastern. Those that have been esteemed such were widows, to whom the name of deaconesses may have been here and there transferred, and dedicated virgins (*sanctimoniales*), who voluntarily assisted them. This is proved by the manner in which Jerome interprets the passages Rom. xvi. 1, 1 Tim. iii. 11, for with respect to both he says by way of explanation, that in the East (therefore not in the West) there are still deaconesses; and adds to this by a passage in the letter of the same Father to Nepotian, in which he advises the latter to let himself be taken care of in his sickness by a brother or sister, or if he has not such relations "the Church maintains many aged women, who give their services and receive support while serving, so that your infirmity will bear the fruit of an almsgiving." [49] This plainly shows, that in the West the aged women, the widows, still performed the services, which had in the East devolved on the deaconesses. The epitaphs too, in which so many deacons and dedicated virgins occur, never name deaconesses in the West. I at least have found but one from Upper Italy, and this, standing as it does alone, cannot prove the existence of an institution of deaconesses.[50] That of widows did not indeed last much longer in the West. If it remained somewhat longer than in the East, it could not but succumb there also. The only difference was, that no compensation for it was made in the West. The times were too stormy, and charity had already assumed another character.

In the oriental churches the deaconesses undoubtedly belonged to the clergy, although only to its lower order. The Apostolical Constitutions assign to them the rank of sub-deacons, and their supplies correspond with this—the bishop receiving four portions, the presbyter three, the deacon two, and the deaconess like the sub-deacon one portion.[51] The deaconess, as belonging to the clergy, was also ordained. This has been questioned, but it is plainly shown by many passages, in which the laying on of hands is spoken of in the case of deaconesses.[52] We have a certainly somewhat later description of the inauguration of a deaconess, which was, however, essentially in use also at the date of the Apostolical Constitutions, which in Book viii. give only the prayer of consecration.[53] The deaconess in a veil comes to the altar. The bishop greets her with: "The grace of God, which is powerful in the weak, be with thee." Then she bends not her knee, but her head, and the bishop prays: "Eternal God, the Father of our Lord Jesus Christ, who didst create man and woman, who didst fill Miriam and Deborah, and Anna and Huldah with the Holy Spirit, who didst not deem it unfit, to let Thine only-begotten Son be born of a woman, who also didst appoint in the tabernacle a witness, and in the temple female guardians of Thy sacred doors, look upon this Thine handmaid, who is chosen for Thy service, give her Thy Holy Spirit, and cleanse her from all pollution of the flesh and the spirit, that she may worthily perform the work committed to her, to Thy glory and the glory of Thy Christ, with whom and the Holy Spirit be glory and worship to Thee, for ever. Amen." After the prayer he puts on her, under the veil, the orarium (the ancient stole) of the deacons. Then follows the celebration of the Lord's Supper, at which the deaconess receives the cup from the hand of the deacon, but on her part does not hand it on, but places it on the altar, this being the sign that she is not to take part in the distribution of the sacrament.

The services of the deaconesses lay first, as already remarked, in the sphere of public worship. They stood as portresses at those entrances of the church which were appointed for women, to keep away unfit visitors; they showed women, especially strangers, their places, and kept order. According to the book of Clement above referred to, they were also to reprove those who came too late, and to pray with them, that they might be more zealous.[54] Then they attended on women at baptism, and, after the priest had anointed them on the forehead, performed the unction of the breast.[55] I do not find that they had also to prepare candidates for baptism by instruction, though a synod in Carthage does indeed prescribe such instruction by widows and God-betrothed virgins. They are to teach inexperienced and uneducated women before baptism, how they are to answer the baptizer, and how they ought to live after its reception.[56] According to the book of Clement, it is also their duty to carry the sacrament to sick women, who cannot go to church. This seems, however, not to have been the general custom.[57]

Besides these Church services, however, the deaconesses were also active in the care of the poor. They occupy, in respect of the female portion of the congregation, exactly the same position which the deacon does in respect of the male. The bishop could not send a deacon to visit the women, because of unbelievers, lest, as the Apostolic Constitutions say, evil reports should arise. Hence he is in this case to send a deaconess.[58] We must therefore conclude, that the deaconess in this case investigated the circumstances of the poor, and then furnished the necessary relief. Also, when a woman on the other hand desired to go to the bishop, she could only do so under the escort of a deaconess, for the sake of decorum.[59] The entire ministrations of the diaconate, so far as they relate to women, are very expressly transferred to deaconesses. After first describing the qualities of a deacon, it is said: "And let the woman (the deaconess) be zealous in assisting the women. But both are to undertake the offices of bringing messages, going out, giving assistance and service. They are not to be ashamed of ministering to the poor after the Lord's example, who came not to be ministered to, but to minister, and to give His life a ransom for many." Nay, if needs be, they too must not hesitate to lay down their lives for the brethren.[60]

It was just this full development of the diaconal office which made it possible for the bishop to practise an individual care of the poor, even to the smallest details. The services of deacons and deaconesses furnished him on the one hand with information of all the distress existing in the Church, and on the other gave him the means of affording to every one who was sick or poor, just the assistance his circumstances required. On the one side strict centralization, on the other the utmost individualization,—such were the advantages of this organization, and those which enabled it to produce so great results.

CHAPTER V.

THE WORK AND ITS RESULTS.

THE work developed by the Ancient Church among the distressed of every kind was abundant and many-sided. Justin Martyr, Tertullian, and the Apostolical Constitutions depict it in quite similar words, a sign that it was pretty much the same in the most opposite districts of the Church, in Rome, in Africa, and in the East. We have already become acquainted with the passages respecting it from Justin and Tertullian, when the collecting of means for the poor was spoken of. In the Apostolical Constitutions the whole sphere of charity is still more fully described. It is there made the duty of bishops to take care for the maintenance of all who are in distress, and to let none of them want. They are to supply to orphans the care of parents, to widows that of husbands, to help to marriage those ready for marriage, to procure work for those out of work, to show compassion to those incapable of work, to provide a shelter for strangers, food for the hungry, drink for the thirsty, visits for the sick and help for the prisoners.[1]

It was esteemed a general principle, that only the really needy were to be relieved, and that these were to be supplied with only absolute necessaries. Gluttons and idlers, who were in distress through their own faults, were excluded from support. They are not worthy to be members of the Church at all, let alone living at its expense.[2] On this side the strict discipline of the Church, by which the unworthy were excluded, was a powerful protection against the waste of means for the poor. A supposed saying of our Lord Himself, which is met with both in Clement of Alexandria and again in the Apostolic Constitutions, is appealed to. In Clement it runs : " Woe to them who have somewhat and yet out of hypocrisy and idleness let gifts be bestowed on them by others," and the Apostolic Constitutions place it as a parallel to the Lord's saying: " It is more blessed to give than to receive." The same Lord, who thus speaks, says also : " Woe to those who have and hypocritically take, or who, while they could help themselves, rather take alms from others, for both will have to give account to the Lord at the day of judgment." He who can himself work and yet receives alms, robs the really poor of his bread, and the Lord will punish him for it.[3] On the other hand the truly poor, who, by reason of the infirmities of age or sickness, are incapable of themselves earning their bread, are highly esteemed and honoured. It is no shame to them to receive alms. They are the altar of God, upon which the Church lays its gifts ; and if they on their part repay it as alone they can repay it, with faithful intercessions for their benefactors, they will receive praise from God in eternity.[4]

Only necessaries were given to the poor. If the Christians of those days were unfavourable to luxury of every kind, and very highly esteemed the virtue of simplicity in all the requirements of life, this was self-evident. Cyprian in one of his letters gives directions concerning an actor, who desires to become a Christian.[5] He must give up his business, and if he can find no other way of earning, he may be received among the number of those supported by the Church, but with the condition that he should be content with frugal and simple food. It is especially inculcated on the poor, that they should be contented, humble, and devoted to God. It is impressed upon them with the utmost confidence, that they have no right to support, but that it is free love which offers it to them: They are always to regard what they receive as the gift of God, who bestows it upon them by means of His faithful ones. "The rich give to the poor, the poor praises God, for sending to him some one, by whom his wants are supplied," as it is said in the Epistle of Clement of Rome.[6] At no time has the Church more strongly insisted on the duty of assisting the poor in love, but at no time also has she more decidedly pronounced, that all is love and to be done with justice. Never has she more highly reverenced the poor, more kindly and lovingly treated them; never also has she been farther from fostering beggary, and making their life easy to idlers. Christian life was then too earnest, and its view too actively directed to another world, for anything of the kind to occur.

The aid afforded consisted first in the distribution of the necessaries of life in natural products. Those presented as oblations were dispensed on the same day, or if anything was left, on the second or third.[7] Those regularly assisted, the aged, the infirm, and those unable to work or not in a condition to support alone a large family, received regular and probably monthly aid, each according to the bishop's appointment. Thus we read, e.g., in Hippolytus, that the bishop Victor, from compassion, allows Callistus a monthly assistance for his maintenance.[8] The lists of the poor, which were probably now drawn up, and in which the names of those assisted and their circumstances were accurately notified, served to prevent any being forgotten, and at the same time any being relieved whose circumstances had not been accurately inquired into. In general, the help of the deacons, as above remarked, rendered a great individualizing possible in the relief of the poor. Every one received the assistance which his necessities required. Efforts were above all made to render the poor again capable of work, and to put them in a condition to earn their own livelihood. They were directed where to find work, and were furnished with tools. Where there were still connections or relatives, their aid was first requested; they were not to suffer the Church to be burdened with those whom it was their own first duty to help.[9] If the more the relief to the poor is individualized, the higher its value, that which was exercised at this period is of a very high rank.

The Agapæ were still at this time a peculiar kind of assistance to the poor. Even after the celebration of the Lord's Supper was separated from them and transferred to the morning service, they continued to be held as occasional love-feasts of the whole Church, to which each contributed according to his means. They were thus at the same time a help to the poor in a most dignified form, which gave the poor a consciousness of forming part of the Church. This is expressly brought forward by Tertullian, in answering the reproach of extravagance brought against these meals by the heathen. Whatever they cost, it is a gain to incur expense in the name of love to one's neighbour, for this refreshment is in behalf of all the poor. We do not, however, receive it like parasites, who hold it no dishonour to sell even their liberty, and will put up with any kind of indignity for the price of being able to cram their bellies, but because the consideration of the poor is highly esteemed by God. Then Tertullian gives a description of the meal, which, though it may perhaps somewhat idealize it, still gives us so true a glimpse of the active brotherly association of all Christians both rich and poor, who were present at the common table : " As the motive of the feast is an honourable one, you may estimate accordingly the regulation of the rest of our conduct, how it corresponds with our religious duty, which allows of nothing mean, nothing superfluous. We do not sit down to table till prayer to God has been first tasted ; we eat as much as the hungry need, we drink no more than serves the modest. We appease our hunger as those who know that we must pray to God even during the night ; we talk with the consciousness that the Lord hears us. After we have washed hands and the lamps are lighted, the summons to praise God goes forth to all, and he who is able to impart anything out of the word of God or from his own mind does so. Herein lies the test as to how we have drunk. The whole meeting closes with prayer, and we do not separate to commit improprieties in the streets, but to continue our practice of decency, because we are not coming from a drinking bout, but from an exercise of propriety and modesty." [10]

Subsequently indeed, when Tertullian had become a Montanist, he would have nothing more to do with these Agapæ, which he had described as so admirable. He applies to them Rom. xiii. 13, and says derisively, " The Agapæ (love) is glowing in your kettles, if faith is hot in the kitchen, hope rests in the plates." [11] In fact all sorts of disorders occurred at the Agapæ, and these were sufficient to bring straightforward minds like Tertullian's to reject them entirely. Clement Alexandrinus [12] too speaks with disapprobation of the little meals "at which there is an odour of roast meats and sauces," and laments, that "the excellent and salutary institution of the Logos, the common meal, is disgraced with overturned saucers." He does not, however, entirely reject them because of their abuse, but only requires "that the meal should be simple and frugal." He then grants, that "the love-feast is an excellent nurse for public spirit, where contentment thereat is as an abundantly filled poor-box." "The pleasures of the common meal possess a certain excitement for Christian love, and are a reminder of eternal pleasures. The essence of Christian love does not therefore lie in the meal, which is but something accessory." Nevertheless, such irregularities as Clement assumes, were the reasons that the Agapæ ceased as meals of the whole Church. They then became meals for the poor, prepared by any benevolent member, and only the poor were invited. It is as such that the Apostolical Constitutions and kindred writings are acquainted with them. Aged women seem especially to have been invited. This, however, was to be through the deacon who knew them. It is strange to find that such presbyters as were present were to receive a double portion, and moreover a sign that the original character of these repasts was pretty well obliterated.[13] We get further details concerning them from the canons of Hippolytus and the book of Clement. These tell us, that they were held on Sundays towards evening. When the deacon had lighted the light, the bishop prayed for the poor and those who had invited them. Then the meal began, but no one was to begin to eat before the presbyter. All were to eat in silence, and not to say anything unless the bishop or presbyter asked them a question. Psalms were sung at the meal, and all were to retire singly before darkness set in. This was indeed no longer the ancient love-feast, at which the whole church had assembled as one family at a common table. The times of such association were over. But it was still an echo from the older times. The honour of eating at the same table as the bishop was still accorded to the poor, although on the other hand, the rules which prevailed made them plainly enough conscious of the distance between him and themselves. It seems also that the bishops then already withdrew from these repasts of the poor, and left their management to the inferior officers of the Church. According to the Apostolical Constitutions, the bishop was no longer present at them.[14]

Of widows, so far as they occupied a position of honour, a sort of office in the Church, we have already spoken above. Whether there were so early as the second century, as Zahn[15] thinks, special widows' houses, in which they dwelt as a community, is, I think, doubtful; on the other hand, such are already presupposed by the Apostolic Constitutions. The manner in which widows are there spoken of as living together leads to this conclusion. They had then yielded their official duties, and much of their position, to the deaconesses, but are still spoken of as a separate corporation apart from the other members of the Church. Only such as were sixty years of age, had been but once married, and were well reported of, were received into it, and they then made a promise to remain unmarried. Younger widows were, if they required it, to be otherwise assisted. To such even a second marriage might be allowed, though this was already regarded with disfavour.[16] It was forbidden to widows to wander about in the church, and this on the ground that they are the altar of God, and the altar does not wander about. They are not to be talkative, not to solicit gifts, but to wait till something is given them, and then to pray for the giver and for the whole Church. Such intercession was set before them as the special duty of their lives.[17] Nay, in the Apostolical Constitutions a liturgical form of prayer is prescribed. If a widow has been clothed by any one, or has received money, food, drink, or shoes, her fellow-widows, on seeing their sister, who has received relief, shall say: "Blessed be Thou, O God, who hast refreshed my fellow-widow; Lord, bless and glorify him who has thus ministered to her, that his good work may come up to Thee in truth, and remember him for good in the day of his visitation. Bless also my bishop, who serves Thee truly, and has taught in due time to give alms to my poor fellow-widow. Increase his honour, and give him the crown of glory when Thy coming is manifested." The widow, too, who has received the gift, is also to pray with her for the giver.

Orphans as well as widows are always commended to Christian love. The bishop is to have them brought up at the expense of the Church, and to take care that the girls be given, when of marriageable age, to Christian husbands, and that the boys should learn some art or handicraft, and then be provided with tools and placed in a condition to earn their own living, so that they may be no longer than necessary a burden to the Church.[18] It would also often happen, that individual members of the Church would receive orphans, especially those whose parents had perished in a persecution. Thus, *e.g.*, was Origen adopted, after Leonidas his father had suffered martyrdom, by a pious woman in Alexandria.[19] Again, the child of the female martyr Felicitas found a mother,[20] and Eusebius tells us of Severus, a Palestinian confessor, who specially interested himself in the orphans and widows of those who had fallen.²¹ In the Apostolical Constitutions, members of the Church are urgently exhorted to such acts. If any Christian, whether boy or girl, be left an orphan, it is well if one of the brethren, who has no child, receives and keeps him in a child's place. They who do so perform a good work, by becoming fathers to the orphans, and will be rewarded by God for this service.²² Of foundlings nothing is at this time expressly mentioned, but with the wide dissemination of the custom of exposing children, which was never esteemed a crime by the heathen, we may safely conclude, that Christians took pity on these unfortunate creatures, and bestowed upon them the care which their unnatural parents had denied them. If Tertullian in his *Apologeticus* represents to the heathen with such terrible earnestness, that the exposing of children is murder,²³ Christians would also regard it as murder not to take charge of a foundling; and if Lactantius ²⁴ reminds the heathen, that it is ungodly to leave children to the compassion of strangers, Christians certainly would not have suffered themselves to be devoid of such compassion. When we first meet with the mention of the adoption and bringing up of foundlings, this work appears not as a novelty, but as one long practised. It is true that the heathen also used to take care of exposed children, but for the purpose of bringing them up as gladiators or prostitutes, or to use them in their own service, for a healthy child belonged as a slave to any who harboured it. Christians brought up the children whom they took charge of for the Lord, and for a respectable and industrious life.

As yet there were no hospitals. The sick were attended to in their own houses. The bishop, the presbyters and deacons, visited them there. "It is a great thing for one who is sick," it is said in the canons of Hippolytus, "to be visited by the chief among the priests. He not seldom recovers from his sickness if the bishop comes to him, especially if he prays over him.[25] A deacon is to accompany the bishop." The book of Clement speaks still more particularly. The deacon is to find out whether the sick person is in distress, and then to provide all that is necessary for his case.[26]

The grandest manifestations of Christian compassion took place in the times of those great calamities, which broke in upon the Roman Empire in increasingly rapid succession during the third century. A fearful pestilence was then going about, and making its appearance now in one place, now in another. In Cyprian's days it broke out in Carthage. The bishop's biography gives us a moving description of the almost entire dissolution of all ties which was the result of the pestilence.[27] "There was a general panic. All fled. All avoided contact with the infected, and let their relations lie without help, as though they could thus keep death at a distance. There were corpses lying about in the street throughout the town. No one thought of anything else than of making horrible profits. No one did to another what he would have wished done to himself." Almost more strongly does Cyprian himself, in his apologetic book to Demetrianus, describe the selfishness of the heathen, which, as is, alas! so often the case, broke out in this general distress. "No compassion is shown by you to the sick, only covetousness and plunder open their jaws over the dead; they who are too fearful for the work of mercy, are bold for guilty profits. They who shun to bury the dead, are greedy for what they have left behind them."[28] He reproaches them with leaving the sick in the lurch for the sake of taking possession of their property after their death. "They run about everywhere to plunder, to take possession."[29] It was quite different with the Christians. Of them Cyprian says, they would more have broken the storm themselves than have been broken by it. With burning words did the bishop summon them to give their assistance, and, as was his nature, himself energetically organize them. Services were allotted to each, says his biographer, according to their individual ability.[30] Some gave money, others their personal assistance. "Who would not have hastened under such a teacher to be found taking some part in this warfare?" Thus the sick were nursed, the dead interred. The heathen, too, had a share in the deeds and sacrifices of love. "For," preached Cyprian, "if we only do good to those who do good to us, what do we more than the heathens and publicans? If we are the children of God, who makes His sun to shine upon good and bad, and sends rain on the just and the unjust, let us prove it by our acts, by blessing those who curse us, and doing good to those who persecute us."[31]

The pestilence raged in Alexandria under the Emperor Gallienus. Eusebius has preserved a letter of Dionysius, then its bishop, in which he describes the conduct of the Christians during this visitation:[32] "Most of our brethren, in the fulness of their brotherly love, did not spare themselves. They mutually took care of each other, and as instead of preserving themselves they attended on the sick, and willingly did them service for Christ's sake, they joyfully laid down their lives with them. Many died after having been by their exertions the means of restoring others. The best among the brethren, many presbyters,

deacons, and distinguished laymen ended their lives in
this manner, so that their deaths, which were the result
of piety and strong faith, seem not inferior to martyrdom.
Many who took into their hands and laid upon their
bosoms the bodies of Christian brothers, closed their
mouths and eyes, and reverently interred them, soon
followed them in death. It was quite different with the
heathen. They thrust out those who were beginning to
sicken, fled from those who were dearest, and cast the
dying into the streets; they let the dead lie unburied in
their desire to avoid infection, which nevertheless they
could not escape." It was the same when this city
suffered from famine and pestilence under Maximus.
While the heathen quite lost courage, and each thought
only of his own preservation, the Christians were active
throughout the whole city. Some distributed bread to
the hungry, others attended on the sick, others again took
care for the interment of the dead, so that even the
heathen praised the God of the Christians, and declared,
that Christians alone were pious and godly.[33]

It was at other times also esteemed a work of mercy to
bury the dead. Lactantius[34] reckons the interment of
strangers and of the poor as among the duties which
humanity imposes on men. He reproaches the heathen
for their neglect of this duty, and for their estimation of
duties only according to their utility. It is indeed
indifferent to the dead whether they are buried or not.
" But we will not suffer the image and creature of God to
be thrown for a prey to the wild beasts and birds, but will
give it back to the earth from which it was taken, and
fulfil to even an unknown man the office of his relations,
into whose place, if they be absent, humanity steps." It
belonged, as we have seen, to the duties of the deacons to

provide for the interment of the poor and of strangers; nay, even the corpses cast up by the sea, found, through the love of Christians, a decent grave.

With special love did the Church, mindful of our Lord's words : " I was in prison, and ye came unto me," interest herself in prisons and prisoners. For this there was plenty of opportunity. There were not only brethren cast into prison for the sake of the faith, of provision for whom we shall soon have to speak more particularly,— there were also prisoners of war, for the inroads of the barbarians became increasingly frequent even in the third century; there were at all times many who were imprisoned for the non-payment of taxes, and debtors who were kept in prison by reason of the severity of the Roman laws of debt, because they could not meet their engagements to private individuals. It is of such imprisoned debtors that we must especially think, when Ignatius and the Apostolical Constitutions name the liberation of prisoners, together with the maintenance of widows and orphans, as a conspicuous portion of the Christian exercise of mercy.[35] That prisoners of war also were ransomed, and often in great numbers, an example has been given in the noble deed of the bishop of Carthage already mentioned.

Among the captives may also be reckoned[36] slaves, whose lot, though it gradually became milder, was still one of great hardship. On them, too, Christian love had compassion, only not in such wise as to labour for an emancipation of slaves, as the Church has been here and there represented to have done. This, on the contrary, lay entirely beyond her horizon. She simply recognised slavery, as well as the other institutions of civil life. Emancipation theories, in connection with communistic ideas, do indeed make their appearance among the

Gnostics, but cannot be found in the Church. She occupied just as neutral a position with respect to the contrast of bond and free, as to that of rich and poor. All might be Christians, all might have a share in the kingdom of God, whether bond or free. "If I am a slave, I bear it; if I am free, I glory in my free birth," is a saying found in Tatian.[37] Nay, Tertullian speaks in a depreciatory manner of civil freedom, as of something which to Christians, who know of a better liberty, is of no value. "The freedom of the man of this world puts on a wreath." (It was the custom for freedmen to put on a wreath to express their joy at their freedom.) "But thou art already ransomed by Christ, and at a high price. How should the world be able to give liberty to one who is in another's service? If it looks as if one were free, it is just as clear that he is still in servitude. All that is in the world is appearance, and nothing in it is truth. For before, thou wast, as one redeemed by Christ, free from the authority of man, and now thou art a bond-servant of Christ, though set free by man!"[38] Or if we are to suppose, that it is the strict Montanist who is here speaking, we meet with essentially the same views in Lactantius,[39] who makes the distinction between bond and free exactly parallel to that between rich and poor. To the objection, that there are still among Christians rich and poor, bond and free, and that it is therefore all over with equality and brotherly love, he replies: "We estimate human affairs not according to the standard of the body, but of the spirit. Hence our servants, though occupying a different position according to the body, are still not our servants, but we esteem them in spirit as our brethren, and in religion as our fellow-servants;" and then he refers to the fact, that in this life everything is transitory and of short duration. Hence it is in truth indifferent, whether a man is a slave or a free man. Let us not forget the powerful attraction towards another world with which Christianity is affected. This life is short, and its aims are upwards. If the slave may, just as much as the free man, have a share in the future glory, it is indeed a matter of indifference whether he is free during the short span of time in this world.

Nowhere then is there found a trace of the keeping of slaves being thought wrong on the part of a Christian. Clement Alexandrinus assumes it as self-evident, that Christians as well as others should have slaves, and when he condemns a large establishment of servants, he does so only in the same sense in which he reproves all luxury. When, in the Apostolic Constitutions, Christians are exhorted to go but seldom to the market, and then only to purchase necessaries, slaves are mentioned among such necessaries without the slightest scruple.[40] The Church, too, never urged the manumission of slaves or made this a Christian duty. Manumissions did occur, but certainly not often, or we should have heard more of them; they were not indeed so frequent among Christians as among heathens. The heathen often freed their slaves from impure motives, for the sake of fame, or pomp, that very many might follow at their funeral with the hat, the token of manumission, and even for the sake of gain, that they might get more profit out of freedmen than they could out of slaves. All these motives were lacking with Christians, nay, they would have regarded it as an act of injustice to give their slaves liberty for such reasons. On the contrary, Christian masters had a special motive for keeping their slaves, viz., that they might have the opportunity of exercising a religious and moral influence upon them, and of winning them for Christ. A slave was much better off with a truly Christian master, than a freedman cast out by his owner into a world in which free labour was so little esteemed. During this whole period, I only find two passages in which the liberation of slaves is certainly spoken of. In the Apostolical Constitutions it is reckoned among the works of love,[41] in what sense we shall hereafter have an opportunity of observing; and Ignatius, in his Epistle to Polycarp,[42] exhorts slaves not to wish to be ransomed by the Church, that they be not found to be the slaves of desire. From this passage it appears, that slaves were then indeed ransomed at the cost of the Church, but Ignatius desires that slaves are not to press for this, lest they thus become slaves indeed, slaves of their own desire. We must conceive of the state of affairs so as to consider, that cases would occasionally occur, in which his relation to his master would make it just impossible for a slave to lead a truly Christian life, or in which this was in the highest degree endangered. Then, indeed, the Church took the case in hand, and liberated the slave from such a condition. But slaves were not to think they had a right to this, they were not to think themselves too good as Christians to perform servile labour, and not to make themselves slaves to an unchristian desire for worldly freedom. In fact, what we find related in contemporary delineations of the efforts of the Church, to give liberty to slaves, is only true of spiritual liberty; if we understand it of numerous manumissions, it is inconsistent with facts. As a rule the slave remained a slave, even when he became a Christian, and the Christian master kept his slaves as before, but the slave served and the master ruled in a different manner from what they formerly did.

N

It was in this respect that the change was effected. Everywhere we meet with exhortations both to slaves to obey, and to masters to be just, kind, and gentle towards their slaves. They are not to be used, says Clement of Alexandria, like beasts, but the Christian master must treat his Christian slave like a son or a brother, for the sake of their common faith.[43] If the heathen treated them like things, like bodies without souls, the Christian was to esteem it his duty to take an interest in his slaves, to bring them to knowledge and to faith. "We reject none," says Origen,[44] "not even the rude slave. We turn to him as to an ignorant woman or child, to improve him;" and in another place,[45] "We instruct the slave how to gain the disposition of a free man, and to obtain through faith true freedom." The Church was as open to the slave as to the free. It is true that at his admission, the consent of his master was, at least in the third century, required, and if the latter were a Christian, required absolutely. If he were a heathen, his refusal was only regarded, in case the master could prove a hostile disposition in his slave towards him. The Church was not to serve as a refuge to slaves, who were either disobedient or of hostile disposition to their masters.[46] But if the slave was received into the Church, there was no distinction between him and the free man. Where the Apostolical Constitutions treat of places in the Church, there is not a trace of separate places for slaves. The slave sat with his master, ate of the same bread and drank of the same cup. Every office too was open to him. Callistus from a slave became bishop of Rome. Slaves, who with free men had obtained the highest crown, were honoured by the Church among the martyrs. With all this the slave continued bound to obey his master, the only difference being, that his obedience was limited by the commandment of God. If his master bid him do anything contrary to the command of God and of Christ, the slave must not obey. In the persecutions of Diocletian, certain Christian masters had caused sacrifices to be offered for them by their slaves, for the sake of escaping persecution. The Church punished the masters with a penance of three years, the slave with a penance of one year,[47] for by their obedience to their masters according to the flesh, they had violated their obedience to Christ. Thus the slave was looked upon as self-responsible, as though a bondservant yet free in conscience even with respect to his master. The Church also came to the slave's assistance with its means of punishment. According to the Apostolical Constitutions,[48] the bishop was to receive no oblation from those who ill-used their slaves, and the Synod of Elvira (305) determines, that a woman who in anger so strikes her slave, that she dies within three days, is to be excluded from the communion for seven years if it were done intentionally, for five if it were done accidentally.[49] It is sad enough to think, that it was necessary to threaten such punishments, and a sign to how slight a depth Christianity had penetrated. While the condition of slaves ought to have been progressively improving, such appointments prove, alas! that it again became worse, and we shall subsequently hear still more of such examples.

Special tasks were imposed on Christian charity in times of persecution. Poverty and distress might easily become a strong temptation to apostasy. Persecution too inflicted material damage on many, their business suffered, they were entirely withdrawn from it, when they were either thrown into prison, exiled, or compelled to flee. Confiscations also took place, or the houses of Christians were plundered by the heathen populace. In such times the bond of love had to prove itself the firmer, and it was needful that those whose lot it was to answer for their faith in prisons, in mines, before tribunals, should know themselves to be supported by the whole community. Hence it is that Cyprian so very specially exhorts to zealous care for the poor during the Decian persecution: "Let neither your care nor your zeal be lacking—as I wrote to you before—to the poor, especially to those who, fighting firmly and bravely in the faith with ourselves, have not forsaken the camp of Christ. We must bestow all the greater care and diligence upon them, because, neither conquered by poverty, nor overthrown by the storm of persecution, they faithfully serve the Lord and give the rest of the poor an example of faith."[50] Meantime have as much care as ever you can for the poor, even for those who, standing in unshaken faith, have not forsaken the flock of Christ, so that what is necessary for their support under their privations may be bestowed on them by your zeal, lest distress should effect in the sufferers what the storm of persecution was, as to their faith, unable to accomplish.[51]

If a Christian were cast into prison on account of his faith, the Church cared for him with the greatest zeal. He was visited, he received necessary provisions, and also the means of procuring from the soldiers and gaolers all kinds of alleviations. Tertullian, speaking of the destination of the gifts of love administered in assemblies, mentions[52] also the maintenance of those who are in mines, in islands, and in prisons, supposing only that they suffer merely for the sake of God. Cyprian, in his epistles,[53] gives directions how the confessors were to be received. The Apostolical Constitutions most impressively lay this duty upon the heart of the members of the Church, certainly not without some admixture of that increased veneration of the martyrs, which appeared in the later times of the persecutions:[54] "If a Christian is condemned to the combat, or to be thrown to the wild beasts, or sent to the mines for the sake of his faith and love to God, you are not to despise him, but to send to him of your labour and of the sweat of your brow, wherewith to live and to pay the soldiers their fees, that he may obtain some alleviation and be cared for. For he who is condemned for the sake of God's name, is a brother of the Lord, a son of the Almighty, a vessel of the Holy Spirit. Therefore, all ye believers, send of your possessions for the help of the saints through your bishop. But if any one has nothing, let him fast, and appoint the day's provisions for the saints. But if any has superfluity, let him give more in proportion to his property. Nay, if any can free them from prison by the sacrifice of his whole property, he will be blessed and a friend of Christ. For if he, who even gives his goods to the poor, is perfect, how much more will he be perfect, who devotes all for the martyrs!" Christians are then also admonished to visit the prisoners at peril of themselves becoming martyrs, and to let themselves be hindered by neither shame nor fear.

The lot of those sent to work in the mines was the hardest. With scanty fare, almost naked, cruelly treated by harsh and unpitying overseers, they were compelled to do the hardest and most disagreeable work, so that most succumbed after a short period. Of these sufferers Christian love then took even extraordinary care. The Romish Church is especially praised by the Bishop Dionysius of Corinth for having sent help everywhere,[55] and among the

Epistles of Cyprian are found many letters of thanks from Christians in the mines, in which they express their gratitude for gifts, which the bishop had sent them through a sub-deacon and several acolytes, together with letters of condolence.[56] It is felt from the letters what refreshment such gifts must have afforded to the poor creatures under sentence, furnishing them besides the assurance, that the Church at home was mindful of them, suffered and struggled with them. It is a touching proof how far Christianity had inwardly altered the relation of master and slave, that at the close of one of the letters, a slave sends special greeting to his master. And how must it have raised the courage of the confessors to know that their belongings were cared for, that wife and children would not be allowed to want, if they themselves suffered death in prison or at the place of execution! Lactantius once expressly refers to this:[57] "God has on this account commanded us to defend and provide for the widows and orphans, that no one may let himself be kept back, by compassion or regard for the pledges of his love, from dying for righteousness' sake, but may without hesitation boldly incur death, knowing that he leaves his loved ones to God, and that help and protection will never be wanting to them."

The highly esteemed virtue of hospitality too is only rightly appreciated, when the condition of Christians in the times of persecution is considered. This virtue indeed seems least of all a novelty or one peculiar to Christians. And yet Christian entirely differed from heathen hospitality. Lactantius calls the hospitality of the heathen just ambition, its aim being not to succour the poor and needy, but by the reception of "illustrious guests," as Cicero expresses it, to oblige others, and to gain respect and power abroad also. Lactantius thinks, that Cicero in hospitality really had his own advantage in view, and yet desired also to be considered humane.[58] With the Christian it is not the important guest who is received, but the Christian brother, independently of who or what he is. It was in this sense that hospitality was inculcated, in this sense that it was everywhere exercised. Bishop Melito, of Sardis, wrote an entire book upon hospitality,[59] and it is always placed in the first rank, in accordance with the apostolic exhortations, wherever the exercises of Christian compassion are spoken of.[60] It is among the chief qualifications of a bishop to be hospitable,[61] and Cyprian not only by word lays it on the heart of the presbyters left at Carthage to entertain strangers, but furnishes them also with means to do so from his own property.[62] Clement of Rome praises the Corinthian Church for receiving those who came there with liberal hospitality,[63] and Bishop Dionysius of Corinth in return praises the Romish Church for the same virtue.[64] It was among the duties of a bishop to receive and provide for strangers. As yet, houses for their reception did not exist;[65] if the bishop's house were not large enough, they were taken to that of some member of the Church. Tertullian assumes it as self-evident of the Christian woman, that she should receive into her house and entertain brethren from a distance.[66] The abuse which was made of the hospitality of the Church, necessitated precautions for keeping away false brethren and also spies and vagabonds. No brother was received, who was unable to authenticate himself as a member of the Church, by a letter of introduction. Only the bishop could issue such letters, for communion with the bishop is Church communion. But afterwards, when even such letters were forged, it was found necessary to give them an appointed form (*Literæ formatæ*) for the purpose of preventing forgeries, or at least making them more difficult. The Synod of Nicæa is said to have passed resolutions on this account, prescribing the use of certain artificial combinations of the three letters representing the Trinity, π υ α (Father, Son, and Holy Ghost), to be placed on the letters. Whether this resolution was, however, of so early a date is questionable.[67] But all, who brought with them proper and genuine letters of introduction, were received and entertained as brethren.

Hospitality thus regulated was of great importance to the development of the Church. As each separate church formed a family, so also did the whole Church through this exercise of hospitality. "The whole sphere was united by the exchange of letters of introduction into one community," says Optatus of Mileve. This was the more valuable, inasmuch as the ties of constitution and government, which serve to otherwise keep the Church together, were at this time lacking. Each church, each bishop, was as yet very independent. Intercourse was, however, very active. There was much travelling, if not as much as with us at present, at any rate more than with us a hundred years ago. Hospitality brought about a constant exchange of intercourse between the different churches. They heard of and learnt from each other, suggestions of all kinds came and went, and in times of distress and persecution they could the more easily assist each other.[68]

By such mutually rendered assistance, love stretched out her hands beyond the individual church. Where a church fell into special trouble, it found prompt and willing assistance from others, who were for the time more favourably circumstanced. When the Numidian bishops could not raise the means for the ransom of the prisoners in their own churches, they applied to Cyprian, and the Carthaginian churches collected what was lacking. Even in the time of Basil the Great, the church of Cæsarea, in Cappadocia, remembered that Dionysius, bishop of Rome (259–269), had sent them a letter of condolence, when they were in great affliction through the incursions of the Barbarians, and accompanied it with money for the ransom of prisoners. The letter was then still preserved in the church.[69] It is also elsewhere said of the eminently flourishing and affluent Romish Church, that it was always ready to succour other churches;[70] and certainly such services contributed not a little to procure for the Church of the world's metropolis, the illustrious and subsequently dominant position which it occupied.

In all these respects we get a view in some degree of the ample blessing with which the charity of this period was crowned. The result already was, that in the Christian churches there were actually no beggars, and none who suffered want. If Julian was constrained against his will to testify this of Christians even in his days, when circumstances had become far more unfavourable, how much more does it apply to those of which we are treating! But that we may not over-estimate this result, we must certainly remember, that the churches were still small, and that financial circumstances did not as yet point to such distress as afterwards. This external result, however, is not the only nor the greatest result. How far the charity of a period may be successful in overcoming its poverty, depends upon other conditions than merely the intense vitality of its love. Far more highly must we estimate the blessing obtained by the Church itself, from this labour of love, and the impression produced thereby upon the heathen. Besides the courageous faith, and happiness in death of Christians, it was above all their love which at last won for the little flock its victory over the enormous power of the heathen world. Athenagoras was right when he declared this love to be the best apology for Christianity: "The Christians make no declamations, but point to good deeds; being struck, they do not strike in return; and being plundered, they do not accuse before tribunals; they give to those that ask, and love their fellow-men as themselves."[71] The heathen themselves could not resist the impression, that here was a new life such as they had not known, and that this life of love was somewhat higher than what they, with their philosophy, their political life, their art and science, were capable of attaining. "See," they exclaimed, "how these Christians love one another!"[72] Here too was the saying fulfilled: "He that is in you, is greater than he that is in the world." The world full of love, which had originated in Christianity, could not but at last gain the victory over the world without love; and it gained it in spite of the human weakness, which certainly was not lacking, and in spite of the obscurations, which now already began to darken the shining light of first love.

CHAPTER VI.

OBSCURATIONS.

It is a still widely disseminated notion, that the corruption of the Church did not begin till its victory under Constantine. Before that epoch nothing is seen but light and brightness, from it is dated its secularization, the relaxation of its strong faith and first love, the obscuration of genuine Christianity by external rites and self-righteousness; and the act of Constantine is made responsible for all, even if a chief argument is not derived from it, against all close connection of the Church with the State. In fact, however, these evils only come out more strongly after Constantine; their commencements existed before, and the Church, which obtained the victory, was already in many respects different from that which began the contest. The turning-point lies, on the contrary, especially if we have regard to Christian life and its development, in the Montanist movement and in its separation. It is just there too, that we perceive those first obscurations of charity, which it is so important to observe and fix, if we are to attain a right understanding of the next epoch.

Montanism made its appearance with a claim, based upon a new revelation by the Paraclete, the Holy Spirit, which, compared with the revelation in Christ, was said to be a more exalted one, of raising the Christian life to a higher level. Under the law, righteousness was in its childhood, under the gospel it was glowing with youth, through the Paraclete it was to be brought to maturity.¹ In truth, however, Montanism was nothing else than the reaction against that making itself at home in the world, which was beginning to take place in the Church. Herein Tertullian quite rightly saw, that the youth of the Church was departing. Towards the end of the second century a relaxation of the first enthusiasm is already plainly traceable; men were no longer so earnest, so strict about their Christianity; much already passed as permissible, which would formerly have been avoided as inconsistent with Christianity; the separation from the surrounding heathen world was no longer so abrupt, the feeling of only sojourning here in a strange land was giving way, arrangements were made with a view to a longer continuance of the Church on earth, and the thoughts of the Lord's speedy return, of a speedy termination to the present dispensation, receded. In Montanism the old stricter but also narrower and somewhat conventicle-like Christianity was reacting. So far, Montanism was not without justification, and it must not be regarded, as its adversaries chose to do, as an antichristian or even a diabolical phenomenon. Nevertheless its pretension to represent a new revelation was a grievous self-delusion, and the way it struck out for healing existing evils, and raising Christian life to a higher level, a fundamentally erroneous one. Montanism knows of no other means than increasing the severity of discipline; the place of the "new law," as Christianity was then universally comprehended, was to be taken by "a newest law," distinguished from the former by greater strictness. If hitherto the principle: "What is not forbidden is allowed," had been current, it was now to be said: "What is not expressly allowed is forbidden." The notion of the allowable, the category of things indifferent, was wholly expunged. The newest law of the Paraclete regulated everything, down to the slightest trifle, as *e.g.* the veil of virgins. Asceticism was increased, fasting made more rigid, and second marriage forbidden. The Christian must entirely break with the world, for the world is approaching its destruction. The expectation of the speedy return of Christ, which was abating in the Church, was revived in glowing colours by the Montanists. These heightened moral claims were made not only upon individuals, but upon all Christians. Only they who satisfy them are genuinely spiritual men; others are the psychical, the sensuous, in fact not Christians at all. The churches must become churches of saints, and the means to make them such consists in increasing the strictness of discipline. Every mortal sin after baptism absolutely and for ever excludes from the Church. There is no more repentance after baptism. By this it is not meant to declare the forgiveness of even such sins impossible, but that they are left to God. The Church forgives no more.

Such a tendency was incapable of becoming the vehicle of the Church's further development. Had Montanism been victorious, the Church could not have become a universal power, and it was to this she was called. She did become such, but not without forfeiting by this step a portion of her original endowment. She separated from Montanism, but this separation did not ensue without some adulteration. She protested against the stricter demands made by Montanism on all Christians, but in place of these, began to make still higher claims upon individuals in the Church. She rejected the contrast set up by Montanism between spiritual and psychical men, but in its place gave currency to a contrast within the Church between perfect and imperfect Christians. It was just this distinction, this double ethic, that of perfect and that of ordinary Christians, which was the chief harm the Church came off with from the Montanist controversy.

Let us endeavour to make this somewhat clearer; for it is the point on which depends the further development of charity in the Christian Church. If the Church was to become a universal power, if it was to exercise a transforming influence upon the world around, its position with regard to the world, to science, to art, to the State, must not continue to be of a purely negative character. A congregation of saints, sharply separated from the world around, is no universal power. The Church had to gain a firm footing in the world, to enter into the natural conditions of life. A Church, such as the Montanists conceived, maintaining the supernaturalness of its origin by its inflexible reserve, would have hovered above the world, and have been utterly incapable of transforming it. It must become larger-hearted, more indulgent to human weakness, "a safety company for a weak generation standing in need of milder discipline." [2] Thus only could it become a Church for the masses, a national Church capable of pervading national life with a new, a Christian spirit. That the Church should after its conquest of Montanism turn into this path, was a thoroughly necessary and right development. Nor is it to be accounted a fault, that it became milder in discipline, and made reconciliation possible to the fallen, that the whole idea of Christian life was somewhat lowered; for what the first enthusiasm had effected in the Church's youth, could no longer be required in the subsequent centuries. But the Church was now in presence of the great task of penetrating the surrounding national life—the State, art, science, social relations—with the Christian spirit, and of transforming them within and without. Against this task the vessel struck, and was thus driven into false paths. Incapable of christianizing the masses, herself on the contrary but too soon caught by the ancient heathen spirit, she surrendered one point after another of her moral requirements, became increasingly indulgent and lax in discipline, and was more and more contented with a Christianity, which consisted merely in a participation in Church ceremonies. In the same proportion, however, in which she thus despaired of the moral transformation of the people in general, did she strain the more tightly her claims upon those who desired to be perfect Christians. As the universal priesthood of all Christians was replaced by the hierarchical priesthood of the few, so was the holiness of all by that of some few saints; the perfection required in Scripture from all became the aim of a select band, of a moral aristocracy, standing as a correlative beside the clerical aristocracy.

The germs of a double ethic, of a distinction between perfect and imperfect Christians, are early to be recognised.[3] They are found especially in the high estimation of the unmarried state. Hence it is here also, that the double ethic, the distinction between commandments binding on all Christians and counsels left to free decision, first comes forth clearly and consciously in Origen and Cyprian, even the counsel of celibacy, which is chiefly brought forward. The firstlings of the Church are according to Origen, virgins, and its tenths those who live continently after marriage. He very decidedly distinguishes between the commandment and what exceeds the commandment. He, who does only that which is commanded, is, according to Luke xvii. 10, an unprofitable servant; but he who adds something to the keeping of the commandments, does something beyond his duty, and receives the praise: "Well done, good and faithful servant." And this work surpassing the commandment is celibacy, which in 1 Cor. vii. 8 is not commanded, but only advised.[4] So too in Cyprian, it is on the counsel of celibacy that emphasis is chiefly laid. The Lord does not command celibacy, but He admonishes to it; and they who follow His monition, obtain thereby a better mansion in the world where there are many mansions, and then are of a higher rank than ordinary Christians.[5]

If then celibacy was regarded as a point of perfection in Christian life beyond the condition of the Christian living in the married state, it was but a short step further, to view in a similar manner the renunciation of earthly property. In both Origen and Cyprian it is plainly seen, how the development is tending this way. How very differently from Clement of Alexandria does Origen[6] already expound the history of the rich young man! It is true that he too quite acknowledges, that wealth does not prevent salvation; but, he adds, that it makes it in many respects more difficult, and is then inclined so to understand the passage, that he, who gives his goods to the poor, is for this supported by their prayers, and thus the more easily brought to perfect virtue—to perfection. The renunciation of earthly goods is thus at least made a way to perfection. While Clement holds him up as the victor, the true hero, who, united with God, conquers sorrow and pleasure in marriage, in the bringing up of children, in care for his household,[7] Origen already says:

"When a man gives himself up entirely to God, when he releases himself from all the cares of the present life, when he keeps himself separate from other men, who live after the flesh, and seeks no longer what is of earth, but only things heavenly, he truly deserves to be called holy."[8] It is as though we already saw monasticism making its appearance. In a similar manner do we find voluntary poverty combined with celibacy in Cyprian. His exhortations to virginity had been opposed by: "I am rich, and must use what God has given me to possess." To which Cyprian replies: "Use it but for salutary things. Let the poor experience, that thou art rich; the needy, that thou hast property. Put out thine inheritance to usury with God."[9] The renunciation of marriage entails that of property. Cyprian already regards property as a burden, and the rich are in his eyes unwise for seeking to increase this burden, instead of to rid themselves of it.[10] He very decidedly demands of those who have fallen away in persecution, that they should give up their wealth: "Let him who has been deceived and conquered by his wealth, neither retain nor love it. Property is to be fled from as an enemy, to be avoided as a robber, to be feared as a sword."[11] The saying of our Lord to the rich young ruler: "Sell all that thou hast!" is now without any hesitation understood of external giving away. If the rich had done this, they would not have perished through their riches. Nay, the notion already makes its appearance in Cyprian, that he who gives away his earthly goods, can more freely serve the Lord, and thus follow the example of the apostles.[12] These are in germ the views, which subsequently had so deep and decided an influence upon charity. To give away property is in itself a good work;

voluntary poverty is a more elevated moral condition than the possession of wealth.

Certainly things could not have come to this pitch, unless the New Testament doctrine of a Christian's fulfilment of the law had already been greatly obscured. According to New Testament teaching, the fulfilment of the law proceeds from faith; the moral conduct of man, his obedience to God, is the intrinsically necessary result of his entering into a right religious relation to God through faith in Christ. Justified by grace through faith, man is a new creature, and he now walks in obedience to the Divine commandments, in love, which is the fulfilling of the law. This connection was, however, soon lost to the Church. Even Clement of Rome, one of the earliest of the Apostolic Fathers, no longer grasps it. He strongly insists on justification through faith, but the fulfilling of the law is in his writings no longer rooted therein, but made to stand unconnectedly beside it. The tie, which unites faith and good works, justification and the fulfilling of the law, the religious relation of man to God and his moral conduct, is dissolved. The consequence is, that the two sides of the Christian life come into a false relation towards each other. Faith dwindles into an obedient reception of the rule of faith; the fulfilling of the law, as something not yet implied by faith, no longer having its roots in faith, exists independently beside it. Two things are required from him who desires to be a Christian: he must accept the rule of faith and fulfil the law of Christ. The less the moral value attributed to the first point, viz. faith, *i.e.* the acceptance of the rule of faith, the more strongly must the second, the fulfilling of the law, be insisted on. Christ is regarded as a new lawgiver, and Christianity esteemed a "new law" in distinction from the old law. The further consequence of this, however, was, that Christian life was no longer comprised as a whole in obedience to the Divine commands, but shattered into a multitude of single good works, and that thus the road was smoothed for the thought, that it was possible for a man to do more than he was obliged to do. For as long as Christian life is comprised as a whole in faith working by love, there is no room at all for such a notion. In other respects too this legal view of Christianity could not fail to have a disturbing influence upon charity. All legality is deficient in constancy. The appointing will remains one alien to man, it is not assimilated to his own will. Hence a fulfilment of this will as a whole is not attained to, but only a performance of single works. This is the reason that charity too, when a legal view of it was taken, was more and more split up into isolated almsgivings. Already in Cyprian it is no longer, as in Clement of Alexandria, upon the community that emphasis is laid, but upon the most abundant possible almsgiving, and in the post-Constantinian period charity is entirely comprised in wholesale almsgiving. And the more so, that now, as a further consequence of legality, almsgiving came to be looked on as meritorious and sin-atoning.

That there is in almsgiving an inherent satisfactory and sin-atoning power, was even in the second century no unheard-of matter. Justification by faith being no longer understood, the forgiveness of sins was soon made dependent on the fulfilment of the Divine commands. "Happy are we," writes already Clement of Rome, "if we keep the commandments of God in the unanimity of love, that our sins may be forgiven through love;"[13] and when we read in the Epistle of Barnabas the admonition:[14]

"Labour with thy hands for deliverance from thy sins," it is meant, that he who does his neighbour service with his hands, thereby obtains the forgiveness of his sins. Hermas represents in a peculiar manner the blessing brought by alms. He compares[15] the rich to the poles to which the vines are fastened. The pole itself bears no fruit, but so helps the vine, that it can bring forth fruit, and the fruit is so far to its advantage, that it indirectly bears fruit. The rich man prays little, and his prayer is powerless. But if he helps the poor, they pray for him, and their prayer is fruitful. God gives to the rich man all good, because the poor pray for him. But these isolated expressions are still something very different from the systematic insertion of almsgiving in the scheme of salvation. This is first met with in Origen and Cyprian, and with it the foundation of what was subsequently so significantly developed, and handed down throughout the whole period of the Middle Ages.

The universally accepted proposition, that baptism procures only the forgiveness of sins committed before baptism, is presupposed. Since then a Christian sins also after baptism, it is asked, how he obtains the forgiveness of post-baptismal sins. According to Origen, a sacrifice, to be brought by man himself, is required for this. Martyrdom is esteemed as such in the first rank. Martyrdom is a continuation of the sacrifice of Christ, and like it,—though certainly only, as Origen adds, in virtue of it,—has atoning power, which may then be applied to others, by the martyr also, in the way of intercession. But even this means of forgiveness is not sufficient, for there are not always martyrs in the Church. Origen then knows of other ways, in which sins may be forgiven, and among these alms stand first. Next to this the forgiveness of offences committed against us by others, the fulness of love, and lastly, public Church penance. While the latter is appointed for grievous and mortal sins, alms are above all the means of covering daily and slighter transgressions.[16]

Still greater stress is laid by Cyprian upon the sin-atoning power of alms, nay, it may be said, that he was the first to strike out the path, which was not again left till the era of the Reformation. His work *On Good Works and Alms* is here in all respects fundamental. He too starts from the proposition, that baptism takes away only the sins which preceded it. Hence baptism and the forgiveness of sins in baptism would have availed us nothing, unless God " had opened to us a way of salvation through works of mercy, that we might by alms wash off the defilements of sin, which we subsequently contract."[17] We plainly perceive in Cyprian also the way in which alms are intruded, in a hitherto unprecedented manner, into the scheme of pardon. Hitherto penitent prayer had been regarded as the means of obtaining pardon. Even public Church penance was only distinguished from penitence for daily sins by the circumstance, that in the former the penitent prayer of the individual was supported by the prayer of the Church. Cyprian now combines prayer and alms. Prayer is unfruitful unless accompanied by alms. It is alms which makes it powerful. "For He, who on the Day of Judgment will give their reward to prayers and alms, now also graciously hears the prayer that is combined with alms."[18] In confirmation of this proposition, Cyprian has now recourse to the Old Testament, and especially to the Apocrypha. Not only are Ps. xli. and Dan. iv. 24 brought in, but Cyprian is also the first to make use of the Apocrypha, and to introduce into the Church that apocryphal estimation of alms, which goes beyond the lines of the Old Testament. We there find, Tob. xii. 9, and above all Wisd. xxix. 12, and iii. 33: "As water extinguishes fire, so do alms extinguish sin."[19] Cyprian introduced into the judgment of the Church, that judgment concerning alms which was peculiar to post-Babylonian Judaism, and it is accordingly characteristic to find him making such copious use of the Apocrypha. New Testament passages are then also applied in a corresponding sense, especially Luke xi. 41. Our Lord here teaches, according to Cyprian, that we are to cleanse not the outside, but the inside, and adds, that this is to be done by alms.[20] Tabitha serves as an example, that alms deliver from death, even the death of the body. Thus alms appear beside baptism as sin-atoning. "As through the bath of the healing water the fire of hell is extinguished, so through alms and good works is the flame of sin put out."[21]

Henceforward the notion that alms are sin-atoning never recedes. We meet with it in the oldest sermon we know of, the so-called Second Epistle of Clement,[22] wherein alms are called repentance for sin; in the Apostolical Constitutions, where we find the exhortation: "If thou gainest anything by the labour of thy hands, give, that thou mayest work for the expiation of thy sins;"[23] and in Lactantius, where it is said: "Great is the reward of mercy, which God promises, that He will forgive all sin." Lactantius, however, lays far less stress upon the sin-atoning power of alms than Cyprian does. On the contrary, he places in the foreground the notion of humanity, which brings forth all the works of love, and is a part of the righteousness required of the Christian.

On the whole, the notions developed by Cyprian take

less effect during the præ-Constantinian era. There was still too much real love to need the impulse involved in this combination of alms with pardon. The era of distress and of conflict offered Christians so much opportunity of showing their readiness for sacrifice, that there was no necessity for special self-imposed sacrifices. "So long as"—again to use expressions of Cyprian—"the purple crown" of martyrdom beckoned, "the dazzling white crown" to be obtained by the voluntary surrender of property in the form of alms, could exercise no great attraction. But when the victory was won, when the Church became dominant, when love decayed in the multitude of nominal Christians, while distress increased, and a wholesale poverty, unknown in former times, set in, these notions began to influence and to obscure charity in ever-increasing proportion. Motives were altered. In the place of simple love, was found a regard to the blessing which alms bestow; respect was had not to the poor, but to self and what was to be gained thereby. This could not but gradually have a pernicious effect upon charity. The care of the poor on the part of the Church was stunted; in its place was found, on the one side, wholesale almsgiving, on the other benevolent institutions, the hospital and the monastery. Other causes certainly contributed to bring about this change, but in truth its main cause is to be found in that view of the atoning power of almsgiving, which was first clearly expressed by Cyprian. The post-Constantinian Age furnished much that was still great, in some respects greater, and at all events more dazzling in the sphere of charity, but it was no longer that simple, purer, and therefore so greatly blessed exercise of love, which prevailed in the earlier centuries.

BOOK THIRD.

AFTER THE VICTORY.

CHAPTER I.

A PERISHING WORLD.

THE history of Christian charity can only be understood in connection with the entire development of ecclesiastical, nay of secular history. For only thus shall we be in a position to comprehend the special tasks imposed upon it in each period, and how in fulfilling them it co-operated, as no small and unimportant factor, in the fulfilment of those imposed upon the world, and duly to appreciate those changes in its character, which corresponded with the changes of the times. Let us then first bring before ourselves that last period of the Roman Empire, which commences with Constantine.[1]

The rule of Constantine and his acts, directed as they were towards a restoration of the Empire, were even then very differently judged of, according to differing views of their results. While the heathen saw in him the destroyer of the Empire, and in all the troubles which from this time onwards increasingly overwhelmed the State, only the result of his supplanting the native religion by Christianity, he appeared to the Christians as crowned with the halo of a restorer of the Empire, and his acts were esteemed by them as in a special sense saving acts. In truth both were right, for as a powerful remedy infused into a sick body, calls forth a salutary reaction, which for the moment checks the progress of disease, but on the other hand, because the body lacks the vitality required for lasting health, produces pernicious effects and makes death only the more certain; so did the acts of Constantine bring about this double result. On the one hand their influence was preservative, the Empire owed to them its last appointed respite; on the other they could not but bring on with greater certainty the dissolution of the decaying body. After Constantine, the Roman Empire, notwithstanding the saving acts of the Emperor, nay in a certain sense by their means, was a perishing world.

There are three points, which chiefly indicate that final period of the Roman Empire, which, already preparing under Diocletian, fully set in with Constantine.

First, the totally altered character of the Empire itself. The forms of the republic, hitherto firmly though only apparently kept up, were now entirely obliterated. The Imperator became the Dominus, the absolute ruler. Oriental pomp, a numerous retinue of court officials, a ceremonial most minutely carried out, were calculated to separate him from the people, and to give a character of sacredness to his person. He was seldom seen by the people, and then only in the greatest pomp, in the purple and diadem of pearls, and surrounded by the bodyguard with their golden shields. It was only from a distance that the multitude could cast a furtive glance on all this glory. Access to him was difficult, a host of officials, by whom everything was brought before him, and his commands obtained in reply, stood between him and the people, while he himself, like an all-directing deity, sat enthroned out of sight in the "sacred apartments" of his palace.

Undoubtedly this nicely calculated and new system of

government exercised a salutary influence. The throne was more secure; the assassinations of emperors, which had, in the second half of the third century, brought the Empire to the brink of ruin, were less frequent. There grew up again a kind of legitimacy, which, though not one according to our conceptions, with a settled hereditary succession, was yet of a nature to bind men to fidelity to the once acknowledged emperor, and to make it esteemed a crime to rise against him. This system of government had, however, its suspicious reverse side. The government proper was in the hands of the bureaucracy. The people sick unto death were no longer in a condition to rule themselves, all self-government having long ceased. Whatever was done, was done from above. But the Emperor too was on his part governed, while he thought he was governing. He saw only what he was to see, and heard only what he was to hear. How things were really going on in the Empire, he never learned, but only that of which his all-notifying, all-enregistering officials thought fit to inform him. Never was a ruler more exceptionally deceived—as Diocletian already complained—than the Roman Emperor; never were the laws more badly obeyed, than in the absolutely governed Roman State. Amidst cringing devotion and apparent subjection to every imperial command, each law, each injunction, was nevertheless evaded. Of these thoroughly deceitful and intriguing officials, but few had the good of the people in view; the majority were only bent upon their own advantage, accessible to every kind of corruption, striving only to raise themselves to large incomes, to brilliant positions, to the utmost possible nearness to the imperial sun, the dispenser of all benefits. The demoralizing influences, which despotism exercises, are most fearfully apparent in the corruption of the official world. The tribunals were no better. They were, as Marcus Ammianus[2] says, not temples of justice, but pits and snares, which those who did not know how to help themselves did not, however innocent, get out of for years, nor till they were sucked to the very marrow, while the guilty, if they only knew the trick, got off with impunity. Everything was to be obtained by bribery. To the rich and powerful it was easy to make their injustice triumphant; to the poor it was difficult, if not impossible, to obtain justice.

Next, it was Constantine, who, conscious of the necessity of infusing young and vigorous blood into the sinking Roman power, was the first Emperor to attract the Germans, to favour their reception into the Empire, the army, the personal service of the Emperor, and thus to bring about a development of the greatest importance to after ages. From this time onwards Germans were mingled in ever-increasing proportion among the Romish population. They came as prisoners of war and slaves, as mercenaries willingly entering the Romish service, as individual adventurers seeking to make their fortunes in the Empire, as hordes settling within its boundaries, and they were soon able to say, as Tertullian makes the Christians do: "We are of yesterday, and we do everything." Germans cultivated the land as colonists, served in the houses as slaves, in the bureaus as officials, in the imperial palace as courtiers, filled the squares of the legions, commanded the army as officers and generals, governed the State as ministers.

Certainly new power was thus infused into the decaying State, and to this it was indebted, in part at least, for its temporary preservation. They were for the most part

Germans, who, now fighting under the Roman standards, with difficulty defended the boundaries of the Empire against their fellow-tribesmen. Still more important was this mingling of Germans and Romans with respect to the future. The Germans, who were thus received into the Empire, were brought into contact with Roman civilization, acquired a sense for it, were educated to become one day its inheritors, and yet remained in sufficient proximity to their kinsmen to civilize them in return. Rome, when receiving the Germans, was unconsciously subserving higher ends,[3] for we really have already before us the beginning of the conquest of the Empire by the Germans, the beginning of the formation of a new Romano-Germanic world; and the same act, which under former emperors had preservative influence, could not fail to fall out subsequently to the destruction of the Empire. When Valens permitted the Goths to cross the Danube, he did nothing else than what many emperors before him had done with advantage to the realm, and yet he then signed, without knowing it, the death-warrant of Rome.

But the act which is specially distinctive of Constantine is, that he gave in Christianity a new religious foundation to the Empire. At first merely acknowledged, Christianity as the religion of the ruler soon became the dominant, and then the only dominant religion. The Empire became externally at least a Christian State. Whatever we may think in other respects of the first Christian emperors, we must at any rate acknowledge, that this act of Constantine was supereminently an act preservative of the State. Without the new religious fermentation, a restoration of the Empire in general would have been impossible. At the same time, it is certain, that the Christian religion could only have permanently strengthened, actually renovated, and longer preserved the Empire, if it had succeeded in really penetrating the national life with the leaven of the gospel. To this, however, it did not even approximate, and hence in other aspects Christianity could not but have a destructive and explosive influence. There is truth in the saying: " The old world died of Christianity."

In endeavouring to explain a proposition at first sight so strange, we must start from the statement, that to be a genuine Roman and at the same time a Christian, was an irreconcilable contradiction. He who became a Christian broke, even if he did not know it, with the entire past; he disowned the whole existing condition of political, civil, social, scientific, and artistic life. For this life was everywhere penetrated by heathenism; at whatever point its roots were followed, heathen ideas were always at last struck against. Hence Christianity could not fail to implant in all the relations of life germs of rupture, the effect of which was a gradual loosening and splitting up, just as water gradually rends asunder even the hardest rocks. Of this Christians themselves had, I repeat, no consciousness, at least no clear consciousness. They esteemed themselves good citizens. How often, in their apologies, do they appeal, in reply to the reproach of being enemies to the State, to their faithful fulfilment of their civil duties, their punctual payment of taxes, their respect for the Emperor, their obedience to authorities. All this was quite true; yet Christians had a secret feeling, that the heathen State was one properly alien to them, and if this feeling did not degenerate into hostility, because they knew themselves to be bound by the apostle's words: " The powers that be are ordained of

God," still their real disposition towards the State was that of indifference. In earnest Christian circles all positive participation in political life, the filling of a magistracy, military service, had long been esteemed sinful. The kingdom of God was more to Christians than the Roman Empire, the Church more than the State. It was there that they found their life's centre, and so long as the State was hostile to Christianity (and we must not forget that this was for centuries), it could not be otherwise. The Church became a state within the State. The Christian found his point of support in the Church, to it belonged first of all his affections and his service; he there sought not only the word of life and what conduced to his salvation, but he there sought also, in the episcopal tribunal, his rights, and aid when he was in trouble.

It might have been expected, that all this would have been changed, when the position of the State towards the Church became a friendly one, when the supreme head of the State himself, and soon afterwards the whole nation, belonged to the Church. But by that time the Church was already a state within the State, and such it continued. For Constantine and his sons, perceiving the power of the Church, and hoping to make this friendly to themselves, aimed rather at still further increasing its power and influence. The jurisdiction of the bishops was recognised and even extended; the Church was overwhelmed with favours, privileges, exemptions from taxation, wealth. Thus the Church increased while the State decreased, nay, it may be said that the Church exhausted the State. A glance at the period shows, that real vitality was on the side of the Church; the State ageing, the Church in youthful vigour; on the side of the

P

State increasing feebleness, on that of the Church an access of power and influence; in the one a slavishly-minded people ground down by despotism, in the other a feeling for liberty. At least it was the office-bearers of the Church who alone ventured to plead the cause of the people before their capricious despots. In the former, moral corruption; in the latter, at all events in the more conspicuous figures, in the rulers of the Church and in thousands of its members, moral earnestness, which, even if it struck out false paths and sought salvation by ascetic self-denial, was still imposing. The State grew poor, the Church became rich; the State lost its influence on popular life, the Church acquired what the State lost; the State broke up into fragments, the Church was compressed into an ever more and more compact unity. While two or three emperors were dividing among them the imperial power in Constantinople, Milan and Treves, Rome, forsaken by its emperors, was becoming the ecclesiastical point of unity and preparing itself, for a second time and in another manner, to rule the world. What intellectual powers the State forfeited, because all intellectually important characters were attracted to the Church! How many thousand citizens were lost at a time when every hand that could guide the plough, every arm that could wield the sword was not to be replaced— lost by the departure of Christians by troops into the wilderness, that they might there in solitude follow after the ideal of a supposed Christian perfection! What material losses did the State incur by privileges and exemptions from taxation granted to the Church, and by the accumulation of such great treasures, such enormous landed property by the latter! A feature of the period was a kind of flight from the State, and this flight set towards the Church. Hither did all who longed to escape from the oppressions of the State betake themselves. The Church indeed requited the State for this, by exercising a moralizing influence upon the people, but not in such proportions as to supply an actual compensation. For just here was the failure,—the leaven of the gospel did not penetrate, an actual christianization of the Roman Empire was never attained, and hence, in the end, Christianity was more a destructive than a conservative agency.

It will now be clear, that the acts of Constantine could not, and why they could not, preserve the Empire; also in what sense they themselves contributed to its dissolution. It is a perishing world that we are contemplating. Everything was falling to ruins. There is something hoary in the character of the age. Population was decreasing both in numbers and strength. Industry, trade, art, science, all were in a state of declension. Financial embarrassments were increasing, the burdens laid upon the people were becoming more and more intolerable. And worst of all, morality was sinking lower and lower. Debauchery, even unnatural crimes were again in vogue. A semi-barbarous luxury swallowed up whatever property still existed. It was as though the desire was to consume time. Falsehood and deceit became fundamental features of the Roman character. How many a German petty king perished through over-confidence in Roman artifice! how many an incursion of barbarians was owing to Roman breach of faith! It was truly felt that morality was sinking; Draconic laws were enacted, justice became, as is always the case in such times, harsh and cruel. It was of no avail, the laws were not kept, and the judges were just as corrupt as the rest of the people. And this internally decaying Empire was encompassed by hordes of Germans, lusting for the glories of Rome and Greece, and only waiting for the moment when they must fall a prey to them. It was now only a question of time, when the hour of ruin was to strike for the Empire.

Strange to say that neither the teachers of the Church, nor the far-seeing men of the age, were conscious of living and working in a perishing world. If we read, *e.g.*, the oration pronounced in Milan by Ambrose on the deceased Emperor Theodosius,[4] we cannot doubt that he really believed in a regeneration of the Roman Empire by the act of Constantine, and nothing is further from his thoughts than its speedy fall. He places Theodosius with Constantine; what Constantine began, Theodosius has completed. The Empire has again one faith. He recalls the circumstance, that his mother Helena presented the first Christian Emperor with two nails out of the rediscovered sacred cross. Constantine placed one in the imperial crown, the other in the bridle of his horse. "Oh wise Helena," exclaims Ambrose, "who assigned to the cross its place upon the head of the Emperor, that in the Emperor the crown might be honoured! Oh good nail, which holds the Roman Empire together!" Ambrose really believed, that the crown had received fresh splendour from the cross, that the Christian faith was the nail that kept the Empire together. How near this Empire was, in spite of the sacred nail, to its destruction, Ambrose did not perceive. And yet the conquest of the Empire by the Germans had already begun. The golden shielded guards, who were keeping watch by the corpse of the Emperor, the generals who were commanding the army, the ministers who were standing by the side of the sons, as yet minors, of the great Emperor, of whom the realm had been too soon deprived, were Germans. The Goths were already in Thrace, and if the eyes of Ambrose had been miraculously opened to behold the future, he would already have seen before him the man who, for the first time since the Gauls, was to enter as a victor into the hitherto unconquered Rome—the mighty Goth, Alaric.

It was with others as with Ambrose. They could not avoid the conviction, that since the Empire had become Christian, distress and misery had increased on all sides, that the christianization of Rome by no means resulted in its revived glory. They often meditated on the question, how this could be; the reproach of the heathen, that this distress was a punishment for forsaking the native gods, constrained them to inquire into it, but they never had a notion, that the Empire could perish, or the Barbarians take the place of the Romans. And well that it was so. For the consciousness of working in a perishing world would have paralyzed their courage for work, and this was necessary not indeed for the preservation of the Empire, but for the realization of the then hidden purposes of God. It was natural also that it was so. Faith in Eternal Rome was too deeply rooted; the Romans were too conscious of their superiority to the Germans in civilization, to have been ever able to conceive, that these Barbarians should supplant them. The thought indeed was not absent, that the present distress was a chastisement of God, a well-deserved chastisement of the degenerate race. Salvian preached thus in touching terms to his contemporaries, and represented to them, that the Germans were victorious because they were chaste, self-restrained and truthful, while the Romans were debauched and deceitful. The fundamental notion of his work *On God's Government of the World*, is: The

government of the world is the judgment of God.
Therefore Africa, a country full of debauchery, fell into
the hands of the chaste Vandals. At the same time,
however, it was always maintained, that the chastisement
was a temporary one, and every glimmer of improvement,
a momentary mitigation of misery, an isolated victory
over the Barbarians, nay, even a gracious letter from the
Emperor to the Senate, awakened the boldest hope, that
troubles were now over, and that a new era of prosperity
was about to dawn upon the Empire. No Roman, and
even no Christian Roman ever entertained the notion
that the Barbarians could ever put an end to the Roman
Empire and Roman civilization. Hence no results were
obtained by their treatises on Divine Providence, its
plans and purposes. Never was the question of Divine
Providence so much discussed as then. Augustine's great
work *On the City of God* starts from it; Orosius, in his
work, *On the Calamities of the whole World;* Salvian,
in his before-mentioned work, *On the Divine Government*,
discuss it. Every fresh trouble again revived this question.
How energetically was it debated after the
defeat at Adrianople, when Valens fell and the Goths
destroyed the Roman army—a defeat which everywhere
made as great an impression as formerly that of Cannæ!
To the assertion of the heathen, that Christianity was the
cause of all this misfortune, that under its ancient gods
Rome had flourished, while under the God of the Christians
there was nothing but misery, the Christians had
nothing to oppose but the retort, that neither had there
been any lack of misfortune under the gods of Olympus.
Calculations and counter-calculations were made, but in
such wise, that one party took no notice of the calculations
of the other. The entire mode of viewing the

matter was somewhat mechanical; the punishments and rewards of heaven were regarded in a very external manner. Neither heathen nor Christians were able to perceive the deeper meaning which events had according to God's hidden counsels. The key was yet lacking for the comprehension of the age.

We have this key, for we can see whither the dealings of God were tending, and just this age in which the saying, "His footsteps are in the deep waters," was so conspicuously fulfilled, and which was therefore so incomprehensible to the generation then living, is to us clear and transparent. If any one were to ask me what period of history he should study, to gain a direct impression of the rule of Divine Providence, I should say the era of the migration of the nations.

It was not the civilised nations of the Græco-Roman world, but the Germans, who were to be the vehicles of Christianity. The old world was too much penetrated by heathen traditions for Christianity to take deep root in it. But if the Germans were to become the inheritors of ancient civilization, and to carry on the work of the Greeks and Romans, a preparation was needed, and this preparation was furnished by the period after Constantine, as also, though without their understanding it, by Ambrose, Augustine, Gregory, and other great men, in whom this period was richer than almost any other. Augustine, in his *City of God*, has, so to speak, unconsciously written out the programme of the Middle Ages; for the Middle Ages are properly nothing else than the effort to realize the ideas laid down in this work.[5] Let us just suppose, that the Roman Empire had at an earlier period—say when Marcus Aurelius with difficulty kept the intruding Marcomanni to the Danube—fallen into the hands of the Germans. They would have extirpated every trace of the civilization of the ancient world, and Christianity with it. Hence the delay, the last respite, which was granted to the Empire by the act of Constantine. The Germans were to be first so far matured as to be capable of fulfilling their high vocation. Not as Pagans but as Christians were they to conquer the Empire. How very differently from Alaric the Goth, would a Marcomannian chief have treated Rome! And the main point, the Church itself, was to be so far strengthened as to be able to furnish a shelter for the treasures of old-world culture. Whatever was saved was preserved in the new world of German culture, *i.e.* by the Church; it was her care that hindered the thread of development from being utterly severed. But if the Church was to effect this, it was necessary that it should strengthen beside the State, become a state in the State, grow rich, gain power and influence. What the Church gained was thus indeed lost to the existent State, but only to be preserved to mankind. The treasures of old-world cultivation, the produce of millenniums of labour, were concealed for later ages in the Church; for when the State perished, the Church did not perish with it, but remained, and was the means of handing over what was saved to the young nations, of raising them to a new culture. And not till the further development was thus prepared for, was the sign for the revolution given far off in Asia. The Huns rushed upon the Goths; the Goths poured into the Roman Empire. The death hour of the ancient world had struck. The Roman Empire might now be destroyed, the thread of culture development was not broken, the new nations became the heirs of the old nations.

It is from this point of view that we can understand the task of charity to have been a double one. It had first to stand, so to speak, at the deathbed of the old world with its aid and comforts. These were such times of most appalling misery, of most wholesale wretchedness, as do not recur in the history of the world. Love, Christian compassion, at least alleviated and mitigated the death-pangs of the dying world; and even if she could not prevent the general misery, she yet dried the tears of individuals, and afforded comfort and repose to countless numbers. But she had also to stand with her aid and service at the cradle of the new age. Christian charity became undoubtedly one of the main educational agencies for the young German nations, helped to win them for the Church, bound them to the Church, and co-operated in the most diverse manners in their transformation.

What Christian love effected towards the fulfilment of this second task, what she did for the education of the German nations, will not be spoken of till we treat of the beginnings of the Middle Ages. What we have in the first place to deal with, is the exercise of charity in the perishing old world.

A perishing world—what a summary of sorrow and misery, of anxiety and distress, is contained in the words! Let us try to take a glance at it, that we may the more plainly perceive how gigantic was the labour now imposed on Christian love.

If we turn over the writings of the time, the sermons of great preachers, their letters and their devotional works, we come upon thousandfold complaints and sighs over the misery which everywhere prevailed; but no complaint recurs so frequently as that concerning the increasingly oppressive taxation. Let us then also first put in the foremost place this feature in the sad lineaments of the perishing world, which is so extremely distinctive of the whole picture. Already, before Constantine, we become aware of such complaints, but they now form the heart-rending cry of the whole people. The State at that period knew of scarcely any other than fiscal interests. The whole land was treated as a domain of the Emperor, from which his officials exerted themselves to extort, by ever new arts and violence, as much money as possible. For money, and much money, was wanted at Constantinople. First, the maintenance of the court swallowed up enormous sums. A brilliant court, oriental pomp and luxury, formed, as we have seen, part of the new system of government begun by Diocletian and carried out by Constantine. Everything was calculated to be imposing in the eyes of the people. The Emperor now sat in his palace in the sacred chambers, surrounded by the seven great dignitaries of the crown and a host of court officials, chamberlains, eunuchs, guards and innumerable attendants of every kind. In the palace there was everywhere the rustling of silk and the glittering of gold and jewels. The dignitaries drew large incomes, the whole crew swallowed up immense sums. An occasional notice informs us, that a court cook received, besides his considerable income, twenty portions from the imperial kitchens; and Julian, who indeed was but a short time at the head of affairs, says derisively, that a court barber was going about in the dress of a minister of finance. Then there was the army, which, though inferior to that of former times, cost incomparably more, for officers and soldiers had become effeminate; then the second army of civilians, the entire many-membered

bureaucracy, which was now looked upon as necessary to
the administration of the Empire, the Pretorian præfects,
the Diocesans, the 120 provincial governors, each of
whom received, besides perquisites, an income of £4500,
the crowds of officials and secretaries of lower rank. If
we remember the cost of the games, which were celebrated
with ever-increasing splendour, the cost of buildings,
always a special fancy of despotic rulers, the heaps of
gold, which the Barbarians, who could no longer be
restrained, carried off under the name of imperial largess,
but in reality as tribute; and lastly, if we take into
account, that there never was a more fraudulent official
world than at this time, that embezzlement and defrauding
were the order of the day, and often brought the imperial
menage into difficulties, we shall be able to gain an
approximate notion of what the State consumed. The
Emperor was no longer in a condition to protect the
people, he could only exhaust them. " The splendour
of one was the ruin of all," says Salvian.[6]

Now all this had to be levied from a population already
poor, and daily growing more so. For the rich, the high
officials, the great proprietors, even the Church and its
officers, rejoiced—thanks to imperial favour—in great
privileges and exemptions. "When a tax is to be raised,"
says Salvian, who may indeed occasionally exaggerate,
but who nevertheless expresses complaints which were
universally diffused, "the rich know how to manage that
the poor may have to bear the main burden, while, when
a mitigation of taxation takes place, they take care that
the poor shall get nothing, the rich everything."[7] The
mass of the people, annually diminishing in numbers, and
whose property was continually being lessened by wars,
by the irruptions of the Barbarians, alone bore the heavy

burdens. Vespasian computed the whole taxation of the Roman Empire as amounting in his days to £30,000,000 annually. The population of the Empire might then be from about ninety to one hundred millions. But now Gaul, which contained at most eight millions of inhabitants, had to raise £19,200,000, *i.e.* about 48s. per head, in land tax alone. Now, though the land tax was the highest of all imposts, a multitude of other burdens were added, poll-tax, customs and rates of various kinds, and many with unusual titles, the furnishing of natural productions, crown-gold on the accession of an Emperor, and many others.

Almost worse than the high rate of taxation was the harshness with which it was collected. Humane Emperors tried, indeed, but were unable to alleviate it. Unless the machinery of the State was to come to a standstill, all that was possible must be extorted from the impoverished people. Besides, what did the Emperor know of the treatment they received from his officers! He only read in his sacred chambers the rose-coloured accounts that were furnished to him, and if a complaint ever penetrated so far, care would certainly have been previously taken by bribery to have it represented as mere falsehood and deception, and the complainers might be glad if nothing worse happened to them, than to be sent home with their ears slit. To the financial and fiscal agents, from the highest to the lowest, every new tax was a delight. For it gave them the opportunity of providing for themselves and filling their own pockets, or even of proving themselves able officials, by extorting from the people more than was prescribed, and sending to Constantinople larger sums than were expected, as a pure labour of love, and to obtain imperial favour in the surest manner. By long routine they had learned the art of discovering and profiting by new sources of finance, and as for compassion, they were unacquainted with it. They would take inexorably the last possession, would deprive the wife of the ornament, the heirloom of better days, which she still wore, the child of the golden amulet with which its mother had provided it as a defence against sorcery, the poor of even his garment. Those who could not pay were thrown into prison, where cruel treatment, hunger and often torture might perchance extort concealed treasures. Whenever a levying of taxes was announced, a cry of grief and despair burst from the exhausted population. The dungeons filled, many fled, some even committed suicide to put an end to their woes. It is related that parents sold their sons, nay, sacrificed the honour of their daughters, to be able to pay their taxes with the proceeds.[8] Basil gives, in one of his sermons, a heart-rending description of a father who, to satisfy the tax-gatherer, has had to sell one of his sons, and is hesitating before the terrible choice, which of the three to part with. The eldest? But he has the right of primogeniture in his favour. The youngest? But he is the weakest and smallest. The middle one? But he is the son who has specially grown round his heart.[9] Certainly this was no dream of the bishop, but a picture drawn from the life. Palladius too on one occasion tells of a knight meeting in the desert a woman, who told him her sad tale. Her husband had been cast into prison and tortured for arrears of taxes, her two sons sold, herself often scourged, until she fled, and had now been wandering three days without food.

It was a special hardship that a tax computed according to landed property and the number of heads was imposed on municipal towns as a lump sum, and that then the Decurions had to advance the money. The only choice left them was, either to be plundered themselves or to plunder others. Things came to such a pitch, that the Decurions, *i.e.* the highest class in the municipal population, the moneyed class, preferred to give up house and grounds, place and dignity, only to be released from taxation. But a whole arsenal of laws prevented this, and bound them with iron fetters to property, which was only a burden. The small landowners were, however, worst off. Now it was money that had to be paid under no one knows how many names, now conveyance to be provided, horses to be in readiness for the imperial post, now corn or other matters to be furnished. If they did not pay, if they did not provide and furnish, they were cast into prison. Thousands of small proprietors chose to sacrifice their freedom, and betake themselves to the great landowners in a relation of bondage. Then the latter would be obliged to provide for them. There was a rush to be rid of freedom, it was sold for a morsel of bread. In other instances they would simply decamp, leave house and grounds behind, and wander about as mendicants in the towns. In Gaul, extensive tracts, which were formerly flourishing fields, lay desolate, vines grew wild without culture. From an investigation made at the turn of the third and fourth centuries, it appeared that in Campania, fertile land which usually yielded its cultivators three harvests per year, 528,642 jugera of formerly cultivated land, *i.e.* about an eighth of the entire province, lay quite waste. The State in vain offered this land to any one capable of paying the land tax imposed on it. No one was to be found. Hence the neighbouring landowners were forced to pay the tax upon this deserted land as well as upon their own, and were thus utterly ruined.[10]

Force was now in general the sole means of government. The Empire could only be kept together by bands of iron. The period of free trade was over. An organization of labour was again attained, but of what a kind! Purely an organization of force. The age was capable of none other. While the lot of the slave was mitigated, all were really becoming slaves. In this development, with the beginnings of which we became acquainted in the preceding period, fiscal interests played a considerable part, nay, were here as everywhere the ruling interests. During the whole imperial period there existed a widely branching system of contributions of natural products, and of labour of all kinds. Hand labour and horse labour had to be furnished, the corn and all the provisions needed by the army had to be delivered gratis, by those who were bound to do so. From the time of Constantine the pursuit after freedom from these burdens begins; whoever could attain it sought release. The result was, that in fact many classes enjoyed this immunity; the palace officials, the lessees of estates, the Church and its property, the professors and the inhabitants of Constantinople obtained it. They thus became a still more insupportable burden to those less highly favoured, and the further consequence was, that these were the more strictly bound to them by laws and penalties, and themselves and their children kept to the position they occupied in the State. Hence arose one of the most characteristic traits of the political economy of the age, the state of obligation in which all classes and associations in any way bound to the State were held. Nay, the children being also bound to occupy the same position as their father, it was in form a system of caste.[11]

The upper classes—to begin with these—were obliged to undertake the office of prætors, of whom there were three in Constantinople and two in Rome. The office itself was no longer of any importance, but combined with it was the duty imposed upon its holders, of giving the public games at their own expense, for the games formed part of the official pomp with which the government was surrounded. For the games actors were required. Hence actors were forbidden to relinquish their business. They were obliged to continue actors, and their children must become such in their turn. Even if they desired to be Christians, which was only possible on condition of their giving up their occupation, their joining the Church was only permitted under strict limitations. The mariners who carried corn to Rome and Constantinople, the store-keepers, the bakers, butchers, and workmen of all kinds, who supplied the wants of the army, the fire-engine men formed corporations, which they might not leave, and the son was in his turn obliged to become what his father had been. The office of the Decurions, formerly a post of honour, had become one of constraint, as we have already seen; and as the Decurions were bound to their office, so too were the Coloni in the country to the sod. The Coloni were partly freemen, partly slaves, to whom a large landowner had delivered up a portion of his land to cultivate, for payment in kind. Hitherto the freemen among them might, if they chose, leave and seek for another and perhaps more advantageous position, while the slaves might be sold by their masters. In fiscal interest, for the sake of ensuring the taxes to be furnished by the property, they were now bound step by step more firmly to the soil (*glebæ adscripti*). At first the masters were forbidden to sell their slaves from province to province, and then to sell them at all. The slave-Coloni could only be sold with the fields which they cultivated. To themselves this was in a certain sense an improvement of their condition. From slaves they had become serfs. But equally had the free become serfs. They too could not leave the land they tilled.[12] Thus all free movement was done away with; every one was bound with fetters to the position which he once occupied, however insupportable might be the burden he had to bear. Only in the region of the Church was there liberty. If any one entered into the service of the Church, or became a monk, settled in the desert, went into a monastery, he was free, he shook off the whole burden at once. Hence that pressure into the Church's service, that fleeing from the world, that rapid increase of monasticism, until the State there too intervened, there too drew limits, forbidding entrance into the service of the Church, or into a monastery to one, and uniting it with certain conditions to another.

That in such a state trade and commerce, industry and agriculture could not flourish, that the lively intercourse of the earlier imperial times should come to a stop, needs no proof. Much wealth still existed. The treasures accumulated in former centuries were not yet consumed. There were families of enormous landed property, in whose numerous palaces incalculable riches were amassed, who, like the senator Symmachus, could squander £400,000 on festivities in the prætorship of his son, or like the senator Maximus, £800,000 on a like occasion, without ruining themselves. But property was unequally distributed, and its distribution became increasingly unequal. The circulation of the blood in the body of the Empire had stagnated. Capital was not invested in profitable undertakings, but squandered in semi-barbarous luxury. Who, too, would invest his money in industrial or commercial undertakings, or employ it in the improvement of estates, when the general insecurity made the result so uncertain? "In the whole Roman sphere," sighs Salvian, "peace and security are equally null."[13] Who, too, would labour only to feed the greedy world of officials, and to have his hard earnings wrung from him by the tax-gatherer, or to lose them at the next inroad of the Barbarians? The nobles, the powerful, and the rich still indeed found protection; the humble and obscure were exposed defenceless to every extortion and oppression. How often in the sermons of this period is the history of Naboth's vineyard brought forward! "The history of Naboth," says Ambrose,[14] "is, if time is considered, old; in fact it is repeated daily. Not one Ahab is born, but one daily, and he never dies in this generation. If one is killed, there are more to take his place. Not one poor Naboth is slain, but Naboths are daily destroyed, the poor is murdered every day." Means and ways enough were open to the rich and respectable to oppress and drain the poor, and besides the testimony of the Church and its discipline, there was no hindrance in their path. Usury especially assumed the largest dimensions. Thus the relation of the rich to the poor became increasingly unequal, thus the numbers of those entirely without property progressively increased. A few rich, who, as Chrysostom so often describes them in his sermons, lived in luxury, ate from gold plate on silver tables, with troops of running footmen, satellites, slaves, around them, rode on golden-bridled horses, or drove in golden decorated carriages, slept on beds of ivory; and beside them were the countless numbers of a proletariat suffering the want of the commonest necessaries. In every town there were crowds of beggars, they filled the high roads, and went from place to place, lay by hundreds in the public places, and especially before the churches, naked, hungry, freezing with cold, sick and emaciated, calling on the passers-by for assistance, showing their wounds, their sores, their deformities, and trying in every way to excite compassion. All courage was extinct in these unfortunates; powerless to rise, they bore in gloomy indifference whatever might happen to them. Many fled to the Barbarians, because life seemed more bearable among them than in the Roman Empire; or, driven to despair, began to rob and plunder like them, thus increasing the general misery. Gaul was for many decades spoiled by hosts of those who had been driven to insurrection (the so-called Bagandæ) by the oppressions of men of office or property. If any unusual calamity were added to the general misery, a drought, as in the time of Basil in Cappadocia, a pestilence like many which visited the Empire, a wretchedness arose which baffles all description.[15]

Distress was brought to a climax by the continual wars and the irruptions of the Barbarians. The struggle of the Germans against Rome assumed after Constantine more and more the gloomy character of a struggle for life and death. The Romans regarded everything as allowable against the Barbarians. If once they succeeded in gaining temporary advantages, often enough more by intrigues and treachery than by valour, they then sought utterly to extirpate their hated antagonists, who in their turn requited them in like manner. They traversed the whole of Gaul as far as into Spain, murdering and plundering everywhere; the Thracian peninsula was for a long time entirely in their power; in their ships they visited Southern Italy, Greece, and Asia Minor. In Jerusalem, the colony of pious men and women, presided over by Jerome, trembled before them. Scarcely was there a place left in the Roman Empire, which the light-haired, blue-eyed hordes had not visited as conquerors and plunderers. Numerous towns and villages lay in ruins, far and wide the country was trampled on, the fruit-trees hewn down, the houses burnt, the inhabitants put to the sword or led away prisoners or wandering about in beggary. We can understand how Gregory the Great exclaims in one of his sermons: "What more can befall us in this world? We see nothing but sorrows, we hear nothing but complaints. Ah, Rome! formerly mistress of the world, what has happened to thee? Where is the senate? Where are the people? Yet why should I speak of men; the buildings are in ruins, the walls are falling;" and how, on another occasion, he concludes a sermon with the words: "You all know how our troubles are increasing. Everywhere the sword! Everywhere death! I am weary of life."[16]

Who was to help in this universal misery? The State could not. It made, during this whole period, no serious attempt to relieve the poor. It provided the Church with large means, it enriched it with donations and privileges, made over to it a portion of the contributions of corn, with which a sort of maintenance of the poor had been carried on, remitted also certain orders concerning the police of the poor, the prohibition of mendicancy, and enactments relating to the treatment of beggars; but as for the relief of the poor, that was entirely abandoned to the Church. The Church alone could help, and to her glory it must be said that she did much, and effected a great result. Her task was indeed quite different from what it had been in earlier days. Then, only isolated cases had to be dealt with, now a wholesale poverty of the most terrible kind. Even this one circumstance could not fail to exercise a most powerful influence upon the whole character of the relief of the poor. It operated upon even the motives of charity. For, undoubtedly, it was under the impression of this wholesale poverty, and in the effort to procure the most abundant possible donations for the poor, that the Church, in whose members the ardour of first love was already considerably cooled, so strongly brought forth the motive of reward, the purification from sin to be obtained by almsgiving. Still more must this wholesale pauperism have influenced the kind and manner of relief. A congregational care of the poor, such as existed in the first period, became increasingly an impossibility. In its place appeared, on the one hand, a wholesale almsgiving; on the other, charitable institutions, of which hospitals and monasteries were the central points. And with these we have already reached the transition to the Middle Ages. As in many another aspect, so too in the sphere of charity, this period is the preparation for the Middle Ages. If the period before Constantine may be characterized as that of congregational or Church relief of the poor, this feature now more and more recedes, till in the Middle Ages it entirely ceases, and hospitals and monasteries become the central-points of a charity, resolving itself into wholesale almsgiving.

CHAPTER II.

PROSPERITY AND DECAY OF CONGREGATIONAL RELIEF OF
THE POOR.

THE first century and a half after the victory form one of the most brilliant periods in the history of the Church. The longer the conflict had endured, the more violent the last persecution had been, the stronger would be the impression of the change, and the Church, elevated by the consciousness of victory, developed her strength on all sides. Under Constantine, while still considerably in the minority, she rapidly won the masses of the people; one hundred and fifty years after, the heathen had become an utterly unimportant minority. In every city churches vying in magnificence with the temples were now built. Worship received during this period its full development; dogma was, after many violent contests, definitely settled at the great Œcumenical Synods. A series of great bishops and teachers, of whom we never find again so brilliant a succession,—Athanasius, the three Cappadocians, Basil the Great, Gregory of Nazianzus, Gregory of Nyssa, Chrysostom in the East, Ambrose, Jerome, Augustine, Leo the Great in the West, to name only the most illustrious,— testify to the power which lay in the new faith. This development of strength manifested itself also in the department of charity. It was both the period of greatest prosperity in Church relief of the poor, and at the same time that which created in the hospital and the monastery the central point of the charity of succeeding centuries.

The change in the condition of the Church could not fail to accrue to the especial profit of the relief of the poor. The Church could now act freely and openly, there was no longer any necessity for acting secretly. Means now came in more plentifully, and powerful personal assistance was more abundantly at command. In place of the State's disfavour, there was now its supreme approbation, the effort to support and promote the work of the Church in every respect. That Constantine already perceived the importance of this work is proved by the fact, that, soon after his recognition of the Church, he awarded to it a portion of the corn contributions.[1] The increasing respect, too, in which the bishops were held, the recognition of their jurisdiction, the many privileges accorded to the Church, the germs even of a christianization of legislation, all contributed to promote its designs. That the Church did not fail to profit by these favourable circumstances is shown by the testimony of its opponent, the Emperor Julian, given just at this time. For he could not help recognizing the charity of the Church, and seeing in it a chief means of that rapid propagation of the Christian faith, which was to him so abhorrent.

The kind of work, its organization, its principles, at first remained the same. All this had indeed been handed down from the times before the conflict. Only now everything was extended and assumed larger dimensions. The direction lay as before in the hand of the bishop, numerous deacons and deaconesses were his assistants, the matricula[2] contained the names of hundreds and thousands to whom the church granted assistance. The larger towns, such as Rome and Alexandria, were divided into districts, each of which was committed to the special oversight of a deacon. Special houses were also erected in the different quarters of the town, in which the poor assembled and were fed. These were called Diakonia,[3] because they also were under the direction of a deacon. The number of deacons and deaconesses was of necessity considerably increased. The resolution of the Synod of Cæsarea (A.D. 314–320), according to which there were to be but seven deacons in each town, was without effect. With the exception of certain cities, in which, as in Rome, this number was kept to, and other kinds of assistance awarded in compensation to the deacons, it was greatly exceeded. In Alexandria there were numerous deacons; in Constantinople Justinian limited the number in the church of St. Sophia to one hundred deacons and forty deaconesses,[4] hence it must before have been still larger. Besides the deacons, who received payment from the Church, there were also those who served voluntarily and without remuneration.[5] The objects of relief were the distressed of every kind, widows, orphans, foundlings, the sick, cripples, those incapable of work, those of decayed fortune through the distress of the times, and all who were unable to earn a living. For all these the church interested itself, and the deacons were especially to search out those poor, who from shame did not venture to come forward and entreat assistance.[6] There were many thousands who thus lived upon the gifts of the church. The matricula of the Church of Antioch numbered in Chrysostom's days 3000 widows and virgins. To these Chrysostom adds many who were in prisons, who were lying sick in the

Xenodochium, the strangers, the lepers, the daily suppliants, to all of whom the church gave food and clothing.[7] At another time he speaks of hosts of registered poor, of multitudes of sick, of tens of thousands of persons in distress.[8] In Alexandria the matricula in the time of John the Almoner included 7500 names,[9] and at Rome, in the time of Gregory the Great, it formed a thick volume.[10] These were, however, only the settled poor of the Church. To these were added in ever-increasing swarms the wandering mendicants, who crowded into the towns, besieged the churches, and who equally expected assistance from the officers of the church. Gregory of Nyssa describes how they assembled in troops, and sought to excite compassion. One would stretch out a withered hand, another would show his swollen stomach, a third his cancerous leg. Each would expose the part in which he was suffering, to show his misery.[11] Chrysostom speaks of the crowds of beggars he used to meet in going to church.[12] Ambrose represents them to us as pressing and crying out aloud, while the most deserving and needy waited silently, till something was given them.[13] So too does Augustine, for there is not a preacher of the time in whose sermons we do not find an echo of the tremendous distress which surrounds him.

In the presence of such wholesale poverty, an individualizing care of the poor, like that of former times, was of necessity impossible. If we even leave out of the question beggars arriving from without, who were satisfied with a single gift, and then went their way, or who found a lodging in one of the benevolent institutions now everywhere arising, in a house for strangers, or an asylum for the sick or poor, if we reckon only the poor belonging to the church itself, their numbers were already much too large to suffer assistance, adapted and proportioned to their circumstances, to be, after due inquiry, extended to all. In Antioch, Chrysostom reckons 100,000 Christians, of whom according to his statement 10,000 were well-to-do, 10,000 quite poor, and the remaining 80,000 in circumstances varying between the two former classes.[14] Even supposing only these 10,000 to be objects for relief, although the former thorough care of the poor would have included many besides within its sphere of operations, it is evident that the numbers are already far too large for an individual care of the poor. A regular administration of relief had to be adhered to, but that separate care of the poor as individuals, which had been possible in the small supervisible churches, which were moreover filled with an active consciousness of their unity, was no longer so in such enormous churches, consisting besides of so many dead members.

There would, indeed, have been one means of obviating this evil state of things. The large churches might have been divided into smaller, and thus better adapted to the development of a genuine church life. It was fatal not only to charity, but to church life in general, that not only was this way not taken, but that, on the contrary, even the existing beginnings of the formation of smaller churches were suppressed. The reason is found in the ascendency of the episcopal office. A Church was only to be thought of as under the guidance of one bishop; churches and episcopal dioceses were coincident. Even if in a larger town several places of worship existed, still the collective Christians of the town, like the 100,000 of Chrysostom's times, at Antioch, formed only one church. The service in the several places of worship, in which the bishop could not himself be present, was provided for by presbyters either appointed thereto once for all, or only for each separate Sunday, by the bishop. The former was, *e.g.*, the case in Alexandria, the latter in Rome.[15] But a severance of churches, and especially a separate administration of property, did not exist. For all the means of the church, and all the gifts of its members, flowed into a common treasury, which the bishop administered, and out of which he provided for the collective clergy of the town, and also for all its poor. Nay, the Church stretched beyond the town, and included the surrounding country district. Where the Church had been planted in the villages from the town, this was naturally the case. But even where, in the smaller places, independent churches under country bishops had for a long time existed, these too now came into dependence. The bishops of the smaller places were either entirely done away with and replaced by presbyters sent by the town bishop, or where they remained as country bishops, their sphere of operations was limited, and they were subordinated to the town bishops, even with reference to the administration of property.[16] As long as Christianity had its professors chiefly in the towns, this might be to a certain degree justifiable. It was otherwise when, in the course of the fourth century, the country population also were converted to the Christian faith. But the bishops of the larger towns, who had now attained to great consideration, knew how to prevent in their own interest the formation of independent country churches. Several synods expressly forbade the appointment of bishops in the country.[17] The frequently recurring prohibition of the alienation of the property of country churches, without the consent of the bishop, was calculated to keep these churches in a state of dependence with respect to the legal disposal of property.[18] The rule everywhere held good, that whatever accrued to country churches of landed or other property, was, according to the ancient canon, to come under the power of the bishop.[19] Not before the end of the fifth century do we meet with the first traces of the legal independence of single churches with respect to property, and in Gaul alone was a proper parochial system arrived at from the commencement of the sixth. Elsewhere this was not effected till still later. But it was then too late, a genuine church life could no longer be developed. During the entire period of the Middle Ages, Christian life was sick of this disorder, that there were indeed parishes, but no churches.

If we recollect in how close a connection church life and charity stand with each other, we shall easily perceive how great an influence this depression of church life would have upon charity. If the latter had in early times borne an entirely congregational, a church character, it now forfeited this more and more. In place of the relief of the poor by the Church, there appeared on the one side a wholesale almsgiving, on the other benevolent institutions.

One symptom of the change which was taking place, was the entire abolition of the Agapæ. For it was on them especially that the family-like unity of the Church was so fully impressed. For a long time, indeed, they had ceased to be the regular common meals of the whole congregation; but even in their subsequent form of meals for the poor, they still made those who partook of them conscious of their Church membership. Ascetically constituted minds had indeed frequently taken offence at these repasts in the churches. The Synod of Gangra (A.D. 360) still protected the Agapæ against them.[20] But still more dangerous to the Agapæ was the offence taken at the combination of the Lord's Supper with these meals. It seemed beneath the dignity of the communion, that it should be celebrated after the meal, and the disorders which occurred served to confirm this. Hence it was at first enjoined, that the Lord's Supper should precede the Agapæ. An exception was made on Maunday Thursday only, in remembrance of the Lord having instituted the Sacrament after the Paschal Supper.[21] The Council of Trulla did away with this exception also. The strictly observed rule, that the communion should be partaken of fasting, allowed of no connection with the Agapæ, which were held in the evening. Next, the holding of the Agapæ in the churches at all was forbidden. The Council of Laodicea[22] first passed the decree, "that the so-called Agapæ are not to be held in churches, and that neither eating nor the preparation of couches must take place in the house of God." In the West it was chiefly by Ambrose and Augustine,[23] that the abolition of the Agapæ was carried out. The Council of Trulla says quite briefly: "The Agapæ in churches are forbidden."[24] Thus was an institution buried, whose existence is as distinctive of the church life of the most ancient church, as its destruction is a sign that such a church life no longer existed.

The altered character of the relief of the poor will more plainly appear, if we consider the manner in which the means for it were now collected. Formerly the main stock consisted of the regular gifts of members of the congregation at public worship, and especially of the oblations offered at the celebration of the Lord's Supper. The church character of the relief of the poor lay just in the circumstance, that it was the congregation who at their public worship laid upon the altar the gifts destined for the service of their brethren. This was now different. The oblations dwindled; compared with the large means in other respects at the Church's disposal, they were scarcely taken into account, and during this period entirely lost their original character of means for the poor. The cause is here, too, to be found in the depression of church life. Formerly it had been the order of Christian life, that every member of the Church came to church on Sundays, participated in the celebration of the Lord's Supper, and regularly brought his oblation at it, but now the decay of church life was already plainly shown by irregularity of attendance on public worship. It was no longer, as before, the whole church that assembled every Sunday. Even such preachers as Chrysostom had to complain of empty churches, especially if it so happened, that races in the circus, or a spectacle at the theatre, presented a counter attraction to the multitude. Chrysostom on one occasion compares Christians to the Jews, who go up but three times a year to worship in the temple. He also complains, that so many, when the sermon is over, noisily crowd out of church without staying to the Lord's Supper. Even those who partook of it did not always bring oblations. It was only on high festivals, on days of martyrs and in memory of the dead, that abundant offerings were still laid upon the altar.[25] This shows that entirely different motives were now operative. The oblations were no longer the thank-offerings of the congregation, offerings of love for the poor, as at first, but gifts by which the individual members of the church hoped to obtain the intercession of the martyrs for themselves or for the dead. Oblations proper now consisted only of bread and wine, and on certain days of the natural products oil, milk and honey, used in public worship on other occasions. These thus inwardly shrunken oblations, which had long ago forfeited the character of alms, thus lost altogether about the year 500 their destination of being for the use of the poor. They devolved as dues to the clergy, partly to the bishop, partly to those who read mass.[26]

There was, however, no lack of gifts and presents to the Church; these, on the contrary, came in with an abundance formerly unknown. The treasure chamber of many a church was filled with expensive garments, gold and silver vessels, even with coined money; in every town were splendid ecclesiastical buildings, whose interiors glittered with jewels and ornaments of every kind; the Church, which had hitherto been satisfied with having what was necessary for the moment, accumulated from donations and legacies a constantly increasing property especially of estates. Constantine began to make the Church rich in these, and frequently as the finances of the Empire were depressed under his successors, means were always found for inclining them to make donations to the Church. Rich commoners vied with the emperors. To give or bequeath anything to the Church was esteemed a specially good work, and one sure to secure the favour of God. Even Chrysostom was obliged to remind his hearers, that salvation was not to be obtained by presenting to the Church a golden chalice set with jewels, and that the Church is not a storehouse of gold and silver wares, but that she far more needs souls dedicated to God.[27] With the increasing dissolution of heathenism, the Church also came into the possession of a great part of the property destined for the temples and the heathen worship. She became in this respect also the heir of the Olympian deities, and many treasures, which had formerly adorned the temple of a Jupiter or an Apollo, now served for the decoration of a Christian altar. The large accumulated property, too, of many collegia was also in the course of time transferred to her, *e.g.* that of the collegium of the Dendrophori.

But an ever flowing and abundant source of earthly possessions was opened to the Church by the legal enactment of Constantine, that testamentary bequests might be made in favour of the Church. According to Romish law, certain gods had the rights of juristic personality, and thus the capacity of being made inheritors by testamentary dispositions; nay, they were in this respect distinguished above private individuals by many privileges. These rights were now transferred to the Church, and were in such wise taken advantage of, that even a few decades later, Valentinian I. had to make a law to restrain the legacy-hunting of the Church. That there actually existed reasons for such a law is seen from an expression of Jerome, in which he, who in other respects well understood the collection of means for the church, complains not of the law, but of the causes of the law.[28] Certainly all bishops were not so conscientious as Augustine, who disapproved of parents disinheriting their children by making wills in favour of the Church and the poor, and refused to accept an inheritance, if the relatives of the testator seemed to him to be injured by it, "for the Church desires no unjust inheritance." Augustine praises in a sermon[29] his friend and fellow-

Bishop Aurelius for restoring to a widower of his Church, who while yet childless had bequeathed his property to the Church, retaining only the usufruct, the legacy without his applying for it, when children were subsequently born to him. "Let him who would make the Church his heir by disinheriting his own son, find some one else than Augustine to receive the inheritance. I hope to God he may find none." But however many bishops might in this respect think and act as nobly as Augustine, the view became increasingly general, that it belonged to a man's care for his soul's salvation to leave by will a portion of his goods to the Church. The more it was hoped that sins committed would thus be covered, and a favourable sentence obtained from the Judge of the world, the more abundant were the gifts presented to the Church. It was decidedly expected of the clergy, virgins and married people who had taken vows of chastity, of monks and nuns, that if they had not already given away their property during their lifetime, they should leave it by will to the Church. Salvian considers their not doing so to arise from covetousness, and their salvation to be endangered thereby. "If the Lord commanded His disciples to go without scrip or purse, how far are those from following His command, who desire to possess their property even after death in their relations; how far are they from the piety which disinherits itself for the sake of God, who will not even disinherit others for their own sake! They disinherit themselves (for eternity) in order not to disinherit others."[30] Salvian also earnestly exhorts other Christians, not living like clerics and monks in a state of special piety, to remember the Church and the poor in their wills. If during their lives they have not done many good works, it the more behoves them to retrieve the omission when they leave the world, so that they may at least have the excuse for their neglect, that by a last act of piety they have atoned for what they had left undone. But if during their life they have already done good works, the same advice must be given; for no one does good enough, and at the moment when they are about to appear before the Judge's throne, they must the more reconcile Him to themselves.[31] Nay, he advises even those who to the end have passed their lives in wickedness, as a last means to give away all their property at death. He will not indeed say for certain, that it will be of any use, but at all events it is better to try something than to do nothing.[32] In this matter Salvian will allow of no consideration for children or relatives. "For in taking care for one soul's salvation, we must love ourselves first of all." "What good does a rich man get, who makes his sons rich and plunges himself into eternal damnation?"[33] Certainly Salvian excuses, but still only excuses, consideration for children; "since in this case faith is placed after blood, and the claims of natural affection conquer religious piety."[34] But he sharply rebukes those who adopt children or leave anything to strangers. It is in general better that children should be poor in this world than parents in the next.

It must be confessed that Salvian is one of those, who lay on the colours somewhat thickly and express themselves strongly. But there can be no doubt that, in his urgency for wills in favour of the Church, he represented the tendency of the times.[35] The appreciation of testamentary liberality is always a sign, and at the same time a consequence, of esteeming the surrender of earthly possessions in itself, and independently of its intention, a good and meritorious work. In times when the life of love is vigorous, as in the first centuries, more is given during life and personally, for the intention is personally to help the poor. As soon, however, as regard to the good work to be performed and the reward to be thereby obtained preponderates, testamentary giving preponderates also; for the end striven for, viz. that of gaining merit by good works, may be thus equally, may be thus, in a certain sense, far more conveniently attained, since there is no need at all for renouncing anything during life. To this is added—a particular not to be overlooked—an after effect of the views of antiquity in this matter as in some others. It had been the custom in Rome to think of friends, of illustrious men, and above all of the emperor in wills. This was now transferred to the Church. If it had been for a period esteemed high treason in Rome to leave nothing to the emperor, it was now regarded as almost treason to the Church, and even to God, for a man not to remember the Church in his will; and as legacies formed an important item in the imperial revenue, so did they now in that of the Church.

Less profitable were the results obtained by the Church by preaching the doctrine of tithes. The notion that the Jewish law of tithes applied to Christians also, that the tenth was the least a Christian should give, is now frequently met with. It was evidently a view now generally held. Eminent Church teachers, such as Chrysostom, Jerome, Augustine, zealously exhort to give the tenth.[36] But it was by no means as yet the general practice, and still less a settled enactment. Many certainly gave a tenth voluntarily, or made the law of tithes the standard of their almsgiving. Thus, *e.g.*, it is with a good intention that Chrysostom says, that God imposed a tenth on the Jews, but a Christian must not stop at this; he must exceed the righteousness of the Pharisees, and give whatever he saves, but at least a tenth. The tithe did not become a really settled law until, in the newly arisen German kingdoms, agrarian circumstances were more favourable to it than in the Roman Empire. In fact it was in Frankish synods, that the law of tithes was first decidedly pronounced. A Synod of Tours, in the year 567, still stops at mere exhortation; the second synod of Macon, in the year 583, is the first which raises the giving of the tenth to a universally binding law, thus opening to the Church a source of revenue, which shows more plainly than anything else how far the once so zealously preserved liberty of giving was departed from, but which was of eminent importance with respect to the property of the Church.

The Church was a good steward. A large portion of the administrative ability and thrifty spirit of the Romans was transferred to the churches of the West, and chiefly to the Romish. The management of Church property was strictly regulated in a series of synods, care was taken to keep it together and to protect it from diminution. Only the bishop could alienate Church property, and he only with the consent of a council or two fellow-bishops, subsequently of the metropolitan.[37] He must neither give away anything nor dispose of it by will, especially to relatives,[38] and might exchange even single appurtenances only to a small extent, and when it would bring some advantage. Relatives had to make compensation for alienated Church property; laymen who alienated it were excommunicated.[39] The management lay exclusively in the hands of the bishop. It now formed one of the most important of a bishop's duties, and was often, as the occasional complaints of just the more spiritually-minded bishops show, felt to be a heavy burden. How frequently are Gregory the Great's letters full of the business imposed by this management; what exact arrangements does he make, down to the slightest details, concerning the administration or letting of estates, the purchase and sale of their produce! He orders on one occasion that the breeding of horses is to be limited, because the grooms cost too much, and too little is made by it, and at the same time does not forget what is to be done with the stock of harness in hand. By a decree of the Synod of Chalcedon,[40] every bishop is, moreover, bound to appoint a steward for the management of Church property. Gregory carries on the administration by a larger number of *defensores*, upon whom a kind of oversight of the bishop is at the same time imposed.

Under careful administration and continual accessions, a considerable property was thus accumulated. Already, in the fifth century, the Church was the greatest landowner in the Empire. The privileges conceded to her considerably facilitated the management and increase of property, and induced many smaller landowners to take refuge in her protection and to transfer their estates to the Church, that they might then receive it again as a Precarium. When Pope Damasus wanted to induce the Romish town-præfect Prætextatus to become a Christian, he replied ironically: Make me Bishop of Rome, and I will be a Christian directly. And yet this Prætextatus was one of the richest of men, and had, besides his large salaries from various offices, an income of £150,000 per annum from his private property. By this we may judge of the amount then at the disposal of the Romish bishop.⁴¹ In the time of Gregory the Great, the Romish Church possessed extensive landed property not only in Italy and Sicily, but also in Gaul, nay in the East. The Church of Milan was also very wealthy, while, in the East, that of Alexandria was eminently so. When John the Almoner was bishop there, he found 8000 gold pieces in the treasury of the Church. Among the heathen, to be a bishop and to be rich meant the same thing. "He who has gained a bishop's see," says Ammianus Marcellinus⁴² derisively, "need take no care for the future, presents make him rich, he drives about proudly in expensive carriages and in raiment that is magnificent, and has such extravagant repasts as to outtrump the Emperor's." But even this heathen was obliged to add, that there were also bishops, "who, moderate in eating and drinking, and simple in their dress, showed themselves to be worthy priests of the Deity."

It is generally a paltry view, which places the increasing wealth and growing power of the Church solely in the category of its augmenting corruption. It was needful for the Church to be rich and powerful, if she was to be equal to the tasks then before her. Even to assist the numberless poor of the times, to give some alleviation to their unspeakable misery, she required abundant resources. She could not have contended with such wholesale poverty with the means at her disposal during the first centuries. Safely invested funds too were required, for voluntary gifts fail most under those unfavourable financial circumstances, which make them the most sorely needed, while the revenues derived by the Church from landed property were still a resource, when all other sources were dried up. But this is a point whose full importance can only be seen in connection with others. The Church was now to be the advocate of the poor and wretched, even in presence of the decaying State. But if so, then it was necessary that the bishops should be respected and endowed with such power and honour as to be imposing in the eyes of Illustrious Highnesses and Excellencies, nay, of the Emperor himself. Even such a man as Ambrose would scarcely have been able to encounter the Emperor in the manner he did, unless he had been at the same time a prince of the Church. If the Church was to bear the culture of the ancient world safely through the storm of the migration of the nations, she must herself become a kind of State, and her bishops powerful lords, and it was a pædagogic moment not to be depreciated, when the bishop appeared before the poor Frank or Goth as a kind of portrait of Lord of heaven surrounded with magnificence, but at the same time mild and liberal, and reflecting the goodness of God by the abundant gifts which he dispensed.

There might indeed be such bishops as Ammianus Marcellinus, in the above-quoted passage, has before his eyes, proud lords in magnificent carriages, whose repasts out-trumped imperial feasts, but at all events they formed the exception. All the great bishops of the time were fathers of the poor, and it must in justice be said of the Church, which had now become wealthy, that she really used her large resources as the property of the poor, and relieved countless multitudes. Ambrose was justified in replying, with a certain degree of pride, to Symmachus, who, in his petition to the Emperor Gratian for the re-erection of the statue of Victory in the Roman Senate, had pointed also to the large revenue of the Church: "Why do not they who appeal to us, as having means, employ their incomes as we do?" "The Church possesses nothing but faith. Her possessions are the support of the poor. Let them point to the prisoners whom their temples have ransomed, the poor whom they have fed, the ruined whom they have assisted. And because what the priests formerly profited by is now applied to the public good, public calamities have, they say, come upon us."[43] He reminds him, as well he might, that they who became priests renounced their property, for he had himself done so. When he became bishop, he gave all that he possessed of gold and silver to the Church for the benefit of the poor, retaining only an annuity for his sister Marcellina. When his brother Symmachus died, the brother and sister gave his property also to the poor. Similar accounts are given of several bishops. Chrysostom individually lived very plainly, and applied all his income to the poor, of whom he regularly supported 7700.[44] Augustine, in a sermon, entreats that expensive garments may not be given him, for he shall only sell them and give their price to the poor. If any one wishes him to wear it himself, he must send him such a coat as he could give in his turn to any poor brother who has none.[45] Basil, Epiphanius of Cyprus, Paulinus of Nola, gave all their private property—nay, it was so far the rule as to be expected of every bishop. After the death of Attilus, the people of Constantinople demanded the presbyter Sisinnius for bishop because he gave so much to the poor. In fact he became bishop.[46]

It is true that Church property was used for other purposes than the relief of the poor. The requirements of public worship, the magnificent churches, their splendid fittings, the rich furniture, the pomp of divine service, made claims upon a large portion. To this was added the maintenance of the numerous church officers, the presbyters, deacons, and sub-deacons, the cantores, readers, doorkeepers, the whole host of lower officials. Most of these, it is true, received but trifling salaries, which merely supplemented the income they already had from their property or the labour of their hands. Many clerics engaged in agriculture or some handicraft, and especially in trade. It was nothing uncommon to see them sitting at stalls, or in apothecaries' shops, or at the weekly markets. Occasionally this was even made their duty by synodal decrees. For a time they enjoyed the privilege of exemption from the trade tax, but this caused too heavy a deficit in the revenue, and the privilege was withdrawn. The demands upon the Church treasury were nevertheless considerable by reason of the great numbers of the clergy. The view was, however, still adhered to, that the property of the Church is the property of the poor. Canon 25 of the Council of Antioch, 341, *e.g.*, determines concerning Church property: The bishop has authority over the property of the Church, so that he distributes it to all the needy with perfect conscientiousness and in the fear of God. It is, however, permitted to him to take what is necessary for himself and his guests. The bishop himself may only have such household furniture, and keep such a table as a poor man. He may also only give to his relations if they are poor, but then in the same proportion as to other poor.[47] The Synod of Agde grounds the prohibition to alienate Church property expressly on the fact, that it is the property of the poor.[48] The same view is found in many fathers, and that this was not a mere form of speech is proved by the fact, that no hesitation was felt at selling even the sacred vessels to feed the hungry and to ransom prisoners. When the Arians reproached Ambrose for having done this, he justified himself with the words: "The Church possesses gold not to keep it, but in times of distress to help with it."[49] And Augustine writes to his deputy Bonifacius: "It belongs not to us, but to the poor; we only direct its administration, and lay claim to no property."[50] Subsequently the custom of quartering the Church property spread from Rome outwards. One quarter was for the bishop, one for the rest of the clergy, one for the maintenance of the Church fabric, and one for the poor. The motives for this division are no longer quite apparent. That the intention was not to limit the poor is guaranteed even by the circumstance, that Gregory the Great was a chief promoter of this custom.[51] Such an intention would not be in accordance with Gregory's character, who fretted for days upon hearing that a man had died of starvation in Rome, and accused himself of being his murderer.[52] The reason of the arrangement may rather be the desire to introduce a certain amount of order into the application of Church property, an order which profited the poor, as assuring to them in any case a fourth of its revenues. The reservation was made, that when need required more might be applied to their use, at least such a reservation was acted on.

Church property then, as administered by the bishop with the help of his steward, now formed the main stock of the means for the poor, and consequently the relief distributed could not fail to assume a form different from that of the times, when the regular gifts of the congregation still funished the means. It lost on this side also its Church character, and took the form of magnificent almsgiving on the part of the bishop. In this respect his steward stood beside him in the front rank. It was he who had the control of the receipts and expenditure;

and if the deacons still helped as of old in the distribution of relief, they were no longer as formerly the eyes and hands of the bishop.[53] Their importance with respect to the relief of the poor could not but diminish, when the steward was inserted between them and the bishop, and when, on the other hand, a large number of individuals were at the bishop's disposal for the service of the poor in the presidents and servants of the benevolent institutions. Besides, a multitude of needy persons, who had formerly been visited and tended by the deacons in their own homes, now found shelter in the xenodochia, the hospitals, the poorhouses, while in the case of those who did not require such care, assistance was confined to regular gifts, the dispensation of which was now the task not of the deacons, but chiefly of the head manager of the Church property, the steward. Ministration to the poor in their homes everywhere fell into the background, the diaconate lost in importance, and after the latter half of the fifth century its gradual decay is clearly perceived.

To begin with the female diaconate. In the East, widows were already in Constantine's time superseded by deaconesses. The Council of Chalcedon quite put an end to the institution of widows by its general prohibition of the appointment of presiding widows.[54] In Basil and Chrysostom widows still occur, but only as persons supported by the Church.[55] With this the institution falls also in the West, where widows had not been, as in the East, superseded by deaconesses. Ambrose and Augustine already no longer know of widows of the former kind.[56] A series of Gallic synods forbids the ordination or consecration of widows, and it is characteristic, that the second Synod of Orleans gives as a reason for the prohibition, the weakness of the female sex.[57]

Hitherto widows and deaconesses had belonged to the clergy, but now such exalted views were entertained of the dignity of the clergy and of ordination, that it seemed an unworthy thing to ordain women. To this was added the increased estimation of the unmarried state, and on this account virgin deaconesses lasted longer in the East. But they too lost in importance with respect to charity and then also in dignity. It is true that we just now meet with several renowned deaconesses of the highest rank, as Macrina, the sister of Gregory of Nyssa, and especially the illustrious Olympias, the friend and disciple of Chrysostom. But their far-famed benevolence was still rather private than official. Neither Gregory of Nyssa nor Chrysostom ever speak of any official agency on their part in this respect. We have several letters of Theodoret to deaconesses, but in these too we meet with no mention of such agency. In the East also advancing monasticism and increased priestly dignity were equally unfavourable to deaconesses. Sozomen [58] tells of a virgin, who, being qualified for the office of deaconess, renounced it to devote herself to a contemplative life. The deaconesses had formerly access to the altar, but this was afterwards done away with and their ordination abrogated.[59] Their agency was after this confined to external services at worship. As female servants of the Church of a lower grade, there were in Constantinople, about A.D. 1200, in the smaller Eastern churches at a later date, still deaconesses.[60]

The deacons also occupied a different position. They ceased to be the vehicles of relief to the poor. Service in the church and at the altar was now their especial duty. It is on this account that they are so frequently compared to the Levites, who served in the temple, and that many appointments concerning the Old Testament Levites, their age and services, were transferred to them. So greatly had the consciousness of the earlier diaconal service vanished, that the Council of Trulla declines the comparison with the seven men, on the ground that deacons are appointed to serve in the mysteries of worship, while the Seven were appointed to serve tables.[61]

We thus see how the old Church care of the poor was dissolved on all sides. It was no longer the Church which, by means of its rulers and deacons, exercised towards her poorer members, with the resources offered in her assemblies, as individual a case as was possible; it was the bishop, who was the great dispenser of alms, who distributed from the property of the Church, and what was bestowed upon the Church, wholesale alms to the deserving and the undeserving, to members of the Church and to the multitudes, whom the common misfortunes had made beggars. It is true that many passages may be adduced from the Fathers, in which they exhort to be careful in the distribution of gifts, and to inquire into their circumstances. Basil[62] says: "Great experience is required to distinguish between those who are really poor and those who beg only that they may collect money. He who gives to a distressed and sick person gives to God, and will receive a reward. But he who gives to a vagabond and parasite, throws his money to the dogs, *i.e.* gives it to men who deserve rather contempt for their audacity, than pity for their poverty." Ambrose[63] speaks of the arts of pretended beggars, and warns to take care lest the portion, which belongs to the needy, becomes the prey of rogues. But it was very difficult, nay impossible, to obey such rules, when unfortunate creatures in danger of perishing with hunger were pressing round in crowds. Ambrose lays down thoroughly excellent rules : " They often say they are overwhelmed with debts, try whether they speak the truth ; they say they have been plundered, try whether this is the case ; in one word, find out whom you are relieving." But he then warns them again not to be inhuman, and reminds them in another passage : " Love does not weigh deserts, but first of all assists distress." [64] " We ought not to be too mistrustful. If Abraham had been mistrustful," says Chrysostom,[65] he would not have entertained strangers, and Gregory Nazianzen [66] comes to the conclusion, that " it is much better for the sake of those who are deserving, to give to the undeserving, than by fearing to give to the undeserving, to deprive the deserving of the benefit." In most cases, then, it must actually have happened, that all were relieved without much distinction. When distress is as great as it then was, all distinction ceases.

The former Church care of the poor was such no longer. The beneficence of the bishop, distributing with open hand to the needy, had, on the contrary, an unmistakeable likeness to what the ancient world also was acquainted with, viz. the distributions of the emperors and the Roman Nobles. When Gregory the Great had corn, oil, wine, meat distributed every month, when he had carts full of provisions driving through the town for the relief of the poor,[67] this looks more like a revival of the old distribution of corn than of the relief of the poor by the Christian Church. The Bishop of Rome had come into the place of the Emperor, the bishops into the place of the Roman nobles ; Christian *caritas* has assumed a suspicious similarity to the ancient *liberalitas.* Still it was a splendid sight to see a bishop daily in the midst of the hungry as the open-handed dispenser of alms, from whom every one expects assistance and receives as much as possible, the poor Roman driven from house and home by the Barbarians, and the German, whom the mild breath of Christian love, now for the first time touches, awakening in his heart the feeling of the Divine mercy therein reflected; a bishop with whom the stranger finds an asylum, and the sick attendance, who sells the Church furniture, the golden and silver vessels for the Lord's Supper, to ransom prisoners, and leads in his home the life of a poor man, to let the poor find that the Church possesses what is hers only for the poor; a Basil, attending himself upon the sick and leprous; a Chrysostom, in the midst of Byzantine luxury himself living simply and modestly, and daily feeding 7000 poor; an Ambrose, a proud Roman, but at the same time a humble Christian, encountering the Emperor and condescending to all the poor; an Augustine, desiring no other garment than such as he can give to any poor brother; a Gregory, taking so deeply to heart the whole misery of the times, and yet fretting when an individual dies of starvation in Rome.

The aim, indeed, formerly attained, that no one suffered want, was no longer attainable. Julian still praises Christians for maintaining, not only their own people, but the heathen also, and for having no beggars among them. This was soon otherwise; the Roman people was resolved into a mendicant multitude. It is characteristic, that the first mendicancy laws were now made. So great a multitude of beggars had in the reign of Valentinian II. congregated in Rome, that the Emperor caused an investigation to be made, and all beggars capable of work to be expelled from the city. Beggary could no longer be suppressed, as, indeed, it never can be by merely compulsory laws; hence the attempt was made to organize it, this age being, in this respect also, the precursor of the Middle Ages. A law was enacted under Theodosius, that no one should in future beg in the streets, until his case had been investigated as to age, health, and circumstances. If incapable of work, he was allowed to beg; if capable of work and continuing to beg, he was deprived of liberty.[68] The enactments of Justinian were still stricter. If the mendicant were a bondsman, he was to be given back to his owner; if a free man, work was to be given him; if he refused to accept it, he was to be expelled. "These commands," says Justinian, "are in favour of the beggars, for their purpose is to preserve them from the crimes to which idleness might seduce them."[69]

Christianity has been reproached with the fact, that not till Christian times did the laws against mendicancy, which were unknown to antiquity, become necessary, the Church having, it is said, by her almsgiving first brought beggars to maturity. This verdict thus boldly stated is an unjust one. The times, in which an ageing civilisation is decaying and dissolving, have ever been times in which mendicancy increases. The age of the Reformation presents a similar spectacle, and ours is making a like experience. To make Christianity and the Church responsible for this is unjust. The Church is not, indeed, without fault in this matter. We shall have to return to the fact, that she did not succeed in renovating the old world by infusing into it the new Christian life. Herself involved in an erroneous estimation of earthly possessions, incapable of rising to a sound moral appreciation of labour, she contributed to this dissolution, and her abundant almsgiving certainly attracted many a beggar. But this shadow should not prevent our acknowledging the light that exists, and admiring the splendid charity of the Church. What would have become of the Roman Empire without Christianity! What numbers the Church assisted, how much misery it alleviated, how many tears it dried! The ancient world must die, Christianity could not prevent it; but it did what it could, it ministered comfort and consolation to a dying world.

CHAPTER III.

ALMS.

SCARCELY ever were alms so much preached, and almsgiving so frequently and so urgently insisted on, as during this period. Distress compelled. The Church was every day besieged by hordes of poor and distressed of all kinds; the hungry, the naked, the sick, the houseless, looked to her and expected help. The Church, however, would not have been able to give so much, if abundant donations had not flowed in; and largely as she distributed, this would not nearly have sufficed, if an extensive private benevolence had not been added. The preachers of the day must often have had the feeling, which impelled Chrysostom to preach his famous sermon for the poor, in which he puts himself in the place of an ambassador from the poor, for whom he is supplicating, to the Church. "I stand up to-day," he begins, "to speak to you for a cause just, righteous and worthy of you. To this I have been summoned by the beggars of this town. Summoned not by words, not by common resolutions, but by the saddest of sights. For, as I was hurrying through the market and narrow streets to your assembly, and saw many lying in the streets, who were mutilated in hands or eyes or covered with incurable sores, I esteemed it the harshest cruelty not to speak of them to your love, especially as the time also invited. For it is indeed at all times necessary to exhort men to mercy towards their brethren, since we ourselves need it on the part of our Lord and Creator, but especially now during the extreme cold."[1] Quite similarly does Augustine conclude a sermon on alms with the words: "Give then to the poor, I entreat, I exhort, I enjoin, I command you. For I will not conceal from you the reason why I esteem it necessary to preach this sermon to you. When I go to church and when I return, the poor call to me and beg me to speak to you, that they may receive something from you. They exhort me to speak to you, and if they see that they receive nothing from you, they will believe that I have bestowed labour upon you in vain. They expect something from you. I give as much as I have, I give as much as I can, but am I capable of allaying their misery? Since then I am not in a condition to appease their need, I am their ambassador to you. You have heard the gospel, you have added the word of thanksgiving: thanks be to God! You have received seed, you have returned words. Your thanksgivings weary me; I support their load, and tremble under it. But, my brethren, your thanksgivings are only leaves, and fruit is required of you."[2] All the great preachers of the day were powerful preachers of almsgiving. How often does Chrysostom say: "Every day, I am told, you speak of alms. Yes undoubtedly, and I shall not cease to speak of it. If you were as docile as I could wish, I should even then speak of it, to preserve you from relaxing. If then you stop half way, whose fault is it? Ought an untractable pupil to complain of the repetitions of his master?"[3] How well did Basil, when Cappadocia was visited by a drought, know how to incline all hearts to give during the distress! "He opened by his sermons," says Gregory Nazianzen, "the granaries of the rich, and like a second Joseph, provided the poor with food and provisions." How well did the two Gregories of Nyssa and Nazianzus understand how to arouse a love for the poor! We have a sermon by the latter on love for the poor,[4] which is one of the most beautiful and touching ever delivered. "If you would listen to me, ye servants of Christ, ye brethren and fellow-heirs, let us," he cries, "so long as we have the time, minister to Christ, feed Christ, clothe Christ, receive Christ, honour Christ!" and then continues, that we too are daily in danger, and do not know what may soon become of us,—a reference to the changes of fortune, which, in those days, in which so many rich and prosperous were often suddenly plunged into beggary, must have made a double impression. "He who is in a ship is near to shipwreck. Therefore, so long as thou art sailing with a favourable wind, hold out a hand to those who are suffering shipwreck; as long as thou art healthy and rich, help the unfortunate. Man has nothing so divine as beneficence. Be a god to the unfortunate, by imitating the mercy of God." Nor are the Latins, Leo the Great, of whom we have a number of collection sermons, Ambrose, Augustine, Gregory the Great, behind the Greek Fathers. From every pulpit in every church the people were exhorted to compassion and to bountiful almsgiving with untiring zeal, and with all the means afforded by the extremely rhetorical style of preaching then in use.

Even this is sufficient to show that the ardour of first love had abated. Almsgiving was no longer self-evident, it needed urging. Nor was there lack of complaints concerning the hard-heartedness of many of the rich. How frequently does Chrysostom turn to them, and reproach them with their injustice in living in the midst of every luxury and squandering their property in superfluities, while so many poor men cannot even be sure of bread! "I am much ashamed," he says, "when I see so many rich men riding about with golden bridles, with gold-laced slaves trailing behind them, and sleeping on silver couches, who, when they are asked to give to a poor man, are poorer than the very poor;" and he thus addresses the church in Antioch: "Through God's grace, the number of Christians in Antioch amounts, I believe, to 100,000. If each of you would give a loaf to the poor, all would have more than enough; if each would give an obolus, we should have no more poor."[5] In Basil, Ambrose, Augustine, we meet with like complaints. They are obliged to refute the thousand excuses, by which hardness of heart, then as ever, sought to justify itself; they have to remind their hearers that it is not right to leave all to the Church, and that the officers of the Church cannot give if nothing is given them. If we add to this the misery which these Fathers had daily before their eyes, how painful it must have been to them not to be able to relieve it, and how often they must have been moved by what Augustine on one occasion expresses: "So many beg daily, so many sigh daily, so many haunt us daily for assistance, that we are obliged sadly to give up the greater part, because we have not enough to give to all,"[6] we shall understand how it was that just that motive for almsgiving was now so prominently brought forward, the motive of reward, which always produces an effect in churches in which love has waxed cold and the deeper Christian motives are no longer powerfully operative. This is not, however, to say that purer motives were absent. The Fathers of those days also often remind, that the poor are our brethren, that they are of the same nature, bear the same image of God, that we are walking with them on the same road towards the same end. "We are all one in the Lord," preaches Gregory Nazianzen, "whether rich or poor, bond or free, healthy or sick, and we have all one head, even Christ. What the members are one to another, each should be to each and all to all."[7] Ambrose often dwells upon humanity and what we owe our fellow-men, and, of course, there is not lacking a frequently recurring reminder of the gratitude we owe to God and to the Lord, or of the fact, that in ministering to the poor we do it unto Christ, that we ourselves must all hope in God's mercy, and are all beggars standing before His gates.[8] Still the motive of reward, that thus we lend to God, that we make God our debtor, that He will repay, is brought far more into the foreground. "Thou hast me for a giver," are the words put into God's mouth by Augustine, " now make me also a debtor. Thou givest me little, I will repay thee much. Thou givest me things earthly, I will requite thee with things heavenly. I will give thee thyself, by giving thee back to Myself."[9] Countless times is the thought expressed, that almsgiving is a safe investment of money at good interest with God in heaven. " Invest thy money above," exclaims Augustine; "do not entrust it to thy servant, but to thy God. God would have thee for His creditor, but His, and not thy neighbour's." One must not say: "I am serving my children when I lay by money." It comes to pass that he loses one of his children, why does he not send his property after his son? Why does he keep it in his purse and dismiss him from his mind? Pray give him what you saved for him. He is dead. Well, he went first to God, his portion belongs to the poor, it belongs to Him to whom he is gone; he is gone to Christ, it belongs to Christ, who says: "Inasmuch as ye did it unto one of the least of my brethren, ye did it unto me."[10]

The notion that alms have an atoning efficacy, which had already made its appearance in the former period, is now universally acknowledged, and is expressed again and again in every variety of form and expression as the motive of almsgiving, which is predominant and preponderant above all others. To put together only a few of the most distinctive utterances of the kind: "Charity," it is said in a homily of Chrysostom on repentance, is "the queen among the virtues, who quickly lifts a man into the atmosphere of heaven, and is the best intercessor. Charity has strong wings, she cuts through the air, rises above the moon, ascends beyond the shining sun, and penetrates to the heights of heaven. But there too she does not remain, but penetrates the heavens also, hastens through the host of angels, the choir of archangels, and all the higher powers, and places herself before the throne of the King Himself." Learn this from Holy Scripture, which says: "Cornelius, thy prayers and thine alms are come up before the presence of God." This "before the presence of God" means: Hast thou even many sins, but hast alms for an intercessor? fear not, for none of the higher powers opposes alms, it claims payment, and brings its bond in its hands. For the Lord Himself says: "What ye have done to one of the least of My brethren, ye have done to Me." "With whatsoever sins then thou mayest be burdened, thy charity outweighs them all."[11] There is a still stronger passage in the same cycle of homilies: "To-day begins a trade in alms, for we see the prisoners and the poor, we see those who wander about the market, we hear how they cry, and weep, and mourn, we have a wonderful fair before our eyes." At a fair, however, there is but one object; the man of business has no other aim than to buy goods cheaply, and to sell them dearly. Such a fair has God opened to us: " Buy the works of righteousness cheaply, to realize in the future a higher price, if indeed it is allowable to call requital realization. Here righteousness is sold cheap, sold for an insignificant piece of bread, for a miserable garment, for a cup of cold water. As long as the market lasts let us buy alms, or rather let us purchase salvation through alms."[12] " Give the poor a piece of money," it is elsewhere said, " and thou hast reconciled the Judge." To say the truth, the benevolent Judge lets himself be gained by money, which he does not take for Himself, but which the poor receive. Repentance, without alms, is dead, and shorn of its wings. Repentance is unable to fly, unless she has the wings of alms. " Understand the goodness of God," it is said in one of Leo the Great's sermons,[13] " and the arrangement of His love. God has therefore willed thy superfluity, that by means of thee another may not starve, and that by the benefactions of thy work of love He may deliver the poor from distress and affliction, and thee from the multitude of thy sins;" and elsewhere: " The food of the needy is the purchase-money of the kingdom of heaven."[14] " Mercy," continues Ambrose, " is a source of salvation for those for whom covetousness has kindled the flame of death, that they, who have kindled the flames by sinning, may extinguish them by almsgiving. Let him buy innocence who formerly bought sin."[15] Still more plainly is it said in another place: " Thou hast money, buy off thy sins. God is not venal, but thou art venal; ransom thyself with thy works, ransom thyself with thy money. Money is a trifle, but mercy is precious."[16] Augustine, too, carries out the thought, that alms give wings to prayer, and that by alms sin is expiated: "The sacrifice of the Christian is the alms bestowed upon the poor. Thereby God becomes indulgent towards sinners. If God is not indulgent to sinners, who is not guilty? Men are cleansed by alms from those sins and transgressions, without which life cannot be passed here below."[17] "Nothing is bought for a lower price than the kingdom of heaven," preaches Gregory the Great; "hast thou no cup of cold water to give to the needy? the goodwill will suffice, for before God no hand is empty, if the heart is filled with goodwill."[18] But most largely, I might say in the most wholesale manner, does the thought, that alms earn merit, appear in Salvian. It must not be thought, he says, that only the wicked ought to give alms, for the purpose of expiating their sins. The good must do it too. For they owe much to God for the goodness which they have experienced, and even they are not sure of their salvation. Therefore they also do well, to give away as much as possible of their earthly goods. "Let it be granted, that they have no punishment to fear, can we then hope for reward without merit? Hence, if we do not sacrifice our wealth to redeem us from sin, let us devote it to purchase our salvation; if we do not give, that we may not be condemned, let us at least give, that we may be rewarded. If there is no evil in the past, for which we have to atone, there are still eternal possessions, which we have to procure; if we have no punishment to fear, we have the kingdom of heaven to obtain; if the saints have nothing from which to redeem themselves, they have something to purchase. The bargain is a safe one, and there is no loss to fear, for God is a faithful requiter."[19]

This may suffice to afford a general impression of the manner in which alms were then preached about, and almsgiving inculcated. The passages quoted are, it must be confessed, after the fashion of the times, highly rhetorical. What is said of redeeming from sin, and purchasing the kingdom of heaven, must not be taken too literally, although (as we shall afterwards have occasion to show) they may frequently have been so understood by the hearers. But they are certainly something more than only a rhetorical paraphrase of the New Testament thoughts, that God rewards beneficence, and that they who exercise mercy shall find mercy. These passages are certainly based on definite doctrines and definite ethical views, doctrines and views which, clearly and sharply impressed, especially by the Latin Fathers Augustine and Gregory the Great, were handed down to the Middle Ages, and became the governing principles of Christian life during that period.

We must remember, that the connection between faith and good works was early lost sight of in the ancient Catholic Church. There is a hiatus between faith and morality. The latter is not the proof of faith, does not grow out of it as a necessary consequence, but stands as second with it. Even Augustine did not rediscover this connection. In his writings also faith and love are separated; faith does not as such work by love, but love is added to faith. There is a faith without love, without hope, without good works. Hence Augustine's doctrine of justification by faith presents a very different appearance from that of the reformers. We are justified by faith, *because* faith works by love. Hence a merit is awarded to love even by Augustine, though he regards this merit as an outflow of grace; and here is the root of the oft-recurring maxim,—found in Augustine also,—"That alms have power to extinguish and expiate sin."[20]

It is true that he very strongly insists, that alms are of no avail without amendment of life. He decidedly rejects the then widely diffused doctrine, that in case a man only believes what the Church teaches, and does not separate from the Church, alms will help to save him, even though as by fire. First of all, he says, must the life be changed for the better. A charter to sin cannot be purchased by alms. All sins are not of such a kind as to be expiated by alms; but when a man continues in the faith and amends his life, then alms are the means of obtaining forgiveness for daily light sins. For Augustine distinguishes three classes of sins—very heavy, heavy, and light. The means of obtaining forgiveness for the first is public penance in the Church; for the second, brotherly correction; for the last, prayer with alms.[21] Among these slight sins he reckons the sins of weakness, by which the Christian is affected even after baptism, the daily sins which none can live without, such, for example, he says, as speaking a harsh word to a neighbour, as laughing immoderately. Even the use of the allowable involves such light sins. They must not, however, be lightly regarded. They are to be feared not for their greatness, but for their numbers. It is their number that ruins men; just as a grain of corn is in itself small, but if too many grains are poured into a ship, the ship is wrecked. These sins are purged away by alms, only care must be taken to keep from committing those sins which separate from the Communion and from the Church, such as murder, adultery, witchcraft, idolatry. Against these alms are of no avail.[22]

We see that in Augustine the maxim, that alms have atoning efficacy, is still surrounded with many precautions.

They have only such efficacy for those who amend their lives, and keep themselves from heavy sins, and for them only when they are actual manifestations of love; lastly, their effect is limited to the third kind of sins—the light, daily, and inevitable. It lay, however, in the nature of the case, that these precautions should not endure, not even in theory, to say nothing of practice. Augustine's threefold division of sins universally gave way to a twofold division into deadly and venial sins, and the atoning power of alms was consequently extended to the whole sphere of sin—the very heavy, such as idolatry, murder, adultery, and those which separate from the Church, alone excepted. Cyprian had already placed alms beside baptism as a means for atoning for sins committed after Baptism, and this thought comes forth far more strongly in Ambrose:[23] "Alms are then to a certain extent a second bath of the soul, so that, if any one has, after baptism, failed through human weakness, there still remains to him the means of purging himself by alms, as the Lord said: 'Give alms, and lo, all things are clean unto you.' Nay, reserving faith, I might say that alms afford still more forgiveness than baptism. For baptism is administered once, and promises forgiveness once, but alms bring forgiveness as often as they are given. These two then are the sources of mercy, which give life and forgive sins. He who avails himself of both is endowed with the honour of the heavenly kingdom. But he who, having stained the living source (baptism) by sins, betakes himself to the stream of charity, will also obtain mercy."

It is true that Ambrose speaks only of sins of weakness. Alms alone are not sufficient to expiate deadly sins. For this Church penance is needed. But even here alms play a great part. Consider, that Cyprian already reckons alms among the proofs of the earnestness of repentance, that he counsels those who had fallen away in persecutions to be zealous in almsgiving. Alms are among the deeds by which a sinner makes satisfaction for his sins. In Gregory the Great, we find this doctrine in as developed a state as that in which it was held in the Middle Ages. The fundamental notion is, that God, while He remits guilt, does not remit punishment. This has to be endured by man, and hence repentance must include the satisfaction of a work, in which man inflicts punishment upon himself. He who has done what is not allowed, must deny himself what is allowed, by way of satisfaction; he who has sinned must make up for it by good works.[24] Three kinds of works, however, are now everywhere deemed good: praying, fasting, and almsgiving, and of these the latter is esteemed the best and most efficacious. "Fasting is good, but almsgiving is better. If any one can do both, both are well; but if he cannot do both, almsgiving is the better. When it is not possible to fast, almsgiving is sufficient. Fasting with almsgiving is doubly good."[25] Thus alms are inserted, as an important item, in the plan of salvation. It is they that expiate venial sins, it is they that, to use a favourite expression, give wings to repentance. All this—I repeat it—under the presupposition of sincere repentance of heart, of which alms alone are said to be the expression. Frequently do the teachers of the Church bring this forward, and often do they recall it to their hearers' minds, that not the external work, but the loving disposition proved thereby, is the main point. Very beautifully says Gregory the Great, in a collection sermon: "Although in this work all the gifts are not equal, still the love must be equal. For the liberality of the faithful is not estimated according to the largeness of the gift, but according to the amount of benevolent love. Let the gift of the wealthy be more abundant, but let not the poor be behind him in love. For though a larger harvest is hoped for from more abundant sowing, yet rich fruit of righteousness may shoot forth from scanty seed;"[26] and in another place: "Property which is unequally distributed, may afford equal merit, if, whatever the extent of the gift, the love is none the less."[27] Augustine still more frequently insists, that by alms he means not only the gifts bestowed upon the poor, but brotherly love, especially the forbearing love which forgives a brother.[28] Ambrose reminds that it is not alms given from ambition that atone for sin, but those whose expenses are provided for by faith.[29] In Matt. xxv. Christ means that those only, who give to hungering Christians as such, give to Christ Himself; and these are they who do not do what Christ disapproves, says Augustine, and delights in carrying out the thought, that we must first give to ourselves the bread of conversion before we give bread to others. Else alms are of no avail. The Lord has regard to the disposition with which we give.[30] To think that we may sin because we give alms, that while paying for our faults we may commit new ones, is, according to Gregory the Great, "to give ourselves to the devil while giving our property to God."[31]

But what could all these reminders avail with a generation only too much inclined to release themselves from the moral demands of Christianity by external works, to regard Christianity in general more as an institution for a magical kind of atonement, than as a power of moral renovation? In effect, countless multitudes sought in the largest possible almsgiving, the safest means of atoning for their sins and rendering God propitious to them, and we need only read Salvian or the pseudo-Augustinian sermons of Cæsar of Arelate, to be convinced that the Church was a participator in their error. It is there said again and again: This or that is sin, but instead of then insisting on a moral change, there follows immediately: But alms atone for sin. How much had not the Church to overlook and actually did overlook, how lax had discipline become! Alms are said to afford a remedy for all, for "as water quenches fire, so do alms sin;" such was the maxim now preached in countless instances. Alms had totally changed their character. They were no longer a moral, but a religious duty; men no longer gave with regard to their neighbours, to serve and to help them in love, but with regard to themselves, to exercise an influence upon their own relation to God, to gain a reward for themselves. "Certainly every one of us does himself and his own soul the greatest benefit, whenever he relieves the distress of others," preaches already Leo the Great;[32] and this motive of benefiting oneself and one's family was ever after more and more strongly brought forward in place of the self-denying, self-sacrificing love, which seeketh not her own.

Nothing more effectively promoted this propensity than the thought, that the sin-atoning power of alms reaches also to the other world. It may be said, that the doctrine of purgatory, and of the influence which almsgiving exercises even upon souls in purgatory, determined more than anything else the charity of the entire mediæval period. This doctrine was now already developed, its outlines were complete in Gregory the Great, and it was thus passed on to the Middle Ages.

We have in the first period already noticed the beginnings of this doctrine. As early as Tertullian's day, oblations were offered for the departed on the anniversary of their death. The intention then evidently was to obtain for them the intercessions of the Church, any merit to be applied to the deceased was not as yet thought of. In Cyprian, however, the stress is no longer laid upon the intercession, but upon the sacrifice offered in behalf of the departed, and it is no longer the oblation, but the celebration of the Lord's Supper, the offering of the mass, which is regarded as such a sacrifice. We have in truth already the mass for souls, the only difference being, that this is not yet severed from the offering of the Church. It now consequently becomes the general custom, to offer for the departed, and the persuasion is generally entertained, that this offering is to their advantage. "It is not to be doubted," it is said in one of Augustine's sermons,[33] "that the departed are assisted by the prayers of the Holy Church, by the saving sacrifice and by the alms, which are offered for their souls, that the Lord deals more mercifully with them than their sins have deserved." Still more amply does he explain this in the *Enchiridion*:[34] "It cannot be denied, that the souls of the departed find alleviation through the piety of survivors, when the sacrifice of the Mediator is offered, or when alms are given in the church for them." "But certainly," adds Augustine, " it only profits those, who have in their lives deserved that it should do so." He distinguishes in this respect three kinds of persons. There are those who do not need it. For them it is a sacrifice of thanksgiving. There are those not entirely wicked. For these it is an atoning sacrifice. There are those quite wicked. Then it is at least a means of consolation for the survivors. But even in the last case Augustine still admits, that a mitigation of their doom may be hoped for. Hence it is in any case, as Augustine says in a work devoted to the subject (*On Care for the Dead*), a universal duty to offer the sacrifice for every departed soul, since one cannot know what is appointed to any individual.

These passages from Augustine already show, that alms were combined with the sacrifice offered for the dead. Alms were given in the Church, when, soon after a death, or on the anniversary of a death, the sacrifice was offered; alms were also given at funerals and at graves, in the hope that their merit might be of advantage to the deceased.[35] Such a custom was the more easily formed, inasmuch as it was connected with an ancient custom, indeed was only an ancient custom remodelled. Scarcely anywhere can we so well trace the continuation and transformation of ancient in Christian customs, as in funerals and the solemnities connected with them, because it is just here that epitaphs afford us a glimpse of prevailing customs. That just in this point ancient customs were retained with special pertinacity, need not surprise us, because the ancient world was distinguished by great reverence for the dead. How highly was the sacredness of the grave esteemed among the Romans, with what attention was a fitting funeral prepared, and how much was expended in permanently honouring the dead and their memory! All this was the more faithfully preserved, inasmuch as it now obtained a fresh and firmer support through the doctrine of the resurrection. To Christians the grave must have become still more sacred, since they believed, that he who was now laid in the grave would not remain there, but rise again. The Christian epitaphs also furnish proofs, that in many respects the ancient custom passed over into the Christian custom.

T

Thus it was the custom among the Romans, to forbid under penalties the subsequent opening of the grave; and we read upon many heathen graves, that whoever presumes to open this grave is to pay such or such a fine to the Romish exchequer, the Vestal Virgins, or whatever other place is stated as authorized to receive such fines. Similarly do we read also upon a Christian grave: Whoever shall open this sarcophagus after my interment, shall pay to the church at Salona fifty pounds silver.[36] Here is the same infliction of a fine, only the receiver is now designated as the Church. Threats are also frequently read. Whoever disturbs the grave is said to incur punishment by the infernal gods. Upon Christian graves it is said: He shall have his reward with Judas, with Gehazi, with Dathan and Abiram, or also, let him be Anathema.[37]

It is especially significant, that, as we saw above, legacies and endowments occur in remembrance of the departed. Money is bequeathed, that the grave of the deceased may on his birthday be decorated with roses and violets, that lights may be lit and a repast held at his grave, or that appointed gifts of bread and wine, or a sum of money, may be distributed at his grave in celebration of his birthday to the members of the collegium to which he belonged, or to his fellow-townsmen. All this was "in remembrance," *in memoriam*, of the deceased. Some heathen memorials so resemble the Christian memorials of the Middle Ages, that they might easily be mistaken for them, but for the certainly important difference, that they are never benevolent endowments, but minister solely to vanity, or, at all events, are only intended to honour the memory of the departed. The particular in which we notice the transformation effected in this custom by Christianity is, that these memorials now became distributions of alms to the poor. Chrysostom already speaks of it as an ancient custom, to keep up the remembrance of a deceased wife, husband, or child, by inviting the poor at the interment, or on the anniversary of the death, and giving them food and drink. Subsequently feasts held at graves became a nuisance to the Church, a scandal to all earnestly-minded Christians. At the graves of relatives, at the graves of martyrs, luxurious banquetings were held on their anniversaries. Augustine had often to contend with this obnoxious custom. It was, however, too firmly rooted to be extirpated, and hence the efforts of the Church were directed so to change it, that the repasts and presents for friends and relatives should be replaced by the sacrifice of the mass, with the oblation and alms for the poor. Thus arose the Christian memorials, endowments for masses for the dead, and distributions of alms on the anniversaries of deaths. For it was part of the transformation of the heathen custom, that the birthday hitherto celebrated, was exchanged for the day of death.[38]

This development reaches its maturity in the doctrine of purgatory. The distinction between heavier and slighter sins is here again at the foundation. Gregory[39] adduces especially the passage of St. Paul, 1 Cor. iii. 11 sqq. The apostle does not say, that every one may be saved, who builds upon the one foundation, instead of gold and silver, iron, brass, lead, *i.e.* great and heavy sins, not to be expiated in another world, but he who builds thereupon wood, hay, stubble, *i.e.* light and trifling sins, which fire easily consumes. These are sins such as those which Gregory adduces by way of example, frequent and useless talk, immoderate laughter, or a sin in the management of property, which can hardly be carried on without sin by those who know how sin must be avoided. All this does not plunge into perdition, but it burdens the soul even after death, if it is not pardoned during life. Such a man therefore goes before the judgment into a purgatorial fire, in which sins are burned like hay and stubble. It is true that Gregory takes for granted, that the man, while in this world, merited purification through his good works, or he will never obtain it in the next. Only under this condition, but then certainly, will the sacrifices and good works performed for him here on earth by others profit him.[40] Gregory's dialogues are full of histories to prove this. He tells of souls who come into the fire burdened with slight sins, who then themselves pray that the sacrifice of the mass may be offered for them, and as soon as this is done are released. It may suffice to give here but one, which is of interest because it involves the commencement of a mediæval custom which became very productive in respect of alms. A monk of the name of Justus, who had applied himself to the study of medicine in Gregory's monastery, had secretly been in possession of three gold pieces. When this was, shortly before his death, discovered, Gregory ordered that none of the brethren should resort to him, and afterwards caused his corpse to be buried in a dung-heap. The three gold pieces were thrown after him, the brethren exclaiming in chorus, "Thy money be thy ruin!" Thirty days after his death, Gregory had compassion upon the monk who had been thus punished. He called Pretiosus, the prior of the monastery, and said to him, "For a long time has the departed brother been tormented in the fire. We must now show our love to him, and help him as much as possible to be released. Go then and order the sacred sacrifice of the mass to be offered for him for thirty successive days from to-day, so that there may not be one on which the Holy Eucharist is not offered for him." On the thirtieth day, then, Justus was actually released from the fire, and testified the same to his brethren by appearing to them.[41] Accordingly, it became the custom, first of all in Benedictine monasteries, to read mass thirty days for a departed brother, during which period his portion was distributed to the poor; and this is the origin of the custom, observed throughout the whole mediæval period, of having masses read and alms distributed for the soul of any one departed in the so-called thirties, *i.e.* thirty days after death.[42]

It is palpable what a strong motive for almsgiving was involved in the notion, that it could deliver oneself and others from the torments of hell. Venial sins, it is said in a pseudo-Augustinian sermon,[43] do not indeed cause death, but they make the soul so loathsome, that it cannot meet the heavenly bridegroom without confusion. Hence they must be expiated by fasting, praying and almsgiving. Otherwise we must remain in purgatory till these sins are consumed like wood, hay and stubble. We must not, however, say: Although I must go into purgatory, what is the harm, if only I be saved at last? Purgatory is worse than anything we can conceive on earth. We would not willingly thrust a finger into the fire now, and we shall then be tormented for years. We must therefore abstain from mortal sins, and expiate pardonable offences with good works. As often as we visit the sick, deliver those lying in prisons and in chains, fast on the appointed days, wash the feet of strangers, come frequently to vigils, give alms to the poor who pass our doors, our smaller sins are daily atoned for by these good works.

Thus was the sin-atoning power of alms extended to this world and the next; they were deemed capable of preserving ourselves and others from the horrors of purgatory. This motive for almsgiving was the more powerfully efficient, inasmuch as it could not be known when a sufficient quantity of good works had been performed. It is easily seen, that in those exhortations which make use of this motive, the uncertainty which impels to do more and more, because it can never be known whether enough has been done, is powerfully brought forward. It cannot be known whether one departed needs or does not need alms, for his deliverance out of purgatory, or whether they profit or do not profit him. Hence the one thing advisable is to give them for all. "Perhaps," says Salvian, "it may even help the quite wicked," and Augustine also concedes the possibility of an alleviation of perdition.[44] Who would not devote as much as he possibly could, if there were but a glimpse of hope, that he might thereby procure for his father, mother, brethren, children, a mitigation of torment? Besides, no one was ever certain of his own salvation. Man does not know whether his works are so constituted, that God judges them to be good works. Hence even the saints have no unmixed joy in their good works. A letter of Gregory the Great to a lady-in-waiting of the Empress, named Gregoria, is in this respect characteristic. Gregoria had written to him, that she would leave him no peace till he wrote to her, that the forgiveness of her sins was revealed to him. Thereupon Gregory replies: Thou hast asked something which is hard to comply with, and moreover unprofitable. Hard to comply with, because I am unworthy to receive a revelation; unprofitable, because thou must not surrender thyself to full security on account of thy sins, till on the day of thy death thou canst weep for them no more. Till that day comes, thou must ever fear and tremble· because of thy sins.[45] No one must be certain, every one must live in fear, and this fear must urge him to do more and more. As much alms as possible, was now the rule. We do not indeed know whether we still need them, but in any case we earn thereby so much the more merit, and if we do not need this merit ourselves, we can apply it to others. It is also but a trifle that we give, compared with the great thing we expect. For who would not rather sacrifice something here, than suffer there unspeakable torments in purgatory? Therefore, as much alms as possible. If the distress of the times urged the teachers of the Church to use every lever to impel to almsgiving, the members of the Church with their now increasing laxity, if they, surrounded as they were by hundreds of poor, expecting everything from them, were already near enough to regard rather the quantity of the alms obtained, than the purity of the disposition in which they originated, what must have been the case with the ordinary Christian? Alms can do everything, atone for everything, help in every need! How often must earnest men, like Augustine, have had to oppose the delusion, that a man might live as he pleased, if only he gave alms to the poor! But the worst harm lay in that uncertainty as to forgiveness and a share in everlasting blessedness, so decidedly declared by the Church to be inevitable, nay, necessary, and which it was sought to obviate by almsgiving. The Church offered to her members expiation upon expiation; these were, moreover, believingly received, but it almost seems as if they were, nevertheless, not really trusted in; men were not at heart satisfied with them, and therefore strove to obtain, or at least to strengthen an assurance of salvation by their own doings, especially by almsgiving.[46]

In order, however, to a right estimation of the almsdeeds of this period, it will now be necessary to take a glance also at the moral views held concerning property, and concerning riches and poverty. It is not quite easy to be certain in this matter, and opinions therefore differ. While some represent the views of the Fathers as more or less communistic, others, on the contrary, maintain, that they always firmly adhered to the scriptural decision concerning property, and that their views on wealth and poverty were still, in a moral point of view, thoroughly sound.[47] The investigation is rendered the more difficult by the highly rhetorical character of our documents. These are in the first rank sermons, and certainly words spoken in ardour and eagerness must not be, without further ceremony, taken as they stand. It would be easy to collect a series of passages which sound quite communistic, and seem to deny all right to private property. " Whom do I injure, sayest thou, if I keep what is my own?" are the words put by Basil, in one of his homilies, into the mouth of the hard-hearted, to whom he replies: " Tell me then what is thine own? Whence didst thou obtain it and bring it into the world? The rich are just like one who has taken his place in the theatre, and crowds all who come in later, as if the playhouse, which is for all, were for him only. For they first take possession for themselves alone of what is common to all, and then lay claim to it as property, because they obtained it first. If each would only take as much as he needs to satisfy his necessary requirements, where, then, would be the rich, and where the poor?"[48] But we should be doing Basil injustice if we should at once conclude from this, that Basil intended to deny the rights of property, and looked upon riches as in themselves sinful. We ought rightly to estimate, and not to turn into doctrinal propositions the words of Ambrose, when, in his sermon on Naboth, he thunders against those who do like Ahab, and thus addresses the rich:[49] "How far will you stretch your mad desires? Do you alone dwell upon the earth? Why do you cast them out, who are by nature your fellows, and seize upon the possessions of nature for yourselves alone? The earth is given as a common property to all, to rich and poor. Why do you, who are rich, claim rights of property for yourselves only? Nature, which brings forth all poor, knows of no rich. Naked did we come into the world, and a grassy hillock equally covers rich and poor." Nor must we take it literally, when Chrysostom, addressing a richly dressed lady, says: "Of how many poor, O woman, dost thou bear upon thine arms the spoil?" Or when Jerome says: "Rightly does Jesus call wealth the unrighteous mammon, for all wealth arises from unrighteousness. The one can only gain what the other loses; hence the saying: 'Every rich man is a rogue, or the heir of a rogue.'"[50]

Nor is the matter settled by opposing to this series of passages another series, in which the rights of property are acknowledged, and the possession of wealth justified. Certainly the Synod of Gangra was protecting the rights of property against hyper-ascetic efforts, when it said in its 4th canon: "We do not despise wealth, if it is combined with justice and benevolence." "It is not wealth," says Ambrose,[51] "but pride of wealth, that is reproved in the rich man, otherwise poor Lazarus would not have been carried to the bosom of rich Abraham." "Paul did not forbid men to enrich themselves; he did not command them to make themselves poor, to deprive themselves of their wealth, but only not to be proud of their wealth," preaches Chrysostom;[52] and in entire agreement with Scripture do we read in Augustine: "Wealth is in itself, and according to its nature, a good, though not the highest, nor a great good."[53] The Fathers also define giving as a matter entirely left to the free-will of the individual. "God might have constrained us to give alms, He chose instead to make it depend entirely on our free-will, that He might have the opportunity of rewarding us." We are at liberty to give or not to give. Ananias and Sapphira were punished only because "they lied unto the Holy Ghost."[54] The Fathers are very far from preaching to the poor: What the rich possess, properly belongs to you. On the contrary, they urgently warn the poor against envy, and energetically as they remind the rich of their duty to give all to the poor, they equally testify to the poor, that they have no right to this.

But all these utterances do in truth prove nothing to the purpose, for what they certainly do prove, viz. that the Fathers had no intention of abolishing the rights of property, is really in no need of proof. This does not, however, show that the views now held of property, of wealth and poverty were still morally sound, that they were still the same as in the early days of the Church, and had not already undergone a great change.

The latter is, on the contrary, shown in the now universally accepted maxim, that the relinquishment of property is the higher state of Christian life. The Synod of Gangra prefixes to its recognition of property the sentence: "We approve of abstinence from worldly occupations, if it is accompanied by humility." To possess property, to be rich, is quite allowable for a Christian, and does not hinder his salvation. The Church most decidedly rejects the view, that wealth is sinful. Still to be poor is a higher moral condition. All the Fathers whom we have quoted lived in this condition, they gave up their property, and so ought it to be with all Christians. Augustine on one occasion explains,[55] that all the strife in the world, wars, rebellion, offences, murder, injustice, arise concerning what we individually possess. Concerning those things which we possess in common, like the sun and the air, no strife arises. "Let us then, my brethren," he continues, "abstain from private property, or at least from the love of it, if we cannot abstain from its possession." The latter is thus evidently designated as the morally inferior condition, and as one only permitted to weakness, and in this connection the above-mentioned utterances on common and private property acquire another significance than that of mere rhetorical treatment. Augustine [56] says, indeed, very decidedly, that it is not a sin to be rich, nor is it a sin if any one makes use of his riches, fares, *e.g.*, better than others; but still it is a weakness, and riches are a burden, which one would do best to cast off. "God did not create thee alone, but also the poor man as well. You find yourselves companions, and are walking on the same road. He carries nothing, and thou art heavily laden. He brings nothing with him, and thou more than is needful. Give him of what thou hast, and thou wilt both feed him and lighten thine own load."

It is everywhere the opinion of the Fathers, that the natural and original order is common property, and that private property first arose from sin. It is for this very reason, that Ambrose, in his work on duties, refuses the ancient definition of justice, which makes it refer also to private property. It refers only to the common life of men. For this corresponds with nature. "Nature has equally poured forth everything upon all, that food might be common to all, and the earth a common possession. Nature brought forth the rights of the community, usurpation first created private rights."[57] Gregory of Nazianzus having, in his sermon on love to the poor, first laid down the proposition: "Love is the shortest way of salvation, the easiest ascent to heaven," explains, that wealth and poverty, like freedom and slavery, are not original institutions of God, but came into the world through sin. Envy, strife, the allurements of pleasure, power first called forth these inequalities. It is, therefore, the duty of the Christian to labour for the removal of the inequality, brought in through sin and for the restoration of the primitive equality. "Do thou, O Christian, look to the former equality and not to the subsequent disunion, to the law of the Creator, not to the law of him, who gained the victory over him. Help the natural order with all thy powers." With Gregory the distinction between rich and poor is therefore entirely parallel with that between bond and free, as a thing contrary to the original ordinance of God, and it is the duty of the Christian to labour by gifts and grants and alms, for the restoration of the original equality.

Chrysostom really paints in lively colours, in a sermon on the Church of Jerusalem, in which there was none that suffered want, the picture of a communistically constituted society. If all the Christians in Constantinople would sell their possessions, they would certainly produce a million pounds gold, perhaps even two or three millions. This would fully suffice, if all would live in common, to satisfy the wants of all, so that no one would lack anything, as was the case in Jerusalem. For as he now shows, with a fair amount of detail and a glance at monastic life, where this is realized, living in common requires far smaller means. If a father, mother, and ten children live together, this costs far less than if each child lived alone and had his separate house, table, and attendants. Certainly Chrysostom did not seriously contemplate the carrying out of such a plan, still he draws the picture with such evident zest, that we feel, that though it is an ideal whose realization he deems impossible, he yet enjoys its contemplation in private. He does but paint the ideal, which in truth hovered before the eyes of all the Fathers, an ideal to become also a reality, not indeed among the multitudes of ordinary Christians, but among the perfect in monasteries. So far, there is a communistic feature in the view entertained by the Fathers.[58]

Hence, when the right use of wealth is spoken of, giving it away is always dwelt on in a onesided manner. Nay, it may be said, that the Fathers see its right use in giving it away. Its use for our own necessities is indeed conceded, and even the adornments and enjoyments of life permitted, but still these are already under a cloud. They are not exactly sins, but they are weaknesses. The Christian must only so far use his property for himself, as the necessaries of life require. It is quite common to meet with the maxim, that all that a man possesses beyond what is necessary, belongs to the poor, and ought to be given away. So Augustine:[59] "All that God has given us beyond what is necessary, He has not properly speaking given to us, He has but entrusted it to us, that it may by our means come into the hands of the poor. To retain it is to take possession of what belongs to others." "Of what God has given you, take beforehand what you need. The rest, which is the superfluous for you, is the necessary for the poor." "Let not what remains after moderate food and modest clothing are provided for, be retained for luxury, but laid up, by means of alms distributed to the poor, among heavenly treasures." And to give only one more example, Jérome [60] quite similarly says: "We are debtors to the poor of all that exceeds necessary food and raiment." As a scriptural proof Luke xi. 42 was now adduced, according to the interpretation, "What is superfluous, give as alms." [61]

Thus the rights of property were limited to the necessary, the superfluous is not the property of him who possesses it, but of the poor. "Thou dost not give to the poor what is thine own, thou restorest to him what is his. The earth belongs to all, not to the rich only. Thou art there for paying thy debt, and givest him only what thou owest him," says Ambrose. And Chrysostom: [62] "The poor beg for their own, not thine." The error is here quite evident. The rich man is truly a debtor; he is only doing his duty, when he does not use his riches for himself, but shares them with the poor. But he is God's debtor, and his alms have a moral worth, just when it is for God's sake, that he gives to the poor what is really his own. To divide property into the necessary and the superfluous, and to limit the rights of property to the former, and consequently to restrict the duty of almsgiving to the latter, is to make a false distinction and one really impossible to carry out.[63] The Christian is in the fullest sense the possessor of all that God has given him, but also on the other hand bound, when need requires, to give away all.

If all that is possessed beyond the necessary belongs properly to the poor, and what is given them is only what is their due, the duty of love has acquired somewhat of the character of a legal duty, and hence we cannot be surprised, if in the treatment of morals, benevolence should be discussed under the category of justice. It now obtains this situation, to retain it during the entire mediæval period. Not only on this account, however, is it important, to take one more glance at this form of doctrine, but because also it is characteristic in the highest degree of the period we are now discussing. For it is a very evident symptom of a development, which deserves the highest degree of notice, if we are rightly to understand the times of the ancient church, a symptom of the fact, that now—as we have already had occasion several times to remark in particulars—a wide current of ancient views and ancient life flows into and mingles with Christian views and Christian life.

The first Christian Ethic is the work of Ambrose, *On Duties*. It borrows its title, and something more than its title, from Cicero's famous work. It might be called a translation of a Ciceronian work into Christian. It is just in the sphere of morals, that the influence of ancient views would make itself more strongly felt than in that of dogma. The Romans had never been strong in theology. Besides, men will sooner part with dogmas than moral aims. The teachers of the Church found a complete and well-worked out philosophical system of Ethic. They had learned this in the schools. The great Cappadocians, Basil and Gregory, had studied in the rhetorical schools of Athens, and Ambrose had been brought up and taught, like any other aristocratic Roman of the day. Hence they accepted the entire framework of ancient Ethic, its categories and definitions, and used it for the insertion of the new Christian matter. The new wine was put into old bottles, and this could not be done without its acquiring their flavour. The form influenced the matter, and the result was not a Christian Ethic, but a mixture, which is perceived to have flowed from two sources, one ancient, one Christian, just as Basil was at once a Christian and a classically educated Greek, and Ambrose a Christian and a genuine Roman, nay, just as the Christianity of those days was of similarly mixed appearance, rooted on the one side in Bethlehem and Golgotha, on the other in Rome and Athens.

This is seen as soon as Ambrose defines the principle and the task of Ethic.[64] Ancient Ethic is thoroughly eudæmonistic; the aim of the philosopher, even in his moral conduct, is his own wellbeing. Ambrose of course had to renounce this principle, but he lays down a more refined eudæmonism in its place. Philosophers, he argues, ask what is "profitable and honourable," but have in this inquiry only this life in view. "We, however, estimate what is profitable and honourable, rather by the standard of things to come, than of things present, and define as profitable not what contributes to the enjoyment of this life, but what helps to attain the grace of eternal life." Here too, then, all turns upon Ethic teaching us not how to prove our faith, how to develop the new life in all aspects, but what we must do for our own weal, with only the difference that our welfare, not in this world, but in the world to come, our eternal salvation, is the question. An enormous difference truly; but that a sound moral estimation of earthly property can never by this means be arrived at, is shown at once by the manner in which Ambrose himself exemplifies the difference. Just because Christians look to another world, earthly possessions appear to them not an advantage, but a disadvantage; they are, unless they are cast away, only a burden. The Christian ethic of Ambrose is the counterpart of the ancient, the latter is an ethic purely of this world, the former purely of another world; but, in truth, their aim is the same, a man's own wellbeing. With this corresponds also the manner in which benevolence is regarded, the aim is always self, the reward to be gained thereby. It is not the necessary working of faith by love, but a means of obtaining salvation.

More plainly still is the influence of ancient ethic shown, when we notice in what position, and how, Ambrose speaks of benevolence.[65] Here, too, he makes use of the ancient framework handed down by ancient ethic. This, as is well known, distinguished four cardinal virtues, prudence, justice, fortitude, and temperance. Ambrose introduced this mode of treatment into Christian ethic, and it continued in force down to the Reformation. Benevolence is discussed under the head of "justice," and is its proper agency, because true justice relates to the common. It comprises two points, benevolence and liberality. Both are inseparably connected, for it is not enough to have a good will, we must also act; and again, it is not enough to do good, but this must also proceed from a good will. Very beautifully does Ambrose say: "Take away benevolence from the intercourse of men with each other, and thou hast taken the sun out of the world." Benevolence becomes a fact in liberality, and Ambrose now describes Christian beneficence as liberality. Undoubtedly much that he here says is genuinely Christian, it could not have grown up out of the soil of antiquity; but it acquires a very strongly ancient colouring from the circumstance, that all is treated of under the ancient title of liberality. How the practice agrees with the theory, we have seen above, for we were already struck by the suspicious likeness between ancient liberality and the almsgiving of the bishops. We may now characterize the charity of the age by saying, that as all Christian life exhibits a mingling of Christian and ancient elements, and as the ethic of Ambrose is Christian-Ciceronian, so too is charity a mingling of Christian *caritas* and ancient *liberalitas.* Men gave with full hands, but more and more lost sight of the purpose for the sake of which they gave. Giving was itself esteemed a virtue. The more any one gave, the more perfect was he.

In saying this, nothing is further from my intention, than to depreciate the charity of this period. On the contrary, I stand admiring before the exalted figures which it produced, before those bishops daily opening their hands to feed the hungry and to clothe the naked, while themselves living simply and sparingly,[66] before those men, who give away millions, and themselves choose poverty, before that band of noble women, whose whole life was a series of good deeds. It would be doing them the greatest injustice not to acknowledge, that it was indeed genuine Christian love, shed abroad in their hearts from the Cross, which acted in them. Nor did they stop at giving, but added to it their personal services. Basil himself took care of the sick, and the scions of noble Roman families did not think themselves too good to put their own hands to the work and to perform menial services in the houses for the sick and for strangers. But it is doing them no injustice to estimate them according to the standard of the gospel, which was itself the source of their life and strength; and when this is done, we must, in the midst of our admiration, confess, that this charity was no longer healthy.

The life of love appears in its purest form during this period in certain women, whom we meet with in the East, by the side of the great teachers of the Church: Macrina, the sister of Basil and Olympias, the friend of Chrysostom, and to name, beside a virgin and a widow, two married women, Nonna, the mother of Gregory of Nazianzus, and his sister Gregoria. Macrina was betrothed, her lover died, and she regarded herself as bound to him. She therefore led an ascetic life with her mother. She assembled about her a circle of like-minded women, but though of both higher and lower class, "the same mode of life, one order, one discipline, one peace, one rank" united them all. Her servants and slaves were now her companions, and she used her abundant means only in benevolence. In the period of famine especially, which came upon Cappadocia, she assisted many, and it was her brave spirit which attracted her whole family, her brothers, Basil, Gregory of Nyssa and Peter, into the same path. Olympias, a woman of most aristocratic birth, rich, intellectual, beautiful, much admired and sought after, preferred, when her husband Nebridius, the prefect of Constantinople, died, to remain a widow, though only eighteen years of age, and to live only for God and for her brethren. The Emperor Theodosius, who wanted to marry her, deprived her, for the purpose of inducing her, of the management of her property. She only replied with thanks. "You have," she wrote to the emperor, "shown towards your humble servant, the wisdom and goodness not only of a sovereign, but of a bishop, by laying the heavy burden of my estates upon an official, and thereby delivering me from the care and disquietude, which the necessity of managing them well imposed upon me. I now only request one thing more, by granting which you would much increase my joy: Command them to be divided between the Church and the poor. I have already felt the stirrings of vanity, which are wont to accompany one's own distribution, and I fear lest the distractions of temporal possessions might make me neglect those true treasures which are divine and spiritual." Theodosius subsequently restored to her the management of her estates, and she then applied everything to the poor and to the Church. Chrysostom directed her beneficence, which seems to have often surpassed all bounds, and might often have been shared by the undeserving, into right paths. He reminded her, that she would also have to give account of how she had given. "If thou wilt therefore obey me, guide thy gifts according to the necessities of those who beg of thee. In this way thou wilt be able to relieve more, and receive from God the reward of thy wisdom and love." When Chrysostom fell into disfavour and was banished, his deaconess remained faithful to him, and proved herein also the genuineness of her love. Olympias is one of the healthiest manifestations of the times. She is always natural, she never coquets with her poverty and her simple apparel; humility and noble elevation of mind are large features in her character. But we meet also with married women, who are zealous in good works. Nonna, the mother of Gregory of Nazianzus, is depicted to us, by her famous son, as a philanthropist, who could never do enough in supporting widows and orphans, in visiting the sick and poor, so that she always found her property less than her impulse to do good, and would, had it been possible, have sold herself and her children to serve the poor. She died, after the death of her husband, the bishop of the church, praying at the high altar "a holy sacrifice." The sister of Gregory was the wife of a burgess of Iconium; but her brother says of her also: "She was eyes to the blind, feet to the lame, a mother to orphans. Her house was the common asylum of all the distressed."[67]

The characteristic traits of the period are encountered in still greater force in the West. As it was the Western bishops, Ambrose, Jerome, Augustine, Gregory the Great, who matured the doctrine of whose development we have been speaking, so are its peculiarities most sharply impressed on the Christian life of the West.

It was an amazing sight,[68] in the last quarter of the fourth century, to see a number of men and women of the highest Roman aristocracy devote themselves to an earnest Christian life, as then understood. Members of the proud old Roman families, who had hitherto adhered to the old gods, who had made Rome great, Marcelli, Scipios, Gracchi, left their palaces to procure their salvation, by the strictest self-denial, in the monastery or the desert, or turned their palaces into monasteries, laid aside the purple toga or the brocaded state dress, to put on the dusky garments of the monk or nun, distributed to the poor the treasures they inherited from their forefathers, and themselves became poor. Rome saw with amazement senators and consulars going along the streets in the garb of monks, and ladies, whose names had been the pride of the republic, ladies who had hitherto led idle and luxurious lives in their palaces, surrounded by troops of attendants, ministering, as widows or virgins devoted to God, to squalid beggars, and to those sick of loathsome diseases. At first the new folly was derided and rebuked, then men began to admire and extol it. At the funeral of Blesilla the multitude was indignant; "the young lady," it was said, "was killed through fasting;" her mother, Paula, was pitied because her daughter had been seduced into becoming a nun; voices were heard saying that "the monks ought to be driven out of the town." A few years later, at the funeral of Fabiola, a triumphal procession was formed, which Jerome compared to the triumphs of Camillus and Scipio. All Rome took a part in it, the streets, the colonnades, could not contain the multitudes, psalms and hallelujahs resounded on all sides.

The spiritual father of this circle, its centre and leader, was Jerome, whose narrow and monastic, but at the same time self-denying and self-renouncing piety, set its stamp upon it. Marcella is said to have been the first who let herself be induced by him to enter the condition of monastic widowhood. In her palace on the Aventine Hill, and afterwards in her country seat near Rome, were found assembled all who had attached themselves to this tendency. It was there that Jerome expounded the Scriptures, there that Epiphanius and others sojourned when they visited Rome. Like Marcella, Furia, of the race of Camillus, preferred a monastic widowhood, and to live only for her soul's salvation and for good works, to a splendid second marriage. But the most prominent figure of this circle is Paula, whose descent on her mother's side was derived from the Scipios and Gracchi, on her father's from Agamemnon, and whose husband was a connection of the Julian house. Moved by care for her soul's salvation, and by love to the Lord, she distributed her abundant possessions with liberal hands to the poor, in the hope, as she said, of thus leaving to her children a better inheritance, even the mercy of Christ. Seeking out the poor through all the city, she reckoned it a loss if the hungry or the sick were fed by another than herself. "What poor man," exclaims Jerome, "has not been buried in raiment supplied by her, what sick man not fed by her?" When she was remonstrated with on account of this excess of beneficence, she replied, that she wished to die a beggar, and at her death to be covered in a shroud bestowed as a gift. "When I have become poor, I shall find many who will give to me; but if that beggar receives nothing from me, and dies, of whom will his soul be required?"[69] Afterwards, leaving her other children in Rome, she went, accompanied by her daughter Eustochium, who entirely entered into her way of life, and shared her sentiments, to visit the holy places where the Lord had sojourned, and then settled permanently at Bethlehem, that she might live and die near His cradle. There she built a house for pilgrims, and a monastery, in which she and her daughter spent the last years of her life in ministering to all. Her second daughter, Blesilla, died before her, the same at whose funeral Rome was horrified at the new kind of life. A third, Paulina, married to a senator, Pammachius, a descendant of Camillus, followed the example of her mother. After her death Pammachius continued her works. He sold her jewels and ornaments, her silk dresses, her costly furniture, to give the proceeds to the poor. Jerome describes his good deeds, and this description, in his somewhat bombastic manner, gives us at the same time a glance of the misery then existing:[70] "That blind man stretching out his hand, and often crying out when there is no one passing, is the heir of Paulina, the co-heir of Pammachius. That man, maimed in his feet, who stumbles along with difficulty, is supported by the hand of a tender girl. The doors, which formerly were beset by tribes of visitors, are now besieged by the wretched. Here is one languishing of dropsy and near to death; there one deaf and dumb, he has not even the organ for begging, but for this very reason supplicates the more urgently. This man, feeble from a child, does not beg alms alone; that one, already corrupting from leprosy, still survives his corpse. Other husbands scatter roses, lilies, violets upon the graves of their wives, seeking consolation in such service. Our Pammachius bedews the beloved body with the balsam of alms."

Pammachius devoted a portion of his means to found a house for strangers in Portus, the port of Rome, in which Fabiola, another woman of this circle, assisted him with both her property and services. Fabiola, descended, as her name already shows, from the Fabian gens, had married a rich spendthrift and been divorced from him. She was then, however, convinced of her sin, did public penance, and henceforth lived only for the sick and poor. She employed the great treasures at her disposal to found the first hospital in Rome. Sufferers, of whom there were then so many,—men with mutilated noses, with eyes thrust out, with half-gangrened feet and mortified hands, those affected with corrupting sores and leprosy,—found there shelter and care. Fabiola herself often carried the sick into the house, washed and bound up wounds, which other ladies would not even have looked at, gave them food, and refreshed them with drink. Her attention to them was so maternal and so amiable, that, as Jerome says, the poor wished to be sick, if only to come under her care.

Besides this circle, gathered around Paula, we must not omit to mention especially the two Melanias, the elder the grandmother, the other her granddaughter of the same name. The elder Melania, descended from a side branch of the Marcelli, the daughter of a consul, lost in one year her husband and two children. Seeking alleviation for her grief, she left her only remaining son in Rome, and went, when but twenty-two years old, to Egypt, there visited the monks, and devoted herself entirely to that kind of life. In Jerusalem she built a convent, in which she gathered around her fifty virgins. Her income was given to the monks and to the poor. She lived there for more than twenty-five years, when care for her son and his daughter, the younger Melania, urged her to revisit her home. Upon her road, she visited Paulinus, her relative, at Nola, who was, even during his lifetime, honoured as a saint, and who lived there in a small house with his wife, Theresia, and passed his time in religious exercises. Paulinus, too, was one of those Roman nobles who retired from the world, nay, was perhaps the most characteristic figure among them. Born in Bordeaux, and immensely rich (Ambrose calls his possessions kingdoms, and Augustine designates him as " the richest of the rich"), he received a liberal education. His tutor was the poet Ausonius, who, with some amount indeed of flattery, declared himself surpassed by his scholars. In the year 378, Paulinus became consul, and afterwards went, as a consular, into Campania. Even then his love for a monkish life seemed to awaken. For Martin of Tours, who loved him, and said of him, that he alone of his contemporaries had entirely fulfilled the command of Christ, and Ambrose, whom he himself honoured as his spiritual father, had taught him, that only as a monk can one become a perfect Christian. When, then, his only son, whom Theresia had borne him, was torn from him by death, both the parents resolved to renounce the world and lead a monastic life. In Spain, whither he first repaired, he distributed a large proportion of his own and his wife's property to the Church and to the poor, because, as he himself said, " it required more strength than he gave himself credit for to renounce the use of possessions while retaining their ownership, than if he cast them from him." He then settled in Nola, where he built a monastery, in which he and Theresia occupied a humble dwelling, and subjected themselves entirely to a strict rule of life. He gradually distributed his whole property. " He opened," says his disciple Uranius, " his barns to the poor, his storehouses to strangers who arrived. It was too small a thing for him to feed whole provinces, he invited from all quarters those whom he fed and clothed. How many prisoners did he not ransom, how many debtors oppressed by their creditors did he not liberate by paying off their debts, by the same pious deed drying the tears of the debtor and rejoicing the creditor !" Nola became a place of refuge for crowds of unfortunates, and what was believed of him, is shown by the legend handed down concerning him by Gregory the Great, that when, on an incursion of the Vandals, all his means for ransoming prisoners were exhausted, he exchanged himself with the son of a widow, and was carried away into Africa. All those, too, who devoted themselves to this mode of life, strangers who admired him, men and women who revered him, flocked to Nola. He corresponded with all the great men of the time, and was looked up to by all as a model of piety. Having become Bishop of Nola, he remained there till his death, the guardian of the grave of St. Felix, to whom he had dedicated his life, showing himself to be in this respect also a man of his age by his excessive veneration of saints and martyrs. Melania greatly delighted him by presenting him with a piece of the true cross, which she had brought with her from Jerusalem.

Melania remained some years in Rome, entirely occupied in leading her relatives, and whoever else came in contact with her, to that path to heaven which she believed herself to have found. She then prepared to return to Jerusalem, and this time not alone. It was a whole colony that accompanied her, her son Poblicola, her granddaughter Melania and her husband, and many others. Before they started, plentiful gifts were distributed to the poor and to the hospitals, and the churches were liberally remembered. The younger Melania set her slaves at liberty, and bequeathed her property in Spain and Aquitania to the poor. They then set off. It was in the year 409, one year before the conquest of Rome by Alaric. It was as though they desired to save themselves from perishing Rome, and what they gave to the poor seemed also to have been snatched at the right season from the "Barbarian Lion."

The party went first to Africa. At Tagaste, Alyppius was greeted, at Hippo, Augustine. The elder Melania then went to Jerusalem, where she soon after died. The younger built a convent at Tagaste, but afterwards went also to Jerusalem, where she lived on, in a narrow cell, for fourteen years.

They are the chief personages of the Western Church of those times, who have thus been grouped before us in a picture, which represents the piety of the age in sharply cut outlines. Strange as much of it appears to us, we must still confess, that they were in earnest about Christianity, that they were sincerely concerned for their salvation. Even from the bombastic descriptions of Jerome, we still feel something of that ardent love which animated them and moved them to give all their goods to the poor. Jerome tells on one occasion of a rich matron, who was, on her way to church, distributing alms. The poor, standing in a row, received her gifts one after another. When, however, an old woman who had had her share, ran forward and placed herself again in the row, she received from the giver a blow on the face instead of a second gift. A Paula or a Fabiola would never have acted thus. When they distributed alms, it was no external and ostentatious work, but done from love. They gave also their personal services. In their convent, Paula and Eustochium trimmed the lamps, swept, and cooked; in her hospital, Fabiola personally attended on the sick. We cannot help admiring the self-denial with which Paulinus distributed all his goods, and then, when the Vandals had devastated Nola, exclaimed: "Lord, I do not grieve for gold and silver, for Thou knowest where all mine is;" and the composure with which Paula, when it was announced to her, that all her great property was given away, and that nothing was now left, answered only in the words of the two passages of Scripture: "What is a man profited, if he shall gain the whole world and lose his own soul?" and: "Naked came I out of my mother's womb, and naked shall I return." It certainly shows what a new world had been created by Christianity, that where once a Livia and a Messalina had indulged in lusts, a Paula and a Fabiola were now ministering to the poor.

Nevertheless, all was no longer healthy; there was a

morbid element which originated neither in love nor in the gospel. An unhealthy state of mind was shown, when Paula left her daughter poor, nay, loaded with debts, and obliged in her turn to claim the charity of others; and when she left her children in Rome, standing on deck, her eyes lifted towards heaven, while her little Toxatius was stretching out his arms to her. It was surely unhealthy, to name the chief point, to forsake the calling directly handed down, and arbitrarily to choose another, or instead of justly administering property, without setting the heart upon it,—which, as Paulinus of Nola rightly observes, is difficult,—to give it away. In all the proceedings of this circle, there is a morbid restlessness, which is indeed perfectly comprehensible in an age when everything was falling asunder, and the present afforded so little satisfaction. They wandered hither and thither, and even their longing after the sacred places was but a symptom of this unrest. Nor could they find actual satisfaction even then. It would at all events have been more productive, more satisfying, to their love-craving hearts, to have retained their property and administered it faithfully for the common good. Besides, let whoever chooses, wilfully close his eyes against the fact, a more refined selfishness will, upon closer inspection, be found to be connected with such self-sacrifice. The unmeasured panegyrics of Jerome must indeed be set to his own account, but Jerome would not have praised after this fashion, unless he had been able to take for granted a certain amount of receptivity for such encomiums. His epistle to Pammachius flows at last into a kind of begging letter for his monastery at Bethlehem, and is certainly calculated to dispose Pammachius to giving; and what interested adulation do we not find in it! He calls Pammachius not only the general of the monks in Rome, he exalts him not merely above all the senators and consuls, but also speaks of the quartett of piety which the family of Pammachius has set forth, and sees the four cardinal virtues incorporate therein. Justice in Paula, prudence in Eustochium, fortitude in Fabiola, temperance in Pammachius. It is a proof of not only the vanity of Jerome himself, when he says: " Blesilla will never die in my books." Nor is this feature absent in the character of Paulinus of Nola. It is still in truth the proud Roman, handing the sportula to his clients, whom Paulinus describes, in his famous discourse "On the Treasury," and not the simple Christian, giving to his brother in love, when it is there said: " Many are expecting thee and looking eagerly for thy arrival, looking about when they see thee. It is one thing when thou prayest alone, another, when a multitude trembling before God, pray for thee. Thou art silent, they cry out for thee. And they see thee and rejoice ; they find thee and salute thee, they pray for thee in every church, they congratulate thee in every street, they keep thee in memory with thanksgiving to God in every place, and kiss thee though absent, when they kiss their hands." If Paulinus thought by such a description of the gratitude, which one who gives alms may expect, to incite to almsgiving, it is allowable to infer, that he was not himself far from entertaining such thoughts. In fact, Paulinus was very well pleased with the encomiums of his adorers, and made no ceremony of sending to Severus, who was about to put up his image in a chapel, as though he was already a saint, an inscription for the purpose. This secret self-approbation is the necessary result of alms having become a meritorious work. The simple works of a man's own calling were not duly esteemed, hence the works of a self-chosen renunciation were over-prized. Such renunciation is in truth only the reverse side of a worldly life, not a victory over it. The unnaturalness of luxury is left for the unnaturalness of an exaggerated asceticism, which does not however yield inward satisfaction, and therefore produces this need of excitement, which we find in almost all the characters described. Their Christianity impels them to great, to admirably great sacrifices, but to serve their brethren constantly and regularly in the position wherein God had placed them, was not even recognised as a duty. Thus a Christian perfection, as then understood, was attained, but not the perfection which the apostle sets before us as the end to be striven for, in the words : " Whatsoever ye do in word or deed, do all in the name of the Lord Jesus, giving thanks to God and the Father through Him."

Undeniably, this estimation of wholesale almsgiving did not continue. It was just the abundant gifts which flowed from Rome to Jerusalem, through the agency of Jerome, for the support of the monks living there, which gave occasion to Vigilantius to oppose it. His work, which is only known to us from Jerome's evidently very partial refutation, was directed against the over-estimation of celibacy, the exaggerated reverence of martyrs, the vigils held at their graves, and against those very alms, which were given for the saints at Jerusalem. He maintained that we should rather feed the poor in our own country. He also declared it better to make a reasonable use of property, to manage it justly, and gradually to apply the profits to the poor, than to sell it and give away all at once. Jerome's manner of controversy is undignified. When he has no reasons to bring forward, he tries to replace them by cheap raillery. He appeals to the history of the rich young ruler, and defends the gifts for the pious at Jerusalem by saying, that it is better to give to these poor than to others, because such poor as are not themselves godly, cannot fulfil the words : " They will receive you into everlasting habitations." Thus the final point is again a regard not to the necessity of those who receive, but to the reward which he who gives hopes for. For the rest, the irritable tone of Jerome gives reason to suppose, that the work of Vigilantius had made an impression. Nor did the refutation of Jerome everywhere find favour, his friends tried to prevail upon him to mitigate it. The attack, however, left no mark upon the prevailing tendency of the times, and Vigilantius was soon forgotten. It could not be otherwise. He had not perceived the deeper cause of the disease, and had fought only against symptoms. Hence his criticism could only be petty censure of single outgrowths, which could not repress the development as a whole. It was not till the connection between faith and love, as its practical proof, was rediscovered at the time of the Reformation, not till men's eyes were open to the true perfection to be striven for by all Christians, that a just moral estimation of earthly possessions, and consequently of alms also, could be arrived at. To require this of Jerome and his contemporaries, is to drag them out of their times. Let us then judge what they did from the standpoint of their age, and we cannot fail to acknowledge that they did truly great deeds, and that in these times also the power of the love of Christ was not left untestified.

Lastly, it will not be without interest to cast one more look upon the epitaphs of the period. They have this advantage over all other documents, that they bring us into most immediate contact with the times. We have, so to speak, the persons who acted before us; we see them in their acts and dealings, not merely the most eminent among them, not those only who fill a place in history, but plain and simple people. The older inscriptions afford us indeed but little information. They are distinguished, in contrast to heathen epitaphs, which detail all the merits of the departed, by their great simplicity. The name, age, day of interment, at most a short expression of Christian hope, a symbol, the fish, the dove, or a palm branch, is all. From the fourth century they are fuller, and follow the ancient custom of eulogizing the virtues and merits of the departed. This affords us the advantage, as we have said, of such a direct glance into Christian life, at this period, as no other documents are capable of furnishing. In numerous epitaphs then of the time, we find love to the poor, benevolence, abundant almsgiving, commemorated. A certain Junianus is called a "lover of the poor," and his wife Virginia, who is buried near him, "a lover of the poor, and zealous in good works."[71] Another married woman is also designated as a "lover of the poor."[72] We read in one of a Christian that "widows and orphans had in him a father," and of a Christian woman, that "noble by birth and rich in possessions, she was the mother of the poor."[73] "Charitable to the poor" is a frequently recurring eulogium,[74] and it is said of a merchant, "He was a refuge to the wretched and a haven to the poor." At the same time he is praised for having often visited the holy places, and diligently addicted himself to prayer and alms.[75] In the case of eminent persons, their charity is described in detail. "The poor went away from him happy, the naked left him clothed, the prisoner rejoiced that he was ransomed," is read in an inscription on Bishop Namatius of Vienna, who died in the year 522,[76] and upon another grave: "Devoting all to the stranger, the widow, the prisoner, he went, rich through pious poverty, to the stars."[77] The thoughts, too, which we have seen to be prevalent in these days concerning alms, the motive from which they were given, the expectations and hopes connected with them, are also reflected in epitaphs. We read: "He conquered avarice, which is wont to conquer all,"[78] and very often: "He sent his treasures before him to heaven," or, "He sent what was superfluous to heaven."[79] Of Bishop Hilarius of Arles, it is said: "A priest of God, who preferred the love of poverty to gold, and took the kingdom of God by force."[80] On one occasion we already meet with the formula "for the salvation of his soul." One Arenberga, it is said on her gravestone, gave liberty to a slave "for her soul's salvation."

Thus do even the gravestones show us the characteristic feature of the age, abundant alms-deeds, but with a view to the reward of eternal salvation, thereby to be attained. The really universal view, the view which had penetrated and was embraced by the people, was,— to conclude with two distinctive expressions of it,—that which Gregory the Great announces, and the Middle Ages countless times re-echo: The poor are not to be lightly esteemed and despised, but to be honoured as patrons, and as Eligius exclaims: "Oh, happy poverty, through which the heavenly inheritance is gained! Happy exchange, to receive the eternal and the unspeakable happiness of reigning for ever with Christ for the transitory!"

CHAPTER IV.

HOSPITALS.

IF the only thing effected by this age had been the creation of hospitals, it would have produced a grand result, and one deserving the gratitude of all future ages.

The old world was not acquainted with hospitals. There were only houses for the sick, for slaves, perhaps also for gladiators and for the army. There were near the temples of Æsculapius houses for the reception of the visitors, who resorted thither to seek for themselves or others advice in sickness by dreams, during the incubation of the god. Such a one, *e.g.*, existed near the renowned and much frequented temple of Æsculapius in Tithorea, and Antoninus Pius built one out of compassion, near the temple of the Epidaurian Æsculapius. But these were only hospices for shelter, and not hospitals for care and attendance.[1] There were also public hospices elsewhere, which were certainly the precursors of the Christian hospital. For the hospital at its first appearance was quite as much a house for strangers, a xenodochium, a hospice, and the first institutions of the kind received all who needed an asylum, strangers, the poor, widows, orphans, the sick, till by degrees there were separate institutions, according to the various classes of the needy; and thus hospitals, in their present sense of houses for the reception and care of the sick and infirm, were formed. Still the separation was not fully carried out. In the smaller places the xenodochia were, as a rule, employed for various purposes; and even in the larger towns, where there were already several institutions of different kinds, the separation was not a strict one.

The rise of hospitals has been regarded as a retrogression in charity.[2] It is said that they arose when love had waxed cold, that they ministered rather to ostentation, than to simple self-devoting love. This is, to say the least, a very partial judgment. What is true in it, I have already taken occasion to acknowledge. Hospitals had now become a necessity, and were, so to speak, the spontaneous result of the circumstances of the time. They were called into existence, on the one hand, by the extreme amount of misery, on the other, by the institutional impulse which then prevailed. It had been possible to provide for the small number of strangers and the comparatively few distressed persons of former times. They had found shelter in the house of the bishop, in the private houses of members of the Church, or, if needed, in inns, where they were provided for. When, since Constantine, the number of Christians rapidly multiplied, and distress at the same time increased, such expedients no longer sufficed; institutions were needed. This is palpable. But I should like to refer also to the other co-operating moment, viz., that the whole period had a strong propensity to institutions. It is a special characteristic of this epoch of civilization, that everything becomes institutional. The time of free movement is past; everything is organized, comprised in appointed forms, and indeed, because vital power is lacking, more in the way of force than of free development. Let us only remember what we have seen to be the case in the organization of labour. In an age in which the bakers, butchers, etc., formed settled corporations, institutions, that is, so to speak, for the maintenance of the public, it is the more explicable, that charity also should become institutional. If this may be in a certain sense a retrogression, compared with the time in which there was no need of institutions, it is in another sense a progress—a progress never again lost to mankind and to the Church. For since then there have always been institutions, hospitals, of different kinds, and just during the periods in which love has vigorously revived, has it shown itself specially active in the foundation and superintendence of such institutions.

Obscurity covers the beginnings of hospitals. It cannot be said when or where the first xenodochium was founded, nor what thoughts and purposes led to its foundation. The supposition, that the difficulty of maintaining the numerous believers whom Constantine released from the mines and prisons, was the occasion of it, is quite without foundation.[3] The notion, that there were formerly in the bishop's dwelling, or connected with it, special rooms for the reception of strangers, and that the origin of the xenodochium was merely the separation of these rooms from the abode of the bishop, the building of a separate house for strangers, may far rather be entertained. I believe, however, that this cannot be proved, and also that there is no need of such suppositions.[4] Quite sufficient starting-points for the xenodochia are to be found in the hospitality, which was always esteemed an eminent Christian virtue, in the obligation of the bishop to receive strangers, which continued even after the existence of xenodochia. Augustine, *e.g.*, still entertained strangers at his table; also in the inns (pandocheia), which had long existed, and which it was the duty of the deacons to visit, for the purpose of giving assistance to certain suffering strangers. Undoubtedly the chief occasion lay in the increasing numbers of poor and suffering who had no shelter, for the xenodochia were from the first not especially intended for strangers, but for poor strangers and the poor in general, so that the house for strangers and the poor-house, the xenodochium and ptocheion or ptochotropheion, were quite synonymous.[5]

It is generally considered that the first xenodochia were already founded in the time of Constantine. There is, however, none that can be certainly proved to have arisen during the reign of the first Christian emperor.[6] The first perfectly authentic information is found in the efforts of Julian to promote the restoration of paganism by the erection of xenodochia and ptochotrophia on the part of the heathen.[7] He commanded Arsacius, the high priest in Galatia, to establish a xenodochium in every city, " so that strangers may experience our humanity, and not our own people only, but whoever is in need." For means he refers him, partly at least, to public property. Of the 30,000 bushels of wheat and 60,000 sextares of wine delivered as imposts, one-fifth is to be applied to the heathen worship, and four-fifths to such humane purposes. But Arsacius is also to teach the Greeks— and this is specially deserving of notice—to contribute to such works of humanity. " For it is disgraceful, when there is not a beggar found among the Jews, and when the godless Galileans support our poor as well as their own, that our people should be without our help." The efforts of Julian himself may evidently be characterized as an imitation of Christians. Hence there must have been already xenodochia and ptochotrophia among them, nay, such institutions must have been already widely disseminated and their efficiency recognized. We must then admit, that their first appearance was still earlier, but the five-and-twenty years of Constantine's reign offer a sufficient period of time for this. On the other side, institutions of this kind were, even in the times of Julian, somewhat of a novelty. It is just during the last third of the fourth century, that we hear much of the foundation of xenodochia. About 370 Basil founded the famous hospital in Cæsarea, which had from him the name of Basilias, and this institution was quickly imitated in all the towns of Cæsarea. Even in the country there were already ptochotrophia.[8] Somewhat later Epiphanius testifies to the existence of xenodochia in Pontus, where they were called ptochotrophia.[9] In Edessa, about 375, there seems as yet to have been none. For when Saint Ephraem came to the town at a time of famine, and saw the great misery which prevailed there, the starving and the sick, he rebuked the Christians for their hard-heartedness. They excused themselves on the plea, that they were indeed willing to give, but did not know to whom to entrust their gifts. Then Ephraem offered to administer their charity. He had three hundred beds provided in a colonnade, and provided for the hungry, and even for the strangers who flocked into the town.[10] In Antioch there was a tolerably large xenodochium, when Chrysostom was preaching there.[11] He exercised in this sphere also his loving, and at the same time practical mind. He employed what, thanks to his economy and simple mode of life, was left from the church revenues, in erecting two hospitals at Constantinople.[12] In Ephesus

Bishop Brassianus, whose episcopal dignity gave occasion to long discussions in the Council of Chalcedon, founded, when he was a presbyter, a hospital with eighty beds.[13] At this very Council of Chalcedon (451), this institution appears, in a canon regulating the position of clergymen in houses for strangers or the poor, as one generally disseminated and regularly met with, at least in the East.[14]

It then spread from the East to the West. Even the reception into Latin of the titles xenodochium (also senodochium, sinodochium)[15] and nosocomium, which were not till afterwards replaced by hospitium and hospitale, points to this origin. The first hospitals in the West are the house for the sick founded by Fabiola in Rome, and the house for strangers founded in Portus by Pammachius. Paulinus of Nola established in that town a house for strangers in connection with a monastery. Thus it was the circle dependent on Jerome, and connected through him with the East, that "transplanted," as he expresses it, "this twig of the terebinth of Abraham to the Ausonian shore."[16] The institution does not appear to have spread very rapidly in the West. In the time of Ambrose there were still no xenodochia in Milan; Augustine on one occasion describes them as quite a novelty. He himself induced Leporius, a presbyter who lived a monastic life with him, to build one in a garden belonging to him.[17] In Rome, Pope Symmachus (498–514) built abodes for the poor near three churches, and Pelagius II., a ptochium; while Belisarius, the general of Justinian, founded and endowed a large xenodochium in Rome.[18] In Gaul the Council of Orleans (549) is acquainted with xenodochia in the towns. There was especially a large institution of the kind at Lyons.[19] From the letters of

Gregory the Great, we obtain the impression, that in his time at least there was a large number of hospitals in Italy. He mentions such in Naples, in Sicily and Sardinia, and when we see, that several of those in Sicily were in the unimportant see of the Bishop of Cagliari, we may well conclude, that the institution had then taken root in the West also, and that a home for strangers and the poor, a hospital, was there also reckoned among necessary ecclesiastical arrangements.[20] They could not indeed be as yet of as splendid a form in the West as in the East. Dr. Lange reckons in Constantinople thirty-five hospitals of all kinds,[21] and the legislation of Justinian shows us, how fully developed the life of such institutions then was. In the West, so long as the storm of the migration lasted, they continued to be both less numerous and simpler; they there produced very specially happy results, and were still more amply developed under the new German forms of government.

As we have already remarked, the institutions in their earlier days combined various objects. They were in general asylums for the needy and homeless of every kind. In them strangers found a shelter, beggars a maintenance, the sick care and attendance. Even the different designations, which seem to refer them to special branches of charity, did not exclude the assistance of other kinds of distress. The homes for strangers were also homes for the sick and poor, and *vice versa*. In Fabiola's house for the sick, the poor also were received, and in that of Pammachius for strangers, the sick also. Chrysostom's homes for strangers were at the same time houses for the sick. The legislation of Justinian shows, even by the multiplicity of their names, the many-sided development of the institutions. We there find Xenodochia (houses for strangers), Nosocomia (houses for the sick), Cherotrophia (houses for widows), Orphanotrophia (Orphanages), Brephotrophia (houses for the rearing of little children, whether bereaved of friends or foundlings), Gerontocomia (houses for the aged). A house of the latter kind was founded, besides others, by Narses, in Constantinople. John the Almoner instituted, in various quarters of the town of Alexandria, besides the Xenodochia and Nosocomia it already contained, seven houses for the reception of poor lying-in women, in which they might find beds and necessary food and attendance.[22] Justinian built in Constantinople a house for the reception of fallen women, called a home of penance.[23] This was not, however, like the Magdalene hospitals of our days, an asylum and an institution for improvement, but on the contrary, a conventual institution of discipline, females in general being in those times often accustomed to undergo their punishment not in prisons but in convents. For the rest, it is going too far to infer, from the occasional mention of the blind, the dumb, and the insane in hospitals and monasteries, that there were there already institutions for the blind, houses for the deaf and dumb, and asylums for the insane. At all events, such were also received and cared for by the monks. Theodoret relates of the monk Thalassius,[24] that he assembled about him blind beggars, and taught them to praise God, and solicited, from all who came to visit him, contributions to supply the blind with necessaries. The insane were also received in the monasteries on the island of Tabennæ in the Nile;[25] but there were as yet no special institutions for their reception.

The means for maintaining these institutions flowed from various sources. If the institution was a direct establishment of the Church, the revenues of the Church were applied to its support. In Antioch, Chrysostom reckons the keeping up of the xenodochium and the maintenance of the sick received into it as among the burdens which the church bears, as well as the support of the poor whose names were on the Matricula.[26] In Alexandria, John the Almoner appointed regular deliveries of corn from the revenues of the Church, for the supply of the hospitals.[27] If private individuals founded an hospital, they also endowed it with either funds or landed property. Basil solicited and obtained from the rich of his church means for the maintenance of the Basilias. Pammachius, Fabiola, Paulinus of Nola, and other founders of homes for the sick and for strangers, gave the sums required out of their private property. To this was added the gifts of Christian people, which flowed in abundantly. Special collections also occur.[28] At first the State also seems to have participated in the maintenance of the hospitals. At least a law of the Emperor Gratian of the year 382 reckons the reparation of the hospitals among the *munera sordida*. But this already fell through under Valentinian.[29] The xenodochia and all kindred institutions are, from his time onwards, treated as matters purely ecclesiastical, and entirely under the management of the Church, and the State confines itself to protecting and fostering these institutions by legislation. The same privileges which the Church possessed were now accorded to the institutions. Their presidents had the same immunities as clerics, the institutions themselves the rights of moral individuals, including therefore the right of acquiring property and receiving legacies. Specially important was the enactment, that in case any one had, in his will, left orders for the building of an hospital, and his heirs did not execute them within the space of a year, the bishop of the place was empowered himself to undertake the building, and arranging, without being bound by any dispositions, that the testator might have made concerning the administration of the hospital, the appointment of officials, etc.

Besides, whatever authority the testator might have given to his heirs with respect to the foundation and management of the institution, the rights due to the bishop were in no wise to be prejudiced. The chief superintendence of all the benevolent institutions of his diocese was allotted to the bishop, whether they were directly founded by the Church, or founded and endowed by private individuals. It was he who nominated the officials, the xenodochi, ptochotrophi, orphanotrophi, had the supervision, took care that the institution fulfilled the ends for which it was appointed; it was to him that accounts were delivered, and by him that jurisdiction was exercised. The letters of Gregory give us a glance into the care devoted by conscientious ecclesiastical superiors to these institutions. How great is his anxiety for the xenodochia, not only in the episcopal see proper of Rome, but also in the wider sphere in which the sovereign position of the Bishop of Rome was already acknowledged. His letters contain copious directions of the kind to the *defensores* by whom he exercises the oversight of the property of the Romish Church, and also already of the bishops. In Sardinia a xenodochium has fallen into decay, he orders its restoration. In Naples a certain Isidorus has left a legacy for the building of a xenodochium. The *defensor* is to see that the will is carried out. If the means are insufficient for the building of a separate xenodochium, the legacy is to devolve to the already existing xenodochium of St. Theodore. In Cagliari the accounts of various xenodochia of the bishopric have not been, as formerly, brought before the bishop. He is to take care that this is done regularly. He is also to give heed, that such men are placed over the xenodochia as have been found worthy by their lives, their morals, and their diligence.[30] The Church knew what a treasure it possessed in the hospitals, and what assistance they had afforded during the fearful times of distress which had overwhelmed the West. But for them, it would have been still less possible to get the mastery over the abounding misery. How many, whom the troubles of the times had driven from house and home, found here a shelter; how many sick and maimed, who would have perished in the streets, found loving attendance; to how many starving was food dispensed; to how many naked, raiment; all knew that here there was a place of refuge for all. "The door of this house is open to all," are the words of an inscription found in Africa, which had probably stood over a xenodochium.[31] Nay, when the storm of an irruption of barbarians raged over the country, when towns and villages lay in ashes, the houses of mercy were certainly the first to rise again from the ruins. A true shepherd of the flock would rebuild "the house of the Christian poor" before his own, and when the storm had passed, these houses were, as well as the churches, the centres about which the flock could assemble.[32] In the East they, together with the whole Church, were ossified; in the West there was still a rich development before them; they were there destined to become for centuries the special vehicles of charity, and we shall hereafter see how this development had now already begun.

Our information is not sufficient to afford a correct picture of the arrangements of the xenodochia. These undoubtedly differed, according to the size and purpose of the institution. There were smaller institutions, such as the houses in large towns, called diakonia, and afterwards matriculæ, where the deacons provided for the poor of the district; and there were larger, up to those which comprised several buildings. The Basilias in Cæsarea is described as a town before the town. In the centre was a church, round it a large number of single houses, arranged in due form in streets, some being for the reception of the sick and needy of various kinds, others for the servants and officials, others for workshops, where all that was required for the institution was prepared by workmen of its own.[33] We no longer possess representations of a xenodochium of this time, still remains are in existence of some, though certainly of only such as served as asylums for the reception of pilgrims, and were in connection with churches situated near sacred places and famous shrines, and these enable us to form an image at least of them. In Central Syria two such buildings have lately been discovered. One of these is, according to the inscription on its portal, a Pandocheion (asylum for pilgrims), consecrated on the 22nd July 479. In Deir Sem'an, where a monastery of St. Simon Stylites, in which was still shown the pillar upon which the saint spent whole years, attracted many pilgrims. Still larger is a Pandocheion in Turamin. It is a stately building, directly connected with the church, surrounded on three sides by a colonnade. It contains on each of its two stories a large hall, evidently for the reception of pilgrims.[34] If small Syrian places can show such asylums for pilgrims, we may imagine that the xenodochia and hospitals of the larger towns, at least many of them, must have been large and stately buildings. As the age delighted in a profusion of decoration in its magnificent ecclesiastical buildings, so too did those which served the purposes of charity testify to the wealth and power now attained by the Church.

But it is the personal attendants that have most interest for us. Besides the physicians, of whom the nosocomia at least had several of their own, many attendants were, of course, required for various services. These were, partly at least, hired. One class of them was the so-called Parabolani or Parabalani, who also played a not very creditable part in the ecclesiastical history of the times, being more frequently the strong guard of tyrannical bishops, and interposing with their fists in the dealings of synods, as *e.g.* at the so-called Robber-synods. This gives no attractive picture of their agency; they appear as rough and excited fanatics. They are probably the same that are called "leaders" in the description of the Basilias,[35] and their duty was to seek out the sick and suffering, to lead them into the hospitals, and then attend on them while there. They, like the Copiates, the buriers of the dead, belonged to the clerical body, as its lowest order. There were hundreds of them. In Alexandria, Theodosius II., 416, reduced their numbers to five hundred, on account of the disturbances they had excited at the Eutychian controversy, and placed them under the supervision of the imperial prefect. Two years later their number was again raised to six hundred. We may hence conclude, that the numbers of those who were received into charitable institutions was very considerable.

Certainly the Parabolani were not the only personal attendants. In the West there seem to have been no

Parabolani. We frequently meet also with those who attended gratuitously on the sick and poor. We have already heard this of Fabiola, and Theodoret tells us the same of the Empress Placilla, the wife of Theodosius the Great. She went herself into the hospitals, made the beds of the poor, gave them their food, and waited on them like a maid-servant. When remonstrated with on this account, she replied: "If the Emperor distributes money, I will willingly do this for those from whom he received the Empire."[36] Similar examples frequently occur. There were also those, who sought to make amends for their former sinful lives by serving in hospitals.[37] Or the intention was to lead in them a monkish and ascetic life.

The close connection between the xenodochia and monachism is, moreover, worthy of remark. It was just the teachers who promoted monachism, who were also the cherishers and promoters of xenodochia, viz. Basil and Chrysostom in the East, and Jerome in the West. The circle of ascetically living men and women assembled around Jerome, and the persons connected with them were just those who transplanted the institution to the West. The xenodochia were often combined with monasteries or were themselves a kind of monasteries. We are often unable to decide whether a monastery or a xenodochium is before us. A sign of this similarity is found in a story told by Palladius of two brothers, both rich, who resolved to lead an ascetic life. The one gave all his money at once to the poor, the churches and monasteries, learnt a handicraft and lived as a monk. The other built "a monastery" with his money, in which with certain brothers, he received the poor, attended to the sick, provided for the aged and fed the poor. The monks were contending together as to which had done best. But St. Pamleo decided: They are both equal, for the one has fulfilled the saying of our Lord: "Sell all that thou hast, and give to the poor;" the other is like the Lord, who says: "I came not to be ministered unto, but to minister."[38] The xenodochium of Paulinus of Nola and that of Severus, mentioned by him, were very like monasteries.[39] We may certainly accept it as a fact, that both the male and female attendants in hospitals (not to mention those who were properly speaking its servants) led a monastic life. This applies especially to the West, where, as far as I see, the monastic element was stronger in the hospitals than it was in the East, with which is connected the circumstance, that there were there no Parabolani. Gregory the Great expressly requires, that such only should be chosen as presidents of the hospitals, as were "*religiosi*," *i.e.* as were monks and nuns; and when he adds, that this is to be the case, that the secular rulers may not have the power of bringing them before the judgment-seats, and of thus finding opportunity for plundering the goods of the xenodochium, this addition only discloses another strong reason, which could not but lead to an organization of personal attendance of a more and more monastic kind. We find here the germs of the ministrant orders, the hospital orders of the Middle Ages.

In other respects too did the development of the hospital resemble that of the monastery. As the monasteries were at first entirely subjected to the regular supervision of the diocesan bishop, so too were the hospitals; and as monasteries, towards the end of this period, already received certain rights and privileges, and became more independent of the diocesan, so too do we

Y

find in Gregory's letters the first example of the exemption of an hospital. Bishop Synagrius and Queen Brunhilde had founded a xenodochium in Augustodunum. The president was called the Abbas, and there were *monachi* as attendants. Hence the xenodochium was a hospital and monastery in one. Gregory now appoints, that nothing of what has been or shall afterwards be given to the xenodochium shall under any pretence be withdrawn from it. The abbot is to apply all, according to his discretion, to the purpose for which it was bestowed. If the abbot dies, none other is to be obtruded upon the institution, than one chosen by the king with the consent of the monks. He can only be deposed on account of a crime. In this case the bishop is not to pass sentence alone, but only in conjunction with six other bishops.

We have here already the beginnings of the subsequent development of the hospitallers. As the monasteries were combined into close orders by the reception of a common rule, so also were the attendants of single hospitals combined into an order of hospitallers. And as the monasteries were released by exemption from episcopal supervision, and became an independent power beside the hierarchy, so did the hospitallers become the self-dependent vehicles of a charity independent of the more and more stunted relief of the poor by the bishop. A compensation was formed for that church relief of the poor which was now extinct, viz. the hospital, and—by its side, and in manifold combination with it—the monastery.

CHAPTER V.

MONASTERIES.

WE have already had frequent occasion to remark, that the charity of this period bears upon it a strongly monkish and ascetic feature. This is in conformity with the character of Christian charity in general in these times. The monk became in increasing proportion the ideal of Christian life. A monkish life was esteemed philosophic, angelic, apostolic, truly Christian, and it follows that the life of other Christians was also judged according to this standard, esteemed the more highly the nearer it approached to the monkish, and thought the less of the more it swerved from it towards the secular side. Hence this character was impressed upon charity. But monachism had a still more direct influence upon the development of charity. It created for it a second centre; the monastery appeared beside the hospital as its abode. Hence we cannot avoid taking a nearer survey of monachism.

The beginnings of monachism have recently been made the subject of much discussion. The attempt has been made to remove its origin and formation somewhat farther back than formerly, even to the second half of the fourth century, and at the same time to seek for all kinds of starting-points in præ-Christian religions. The Therapeutæ, the servants of Serapis, even the Buddhists and Indian Fakeers, are said to be the models of the Christian monks. Neither of these questions is here of concern to us, for however early or late we may place the first beginnings of monachism, it is certain that in the last quarter of the fourth century it was already a power, which determined the type of Christian piety; and even if such præ-Christian starting-points did actually exist, they would at most have been able to afford an occasion for the rise of monasticism, while the real inward impulse, which caused its rapid growth, which drove thousands into the wilderness and into monasteries, must have been one existing within Christianity, and lying in the state of the Church itself.

The key to the right understanding of monachism, as well as of the tone of Christian piety in general in this age, is found in the fact, already frequently touched on, that the leaven of Christianity never thoroughly penetrated the mass. A transformation of national life by the spirit of Christianity was never attained. Now it is a law of Christian life that if the leaven of the gospel cannot penetrate the national life, it will draw back. The more public life proves itself impenetrable with respect to the Christian spirit, the greater is the tendency to separation. And this was then also the case. Those who were in earnest about their Christian life, began to retire from association with the rest, whether entirely, by going into the desert or the monastery, or partially, by at least leading a more or less isolated life within the Church. Men despaired of pervading the whole mass with the leaven of the gospel, and were contented, that there should be individual saints and perfect Christians. With this was then connected a second element. The genuinely ancient notion, the distinction between philosophers and the common people, the aristocratic feature by which ancient ethic is predominated, again found acceptance in Christianity, and in entire correspondence with ancient ethics, the contemplative life of the Christian philosophers, of the monks, was esteemed as higher and better than the life of ordinary Christians, living and working in the world. But we here encounter a phenomenon, which is at first sight a very strange one, viz., that just monasticism, which flees from the world, should create in the cloister a new centre for charity, from which immeasurable blessings have accrued to society; and that the circles addicted to contemplation should become the starting-point for a new development of labour; that the cloister was the school in which the world learned again to work.

The Roman Empire was now externally Christian,—much, indeed almost everything, was wanting for it to be internally so; indeed, Christianity did little more than graze the skin of the ancient world. What we have before us is in truth only a turbid mixture of heathenism and Christianity. Even the widely disseminated custom of deferring baptism as long as possible, and till just before death, is characteristic. Men desired to remain as long as possible in the mongrel position between heathenism and Christianity, to shun the obligation of being entirely and fully Christians, and were willing rather to reserve the absolute expiation of baptism for the effacement of all preceding sins, than to labour for their sanctification in its power. For a long time even Christian emperors were still invested with the office of *Pontifex Maximus*, and were thus as Christians still at the head of the heathen cultus. When consuls entered into office, auguries were still employed, and even in Salvian's time, the sacred fowls which generals took to battle with them for the purposes of the oracle, were fed at the expense of the State.[1] Nor was the case different in private life. There too, heathen and Christian ways were strangely intermingled. Prayer was now made to the Christian God, but if He did not help immediately, and as desired, recourse was had to the ancient gods, and they were still honoured according to the old custom, though only from fear lest they perhaps might do some mischief. A Christian as well as a heathen mother would hang an amulet round her child's neck, to protect it from witchcraft, only she liked to take a text from the Bible or Testament for the purpose. The Synod of Laodicea had even to forbid the clergy to practise astrology, or prepare amulets. The undoubtedly Christian epitaph on a child, of the year 364, discovered in Rome, designates the hour of its birth as, according to astrological maxims, an unlucky one, evidently for the purpose of accounting for its early decease. On the birth of a child, even in Christian families, a number of candles were lighted, and a name given to each. The child then received the name of the candle which burned the longest; this was said to ensure him a long life.[2] The churches were frequented, favourite preachers were applauded by the clapping of hands, pompous worship was delighted in, but to the multitude it was but a spectacle like any other. The crowds that flowed into the circus or the theatre were as numerous as ever, and often more so,[3] and were just as passionate as formerly in their partisanship for the different colours in the chariot races. The gladiatorial games were not abolished, until in Rome a monk once rushed in between the combatants and thus sacrificed his life. The true faith was contended for, dogmatical propositions excited passionate strife, the formula of the then prevailing orthodoxy was in the mouth of every artisan in his stall, of every female seller in the vegetable market in Constantinople. It was, as Theodoret on one occasion complains, as if our Lord and Saviour had only commanded us to hold certain doctrines, and had given us no precepts at all concerning our life and walk.[4] Chrysostom once compares the Church to a woman formerly rich, but now in reduced circumstances, still showing indeed the chests in which formerly lay the treasures which she had long ago lost.[5] Of moral amendment little or nothing could be traced in the masses. Debauchery, covetousness, deceit, were now as formerly prevailing crimes. "Where is the catholic law, in which they believe?" exclaims Salvian; "where are the examples of chastity and piety which they learn? They read the Gospels and commit lewdness; they listen to the apostles and intoxicate themselves; they follow Christ and are plunderers; they lead a life full of all unrighteousness, and yet boast, that they possess the pure law."[6] In Carthage it was the Vandals, who after their entry, first abolished the utterly shameless debauchery, and, as owned by the better-minded Romans, restored chastity and morals. An incredible levity possessed the people; even the fearful chastisements with which the Empire was visited, were unable to suppress it. The theatre was the first building restored in Treves after it had been burned by the Germans, and it was soon filled again with a joking, laughing crowd. "Rome is dying and laughing." says Salvian with bitter irony,[7] and we are even more touched than by this saying, by the melancholy lament of Chrysostom: "When I think of this frivolous multitude, who clap their noisy approbation of my words, my heart is deeply grieved; and when I return to my solitary chamber, I begin to weep bitterly."[8]

Let us not, however, imagine that the word of God then bore no fruit. There were besides the frivolous, light-minded, morally perishing multitude, many active Christians fully in earnest about their Christianity. The Church has never been richer in great moral characters, both male and female, than then. We can comprehend, however, how obvious it seemed to such, to separate themselves as true Christians from the corrupt mass of ordinary Christians; we can understand how it came to pass, that in an age in which the contrast between heathens and Christians was gradually disappearing, and the former impulse to an earnest Christian walk had been lost, the contrast in Christendom itself, between perfect and imperfect Christians, should impress itself with ever increasing distinctness. This contrast had indeed long existed; long had it been the custom to distinguish between commandments binding upon all, and counsels, which it was the way of perfection to follow; long had there been an inclination to place the contemplative above the active life, to prefer a meditative to a practical Christianity. It was now, however, that these notions first attained, so to speak, a palpable form, that the severance was also externally effected in monachism, that the ideal of the Christian life was incorporated before the eyes of other Christians, in the monk and the nun, and that even those who did not go into the desert or the cloister, still strove as far as possible after this ideal, and led, even while living in the congregation, a really separate life. Such a contrast, however, if once introduced, would, by an inward necessity, be step by step increased. The leaven had withdrawn from the mass; it was self-evident, it was quite in order, that it could not be pervaded by the Christian spirit, that it was and must remain the corrupt world. The fulfilment of the duty of Christianizing the life of the people was entirely given up, nay, it was no longer recognized as such; that the multitude should be what it was, was regarded with indifference, nay, to a certain extent, with inward satisfaction, because this dark background brought into more prominent relief the holiness of the few perfect Christians.

It was just the soil of the decaying ancient world, that was favourable to such a process. In monachism also, as everywhere in these times, ancient and Christian ideas were mingled. Here too do we come upon a reaction of that ancient life, which was repressed in the earlier times of Christianity. For it is very characteristic to find monachism called philosophy, and the admirers of a monkish life so willingly applying the analogy of the philosophic life. In fact, it belongs to the ancient circle of thought to place the contemplative above the practical, the active life. Aristotle expressly declares dianoetic to be higher than ethic virtue, *i.e.*, a life passed in contemplation superior to a life of action. True happiness is found in leisure; a life of thought is, compared with an active, a busy life, godlike.[9] Quite in accordance with this, the contemplative life of the monk was now set up in Christendom as angelic, as higher than that of the Christian active in the world, while according to the gospel the ideal is the mutual interpenetration of the contemplative and the active life, the union of prayer and work. The distinction too between counsels and commandments, between the duties of the perfect and the ordinary Christian, finds its starting-point in the ancient view. Ambrose exactly adopts in his ethic the distinction of the Stoics between perfect and medium duties. He regards as perfect duty what the Lord required of the young ruler, viz. to forsake all.[10] It was a fundamental thought of ancient ethic, that there were different kinds of virtue, a virtue of masters and a virtue of slaves, a virtue of men and a virtue of women, the virtue of the multitude and that of the wise, while the gospel on the contrary declares all these distinctions indifferent, and knows of but one duty, one virtue for all. How decidedly did the Church in the first centuries oppose this aristocratic feature of the ancient world! While the adversaries of Christianity made it a reproach, that artisans, women, and slaves are by it instructed in the same wisdom, directed to the same life, the apologists boast of it as the glory of Christianity, that it fills even the poor and simple with the same spirit, adorns them with the same virtue. The ancient spirit was now reacting, and we come, in the midst of Christendom, upon the same distinction between Christian philosophers practising a more exalted virtue, and the masses who must be contented with a lower, against which Christianity once contended. From this point of view it is also intelligible, that just the men, who were most strongly imbued with the ancient spirit, who had appropriated the culture of the philosophical schools, were such special admirers of the monastic life. To mention only Basil and the two Gregories, whose path led from the schools in Athens to solitude, to the monk's cell, whose whole type is properly a combination of the philosopher and the monk, and in the West men in whom, as in Ambrose, the old Roman spirit can be so strongly traced, and who, not in spite of it, but because of it, so energetically advocated the monastic life. To just such natures must the monastery have appeared a release from all the misery, the unnaturalness, the hollowness of the life of those times. In fact, we are reminded of Rousseau's flight from civilization, when Jerome depicts to Pammachius in Rome, how charming life is in the fields of Bethlehem,[11] or when Gregory of Nazianzus reminds Basil[12] of the days when they "revelled in privations," the vigils, the prayers "of that superterrestrial and incorporeal life," that community, that spiritual harmony of the brethren, who were raised to a godlike life. We get a deep insight into the motives which then drove many into monasteries, in a narrative which occurs in the *Confessions of Augustine*, of two attorneys at the court of Treves, who in a walk come upon monks, and find with them the work of Athanasius upon monasticism. "Tell me," says one to the other, "what do we attain by our efforts? What are we seeking? Why are we serving? What better hope can we have than that of gaining a closer friendship with the Emperor? And even if we do so, how fragile is fortune! Through how much danger are we striving after greater danger! And when shall we attain this object? On the other hand, if I desire to be a friend of God, I am so at this very moment." They forthwith resolve to renounce the world and become monks.[13]

In fact, it was freedom that was sought in the cell of the hermit and in the monastery, freedom from the misery of a decaying world, from a state which was but an institution for the employment of force, and left no space for free activity, from a society in which only deception and appearance bore rule, from a civilization which had become hyper-civilization and was therefore unnatural. It was this that drove the decurion unable any longer to bear the burden of taxation, the artisan who had become the slave of the State, the impoverished small proprietor, nay, even the aristocratic and wealthy Roman educated in the schools of Athens, into the cloister. For even the possession of wealth, even a liberal education was in this perishing world a burden which men sought to get rid of. He who built a cell in the desert, who entered a monastery, was released at a stroke from the whole burden, was free from all bonds. For monachism denied on principle the whole existing order, it denied the State and marriage, all social and civilized life, and strange as it may seem, it was for this very reason in a condition to become the starting-point of a new civilization.

The rise of monachism set a seal on the renunciation of penetrating the entire national life with the Christian spirit. Not that such renunciation was consciously, though it was actually made. It is quite self-evident, that an avowedly Christian life was now a demand made only of monks or of those who lived a monkish life. It was they who were the converted, the followers of Christ, the religious; they who lived after the Spirit, who were the special militia of Christ, contending for eternal life. Others were indeed Christians, but Christians of a lower grade. Christians properly so called, were only those who had renounced the world—widows, virgins, those who had taken vows of chastity, monks, ecclesiastics. We need only read Salvian to be convinced, that he looks upon these as alone such. A separation of this kind must have had a destructive effect upon Church life. A Church life like that of the first centuries became thereby impossible. All active Christianity exhibited a more or less monkish impress, separated itself from ordinary Christians and thus lost its influence over them. Even so zealous a favourer of monachism as Chrysostom felt it necessary to warn the pious in his flock, not to withdraw from the society of other Christians, whom they might influence for good.[14]

But the appearance of monachism has also another side; its influence was not merely destructive, it was also promotive of Christian life. The monasteries became its home and hearth, in them was assembled all that still remained of decided Christianity, to recommence from them the process of penetrating national life with the Christian spirit. The proper destiny of the cloister still lay in the future. Even monachism and monastic life can only be understood in the light of the divine purposes. The ancient world was now impenetrable by Christian truth. It was the German world which was to be and could be a really Christian one. The transmission thereto of Christianity, and in connection with Christianity, of the ancient culture as the foundation of a new culture, was to be effected especially through the co-operation of the monasteries. The hand of God was building in them the fortresses, in which Christianity might maintain itself, when the Barbarian deluge should overwhelm the Roman Empire, and from which should proceed the Christianization and civilization of the new nations. Monachism, whose principle it was to flee from the world, became the world-conquering power, and all that Christian life, of which the old world was deprived by the cloister, turned to the advantage of the new German world.

It is truly a strange world, that we get a glance of, by reading the history of the fathers of monachism, the description of the life of Antony ascribed to Athanasius, Palladius's *Historia Lausiaca*, the *Historia religiosa* of Theodoret, or the life of St. Martin by Sulpicius Severus, and his *Dialogues*, and at first sight we seem to have before us anything but the beginning of a new development of Christian civilization. Everything seems, on the contrary, antagonistic to civilization, nay, to be directed towards the abolition of all civilization, of all existence worthy of human nature, while all that is put forward as Christian life, nay, is admired and honoured as holiness, as a godly and angelic life, has not the slightest similarity to primitive Christianity. These anchorites living apart from all men in deserts and forests, in caves and leafy huts, these recluses who, immured for life, receive their scanty sustenance, perhaps a handful of barley, through a small aperture, these swarms of monks, men of uncouth manners, roaming through the country, and feeding like cattle on the herbs of the field, make upon us at first a revolting impression. Here is one who has carried fasting so far as only to require food once a week; another who does not eat his barley till it is halfrotten; this man sprinkles his food with earth and ashes to make it less palatable, while that one lies all day long in a swamp and exposes his body to the stings of insects. They are on more intimate terms with the beasts than with human beings. A she-wolf bears one of them company, a chamois selects herbs for another, that he may eat nothing poisonous. St. Martin commands the birds, who are catching fish in a pond, and they fly away; he rebukes a dog, and he ceases from pursuing a hare. Miracles everywhere take place, the strangest, most fantastic, and at the same time most purposeless of miracles. Especially are these holy men constantly contending with demons, who wander about in the desert, sit on the rocks, and annoy men in their homes. St. Martin even delivers a cow from a demon who is riding her, and an imperial post-horse on whose neck a demon is seated. But we should be dealing very unjustly to judge of monachism by such circumstances. This often tumultuously fermenting movement clears, and monachism assumes quite a different appearance in a well-ordered monastery, in a society of monks living according to an appointed rule. Decidedly as we must reject the claim that the apostolic life is here realized, we cannot still mistake the existence of a certain similarity between such a brotherhood of monks and the earliest Christian churches. We here again meet with that which the existing churches no longer exhibited, viz. a society of men and women, all Christians and desiring to live as such. However much the requirements of Christianity might in several points be misunderstood by them, they were still in earnest about them; and though they secluded themselves from all who did not belong to their society, there was still within it a fellowship of love, common prayer and work, each serving the whole in self-denial and obedience. And these monastic communities were free from all the hindrances which elsewhere opposed, as insurmountable barriers, the development of a Christian life. For them this whole corrupting civilization had no existence. Within the walls of the cloister, it was possible to make an entirely new beginning.

Nowhere did this new beginning come forth more illustriously, than in a department of moral life, most closely connected with charity, viz. in that of labour. The monasteries were the birthplaces of free labour. In them was felt for the first time full earnestness concerning the moral duty of work as an evidence of Christian life, and for this very reason are they of such vast importance to the further development of charity. For as we have often had occasion to remark, and as Scripture directly shows, labour and benevolence are inseparably united.

Where there is no work, there will be no energetic, permanent exercise of benevolence, and it is in this, that work first fulfils its higher moral purpose. It is Christian to work that we may have to give to him that needeth.

If we remember the economical condition of the Roman Empire at this period, we shall easily perceive that free labour could not thrive in it. Where all was force, where the Decurion was bound to his office, the *colonus* to the soil, the artisan to his *collegium*, there was no room for free labour. The monk was free. The State indeed did not allow every man to become a monk. When harassed and oppressed peasants and townsmen fled by thousands to monachism from the control of the State, it was forced to interfere, to save its own existence. But he who had once become a monk had all this constraint behind him. In the monastery was to be found, what was to be found nowhere else, a place for free work. As long as monachism appeared only in its first irregular form of anchoritism, work, at least profitable and useful work, was out of the question. As soon, however, as a regular monastic life was formed, labour was one of its fundamental ordinances. As the quickly perceived moral dangers of solitude led to the gathering of isolated monks into monasteries, so did the dangers of idleness impel to work. "Be always working at something," writes Jerome to Rusticus, "that the devil may always find you employed." In Egyptian monasteries it was the custom to receive none who would not bind themselves to work, and this not so much for their necessary support, as for their souls' health.[15] And a proverb much in use was, "A monk who works is troubled by one evil spirit, an idle monk by countless ones."[16] "Solitary life," says Basil, "is contrary to the nature of true love, since each cares only for what himself needs, nor will such a one easily perceive his faults." In his rules for monks, Basil already lays great stress upon work.[17] "It is among the duties of a monk to work."[18] Idleness is a great evil; work preserves us from evil thoughts. We are not to think that the aim of a pious life gives countenance to idleness and avoidance of work; it is, on the contrary, a life of conflict and of much labour. The object of work is certainly, in the first place, to earn a livelihood; still this is not its only object. We work to please God, and that we may fulfil the Lord's command: "I was hungry and ye fed me." "Every one must in work keep in view as his object the support of the needy."[19] Work also must have its appointed order, and must alternate with prayer and singing psalms. Each is to do the work he is fitted for, and which the head of the monastery gives him to do. None is to go from one thing to another, none arbitrarily to give up his own handicraft.[20] According to locality, such work as the material may be easily procured for, and as will find a ready sale in the neighbourhood, is to be chosen; also such as will not disturb a peaceful and quiet life. Basil esteems the weaving of simple stuffs as the best; carpentry, cabinetmaking, and forging, also agriculture, are in themselves useful, but they make too much noise and disturb the brethren. Only as much art is to be employed as is necessary in the article required, simplicity and cheapness must in every case be the rule.[21] If we may consider, as we may, that these rules of Basil were even approximately put in practice, nay, if they were probably for the most part taken from what was already acted upon, we have before us a society of free workers, such as the ancient world knew not of. Though at first only in small circles, secluded from the rest of the world, the New Testament ideas of work are here realized. Work is done, because God commands it; each perseveres in the work of his own vocation, work and prayer are combined, labour alternates with rest, and the object of work is not the merely selfish one of earning for oneself, but also that of serving others.

Elsewhere, too, do we learn, that the monks of the East were workmen. They make baskets, sew sacks, weave, and carry on, to a small extent, agriculture and horticulture.[22] Chrysostom describes them as follows:— "Having renounced all earthly possessions, they use the labour of their bodies for the support of the needy. They divide the day between prayer and handiwork. They put us all to shame, both rich and poor, when they, who have nothing but their hands, earn money for the poor."[23] Theodoret tells us of the monk Theodosius in Cilicia, that he directed those who came to him to work. "For," said he, "it is not fitting, that they who live in the world, should support their wives and children, bear the burden of taxes and customs, offer the first-fruits to God, and assist the poor, while we put our hands in our bosoms and live upon the work of others."[24] In the East, however, the monasteries did not become a civilizing power. The contemplative tendency was there stronger than the active. Idle meditation and fantastic asceticism got the upper hand. Pillar-saints, who passed whole years standing on a column, recluses who had themselves immured, anchorites who renounced in solitude all participation in the products of civilization, here passed for great saints; while the Western monks were carrying on in silence the work of civilization, clearing forests, draining morasses, converting barren tracts into fertile fields, and becoming the instructors of the young German nations. It was in the West that monachism first fulfilled its vocation, it was there that the cloister first became a school of work.

It cannot indeed be said, that work was made more prominent in the rule of St. Benedict of Nursia, which prevailed in the West, than in that of Basil. Western monachism was in the first instance a growth transplanted from the East to the West, but it there found a different soil. A Gaul, who became a monk, was already very different from an Egyptian or a Syrian, and, as must be well considered, the tasks set before monachism in the West were also different. Both circumstances are brought forward in the comparison made by Sulpicius Severus between Eastern and Western monachism. With a certain amount of wholesome humour, he dwells upon the fact, that the Gaul, with his often derided appetite, cannot live like the monks in Egypt,[25] and brings it forward as the greatness of St. Martin, that "in the midst of the throng and in the company of people," he did just as much as those anchorites, who in their solitude were hindered by nothing.[26] Western monachism was from the first placed in the midst of the great problems of civilization. While the East, ossifying in Byzantinism, was becoming a mummy, and monachism was accordingly stiffening in resultless contemplation and unnatural asceticism, a new era of civilization, with new duties, was setting in in the West with the entry of the Germans, and the important feature in Western monachism was just the fact that it entered into these duties of civilization. The same maxims concerning work in the rules of St. Benedict as in those of Basil, could not but be carried into practice quite differently in the West from what they were in the East.

On the first appearance of monachism in the West, we

meet there too with the same inclination to idle contemplation. Men sought in the monastic life a wished-for opportunity for inaction, and to be supported by the charitable gifts of others, instead of earning their own living. Scripture was appealed to, and idleness was given out as the fulfilment of Christ's command, to take no care for the morrow, while the apostolic rule: He that will not work, neither let him eat, was set aside by a spiritual interpretation. This inclination to holy idleness is energetically opposed by Augustine in his work *On the Work of Monks*. He replies to the monks, who appealed to our Lord's words about the birds of heaven, that they ought then neither to grind nor to cook, for the birds do neither, nor ought they to lay up in storehouses. He says banteringly, that then God must give them wings, that they may seek their food in the fields. No man, he continues, can live without stores, without property, hence it is every one's duty to work. If any one is weak and unable to work, God will provide for him by the gifts of others; but if he can work, God provides for him by giving him work and blessing it.[27] He brings to bear upon the monks in the most decided manner the plain and literal meaning of the apostolic rule: " He that will not work, neither let him eat." He who has entered a monastery as a slave, a freedman, or an artisan, is to go on working there; he who has entered as a rich man is, after giving away his property, to begin working, if he possibly can, that, by such an example, he may show still more mercy, than by even giving away his goods. " For the rich do not humble themselves in the warfare of Christ, that the poor may be exalted. In no wise is it becoming, that in the life in which senators become workers, artisans should be idlers, and that when landowners give up all the enjoyments of life, peasants should live in luxury. If those out of the upper classes work themselves, they deprive the humble of every excuse."[28]

That it should be just Augustine, whose credit in the Church was for centuries so decisive, who should so write about the work of monks, as to make labour their duty, was of the greatest importance in the development of the Western monasteries. In fact we hear far less of idle monks in the West than in the East. Asceticism was here less strict. "The Gallic appetite" must be taken into account, but work was also more zealously pursued; and when Benedict gave a single settled rule to monastic life, which had before been multiform, it gave full expression to just these characteristics of Western monasticism, moderate asceticism, and a prescribed combination of meditation and labour. Seven times a day did the brethren, according to Benedict's rule, assemble at the seven canonical hours in the church. Their remaining time was divided between work and meditation. The day began with four hours' work, the next two were devoted to the reading of the Scriptures or good books. After dinner there was a time of rest, then work again till supper, and again a shorter period of work till bed-time; for "idleness is the enemy of souls."[29] The diet was more or less nourishing in proportion to the work, and in the time of summer labour rations were increased.[30] While in Eastern monasteries agriculture fell into disfavour, as too noisy and too alien to meditation, it took the first place in the Western, and it was just in this respect that the monks produced such great results. Gaul, which had become almost a desert, was re-cultivated by them, the monasteries became everywhere the advanced posts of civilization, the monks made roads and built bridges, and it was from them that the

Franks and other German races learnt agriculture, handicrafts, and arts.

By work the monasteries obtained the means not only for their own support, but for extensive benevolence. We have already seen how Basil lays down, in his rules, as the proper object of work, not merely the earning of our own maintenance, but also the assistance of the needy. Certainly what was earned went in the first instance to the support of the brothers, but what was over was then to go to the poor outside the cloister, that, as it is written, the sun may rise upon the evil and the good.[31] It is generally interesting to observe, how, notwithstanding the high estimation in which asceticism was held, the consciousness that love is of higher value and greater use breaks through. When St. Spiridion was once visiting an exhausted stranger, he, saint and great pastor as he was, had meat brought up, although it was a fast-day, nay, ate himself in company with the stranger. "For," as he explains, "to the pure all things are pure. To show love to a stranger is more than fasting."[32] It is said of Evagrius, a monk, that he advised a brother, who was greatly tormented by night visions, to attend on the sick, and that, being asked the reason of this advice, he replied: Such visions are more certainly dispelled by works of mercy than by anything else.[33] Such traits are evidently reported with approbation, a proof that a feeling still prevailed, that the exercise of mercy more promoted the inner life than any chastisement of the flesh. Hence much is related also of the charity of the monks of the East, in spite of their tendency to contemplation. Cassian[34] tells us, that the monks of Egypt not only supported themselves by their labour, but also assisted those districts of Libya which were suffering from famine, and supported the

Christians who were languishing in prison for their faith's sake under Valens; and Augustine relates,[35] that the monks in Syria were able, by diligent work and moderate living, to send whole ship-loads of provisions to different districts. Strangers, beggars, the sick, found reception in the monasteries. A xenodochium for their use was combined with many cloisters. The monk Thalassius collected blind beggars about him in the district of the Euphrates, built them dwellings, taught them to sing psalms and Christian hymns, and procured them a maintenance from his many visitors.[36] Even children were often brought into the monasteries to be taught. In these rude times wealthy parents thought their children were most securely concealed in monasteries, and were glad to see them led from their earliest years to monkish piety. Basil in his rule gives precepts, as to how the children are to be brought up in separate dwellings, and Chrysostom boasts of how much the monks did in education.[37]

All this was in the West comprised in settled orders. Among good works, or more strictly speaking, among the "the tools of the spiritual art," by the handling of which eternal life is obtained, Benedict reckons, immediately after naming fasting, feeding the poor, clothing the naked, visiting the sick, burying the dead.[38] According to his rule, the care of the children, the sick, the strangers, and the poor is imposed upon the cellarius of the monastery, and he is to interest himself in them with all diligence, in the consciousness that he will have to give account at the day of judgment.[39] The porter is to answer every stranger who knocks, every poor man who begs, with "Thanks be to God!" and then to give him a kind reception. The poor and strangers are to be received with respect, and attended to with care, for in them is Christ received. The prior is to eat with them, and is for their sake to break off fasting, except on the great fast-days. Spiritual food, reading of the Scriptures and prayer, is to be added to bodily.[40] Many a poor man, many a stranger, many sick found shelter, food, and restoration to health in the cloister. Other kinds of benevolence were also among monastic virtues. The cloister was a source of blessing to its neighbourhood far and near. In times of scarcity, in the irruptions of the barbarians, it was the monasteries that preserved the miserable remnant of the population from starvation, that sheltered them, that inspired them with fresh courage. Benedict himself, during a famine in Campania, made no ceremony of causing all the stores of the monastery of Monte Cassino to be distributed to the poor, trusting to God to bestow fresh ones. One Abbot Suranus acted in like manner, on the occasion of an invasion of Upper Italy by the Lombards.[41] And when the floods of the migration gradually subsided, the monasteries were capable of becoming the centres of a new civilization, and the monks of becoming, as indeed they did, the instructors of the young nations.

CHAPTER VI.

THE CHURCH THE REFUGE OF ALL THE OPPRESSED AND SUFFERING.

AMBROSE reckons it among the duties of an ecclesiastic to take an interest in the oppressed and suffering. "Your office will shine gloriously, if the oppression of widows and orphans attempted by the powerful, should be hindered by the servants of the Church, if you show that the command of the Lord is more to you than the favour of the rich."[1] In fact the command of the Lord was more to the Church, than the favour of the great and powerful, of imperial officials, and of the Emperor himself, when the question was to protect the oppressed, and to assist the poor and needy. Not that there was, even in such action, any lack of hierarchical presumption and self-complacent monkish exaltation. When Bishop Cyril of Alexandria offered violent resistance to imperial officers, when a monk of Constantinople, in arrogant conceit of his own sanctity, excommunicated the Emperor Theodosius II. (who did not rest till the ban was removed), the canon of Ambrose, enjoining that "we must not, in our obedience to the Lord and our love to the brethren, appear to act more from vanity than from mercy," was not observed, and transgressions of the kind frequently occur. In spite, however, of such transgressions, it is one of the most brilliant and honourable pages in the history of the Church which we are now about to turn over. It was when misery became greater and greater in the perishing world, when the arm of the State was more and more paralyzed, when the authorities no longer offered assistance to the poor and the oppressed, nay, themselves took a part in oppressing and exhausting them, that the Church became on a grand scale the refuge of all the oppressed and suffering.

Among the means at the command of the Church, for the fulfilment of her destiny in this respect, the preaching of the Word of course stands first. Boldly did such men as Gregory Nazianzen, Chrysostom, Augustine, who, in spite of their pompous rhetoric—a rhetoric characteristic of the period—will always be reckoned among the greatest orators of any age, rebuke the vices of the times; boldly, too, did they openly and specially reprove the sins of the rich, the great and the powerful. To this was added the means of discipline. The oversight, which the Church exercised upon the behaviour of all her members, now extended, so far as they were Christians, to the imperial officials, nay, even to the Emperor himself.

Even in the year 305, the holding of a magisterial office was held to be so incompatible with church membership, that, according to a canon of the Synod of Elvira,[2] any one invested with the office of duumvir, was obliged, during the period of his magistracy, to withdraw from the Church. In the year 314, however, a Synod of Arles decrees,[3] that if a Christian becomes prefect of a province, a testimony to his church membership is to be given him, for the bishop of his seat of office. This bishop is to watch him, that he may commit no injustice, and not till he does something inconsistent with church discipline, is he to be excluded from the Church. To be a Christian and to fill a magistracy were, since the relation of the State to the Church had become a friendly one, no longer regarded as incompatible. But the Church by no means gave up the claim to inspect the behaviour of such of her members as filled magisterial posts, and if necessary to exercise discipline upon them, as upon any other member. Athanasius excommunicated the viceroy of Lydia, notorious for his cruelty and excesses; and Basil, who had made this excommunication known to his flock, could testify to him, that the Church agreed with it.[4] After Synesius of Ptolemais having in vain warned the Prefect Andronicus to cease from his injustice and his oppression of the people, excluded him from the Church. No church was to be open to him, no priest to enter his house.[5] Even the Emperor was not too high for the word of exhortation and, if necessary, the discipline of the Church to reach him. When the inhabitants of Antioch were trembling before the wrath of the Emperor, because they had overthrown his statues in a tumult, Bishop Flavian went to Constantinople to intercede for the town, and to dispose the Emperor to leniency, while his presbyter Chrysostom comforted the people and kept up their hope by daily sermons, the famous "statue sermons" of the great orator. When, however, judicial proceedings began, and hundreds were thrown into prison and cruelly tortured, a monk seized the bridle of the judges, as they were riding through the streets, and cried to them: "Tell the Emperor: You are not only an emperor, but a man, and those you reign over are your fellow-men. Human nature was made in the image of God; do not then so mercilessly and cruelly destroy the image of God." Chrysostom had the pleasure of being able to proclaim to the people the Emperor's pardon, and they were expressly Christian motives, which led the Emperor himself to this decision. "What merit is it in me," are his words, "who am but a man, to renounce my revenge upon other men, when the Lord of the universe, who took for us the form of a servant, and who only did good to men, prayed to His Father in heaven for those who crucified Him?" Nay, when Theodosius the Great had not so moderated his easily-excited wrath, but had taken fearful vengeance on the city of Thessalonica on account of a tumult, thousands of innocent persons, women and children, having been massacred by his soldiers, and was afterwards about to visit a church in Milan, Ambrose met him at the door, and expelled him from both the church and the sacrament, until he did public penance, a step which honoured the Emperor no less than the bishop, and proved to the whole people, that there existed in the Church a spiritual power, which afforded protection against even the absolute ruler of the world.

Far-seeing statesmen could not but perceive, that such action on the part of the Church would at last be to the advantage of the State, that the Church was in this sense a power protective of the State. Theodosius was well aware of it. When Ambrose, a few days after his ordination as bishop of Milan, remonstrated with him on account of the conduct of some of his præfects, he answered him: I have already experienced your candour, and yet I consented to your elevation to a bishopric; therefore give us help, as the divine law prescribes, in our sins.[6] The feebler the State became, the more was its power transferred to the Church, and that with its own consent. The interposition of the Church in favour of the oppressed became the subject of legislation. Already, before Constantine, an episcopal jurisdiction, independent of the Church, had been formed within the Church, and this was now formally recognised, and still further extended by the State. Ecclesiastics were bound by it, it was free to other members of the Church to apply to the bishop's court, if they chose; but if they had once subjected their cause to it, the sentence of the bishop was binding and unalterable. If the poor and humble could, in the increasing corruption of imperial tribunals, scarcely obtain justice, it was of the more importance that recourse to the tribunal of the bishop should be open to them. It was also the right and duty of the bishop, to interest himself in those who had been condemned by imperial justice, especially those condemned to death; and if they often asserted this right to a wider extent than was consistent with a strict administration of justice, nay, occasionally sought to obtain, in spite of it, favour for the guilty, it still often afforded them the means of interposing in behalf of those unjustly condemned, or of mitigating a jurisprudence which, as often happens in times of decaying civilization, had again become barbarous. The thought lying at the basis of all these enactments is, that it is the part of the Church to exercise humanity and advocate mercy in opposition to strict justice. Hence the oversight of the prisons and the duty of providing for the humane treatment of prisoners were also transferred to the Church, as well as the care of widows, orphans, and exposed children, and that of the chastity of women and young girls. Finally, and this is a point deserving of special attention—the State recognised the Church's right of sanctuary. This right it was, which furnished her with such powerful assistance in the fulfilment of her task, for in sanctuary a temporary refuge at least was open to all, who desired protection against violence and oppression.

The temples and altars of the gods, the images also of the Emperor,—for he was esteemed a god,—had rights of sanctuary among the heathen. He who fled to them might not be violently taken away. This right was transferred to the Church, when Christianity became the dominant religion.[7] At first it was the altar—the holy table—that was esteemed a sanctuary. Afterwards, because it seemed unfitting that fugitives should sleep at night in the church, by the altar, or should eat and drink in the church, the accessory buildings, the court, the bishop's dwelling, and the surrounding space to thirty paces' distance, were admitted to the right of sanctuary. The Church insisted strenuously, that here there was peace, and imperial legislation acknowledged it, with certain limitations. No one might take refuge in a church with arms; he must deposit these in front of the church. Nor might any one incite to tumult and rebellion from the church. The sacred places were to be places of peace with regard to both sides. Nor was an asylum open to all without distinction. Murderers, adulterers, carriers-off of virgins and public debtors were excluded. Sanctuary was not to contribute to the escape from punishment of the really criminal. It was only to afford a refuge to those who were unjustly pursued, and to enable them to assert their rights; it was to secure to them the first necessary protection, that they might take steps towards reconciliation with their adversary; by the temporary safety of the pursued, time was to be won, that meantime the first wrath might blow over, and room be obtained for mediation and intercession. Hence the sojourn in sanctuary was limited to thirty days. During this time, the fugitive, if poor, was to be maintained at **the expense of** the Church. The Church, however, not merely received the fugitive into her peace, but also advocated his cause. When an unjust judge was desirous of forcing a rich widow to marry him soon after her husband's death, she fled to the church, and Basil protected her.[8] When a debtor, sued for about seventeen solidi (£10, 15s.), fled to the church, Augustine paid the debt for him.[9] When the quarrels of individuals were in question, the Church did not deliver up a fugitive until his adversary had sworn on the Gospels, that he was willing to be reconciled to him. The fugitive had on his part to take the same oath.[10] The Church vindicated this right, if needful, with all energy. He who violated the right of sanctuary was excommunicated. It was just because the Præfect Andronicus despised the right of sanctuary, and issued a decree forbidding fugitives to take refuge in the church, declaring that he knew where to find them, even if they were embracing the feet of Christ, that Bishop Synesius was induced to pronounce excommunication against him. Nor was Basil terrified by the threats of the præfect, who cited him before his tribunal, from defending the fugitives who had fled to the church.[11]

Equipped with such means for the protection of the oppressed and suffering, the Church extended her shelter to them in the most various ways, and exerted herself on every side in mitigating the immense mass of misery with which the Roman Empire was filled. As we are about to survey what she did in this respect, as the advocate of all the suffering classes of the population, we must in reason begin with those who belong to its lowest grade—the slaves.

We have seen above (p. 190 sqq.), that the notions of the Church concerning slaves were far removed from emancipation, and this was still more the case during this period, than in that of the conflict. The Church was now living at peace with the State, and had itself become a power preservative of the State. But the institutions of slavery, and the bondage now to so large an extent existing and continuously increasing, were inseparable from the State of those days. The Church then recognised these institutions so far as herself to enter into them. She was herself a slaveowner. In the canons of Councils in which Church property is computed, slaves are, in conformity with the laws of the day, reckoned, as well as estates, houses, moveables, as a part of her possessions, and the bishop was just as much bound to retain the slaves as to preserve the rest of the Church property. He was as little able to alienate them as any other possession, except such as fled, and were, after they had been recaptured, troublesome to keep:[12] these he might part with, as other masters also did with refractory and unmanageable slaves. He might not give them their freedom, for this would be a deterioration of Church property. He was only permitted to do so to a very small extent, viz., when individual slaves had deserved especially well of the Church. He might then also settle landed property upon them, but not above the value of twenty solidi (£12, 10s.). To this extent his successor had to recognise the manumission and donation.[13] Nay, the Church was as decided in the assertion of her rights as any slaveowner could legally be. If the descendants of slaves—decrees the Synod of Orleans, 541[14]—are again found in the place to which they belong, the bishop shall demand them back, and they shall remain in the same condition in which their parents were. Laymen who keep back the offspring of Church slaves are excommunicated. Gregory the Great makes no ceremony of having a fugitive slave brought back "by any means" from Otranto, though he was also torn from wife and children, to serve as a baker in Rome.[15] The monasteries also possessed slaves. Here the rights of property were even increased. The bishop might, under certain circumstances, give freedom to individual slaves, the abbot not at all, "for it is not fair, that, while the monks work, their servants should be idle."[16] As the Church asserted her own right in the matter of slaves without scruple, so did she also protect the right of others. If in the preceding period a slave might be ordained, even against the will of his heathen master, this was now unconditionally forbidden. A bishop who ordained a slave, or a *colonus* who was a bondsman, against the will of his master, had to pay double his value as a compensation, and was subject to Church penance.[17] Nor could the monasteries admit a slave or bondsman as a monk, against the will of his master.[18] The consent of their masters was unconditionally required for the marriage of slaves. If a male and female slave were to flee to a Church to be married, against the will of their owners, such marriage was invalid, and ecclesiastics are not to defend such a connection.[19] These facts must warn us, that certain passages in the Fathers, which speak of the original freedom of all men, are by no means to be understood in the sense of the emancipation theories of later times. Many such expressions are also found in this period. It is much dwelt upon, that God created all men free, that the distinction between masters and servants first entered the world through sin, that Christ redeemed and made all men free, that in Him all men are brethren, all equal. But these words would be entirely misunderstood, if the conclusion were to be drawn from them, that it is therefore wrong to possess slaves, or if they were used to prove, that it was the duty of Christians to set their slaves at liberty. Even Chrysostom, who so frequently brings forward these very thoughts, does not demand of his hearers, that they should release their slaves, but only declaims against the keeping of numerous slaves, as against all luxury, and recommends his auditors to limit themselves to a few. But these few a Christian may keep with a good conscience, if only he takes care of them and treats them in a Christian manner. A document, in which Gregory the Great gives their freedom to two Church slaves, is in this respect very characteristic.[20] "As our Redeemer, the Author of the whole creation, took upon Him human nature for the purpose of releasing us by His grace from the chains of bondage, in which we were held, and of restoring us to our original liberty, so is a salutary action performed, when men, whom nature from the beginning made free, and whom the rights of nations have subjected to the yoke of slavery, are restored to the freedom in which they were born." This saying is often quoted[21] to prove, that the Church regarded slavery as a relation antagonistic to the universal dignity of man, as an injustice, which it was the duty of every Christian to repair. But it is not so often noticed, that Gregory, immediately after these words, carefully defends the rights of the Romish Church under certain circumstances to the property of the manumitted slaves, that he therefore, as his conduct at other times sufficiently shows, does not intend to abolish entirely the right of slave-owning, nor by any means feels it against his conscience for the Church to possess slaves and to deal with them according to prevailing laws.

Such expressions concerning the original freedom of all

men are to be understood from the standpoint of the views of the time, and not till we try thus to estimate them, shall we, instead of spuriously imputing to the Church notions of an abolition of slavery, of a compensation for it by a powerful middle class, which she never entertained,[22] perceive what she really effected for the slave, and this was something truly great. Let us not forget, that the teachers of the Church also regarded the unequal distribution of property, the distinction between rich and poor, the subjection of the wife to the husband, nay, the existence of the State as opposed to original Divine order, and first entering into the world through sin. Chrysostom on one occasion[23] even declares the bondage inflicted by the power of the State upon the freeborn to be the harder, compared with slavery, and Gregory Nazianzen, in a sermon on love to the poor, places poverty and wealth quite on a level with freedom and bondage, and says: "Poverty and wealth, freedom and bondage, are not original institutions of God, but came into the world through sin." The Church had just as little notion of abolishing slavery, as of doing away with the distinction between rich and poor. She expected the abolition of all these conditions in the perfected kingdom of God; till then, the Christian must bear them with patience. But as the Church strove to mitigate the hardships existing in these conditions, and so too the hardships of slavery, and as she took under her protection all the oppressed, all who were suffering from the troubles of this life, so also did she extend it to slaves.

This she was now capable of doing to a far greater degree than formerly, for, as the dominant Church, much greater resources were, as we have seen, at her command. Above all, however, she sought now as formerly to influence both masters and slaves by the preaching of the Word. How frequently does Chrysostom, how frequently does Augustine, speak in his sermons of the relations of masters and slaves! The slave is exhorted to faithful service, and referred to the example of Christ, who Himself became a slave. "Only see," cries Augustine [24] to slaves, " Christ did not make slaves free masters, but bad slaves good slaves. What thanks do not the rich owe to Christ, for keeping their households in order! If they have an unfaithful servant, Christ converts him, and does not say to him: Let your master go, you now know your true master; your master is ungodly, you are believing and righteous, it is not fitting that the believing and righteous should serve the unbelieving and unrighteous. Christ speaks not thus, but says: Slaves, look to my example, for I too served the unrighteous! for from whom did the Lord, who endured so great sufferings, endure them but from the slaves, and the bad slaves, whose master He was." By the Word of God the Church dispensed moral power to slaves, to prove themselves, even in this condition, truly free, to bear in faith and hope the hardships it involved. They were taught, that to be born in slavery was a temporary matter, that true nobility consisted in willingly humbling themselves to serve their neighbours. As Christ destroyed death, so that now only the name of death remains, and it has in truth become but a sleep, so too only the name of slavery remains, and in truth slaves have become free men and brethren through Christ. The stain of slavery is removed from him who serves not against his will, but from the resolve of his will, for Christ's sake, he is a free man.[25] "Slaves," as Augustine [26] says, "are themselves to exchange their bondage for liberty, by serving not in slavish fear but in true love," and he comforts them with the hope of the time "when all unrighteousness shall be over, when all dominion, all human power shall be done away, and God shall be all in all." On the other hand also, the Church sets before masters in good earnest, their duties towards their slaves. This was, alas, but too much needed; and this continued harsh treatment of slaves was another symptom how little the spirit of Christianity had penetrated Romish society. The stick ruled even in Christian houses, and many a Christian woman was as little ashamed as a heathen lady, of cruelly chastising her female slave for the most trivial fault. Augustine even maintains the right of a master to strike his slaves,[27] "only it is to be done in just and allowable measure;" and Chrysostom felt it necessary frequently to exhort to more lenient treatment in his sermons—on such occasions it is striking to find that he especially addresses himself to the female portion of his audience. He concedes, that the slaves have faults, but reminds his hearers that "there are other means of correcting them than the stick. Kindness would effect more than fear." "They are inclined to drunkenness: take from them the opportunity of getting drunk. They are inclined to unchastity: marry them. This slave is thy sister in Christ. Has she not an immortal soul like thyself? Is she not honoured by the Lord Himself? Does she not sit at the same table of grace with thee?"[28] What the preachers of the day inculcate upon masters is, that it is their duty to improve their slaves, that they are responsible for their souls. A father of a family, says Augustine, takes care also for his slaves like a father for his sons, to lead them to the true worship of God;[29] and when interpreting the text, "He that will take thy coat, forbid him not to take thy cloak also," he seeks to apply it to a man's whole property, but excepts his slave, " if he is brought up better, more morally and more consistently with the honour of God, by thee than he can be by him, who would take him from thee." [30]

Where her words produced no effect, the Church gave them emphasis by punishments. He who treated a slave cruelly, or killed him without a judicial sentence, was excommunicated.[31] The sanctuary of the Church protected also the fugitive slave. If a slave fled to a church, he was not delivered up to his master, till the latter had taken an oath on the Gospels, that he should not be punished.[32] Even if the slave was guilty, the Church protected him, at least from the worst. The master had thus only to swear that he would not corporeally chastise him by strokes or death; but he was allowed to cut off his hair or to keep him to hard labour.[33] The clergy, too, often interposed as mediators for the slave. Basil succeeded in inducing one Callisthenes by his intercession to spare the lives of two slaves.[34]

That the manumission of slaves was esteemed a good work, is already shown by the before-quoted document of Gregory the Great, though quite other notions prevailed in it than that of a general though gradual abolition of slavery. The Church as little contemplated this, as an abolition of property, when she declared it a good work for any one to renounce his property. Under this point of view, it may be stated that the Church approved of manumission, exhorted to it, gave the act the appearance of an ecclesiastical one, by having it take place in the church, and so imparting to it a religious consecration. Hence Chrysostom, in speaking of luxury in general, exhorts to an emancipation of superfluous slaves. Necessary slaves might be retained, only the superfluous were to be set at liberty and taught a trade.[35] It is on this account that we meet with the circumstance, that those, who desired to enter upon a monastic life, first deprived themselves of their slaves, as of the rest of their property. Augustine and his clerics gave freedom to their slaves, when they were about to commence in common their monastic life.[36] Melania freed all her slaves— according to Palladius, 8000,—when she left Rome to begin a conventual life. In epitaphs also we meet with the manumission of slaves, "for the soul's health."[37] It is in this sense too that we must understand the reply of Abbot Isidor of Pelusium, to a man of rank, who applied to him to be allowed to retain one of his slaves: " I should not have thought, that one who loved Christ, who knew the mercy that makes all men free, would have a slave."[38] It is the monk, in whose eyes one who loves Christ is, one who has renounced the world, who speaks in these words. This too accounts for the important influence of monachism upon slavery; and here we come upon as apparently contradictory a phenomenon as before. An institution calculated in the first place entirely to deprive men of liberty, utterly to absorb freedom in monastic obedience, was essentially to contribute to its restoration.

He who became a monk, quitted a secular for an "angelic" life. For him, therefore, all that is distinctive of life in this world no longer existed. For him there was no State, no marriage, no property, and therefore no longer the distinction of rich and poor, of bond and free. In the sphere of monachism slavery was virtually abolished. It was on this account, that so many, who desired to escape from the fetters of the life of those times, streamed into the monastery. This was especially the case with slaves, many of whom ran away from their masters under the pretence of "leading a pious life." The matter became so serious, that not only had Emperors to interfere with the secular arm, but the Church also. One Eustathius, probably the same whom we meet with as bishop of Sebaste, consistently carrying out monastic notions, invites slaves to leave their masters and assume the monastic habit, that they may at a stroke abolish their servitude. On the other hand, a council held at Gangra, the capital of Paphlagonia, interposes and decrees: " If any one, under the pretence of piety, advises a slave to leave his master and run away from his service, and not to serve his master with good-will and full respect, let him be anathema."[39] This canon, which obtained universal validity in the Church, was quite consistent with those views of slavery, which, as we have seen above, prevailed in the Church. But the consistent carrying out of a monkishly ascetic isolation from all secular life, could not fail to result in the entire dissolution of all human relations.

Hence the idea of monachism could not be in every respect carried out, and monachism, if it had continued in anchorite isolation, would never have become the civilizing power it did. It was obliged to take up its position in the world, in a certain sense to re-enter the world, and consequently to give up that entire renunciation of slavery, which its principles involved. In the East these principles were so far carried out, that the monasteries kept no slaves. In the West, no scruple was felt on the point.[40] Nay, slavery was in this case even more stringent, inasmuch as the slaves of a monastery had no chance of being set at liberty. This apparently unfavourable distinction of a

Western monastery turns out upon closer observation to be in its favour. The monachism of the East, which retired entirely from the world, and was in its purely contemplative character without influence or result, could well dispense with slaves. That of the West needed them for its work of civilization. But it was just through this work of civilization, that it contributed far more than Eastern monachism to the internal conquest of slavery. The fruit, indeed, was not reaped till centuries afterwards. But still the idea of monachism was even now working itself out in this direction. Whoever became a monk—for which certainly in the case of a slave, the consent of his master was required—was free, and that for ever. The slaves of monasteries were treated with absolute kindness. The monks themselves shared their labours in the field. Besides, the high respect in which monachism was held, could not but influence masters the more willingly to give their freedom to such slaves as desired to become monks, while the Church, if needful, exercised a certain amount of pressure to obtain their consent. Lastly, the idea, that it was a step towards perfection to deprive oneself of slaves, as of any other possession, could not fail to extend itself far beyond the sphere of the convent, and to dispose many to the manumission of their slaves. It was the persuasion that they were thereby doing a work well-pleasing to God, that induced many of the rich and great of this world to give freedom to their slaves, and often in great numbers, especially by testamentary disposition; and the Church, decidedly as it maintained the lawfulness of slavery, energetically promoted this tendency. The manumission took place in church, in order to make it clear that the slave owed his freedom to the Church and its influence; and when once he was free, it was the Church again who protected and defended him in his freedom in these rough times. It is often laid down in the canons of Synods, as being expressly the duty of the Church to protect those who have been legally emancipated by their masters.[41] And if the freedman, for whom his master no longer has to provide, should, as so often happened, fall into distress, it was once more the Church who assisted him with her exercise of mercy, with her gifts and benefits.

There was yet another point of view, which induced the Church to take an interest in slaves. Their servile relation must not be allowed to hinder them from fulfilling their church obligations, must not endanger their salvation. It was on this account, that the Church so often impressed upon masters the duty of allowing their slaves to attend public worship and to keep holy days. Thus, *e.g.*, the Council of Orleans, 511, decrees that slaves are not to work on the Rogation Days, held at Ascensiontide.[42] It is true that Constantine had already forbidden the Jews to keep Christian slaves,[43] but this prohibition seems not to have been carried out. In the 5th and 6th centuries we frequently find Jews owning Christian slaves; indeed, the slave-trade of the times was chiefly in their hands. It was they who bought prisoners of war from the barbarians, and brought them into the slave-market in the Roman Empire. Among them were also Christians, or slaves who, at first heathen, afterwards became Christians. But that a Christian should be in bondage to a Jew, seemed not only unworthy, but with the hatred still borne by Jews towards Christians, dangerous to his faith and salvation. Hence the Church regarded it as a duty to take a special interest in such slaves. The Council of Orleans, 538,[44] insists that they shall be protected, if their

Jewish master exacts from them anything contrary to the Christian religion, or if he punishes them for a fault which has been already remitted by the Church. A Synod held three years later in Orleans, goes still further. It appoints, that if a Christian who is slave to a Jew, flees to a church or to another Christian, he is to be ransomed according to a just valuation, which appointment the Synod of Macon extends to the decree, that every Jew must submit to the redemption of his Christian slaves at the settled price of ten solidi (£6, 7s.).[45] If he refuses to accept this price, they are without further ceremony free. Finally, Gregory the Great entirely forbids the keeping of Christian slaves by Jews. He declares it to be an objectionable and abominable thing. He even permits such slaves as only intend to be Christians, to flee from their masters, and assures them of the protection of the Church. He likewise limited the trading of the Jews in Christian slaves, a limitation [46] which was the more important, because, as it was just the Jews who carried on so flourishing a trade in slaves, the prohibition must have directly co-operated in the limitation of slavery itself.

Next to the slaves were the serf-coloni and the tenants who held estates by hereditary tenure for a rent of natural products.[47] These were frequently treated in an unjust and arbitrary manner by their landlords. Even when the year was a bad one, when the harvest failed, the same supplies were demanded from them, or a money payment according to high market prices. When, on the other hand, there was a good harvest, money payments at the lowered market prices were refused, and more demanded. Rent was arbitrarily raised, demanded twice over, or the supplies required to be delivered in larger proportion. If the tenants had to deliver them at an appointed place, which was often across the sea, and if the corn already sent were lost on the way, through shipwreck or any other misfortune, it was not credited to them, but they had to send it once again.[48] In short, as much as possible was, without consideration, got out of them. "How they ill-use the poor farmers," exclaims Chrysostom; do they treat them more humanely than the barbarians do? They do not hesitate to impose insupportable burdens, daily heavier, upon those who are perishing with hunger, who are toiling away their lives. Whether the land yields anything or nothing, they always demand the same.[49] In them too the Church took an interest. Theodoret in a letter entreats a landowner for some indulgence towards the coloni of his flock: "Have pity on the labourers who have laboured in the fields and have gained but little. Let the scanty harvest be an occasion to thee of a plentiful spiritual harvest."[50] Augustine seriously appeals to the conscience of one Romulus, concerning his oppression of coloni, on whom double supplies were about to be imposed, and threatens him with eternal judgment. "They toil for a short time, but do thou look to it, that thou heap not up treasure against the day of wrath and revelation of the righteous judgment of God." Gregory the Great's letters show how careful he was about the welfare of the country people, and contain a number of directions to his *defensores*, for the alleviation of their condition. "Not only by frequent injunctions," he writes to his sub-deacon Anthemius,[51] "but also personally, have I, as I remember, exhorted thee, to have less in view, in thy deportment as our vicar, the temporal profit of the Church, than the alleviation of the miseries of the poor, and on the contrary, to protect them against whatever oppression may be inflicted on them." To the sub-deacon Peter, too, who administered the Church property in Sicily, he gives the excellent advice: "I desire, that the noble and respectable may honour thee for thy humility, and not loathe thee for thy pride. But if thou shouldest see them commit an injustice against the poor, then quickly raise thyself up from thy humility, so that thou mayest be submissive to them as long as they act justly, but their opponent as soon as they do evil."[62]

There were two kinds of evils, which pressed heavily upon the humbler, and especially the rural classes, oppressive taxation and the prevailing usury. The taxes grew more and more exorbitant; the arbitrariness of officials, their efforts to enrich themselves, increased the oppression. Many among them had employed large sums in obtaining an office, and of course thought it no harm to extort all the more.[53] It was difficult, almost impossible, for the people to make their complaints heard. Only from the bishops, if they could help them in no other way, did they find at least audience and sympathy; they also made use of their high position, their relations with the court, to appear as intercessors for the people, and to make their often too well-founded accusations heard. When a tax-collector in Cappadocia, for the sake of extorting more from the people, had recourse to the means of requiring a statement on oath of property, Basil earnestly remonstrated with him on the perniciousness of this proceeding, on the temptation to perjury it involved, and actually required its abolition. The letters of Basil also show in many other places, how actively he interposed in behalf of the heavily-taxed members of his flock.[54] We possess a heart-moving letter of Theodoret to the Empress Pulcheria, in which he describes to her the misery in his diocese, and begs for a mitigation of taxation. "The whole district is heavily oppressed. Many estates are forsaken by the coloni, and are lying waste. And yet the unfortunate decurions are held responsible for it, who, incapable of bearing such burdens, either become beggars or escape from them by flight."[55] Gregory the Great represents to the Empress Constantina the great misery of the island of Corsica, where the taxes are so high, that "many are scarcely able to meet the demands by the sale of their children." "Would that the most gracious Empress would take all this into consideration, and stop the sighs of the oppressed. For I do not believe that these things have hitherto come to your most gracious ear. If this had been the case, they would not have lasted till now. Representations ought to be made concerning them to the most gracious Emperor at a fitting season, that he may remove this dreadful burden of sin from his soul, from his Empire, from his children."[56]

Woe to him who should in his necessity have recourse to a loan; what with the high rate of interest, the severity of the laws against debtors, and the greed of usurers, he was almost hopelessly ruined. Productive loans were at this period out of the question. It was only distress which forced a man to borrow, and only the endeavour to get profit out of others which induced any one to lend money. The poor, urged by hunger, were obliged, as Gregory of Nyssa expresses it, "to swallow the barbed hook of interest."[57] We everywhere meet with complaints of the insatiable avarice of usurers. They profited by the distress of their fellow-men, and made "the miseries of the unfortunate a source of gain." "The poor man comes to seek help from thee and finds an enemy, he seeks a remedy and finds poison." "What can be more cruel than to derive advantage from the poverty of a neighbour, and under the

CHAP. VI.] THE CHURCH THE REFUGE OF THE OPPRESSED. 383

pretence of obliging him, to plunge him into the abyss?"[58] The usurers well knew how to take advantage of the distress of some, and the inexperience of others. "They inquire," says Ambrose in describing their guile,[59] "where an heir to wealth may be found. Then they go to him under a pretence of paternal friendship, and find out his inclinations and needs. They call his attention to some fine estate, to be sold on advantageous terms. If he says: I have no money, they answer: Use mine, as if it were yours. Thus they draw him into the net. Then begins the torture. Interest is heaped upon interest, the poor man is forced to sell everything, and yet this is not enough to satisfy the creditor. He is thrown into prison, and often driven to suicide. Oh insatiable avarice, worthy of Satan, whose most faithful portrait thou art!"[60] It must be understood, that the teachers of the Church did not distinguish between fair and just interest and usury; that in their eyes all interest was unrighteous usury. They taught, that to a Christian the reception of any interest was sin. Proof was adduced from Luke vi. 34, 35, but especially from the Old Testament (Ex. xxii. 25; Deut. xxiii. 19). The fact that it was allowable to lend to an enemy could not be appealed to. "Thou mayest kill him with whom thou livest in a state of war, and thou mayest lend to him whom thou mayest kill, for it is but another kind of killing."[61] Interest being allowed by the civil legislation, the Church confined, indeed, its express prohibition to ecclesiastics,[62] but made it a moral duty to the laity also, to lend without interest.[63] While thus usury in general was opposed by the Church, she at the same time assisted, as far as possible, the unfortunate debtor. To deliver debtors out of the hand of usurers was esteemed an especially good work. Thus Augustine pays seventeen solidi, for which sum a certain Fascius, pressed by his creditor, had taken refuge in the church, and then begs his flock to replace the money which he has had to lend, by a collection.[64] Gregory the Great having learnt, that many farmers, constrained to pay their taxes before selling their harvests, were having recourse to loans, and thus falling into the hands of usurers, commissions Peter, the sub-deacon, to make them an advance out of the Church resources, which they may repay by instalments.[65] The deacon Cyprian receives a like commission. He is to make advances to the farmers, that they may not get money elsewhere, since they will then either have to pay interest or have their produce undervalued. " For thus neither will the Church treasury be ruined, nor the prosperity of the farmers destroyed." [66]

The Church, which thus denounced the oppression of the poor by the usurers, also opposed whatever violence was exercised by the rich and noble against the poor and humble; and, as Ambrose says, protected the Naboths against the Ahabs, of whom a new one rose up every day.[67] Especially did she grant her protection to those who needed it above others—to the widows and orphans. The Synod of Sardica, which in other respects endeavoured to limit the superfluous journeys of bishops to the imperial court, allowed them to travel thither for the purpose of interceding, if a widow were oppressed, or an orphan plundered; and Ambrose, as well as Augustine, reckons it among the most pronounced duties of bishops, to protect them against injustice.[68] It was among the circumstances by which Chrysostom drew down upon himself the wrath of the Empress Eudoxia, that when the Empress, relying upon a law, desired to possess herself of the vineyards of certain poor widows, for a payment in money, he protected them in their possessions, unconcerned about the wealth of the Empress.[69] The property of widows and orphans was frequently entrusted to the Church for preservation and management. Augustine once mentions this, and adds: "The bishop protects the orphans, that they may not be oppressed by strangers, after the death of their parents."[70] In Pavia, a respectable man had surreptitiously obtained an imperial rescript, by which the property of an orphan, held as a deposit by the Church, was adjudged to him. Nevertheless, Ambrose refused to deliver it up, withstood all the threats and annoyances of the corrupted officials, and at last effected the withdrawal of the rescript. Many of Augustine's letters treat of the proposed marriage of an orphan girl, who had been entrusted to the Church, and the care of whom the bishop, notwithstanding his numerous cares and labours, did not neglect. "For your piety knows," he writes to Felix, "what care the Church and the bishops should take for the protection of all men, but especially of orphan children."[71]

The exposing of children was still of frequent occurrence. The consciousness that it was a duty of a parent to bring up a child, and a wrong to leave it to accident, only gradually made way. Nor did the laws punish the exposing of children. Valentinian I. was the first to promulgate a law, by which the rearing of children was made an obligation, and exposing them forbidden. Still, for a long time this did not put an end to the crime. Diocletian sought to dispel the evil by declaring all foundlings free, and by thus thwarting that love of gain which led to the bringing up of these poor creatures for shameful profit, to abolish indirectly the evil itself. But this, too, was of no avail. Constantine, in the first zeal of his humanity, appointed that to such parents as declared that they did not possess the means of bringing up their offspring, assistance should be given from the public treasury. This seems for a long time not to have been done. The resources required surpassed the power of the State. There remained only the help of the Church, and a field of labour was here opened to Christian charity, which the remembrance of the high value of children in the eyes of the Lord, induced her to cultivate with special zeal. The care also of foundlings was incumbent on the bishop. They were transferred to him by both ecclesiastical and civil laws. The emperors Honorius and Theodosius II. appointed, that whoever took in and brought up a child should keep it, if witnesses declared that it had not been claimed, and the bishop signed this declaration. Whoever found a child was to announce it to the Church. On the following Sunday this was proclaimed by the clergy from the altar, and the relatives were summoned to claim the child. The finder was to keep it for ten days, and to receive payment for so doing from men, or, if he preferred it, from God. If no one came forward, it was awarded to him. Whoever subsequently claimed such a child and slandered the finder, was exposed to the punishment of the Church. The Church itself brought up those children whom no one would receive. In Africa, the nuns collected foundlings and brought them to baptism.[72] The desire of procuring for children the blessing of baptism, must specially have impelled to this work. The brephotrophia also received such children. Houses specially for foundlings did not as yet exist. The Church also contended with all her power against the crime of exposing children, and the still more frequent one of infanticide. "The clergy," says the Synod of Toledo, 589, "and the secular judges must unite, in extirpating the widespread and terrible crime of parents' killing their children to escape the trouble and cost of bringing them up."[73]

Certainly many an orphan girl and many a foundling were preserved by the good offices of the Church, from sinking into the abyss of prostitution, which had in the heathen world demanded so many sacrifices, and which, alas, still demanded them in the Christianized world. The complaints of many Fathers, the dark pictures drawn by **Salvian of Aquitaine**, by **Augustine** of Africa, prove how general this evil still was. Unconscientious dealers bought up girls and women, to carry them to Constantinople and other large towns. It was incumbent on the Church, at least, to watch that this was not done against the will of the persons in question, and to defend chastity from this disgraceful speculation. Other attempts, too, were made to check the evil, especially by assisting young girls to marry early, and by giving some contributions towards their dowry.[74] I have already had occasion to mention the "House of Penance," which was erected under Justinian for fallen women. It was indeed scarcely a Magdalenium in the present sense, an asylum and an institution for improvement, but rather a conventual house of discipline. It frequently occurred in those days, that women had to pass their time of imprisonment in conventual institutions.[75]

It was now, too, that the influence of Christianity was first felt in the mitigation of imprisonment. An imperial decree of the year 400 imposes upon bishops the duty of ascertaining, by regular prison visitation, that no one was detained there unlawfully, and that the prisoners were humanely treated.[76] A canon of the Synod of Orleans, of the year 549, goes still farther. The prisoners are to be visited every Sunday by the archdeacon of the Church, that their misery may, according to God's commandments, be alleviated by compassion. The bishop is to appoint a faithful and diligent person to care for the wants of the prisoners. They are to receive necessary food from the Church.[77]

Christian love turned, however, still more to those who had been taken captive by their enemies, than to those whom the arm of justice had cast into prison, and the ransoming of such captives takes a very prominent place among works of mercy at this period. "It is the highest act of liberality," says Ambrose in his work on duties,[78] "to ransom prisoners, to withdraw them from the hands of their enemies, to rescue men from death, and women from shame, to restore parents to their children, and citizens to their native land." We feel here the heart of the Christian and that of the Roman, beating in unison; in the eyes of the Roman, prisoners are citizens whom he restores to their native land, in those of the Christian, fellow-men whom he benefits. Opportunities for such deeds were but too abundant. When the barbarians made inroads, they made prisoners of all who were not slain by the sword. When the Goths overran Thrace and Illyria, after the fall of Valens, there were so many prisoners, that "if you could ransom them all, they would fill a province." What hosts the Vandals carried away from Italy to Africa, how had Gaul constantly to suffer from this calamity, and afterwards Italy, when the Lombards took the place of the Goths, who were but just driven away! All who were not ransomed, incurred slavery, and were treated in the most cruel manner, or ruthlessly slaughtered. It was a sad spectacle to behold the former masters of the world, with chains on their hands and feet, bound to the chariots of the barbarian hosts, and carried off covered with blood and dust. They often succumbed to their miseries and to hunger, and if their ransom was too long in arriving, were hewn down in troops. Or some would return with mutilated limbs, with noses and ears cut off, to bring intelligence of the misery of others. How deeply all hearts were moved by such distress, is testified by the litanies of the time, which contain special intercessions for prisoners. " Remember, O Lord, the faithful, who languish in prison, and grant them to see their native land again."

All the more did the Christians of those times feel a lively interest in granting their aid in such cases. Ambrose zealously urged the ransoming of prisoners from the Goths. Chrysostom applied, even in banishment, a portion of the sum, which Olympias sent him from Constantinople, to ransoming captives from the savage Isaurians; Paulinus of Nola gave all that he still possessed to rescue as many as possible from the hands of the Vandals, and to save them from the fate of being sent away into Africa; the letters of Gregory the Great contain numerous directions and injunctions in this respect.[79] At one time he sends thanks for sums received for this purpose, at another he directs a bishop how to get money for it, at another he himself gives money for this work of love. Even when the prisoners had already been carried off to the abodes of the barbarians, presbyters were sent after them to deliver them from slavery.

Large sums were required for such a purpose. The barbarians kept up the price of their captives in the hope of large ransoms. Gregory at one time complains, that the Lombards are demanding too much. For one prisoner, certainly a cleric, for whom a specially high sum would be demanded, 112 solidi (= £71, 11s.) were paid,[80] and it was a question of thousands. For two bishops carried away from Cilicia, the barbarians had taken 14,000 gold pieces (about £9000).[81] But the Church made no scruple about employing her resources on a large scale. She was also frequently assisted in this work by individuals. One Rusticiana, a patrician lady, sends Gregory ten pounds of gold for this purpose, and Theotistus, a patrician, sends thirty for this and for the poor in general. Gregory applied half of the gold to the ransoming of prisoners from the Lombards, the other half he used in purchasing warm beds for the female servants of God in Rome, who were suffering much from the cold winter. He sends Theotistus, out of gratitude, a key, which, having been brought in contact with the relics of St. Peter, had thereby acquired great miraculous powers. If no means were at the Church's disposal, no hesitation was felt at borrowing money, contracting debts, nay, selling the sacred vessels. It is related of a whole series of bishops, that they did not shrink from this act. Exsuperius, bishop of Toulouse, had cut glass vessels for the celebration of the Lord's Supper. All gold and silver had been used for the ransom of prisoners.[82] No one more excellently defended this act than Ambrose, whom the Arians had reproached with it. "It is far more useful, to preserve souls for the Lord, than to keep gold. For He who sent out the apostles without gold, also collected the Church without gold. The Church does not possess gold to hoard, but to distribute it, and to help with it in distress. Would not the Lord ask us: Why did you let so many die of hunger? why were so many prisoners carried away and not ransomed? why were so many killed by the enemies? it would have been better to preserve the living than the metal vessels. And what wilt thou answer? Will it be: I feared lest the temple of God should lack necessary adornment? Would He not reply: The sacraments being not bought for gold do not need gold, nor find acceptance for the sake of gold. The adornment of the sacraments is the ransom of prisoners. How glorious to be able to say, at the sight of the prisoners ransomed by the Church: Christ has ransomed these! Behold a kind of gold of great value, useful gold, the gold of Jesus Christ, which delivers from death, which ransoms modesty, preserves chastity. I would rather set these prisoners free than keep the gold. The long lists of the ransomed are far nobler than the splendour of the gold."[83] Besides, the canons of the Church declared it allowable to sell the treasures and jewels of the Church for this object, and Gregory the Great often praises bishops who have done so, for "it would be a sin and crime to esteem the furniture of the Church above the prisoners," while he severely blames a bishop, who had refused to pay the money needed to ransom a boy.[84] Hence the Church was able to restore large numbers to liberty. Candidus, bishop of Sergiopolis, on one occasion ransomed 12,000 prisoners for 14,400 solidi (£9136, 16s.). Especially, as the inscriptions show, was the Gallic Church zealous in this work, to which private individuals also contributed. " With her treasures she delivered prisoners from unjust fetters," is read on the gravestone of Eugenia, a Christian woman.[85]

This work of mercy extended beyond the boundaries of the Roman Empire, a sign that it was prompted by more than mere patriotism, and that something more was thought of than restoring citizens to the country, and clergy to the Church. When, on the occasion of a great victory of the Emperor Theodosius II. over the Persians, many prisoners had fallen into the hands of the Roman soldiers, Acacius, bishop of Amida, called his clergy together, and represented to them: "Our God needs neither the plates nor the cups, for as One who needs nothing, He neither eats nor drinks. What then do we want with so much silver plate? It is right that we should sell it and ransom and feed the prisoners." And this was done, the prisoners were ransomed and sent back to the Persian king supplied with necessary provisions for the journey.[86]

And how much more may have been done in private! Theodoret tells us on one occasion, in his letters, all of which are pervaded by the remembrance of the miseries inflicted on Africa by the Vandals, a little history of the kind, which well deserves to find a place here. Mary, a noble lady, was taken prisoner by the Vandals, dealers had brought her to Cyrus in Syria, and there sold her and her maid. The maid, though now her fellow-slave, still continued to serve her mistress faithfully. When this was known, certain Christians ransomed her, the bishop commended her to the care of a deacon, and assigned her a certain supply of corn for her support. She then heard that her father was still alive and invested with an office in the West. She therefore set out to go to him, and Theodoret gave her a letter of introduction for the journey.[87] In several other letters Theodoret recommends one Celestiacus, who had formerly been rich, but having lost everything at the conquest of Carthage by the Vandals, was now wandering about in poverty with his wife and child, and entreats that he may be assisted.[88]

We must now just turn our attention more directly to the misery of the perishing world, and survey that which is, in the times when great revolutions are effected, so easily overlooked, the manner in which this misery

affected the lives of individuals. Those who suffered
were countless multitudes. It was amid thousandfold
calamities, in such wretchedness as scarcely ever recurred,
as was perhaps just at one time approximated during the
Thirty Years' War, that the old world perished, and all
its glory was buried. Like successive floods did the
German nations inundate the Empire, wrecking the old
forms and ordinances of political and national life, and,
themselves as yet incapable of creating new and
permanent ones; they came in the vigour of youth,
and but too soon enervated by the mild climate, to
which they were unaccustomed, weakened by the in-
dulgences of a foreign civilization, consumed by the sins
of those whom they had subdued, were drawn down
with them to destruction. How soon were the Vandals,
to whom, as Salvian says when rebuking the Romans,
God gave the victory because of their chastity, quite as
morally corrupt as the Romans! How did the Ostro-
goths perish in Spain, how tragically the Visigoths in
Italy! At first an unparalleled chaos ensued. The
new, the Christianized, German world was born amid
thousandfold pangs; centuries passed before settled and
permanent policies and nations emerged from the deluge
of the migration of the nations. And in the midst of
this chaos, stood the Church as the sole power which
survived the universal ruin, and continued to perform its
office of being the refuge of all the oppressed and
suffering. In these times of confusion, when every other
support failed, she alone still held out a helping hand to
the poor, pursued, and alarmed people. Did an invasion
rage over the land, and towns and villages lie in ashes,
the Church was still there, and immediately recommenced
her work. Churches, chapels, hospitals and monasteries,

the houses of mercy, were the first to be rebuilt. There distributions again began, there did the poor daily find the storehouses of the Church open to them, and receive such food, shelter and assistance as she could give. Besides material help, however, they also received spiritual gifts. Distributions of alms were combined with public worship. The poor, who came to get bread to appease their hunger, or a garment to cover their nakedness, or medicine and advice for their sickness, heard at the same time the word of God, preached as well as the Church knew how, received comfort from this source of all comfort, and acquired strength to go on suffering and hoping. If the people did not utterly despair, they owed this to the never-ceasing charity of the Church. In fact, it was a great, a marvellously great, work which the Church effected at that time, a work which proves, that in the love of our Lord Jesus Christ, a new power had entered the world, which even these tempests could not destroy, which, on the contrary, only manifested itself the more great and glorious in the midst of the tempest and the universal misery. The Church could not save the old world, but she sat at its death-bed with help and comfort, and lighted up its last hours with such an evening glory as the old world had never known in the times of its greatest prosperity.

At the same time she stood also at the cradle of a new world, of the German Christian world, at the cradle of the Middle Ages.

The work effected by the Church with respect to the German nations, falls indeed outside the limits of the picture, which I proposed in the first instance to paint, of charity in the ancient Church. We may, however, just cast a glance at it. They were young nations in unbroken, but still rude power, who now intermingled with the remnants of the ancient nations, occupied their place, were their heirs, and at the same time the continuers of their work. To educate them to this was the task of the Church, and among educational forces compassionate love was one of the most prominent. Nay, I might in a certain sense say, that hospitals and cloisters were, together with the house of God, the episcopal cathedral, or the quiet forest chapel, the two national centres of education. Love in the hospital, work in the cloister,—these were the educational powers. The Church made no distinction between Germans and Romans. The poor German, equally with the poor Roman, received her alms, or was welcomed into her hospitals. But what he saw and experienced made a far deeper impression upon him. To the Roman, charity was already a thing with which he had long been familiar; to the German it was entirely new. For whatever kindness there was in the German nature, expressed as it was by the old word "*Milte*," which means especially liberality towards the poor, it was still something very different from Christian love. Besides, all that was best and most excellent about it had been long since lost amidst the migrations and invasions. It was a far more savage race, that was now sojourning within the Roman boundaries, than that which had formerly settled in the German districts. How then must the Church's work of love have bound the young nations to her, how must it have rendered them accessible also to her doctrines and ordinances, and have gained their hearts for the exalted Lord of heaven, who once walked on earth as a poor man! And in the monasteries and from the monasteries, the people, now alienated from and despising work, again learned to work. The monasteries became everywhere the starting-points of a new civilization. There was the field again tilled, the vine again cultured; there, too, was also cultivated whatever of art and science had been rescued from the overthrow. Thence originated that new Germanic civilization, which everywhere had its roots in the ancient civilization, but with this difference, that Christianity now penetrated far more deeply into national life, than it had ever done in the Roman Empire, and that the Church became for a thousand years almost the all-dominating power.[89]

It was in the Church life of the Middle Ages, that all that had hitherto existed only in germ, was developed in full maturity. To the Middle Ages were transferred those ethic views of riches and poverty, of earnings and alms, and of the meritorious and expiatory power of the latter, of which we have spoken. In Thomas Aquinas and in the ethical works of the Middle Ages, we find again, at least on the whole, the same views which we have already met with in Ambrose, Augustine, and Gregory the Great, only they are now systematically developed into a complete view of the world, which influenced the entire social life of the Middle Ages. To these were also transferred the forms of charity, as they had been already fashioned, the combination of alms with masses for the departed, the memorials, the charitable endowments for the soul's salvation of the deceased, together with the hospital and monastery as centres of charity, but all was developed in infinitely more copious variety. No period has done so much for the poor as the Middle Ages. What wholesale distribution of alms, what an abundance of institutions of the most various kinds, what numbers of hospitals for all manner of sufferers, what a series of ministrant orders, male and female, knightly and civil, what self-sacrifice and devotedness! In the mediæval period all that we have observed germinating in the Ancient Church, first attains its maturity.

The Middle Ages, however, also appropriated whatever tendencies existed towards a one-sided and unsound development. Church care of the poor entirely perished, and all charity became institutional; monks and nuns, or members of the ministrant orders, took the place of the deacons—the diaconate died out. Charity became one-sidedly institutional and one-sidedly ecclesiastical. The Church was the mediatrix of every exercise of charity, she became in fact the sole recipient, the sole bestower, for the main object of every work of mercy, of every distribution of alms, of every endowment, of all self-sacrifice in the service of the needy, was the giver's own salvation. The transformation was complete. Men gave and ministered no longer for the sake of helping and serving the poor in Christ, but to obtain for themselves and theirs merit, release from purgatory, a high degree of eternal happiness. The consequence was, that poverty was not contended with, but fostered, and beggary brought to maturity; so that, notwithstanding the abundant donations, the various foundations, the well-endowed institutions, distress was after all not mastered. The mediæval period first works out, in this respect also, what was begun in the period we have been observing, and furnishes in its issue, in its utter bankruptcy with respect to poverty, a proof that charity, like all Christian life, no longer corresponded with the gospel, no longer sprung from it alone, but was contaminated by the reception of extra-Christian, of Jewish, and ancient elements.

Not till the Reformation was the source returned to, the primitive Christian notions of riches and poverty, of property and alms, of work and vocation revived, and consequently new fountains of active love unsealed. These notions, however, are very far from having been fully carried out; we must on the contrary confess, that our Church has in this respect also, and perhaps most of all in this, come short in practice of what has been given her in knowledge. The first duty of our age is to realize in action the evangelical and reformed ideas concerning charity and the relief of the poor, in connection with those concerning calling and work, wages and property. Beginnings, thank God, exist. Would that they may but develop with increasing power! Then alone can we contemplate, if not without fear, yet still with hope, the changes, the new formations of social life, which we or our children will experience. As in those times, when the Christian Germanic world came forth from the destruction of the ancient world, so now again has love a great task to accomplish; God grant that we may be equal to it! In Christianity is given us the remedy for all evils, the inexhaustible source of healthy life, but let us not forget how our Lord says: " By this shall all men know that ye are My disciples, if ye have love one to another."

ced.

NOTES.

BOOK I.

CHAPTER I.

(1) Lact. Inst. vi. 10.—(2) Tacit. Ann. iv. 63.—(3) Quinctilian Declamat. 301, ed. Bipont. p. 175. Plautus, Trinummus, act iii. sc. 2.—(4) Staatshaushalt der Athener, ii. 260.—(5) *E.g.* Corp. Inscr. Lat. ii. 1270; 4511; viii. 4202 and 5148. Orelli, 80; 4042, etc.—(6) Bœckh, Staatshaushalt der Athener, i. 260 sqq.—(7) Idem, ii. 83.—(8) Isocrates, Areop. 38.—(9) Bœckh as above, i. 235 sqq.—(10) Plebs. frumentaria, ὄχλος πλῆθος ἄπορος πένητες. Comp. Dio Cass. 38, 23; Appian B.C. ii. 120.—(11) Vit. Sever. c. 18.—(12) Vit. Aurel. c. 35, 48.—(13) Comp. Hirschfeld, die Getreidelieferung in der Röm. Kaiserzeit, Göttingen 1869, pp. 20, 21.—(14) Hirschfeld's above-named work, p. 44.—(15) Comp. Mommsen's Röm. Gesch. 491 : " Cæsar first developed into an organic institution of the State, that which in the narrow restriction of Athenian life had remained an affair of the community, and transformed an arrangement which was a burden and disgrace to the State into the first of those innumerable institutions so rich in blessing, in which infinite human compassion contends with infinite human misery." This is certainly saying too much, but it correctly points out the path this institution was taking.—(16) Mommsen and Marquardt, Handbuch der Röm. Alterthümer, v. 106 sqq.—(17) Plin. ix. 81; xiv. 27. Friedländer, i. 421.—(18) Sueton. Nero, c. 9, 18.—(19) Häser, Gesch. der Krankenpflege, p. 3.—On the houses for suppliants at the temples of Æsculapius, comp. Paus. ii. 27, 2 ; x. 32, 8.—(20) Tac. Ann. ii. 47 ; Marc. Aurel. Vit. c. 11.—(21) Innumerable inscriptions testify to this fact. Comp. *e.g.* Or. 80, 748, 2172, 3848, 5323 ; C. J. i. 190 ; ii. 4514 ; v. 5651, 7881 ; viii. 967, 6948, and elsewhere.—(22) Comp. Marquardt and Mommsen's above-named work, 137 sqq.—(23) Corp. Inscr. ii. 1174.—(24) C. J. viii. 1641.—(25) Ep. vii. 18.—(26) Bullet de l'Inst. 1839, 153.—(27) Comp. on the *collegia* especially, **Mommsen, De collegiis et sodaliciis Romanorum, Kiliæ** 1843, and Boissier,

La Religion Romaine, ii. 277-342.—(28) Comp. Bœckh's above-named work, i. 267 sqq.—(29) Comp. on these especially, Marquardt and Mommsen's above-named work, vi. 137 sqq.—(30) Tertullian, Apolog. c. 39.—(31) Or. 6086.—(32) C. J. viii. 2557.—A passage in Plin. Epp. x. 93, 94, is also interesting. Pliny is entreating permission for an Eranos, a collegium in the town of Amisus, and Traja,i grants it, with the words, "eo facilius, si tali collatione, non ad turbas et illicitos coetus sed ad sustinendum tenuiorum inopiam utuntur." Hence the question was concerning a collegium for mutual assistance. In spite of which Trajan objects : "In cæteris civitatibus, quæ nostro jure obstrictæ sunt, res hujusmodi prohibenda est."—(33) Or. 3999 ; 4107.—(34) C. J. v. 5907.— (35) Or. 7215.—(36) Or. 3999.—(37) Or. 4366.—(38) C. J. viii. 9052.— (39) C. J. v. 5272.—(40) C. J. ii. 4511.—(41) Or. 2417.—(42) Comp. *e.g.* Or. 1485 ; 1238.—(43) C. J. ii. 1976.—(44) "Zur Geschichte der römischen Tributsteuern seit Augustus " in Hildebrand's Jahrbüchern für Nationalökonomie, viii. 461. — (45) Marquardt and Mommsen, vi. 254 sqq.—(46) Liv. xvi. 23 ; xxxiii. 2, 25. Varro in Non. s.v. pandere. Marquardt and Mommsen, vi. 347, note 2.—(47) Comp. Ovid ex Ponto, i. 1, 39 ; iv. 352 ; Cicero, de Leg. ii. 9, 22 ; Minuc. Felix Octavius, c. 24 ; Tertull. Apolog. c. 13 ; Liv. xv. 12 ; xxii. 1.—(48) Liv. ii. 33 ; iii. 18.— (49) Plin. H. N. xxxiii. 10. Among the inscriptions are found many which speak of the erection of a statue "*stipe collata.*"—(50) Republ. vi. 508. — (51) Definit. p. 414 ; Republ. vii. 517. — (52) Tim. 29 ; Republ. x. 613.—(53) Rep. vii. 519.—(54) Rep. iii. 168.—(55) Eth. Nicom. iv. 1.—(56) Ibid. c. 2.—(57) Ibid. viii. 2 ; ix. 5, 9.—(58) Ibid. viii. 2.—(59) Diog. Laertius, v. 1.—(60) Eth. Nicom. ix. 8.—(61) De beneficiis, ii. i. 9, 14.—(62) De benef. iv. 3, Non est beneficium, quod fortunam spectat. C. 9 : Ergo beneficium per se expetenda res est. Una spectatur in eo accipientis utilitas ; ad hanc accedamus, semotis commodis nostris.—(63) iv. 11.—(64) iv. 9.—(65) iv. 29.—(66) iv. 26-28.—(67) iv. 29 : "negligente " "non homini damus sed humanitati."—(68) vii. 32.— (69) iv. 12.—(70) De clementia, ii. 5, 6.—(71) Giornale Arcadico, t. 39, p. 223.—(72) C. J. v. 6668.—(73) Or. 3177.—(74) Or. 114.—(75) C. J. viii. 7384.—A similar inscription is found in Le Blant, Inscriptions chrétiennes de la Gaule, i. 171. The last-named inscription is in the Journal de l'instruction publique, Feb. 26, 1853.—(76) Philostratus, Apollon. iv. 3.

CHAPTER II.

(1) Comp. Diestel, Die Idee der Gerechtigkeit im alten Testament. Jahrb. f. deutsche Theologie, 1860, p. 214. — (2) Comp. Eisenmenger, Entdecktes Judenthum, ii. 287.—(3) Tractat. Rosch haschana.—(4) Pirke

Aboth, v. 13. Comp. also the same, v. 10 : "Many qualities are found in men. Some say, What is mine is mine, and what is thine is thine. These are the medium sort. Some say, What is mine is thine, and what is thine is mine. That is the way of the ignorant. Some say, What is mine is thine, and what is thine is thine. That is a Chassid (a pious person). Some say, What is mine is mine, and what is thine is also mine. That is the way of the ungodly."—(5) Eisenmenger's above-named work, i. 617 sqq. Rabbi Israel says: Show no kindness and mercy to the nations of the world.

CHAPTER III.

(1) It is utterly unsatisfactory, though from his point of view quite intelligible, when Ratzinger, in his "Geschichte der Armenpflege," (Freiburg in Brisgau 1868), discussing the beginnings of Christian relief of the poor (p. 4 sqq.), can speak of nothing but the teaching and commands of Christ. This shows beforehand the character of his otherwise very meritorious and useful work. He has carefully collected materials for a history of the relief of the poor, but he is not in a condition to represent its development, because his Roman Catholic standpoint obstructs his view of the development of Christian life and of ethic views. Also Chatel, "Etudes historiques sur l'influence de la Charité durant les premiers siècles chrétiens" (Paris 1853), dwells in far too one-sided a manner, livre i. chap. i., upon "la prédication de la charité par Jésus Christ," as though the teaching, the preaching, could of itself have called forth a life of love. The consequence of this is, that he too does not attain to a deeper insight of the development. Comp. my "Vorstudien zu einer Geschichte der Liebesthätigkeit im Mittelalter," Zeitschrift für Kirchengesch. iv. 1.—(2) In the Middle Ages the seven works of mercy were comprised in a *versus memorialis* : "Vestio, poto, cibo, redimo, tego, colligo, condo," and besides these *eleemosynæ corporales*, were also placed seven eleemosynæ spirituales : "Consule, carpe, doce, solare, remitte, fer, ora," to advise, admonish, teach, and comfort one's neighbour, to forgive him, bear with him patiently and pray for him. This whole method of teaching is already hinted at by Augustine.—(3) Comp. the excellent saying of Nitzsch, Pract. Theol. i. 1, p. 214 : "Christianity could not but become habitual love of the poor and active compassion, just because human nature and personality were regarded according to a higher destination than a merely worldly one."—(4) The Vulgate translates the words τὰ ἐνόντα, which must either be understood as "what is in it" (namely in the cup and platter), or with Luther, "what there is," by the words "*quod superest*." This view already appears in Jerome, Epp. 150. Whatever is

left beyond what is necessary for food and clothing, you owe to the poor. So, too, Augustine, p. 249, *de temp.*: "Quidquid excepto victu mediocri et vestitu rationabili superfuerit, non luxuriæ reservetur sed in cœlesti thesauro per eleemosynas pauperum reponetur." Comp. p. 219, *de temp.* in Ps. cxlvii. In the Middle Ages this was the sole prevailing interpretation.

CHAPTER IV.

(1) So *e.g.* Löhe in his work On Mercy, Nordlingen 1877; also Chatel in his above-named work, p. 53; Ratzinger, p. 33, also has a correct view. Comp. on this question in general, its thorough discussion in Ritschl's Entstehung der altkathol. Kirche, p. 354.—(2) Comp. *e.g.* Acts xx. 24, xxi. 19; Rom. xi. 13, xv. 31; 1 Cor. xii. 5; 2 Cor. iii. 8, 9, iv. 1, v. 18; Eph. iii. 7; 1 Thess. iii. 2; 1 Tim. iii. 10, 13; 1 Pet. i. 12, iv. 10.—(3) 1 Cor. xii. 28, Ἀντιλήψεις κυβερνήσεις. This corresponds also with classical usage. Διακονίαι δημοσίαι are in Demosthenes: Munera publica et administrationes publicæ.—(4) "*καὶ τίς διακονίαν τοῖς ἁγίοις ἔταξαν ἑαυτούς,*" Ritschl (above-named work, p. 348) understands the passage so as to make them the presidents of the Church. But the plural seems to include women also, hence it seems to me more correct to think of a ministration of service. So, too, should I understand Col. iv. 17.—(5) My reasons are these:—(*a*) That ὡσαύτως must, according to the whole plan of the sentence, introduce a new category of church officials; comp. ver. 8. (*b*) At ver. 12 διάκονοι is repeated, but why if ver. 11 too was speaking of them? This is only explicable if something else, certainly of a kindred nature, was inserted, and vers. 12, 13 resume the previous subject. (*c*) The family relations of the deacons are first spoken of, ver. 12. (*d*) The wives of the bishops are not mentioned. Why then the wives of the deacons? It is said they were of more importance to church life. This is, however, neither proved nor capable of proof. (*e*) If the wives of the deacons were designated, αὐτῶν would absolutely be found, if the designation is to be intelligible. (*f*) γυναῖκας may well designate deaconesses. The "διακόνους" must be completed from the context. Exactly similar is a passage in the Apostolic Constitutions, iii. 19: "'Η γυνὴ τὰς γυναῖκας σπουδάζουσα θεραπεύειν." Here too the mere γυνή denotes the deaconess, after deacons had been immediately before spoken of. Where this is not the case, iii. 15, "γυναῖκα διάκονον" stands in full.—(6) This strikingly accords with the description given in the Apostolic Constitutions of the widows, whose chief duty also is to pray for the congregation.—(7) That the passage is not grammatically to be otherwise understood, comp. Meyer *in loco*, and also Heinrici. Certainly no other exposition would have been arrived at, but for the preconceived opinion, that it was unworthy of the apostle

to estimate civil freedom so slightly. What we shall afterwards hear of the attitude of the Church towards slavery, entirely coincides with the view taken of this passage.

BOOK SECOND.

CHAPTER I.

(1) The population of Rome is still very variously stated. I have made the computation of Marquardt and Mommsen (Röm. Alterthum. v. 120) the foundation. According to this work, the population is represented as follows :—Roman citizens, 320,000 ; women and children, 300,000 ; senators and knights, 10,000 ; garrison, 20,000 ; slaves, 900,000 ; strangers, 60,000—total, 1,610,000. Whether boys are included in the number of those who received the largess of Augustus, is very uncertain. To be quite sure of not painting too dark a picture I have assumed this, and have hence reduced the number of women and children. Thus the actual condition was formerly still more unfavourable than stated in the text.—(2) Chrysostomus Hom. in Matt. lxvi. 3.—(3) Comp. Friedländer, i. 281.—(4) Seneca, de vit. beata, c. 25.—(5) Martial, xii. 32.—(6) Polyb. i. 15, comp. Bœckh's above-named work, i. 65 sqq.—(7) Marquardt and Mommsen's above-named work, v. 2, 82 sqq.—(8) Suet. Nero, 16 ; Dio, 62, 14. Comp. Schiller, Nero, p. 518.—(9) Comp. Friedländer, iii. 8.—(10) Petronius. Sat. c. 45.—(11) Comp. Rodbertus : Zur Geschichte der röm. Tributsteuern seit Augustus ; Hildebrand's Jahrbücher für Nationalökonomie, viii. 461 sqq.—(12) Hippolyt. (Pseudo-Origenis) Philosophumena, ix. 12.—(13) Juvenal, i. 24 ; x. 224.—(14) ix. 73.—(15) Juv. iii. 32-40 ; Martial, iii. 16, 59, 99. —(16) Senec. de tranquillitate animi ; Plin. H. N. xviii. 35 ; "Latifundia perdidere Italiam."—(17) Comp. Streuber : Der Zinsfuss bei den Romern. —(18) Dio, lxiii. 2, 3.—Pliny the younger advises the Emperor Trajan to lend the State funds under 12 per cent., as otherwise no creditors will be found, Ep. 62, 63. Horace, Sat. i. 2, 12, censures a usurer who took 60 per cent.—(19) Comp. Schiller, Nero, p. 488 sqq.—(20) Plin. H. N. vi. 101 : "Tanti nobis deliciæ et feminæ constant" ("So much do pleasures and women cost us ").—(21) Vopiscus Probus, c. 10.

CHAPTER II.

(1) Justin, Apolog. i. 14 ; comp. Barnabas, Ep. 19, 8.—(2) Pastor. Hermæ Mand. ii.—(3) Quis dives salvus, c. 13.—(4) Barnabas, Ep. 19.—(5) Clem.

Rom. ad Cor. i. 49 ; Barnab. c. 19.—(6) Clement, Homil. Ep. Clem. c. 8.—(7) Clem. Alex. Strom. iii. 4, 5.—(8) In the Testaments of the Twelve Patriarchs, belonging to Nazarene circles, are frequently found opinions adverse to wealth. Also in the portions preserved, though touched up, in Mellitus, de passione S. Joannis ap. (Fabricius, Apocryph. N. T. iii. 609), from the Acts of the Apostles of Leucius, which may be of about the middle of the 2nd century. Comp. Zahn, Acta Joannis, p. xciv. and p. 238. It is striking, that the Clementine Homilies, which certainly originated from Essenic Judaic Christianity, do not reject property. It is also one of the points in which the author of this book accommodates himself to the views of the Catholic Church, in order to gain room for his Judæo-Christian Propaganda, and is consequently also a sign, that the Church kept itself free from such views, which flourished only in sectarian narrowness.—(9) Barn. Ep. c. 19, 8.—(10) Tertullian, Apolog. 39.—(11) Similit. i.—(12) Hermæ Pastor. Vis. iii. 86.—(13) Euseb. H. E. v. 3.—(14) Tertullian, de cultu fem. ii. 9.—(15) Hermæ Pastor. Vis. iii. 2 and 6.—(16) Tertullian, Apolog. 42.—(17) Clem. Alex. Quis dives salves, c. 11, 12.—(18) Idem, c. 13, 14.—(19) Idem, c. 32.—(20) Pædagogus, ii. 12.—(21) Pædagog. iii. 7.—(22) Pædagog. i. 1. —(23) Pædagog. i. 2, 3.—(24) Tertull. de cultu fem. i. 8.—(25) Pædagog. ii. 12.—(26) Pædagog. i. 8.—(27) Pædagog. ii. 1.—(28) Pædagog. iii. 7. —(29) Pædagog. iii. 4.—(30) Pædagog. iii. 10, 11, i. 10.—(31) Pædagog. iii. 10.—(32) Const. Apost. ii. 63.—(33) Comp. Cotelier on Const. Apost. ii. 63.—(34) Const. Apost. iv. 2.—(35) Philosophum. ix. 12.—(36) Const. Apost. i. 4.—(37) Cyprian, Ep. 41 : "ut jam nunc ego cui cura incumbit, omnes optime nossem," Cypriani Opp. Vindobonæ 1868.—(38) Philos. ix. 12.—(39) Tertullian, Apolog. 42 ; ad uxor. ii. 4.—(40) Const. Apost. ii. 28.—(41) Const. Apost. ii. 35.

CHAPTER III.

(1) Comp. Heinrici, The Christian Church of Corinth and the Religious Communities of the Greeks, in the Zeitschrift für wissenschaftliche Theologie 1876, iv.—(2) Apolog. c. 39.—(3) Justin M. Apolog. i. 67. This statement is usually referred to the oblations, but then it is not to be explained why Justin does not come to the contributions till after he has concluded his description of the Lord's Supper. Neither the view embraced by Neander, that (K. G. i. 2, p. 387) the oblations were not offered till after the Lord's Supper, nor Harnack's (der christliche Gemeindegottesdienst, p. 256 sqq.), that Justin is not observing the succession of the transactions, but stating here what properly, according to the sequence of time, belongs to a former passage, is satisfactory. In fact the oblations are not spoken of at all here, but stand in Justin in the usual position

(ἄρτος προσφέρεται καὶ οἶνος καὶ ὕδωρ). Justin just means the contributions, which Tertullian calls *stips* and describes them exactly as he does. Even the several words remind us of Tertullian, *e.g.* the "τὸ συλλεγόμενον παρὰ πρεστῶτι ἀποτίθεται" of Tertullian's words, "haec quasi deposita pietatis sunt."—(4) Cyprian, Ep. 64, 3, where it is said of the apostate bishops, who still desired to continue in office, "stipes et oblationes et lucra desiderant." Also de op. et eleemos. 14 : "Locuples et dives es, et dominicum celebrare te credis, quae corban omnino non respicis quae in dominicum sine sacrificio venis quae partem de sacrificio, quod pauper obtulit sumis." Here *corban non respicere* relates to the *stips*, *sacrificium* is the oblation.—(5) Cyprian's above work ; comp. note 4. Const. Apost. ii. 36. Ratzinger (in his above-named work, p. 39) thinks it was afterwards called *concha*, and appeals to Canon 48 of the Conc. Elib. This is a mistake. Concha there means the baptismal basin. So, too, Krauss in the R. Encyclop. of Christian Antiquities under this word.—(6) Const. Apost. ii. 36.—(7) It is well known that the letter of Pliny to Justin denotes the time of this transference. Justin and Irenæus already know of it at no other time. The custom, however, seems not to have become at once general, but to have spread at first gradually. Even at a later period a celebration of the Lord's Supper was combined with the agapae. Eus. H. E. 19 ; Augustin, ep. ad Januarium.—(8) Comp. Harnack's above-named work, p. 285.—(9) Liturgia divi Marci in Bunsen's Anal. Antinicaena, iii. 163. In the liturgy of St. Basil the prayer runs: "Lord, remember those who offer these gifts, and those for whom and for whose sake and for whose profit they offer them. Lord, think of those who bring forth fruit and do good works in Thy holy Church, and who remember the poor. Requite them with Thy treasures and Thy heavenly gifts. Give them for the earthly the heavenly, for the temporal the eternal, for the corruptible the incorruptible," Bunsen, iii. 226 ; comp. also Const. Apost. viii. 10.--(10) Conc. Elib. can. 49.—(11) Const. Apost. iii. 4 ; viii. 13.—(12) Polycarp, ad Philip. c. 4.—(13) Clem. Rom. i. 59.—(14) Const. Apost. viii. 10.—(15) Comp. the Liturgia Marci, Bunsen, iii. 188. Similar words are also found in the Coptic liturgy.—(16) Comp. also Höfling, Lehre vom Opfer, p. 156 sqq.—(17) Irenæus, adv. Hær. iv. 18, 2.—(18) Cypr. Ep. 15, 34. —(19) Const. Apost. iv. 8, 10.—(20) Tertullian, de praescr. Hær. c. 20.—(21) Apol. i. 13.—(22) Adv. Hær. iv. 17.—(23) Strom. vii. 6.—(24) Comp. Ritschl's above-named work, p. 397.—(25) Tertull. de monogam. c. 10 ; de exhortat. castit. c. 11 ; de corona mil. c. 3.—(26) Cyprian, ep. 1.—(27) Cypr. Ep. 60 at the end.—(28) Origenes, τῷ εὐχῆσ. c. 11.— Tertullian, de monog. c. 10. The refreshment (*refrigerium*) is not a mitigation of punishment in purgatory, of this Tertullian as yet knows nothing, but eternal happiness.—(29) Tertullian, ad uxor. ii. 8, where it is said, *matrimoniam confirmat oblatio et obsignat benedictio*.—(30) Comp

Harnack's above-named work, p. 393 sqq.—(31) In Levit. ii. 4.—(32) Cyprian, de op. et eleemosyn. c. i. 2.—(33) Cyprian, de domin. oratio, c. 32.—(34) Cyprian, de op. et eleemosyn. c. 5.—(35) Comp. above, p. 28. Examples: a statue, Or. 1572, 1971, 2086; a monument, 13, 1348, 1380, 2022; a bridge, 760; a temple, 5659.—(36) De jejuniis, c. 13.—(37) Const. Apost. iv. 8. The same injunction is found in Hom. Clem. iii. 71, a sign that this was a general mode of procedure. —(38) Cyprian, Ep. 62.—(39) Vita Cypriani, c. 2.—(40) Cypriani Ep. 7; comp. Vita, c. 15.—(41) Euseb. H. E. iii. 37.—(42) Const. Apost. v. 7: "'Ἐκ τοῦ κόπου καὶ ἐκ τοῦ ἱγρῶτος."—(43) Sim. v. 3.—(44) Levit. x.— (45) Const. Apost. v. 1.—(46) Similar acts are also met with in ancient times. The whole population of Sparta fasted and gave what was thus spared to assist the Samnites, who were seeking to reconquer their native land. Aristot. Œcon. ii. 2, 9; comp. Bœckh's Staatshaushalt d. Ath. ii. 131.—(47) Iren. adv. Hær. iv. 18, 34.—(48) Cyprian, de cathol. eccl. unitate, c. 26.—(49) Origenes in Num. Hom. xi. 1; in librum Josue Nave, Hom. xvii.; comp. in Prov. iii. 9.—(50) Lagarde, Reliq. jur. ant. p. 88.—(51) Can. Hipp. 36.—(52) Const. Apost. ii. 34, 35; vii. 29.— (53) Euseb. H. E. vi. 43. The sum supposed in the text is purposely very low. In the first century, the cost of a slave's maintenance is computed to have been £7, 10s. (Marquardt and Mommsen, v. 52). If we take this sum for granted, it would amount to £11,250 per annum.

CHAPTER IV.

(1) Valens, a deacon, embezzles some of the money for the poor. Polyc. Ep. ad Phil. c. 11, 12; comp. Herm. Past. Sim. ix. 26.—(2) Polyc. Ep. ad Phil. c. 6.—(3) Herm. Past. Sim. ix. 27.—(4) Cyprian, Ep. 41.—(5) Cyprian, Ep. 5.—(6) Cyprian, Ep. 7.—(7) Anastasius, Vit. Pontif. p. 21 (Romæ 1728).—(8) Ambrosius, de off. min. ii. 28.—(9) Const. Apost. ii. 26, 31.—(10) Const. Apost. ii. 35, 3, 25.—(11) Euseb. H. E. vi. 43.— Sozomenus, H. E. vii. 19.—(12) Conc. Neocæsar. can. 15. The canon appeals to the Seven in Jerusalem.—(13) Const. Apost. iii. 19. The number is to be in proportion to the size of the Church, that so they may be able to support the weak, as workmen in whom there is nothing to blame.—(14) Euseb. H. E. vi. 43.—(15) The older books of the Const. Apost. are unacquainted with them, they are first mentioned in the post-Constantinian eighth book.—(16) Const. Apost. ii. 44.—(17) Const. Apost. iii. 19; ii. 31, 32.—(18) Const. Apost. ii. 44. The matricula is expressly mentioned in Ep. Clem. c. 151; it is, however, doubtful what date should be ascribed to this book. But Cypr. Ep. 2, where the admission of an actor who had become a Christian is spoken of, certainly gives the impression

that a matricula was then kept.—(19) In Philosoph. ix. 12 is also found a similar allusion. At any rate there was a list of the widows to be maintained, and a general catalogue of all to be relieved would soon be made.—(20) The Βίβλιον Κλήμεντος is found in Lagarde's Reliq. p. 80 sqq. To what date it belongs is uncertain. Bunsen ascribes it to the reign of Caracalla and Geta, whom he finds in the book. This can hardly be correct. In its present form, I feel inclined rather to regard it as contemporaneous with Book viii. of the Apost. Constitutions. To this date the injunction to communicate fasting points. It, however, evidently contains older passages.—(21) Const. Apost. iii. 7.—(22) Certain remarks of Zahn in his "Ignatius von Antiochen," pp. 148, 325, and above all Dieckhoff's excellent treatise "die Diakonissen der alten Kirche," in Schäfer's Monatschr. f. Diakonie, 289, 348, 391, have for the first time thrown more light upon the history of the ancient deaconesses. But much still remains obscure. Dieckhoff especially has so far not yet disengaged himself from the former view, as still to suppose that there were subsequently also deaconesses in the West.—(23) Plin. Ep. x. 97 : "Quo magis necessarium credidi, ex duabus ancillis, quæ ministræ (deaconesses) dicebantur, quid esset veri et per tormenta quærere."—(24) In Luc. Hom. 17.— (25) Ignatius, ad Smyrn. 6 ; ad Polyc. 4 ; Polyc. Ep. ad Phil. c. 4. The much discussed passage in Ignat. ad Smyrn. c. 13 : "'Ασπάζομαι τὰς παρθένους, τὰς λεγομένας χήρας," I consider corrupt and in the present text unmeaning.—(26) Vis. ii. 4.—(27) Hom. xi. 36 ; Recogn. iv. 15.—(28) Pædag. iii. 12.—(29) Orig. in evang. Joann. Hom. 17, in Jes. Hom. 6.— (30) Tertull. ad uxor. i. 7 : "cum viduam adlegi in ordinem nisi univiram non concedit." De virg. vel. c. 9 ; de exhortat. castit. c. 7.—(31) Tertull. de monog. c. 11.—(32) Origen, in Jes. Hom. 6. Quite so subsequently the Conc. Carthag. can. 12.—(33) Lucian, de morte Peregrini, c. 12.— (34) Grapte also in Hermas, Vis. ii. 4, appears as commissioned with the instruction of orphans.—(35) Const. Apost. iii. 1, 3, 5, 7, 14, 15.—(36) The Διατάξεις of Hippolytus in Lagarde's Reliq. p. 5.—(37) Ignatius ad Tarsenses, c. 9 ; ad Antioch. c. 12.—(38) Tertull. de virg. vel. c. 9.—(39) Clem. Alex. Strom. vii. 12 (ed Potter, p. 875) : "'Η χήρα διὰ σωφροσύνης αὖθις παρθένος."—(40) Epiphanius, Expos. fidei, c. 21 ; Const. Apost. vi. 17.—(41) Const. Apost. iii. 15. It is complained that the widows stroll about and gossip, that they beg, are shameless in begging, insatiable in taking, so that by such behaviour they have already made many believers slack in giving. They are then threatened with punishment, especially with that of fasting ; comp. iii. 7.—(42) Διαταγαὶ αἱ διὰ Κλήμεντος in Lagarde, Reliq. p. 78 : "καὶ εἴ τινα ἑτέρα βούλοιτο ἐργαζέσθαι." The text gives thus no meaning. According to Bunsen, the Syriac translation has the addition : τοῖ εἴτε κατὰ τὴν προθυμίαν αὐτῆς, which brings out the meaning given.—(43) Lagarde, Reliq. p. 79.—(44) iii. 15.—(45) Epiph. Expos.

fid. c. 21 : "Καὶ διακονίσσαι δὲ καθίστανται εἰς ὑπηρεσίαν γυναικῶν μόνον. διὰ τὴν σεμνότητα ἂν χρεία καταστάιη λουτροῦ ἕνεκα ἢ ἐπισκίψεως σωμάτων."—(46) Lagarde, Reliq. p. 74.—(47) Const. Apost. iii. 15.—Const. ii. 25 has the plural, but the passage has also certainly been retouched, as even the reference to the persecutions having passed over shows.—(48) So I understand the canon when it says, that the deaconesses who turn to the Catholic Church retain their dignity. "We speak, however, of such deaconesses as have been regularly ordained ; if any have received no ordination, they are to be treated entirely as laity."—(49) Jerome on Romans xvi. 1 : "Sicut etiam in Orientalibus diaconissæ mulieres in suo sexu ministrare videntur in baptismo sive in ministerio verbi, quia privatim docuisse feminas invenimus sicut Priscilla ; " ad Tim. iii. 1 : "Similiter eas ut diaconos eligi jubet.—Unde intelligitur, quod de his dicat, quæ hodie in Oriente diaconissas appellant." These passages evidently prove that the institution of deaconesses was, at least in Jerome's time, peculiar to the East, and on the other hand was unknown in the West. We may infer the state of things in the East from the following passage, Ep. ii. ad Nepotianum : "Multas anus nutrit ecclesia, quæ et officium præbeant et beneficium accipiant ministrando, ut infirmitas quoque tua fructum habeat eleemosynæ." Certainly deaconesses are subsequently mentioned also in Gallic synods. Council of Orange (441), can. 26 : "Diaconæ omnimodo non ordinandæ, si quæ jam sunt," etc. ; Epaon (517), can. 21 : " Viduarum consecrationem, quas diaconas vocitant, ab omni regione nostra penitus abrogamus ; " Orleans (533) : " Placuit etiam ut nulli postmodum feminæ diaconalis benedictio pro conditionis hujus fragilitate credatur ; " Worms, can. 73. Fortunatus also tells us, in the Vita Radegundis (Surius Aug. xiii.) of Bishop Medardus, that "feminam manu superposita consecravit diaconam." Except in Gaul, the only trace is found in a quite isolated mention in a Romish Council of 721. Hence I feel certain, that in the rest of the West there were no deaconesses. It is just possible that the institution passed over into the Gallic Church, which had special relations with the East. I scarcely even think this, but suppose that the so-called *diaconæ* in Gaul were only widows and *sanctimoniales* whom those acquainted with the Oriental deaconesses called by this name as resembling them. In this respect can. 21 of Epaon, which says precisely this, is conclusive. With it entirely agrees can. 12 of the Conc. Carthag. iv., which exhibits the "viduæ vel sanctimoniales" as entrusted with the services elsewhere performed by deaconesses. It is also to be observed that all these canons are but the echo of can. xi. of Laodicea, which relates to widows. Nor would it be intelligible why the institution of deaconesses should have been abolished in the West (and it should be remarked that the above canons deal with its abolition), while it was still in a very flourishing condition in the East. All is, however, consistent if the "diaconæ" are widows, since the institution of widows was abolished at the same time in the East also. Lastly, all other church dignities are found mentioned in epitaphs of Italy, Spain, Africa, and Gaul, but not once a deaconess, with the exception of the one case quoted in the text. It is especially important, that also in Le Blant's extremely careful work, Les inscriptions chrétiennes de la Gaule, also a deaconess never occurs.—(50) C. Inscr. v. 2, 6467. The inscription is from Ticinum, "Hic in pace quiescit B. M. Theodora diaconissa quæ vixit in seculo annos pl. m. xlviii." Its date is 539.—(51) Const. Apost. viii. 31.—(52) So especially Conc. Nicæn. c. 19.—(53) Matthæus Blastaras im Syntagma, c. 11 ; comp. Ziegler, de diaconis et diaconissis, p. 362. Const. Apost. viii. 20.—(54) Const. Apost. ii. 57 ; viii. 28. Lagarde, Reliq. p. 89.—(55) Const. Apost. iii. 15, 16 ; viii. 28. Διατάξεις of Hippolytus in Lagarde, p. 9 ; Jerome on Rom. xvi. 1.—(56) Conc. Carthag. iv. can. 12.—(57) Lagarde, Reliq. p. 89.—(58) Const. Apost. iii. 15.—(59) Const. Apost. ii. 7.—(60) Const. Apost. iii. 19. Dieckhoff (in his above-named work, p. 405) does not refer this passage to deaconesses, but, incorrectly as I think, to the wives of deacons. Epiphanius, too, Hæres. 79, 3, and expos. fid. c. 21 (comp. note 45 above), treats (against Dieckhoff, p. 406) of attendance on the sick by deaconesses. Λούτρον here is medicinal waters.

CHAPTER V.

(1) Const. Apost. iv. 2. Quite similarly Clem. Hom. ep. Clem. c. 8. —(2) Const. Apost. ii. 4.—(3) Const. Apost. iv. 3. There is a quite similar passage in Clem. Alex. Fragm. Comm. in Matt. v. 42.—(4) Const. Apost. ii. 26 ; iii. 7 ; iv. 3.—(5) Cyprian, ep. 2.—(6) Ad Cor. i. 38. —(7) Can. Hippolyt. 32.—(8) Philosoph. ix. 12.—(9) Const. Apost. iv. 2.—(10) Tertullian, Apolog. 39.—(11) Tertull. de jejun. 17.—(12) Clem. Alex. Pædag. ii. 1.—(13) Const. Apost. ii. 28.—(14) Βιβλίον Κλημ. in Lagarde, p. 88 ; Hippol. c. 32 ; Const. Apost. ii. 28.—(15) Zahn's Ignatius of Antioch, p. 336. Τὸ χήριον is not a house for widows, but the order of widows, the Viduage.—(16) Const. Apost. iii. 1, 2.—(17) Const. Apost. iii. 5 : "The widow is to think of nothing but praying for the givers and the whole Church ; " Const. Apost. iii. 13.—(18) Const. Apost. iv. 2.—(19) Euseb. H. E. vi. 2.—(20) Euseb. H. E. v. 17.—(21) Euseb. de mart. Palæst. c. 11.—(22) Const. Apost. iv. 1.—(23) Tertull. Apolog. 9. —(24) Inst. vi. 20.—(25) Can. 24.—(26) Lagarde, Reliq. p. 84 ; comp. also p. 164 above.—(27) Vita Cypriani, c. 9, 10.—(28) Cyprian, ad Demetrianum, c. 10.—(29) Id. c. 11.—(30) Vita Cypriani, c. 10.—(31) Id. c. 9.—(32) Euseb. H. E. vii. 22.—(33) Euseb. H. E. ix. 8.—(34) Instit. vi. 12.—(35) Ignatius, ad Smyrn. c. 6 ; Const. Apost. iv. 9.—(36)

Comp. on slaves, Overbeck's article in the Studien zur Geschichte d. alten Kirche, i. p. 158 sqq.—(37) Orat. c. 11.—(38) Tertull. de corona mil. 13.—(39) Instit. v. 15.—(40) Const. Apost. ii. 62.—(41) Const. Apost iv. 9.—(42) Ignatius ad Polyc. c. 4.—(43) Pædag. iii. 11.—(44) Contra Celsum, iii. 49.—(45) Id. iii. 55.—(46) Const. Apost. viii. 32 ; Lagarde, Reliq. p. 87. —(47) Petrus, Alex. lib. de pœnit. can. 6, 7, in Routh, Reliq. iv. 29.—(48) Const. Apost. iv. 6.—(49) Conc. Elib. can. 5.—(50) Cypr. ep. 12.—(51) Cypr. ep. 14 ; comp. ep. 5, 7.—(52) Comp. above, p. 40.—(53) Cyprian, ep. 5, 12, 14.—(54) Const. Apost. iv. 9 ; v. 1.—(55) Euseb. H. E. iv. 23.—(56) Cyprian, ep. 76-79.—(57) Instit. vi. 12.—(58) Id.—(59) Euseb. H. E. iv. 26.—(60) Clem. ad Cor. i. 11, 12 ; Hermæ Past. Sim. ix. 27.—(61) Const. Apost. ii. 3.—(62) Cyprian, ep. 7, 8, etc.—(63) Ep. ad Cor. c. 1.—(64) Euseb. H. E. iv. 23.—(65) In the oft-named Βίβλιον Κλήμεντος (Lagarde, Reliq. p. 80) a πανδοχείον certainly occurs, but it is an ordinary inn, such as existed for travellers of the lower class. Ratzinger (in his above-named work) speaks of a special fund for strangers. But Const. Apost. ii. 38 does not prove its existence. The expenses of lodging, when a member of the Church did not undertake it, were met from the Church fund.—(66) Ad ux. ii. 4.—(67) Comp. Herzog's Real-Enc. under the word literæ formatæ.—(68) Comp. on the whole section Zahn, Christenthum und Weltsverkehr in dem ersten Jahrhunderten.—(69) Basil, ep. 70.—(70) Euseb. H. E. iv. 23.—(71) Athenagoras, Legatio, c. 11.—(72) Tertull. Apolog. c. 39.

CHAPTER VI.

(1) Tertull. de virg. vel. c. 1 ; comp. on Montanism in general, Ritschl, altkathol. Kirche, p. 462 sqq.—(2) Hase, K. G. § 70.—(3) The distinction between commandments and counsels is generally already found in Past. Hermæ, Sim. v. 3, where I cannot as yet find it, but only the contrast between what is always required and what is required under special circumstances, but under these from all.—(4) Orig. in Num. xi. 3 ; ad Rom. iii. (ed. de la Rue, iv. 507).—(5) Cyprian, de habitu virg. c. 23.—(6) Origenes ad Matt. xv. 15 sqq.—(7) Strom. vii. 12, 70.—(8) Origenes in Lev. xi. 1.—(9) Cyprian, de habitu virg. c. 11.—(10) Cyprian, ad Donatum, c. 12.—(11) Cyprian, de lapsis, 35.—(12) Id. c. 11.—(13) Clem. Rom. ad Cor. i. 50.—(14) Barnab. Ep. 19, 8.—(15) Hermæ Pastor. Sim. ii.—(16) Origenes in Lev. hom. ii. 4.—(17) Cyprian, de op. et eleem. c. 1. —(18) Cyprian, de orat. domin. c. 32.—(19) Cyprian, de op. et eleem. c. 2, 5.—(20) Id. c. 2.—(21) Id. c. 6.—(22) Clem. Rom. Ep. ii. 16, 4.—(23) Const. Apost. vii. 12 ; Lactantius, Instit. vi. 12, 41 ; Cyprian, de op. et eleem. c. 26.

…

BOOK THIRD.

CHAPTER I.

(1) Compare on this whole period, especially Richter, Geschichte des weströmischen Reiches.—(2) Ammianus Marcellinus, lib. r. gest. xxx. 4.—(3) Comp. besides Richter Ozanam, Etudes Germaniques, i. 343 sqq.—(4) Ambrosius, Oratio funebria de morte Theodosii M. (Opp. Paris 1569, p. 491).—(5) Compare Harnack's lecture on Monachism.—(6) Salvian, de gubernat. iv. 4.—(7) Salvian, de gubernat. v. pp. 148, 155.—(8) Zosimus, Hist. ii. 38.—(9) Basilius, Hom. in div. c. 5.—(10) Palladius, Hist. Laus, c. 36.—(11) Comp. on this, Hegel, Gesch. der Städtverfassung von Italien, i. 79; Kuhn, Die städtische und bürgerliche Verfassung des Rom. Reiches, i. 77 sqq.—(12) Comp. Rodbertus on the history of the agrarian development of Rome in Hildebrand's Jahrb. ii. 1864, p. 239 sqq.—(13) De gubern. vii. 1.—(14) Ambrosius, de Nabuthe, lib. c. 1.—(15) Compare in general Dureau de la Malle, Economie politique des Romains, vol. ii.—(16) Gregor. M. Hom. in Ezech. 18, hom. ult.

CHAPTER II.

(1) Theodoret, H. E. 1, 10. Julian abolished this award. His successor restored it, but only to one-third the amount. The financial condition of the State had already considerably deteriorated. Besides, the supply of corn was not appointed directly for the poor, but for the Church and its ministers, including virgins and widows.—(2) Chrysostom in Matt. Hom. 66: "ὁ κατάλογος;" and in 1 Cor. Hom. 21: "τῶν ἐγγεγραμμένων πενήτων τὰς ἁγίλας;" Joann. Diaconi Vita Gregorii M. ii. 28; comp. Ducange under the word matricula egenorum. — (3) The diakonia were also called matriculæ, because the poor entered in the matricula, hence called the matricularii, were there provided for. They were a kind of xenodochia or ptochia. Comp. Ducange under the word diaconia. Baronius in martyrolog. ad d. 8 Aug.; comp. Ziegler, de diaconis, p. 36.—(4) Can. 14 of the Synod of Neocæsarea, Nov. 3, c. 1.—(5) Can. 62 of Nicæa, "ut sint septem diaconi, qui ecclesiæ sumptu vivant ac reliqui gratis ministrent."—(6) Ambrosius, de off. min. ii. 15, especially lays this to the hearts of the clergy.—(7) Chrys. in Matt. Hom. 67.—(8) Hom. in 1 Cor.—(9) AA. SS. ad 23 Ian. ii. 499.—(10) Joann. Diac. Vita Gregorii M. ii. 28. 11) Gregor. Nyssa, de paup. amandis, Or. 2.—(12) Chrysost. Sermo de elecm. —(13) Ambrosius, de off. ii. 10.—(14) Chrysostomus, Hom. in Matt. 66, 3. (15) Epiph. Hær. 69, 1; Innocentius, ad Decent. c. 5; comp. Bingham,

Origenes, iii. 599. In Constantinople, Gennadius first orders, that at least the oblations should be left for the clergy of the several churches. Excerpt. Nic. Callisti, i. 13.—(16) Council of Laodicea, can. 57.—(17) Sardica, can. 7.—(18) Cod. can. eccl. Afric. ; comp. Hefele, Conciliengesch. ii. 115; Council of Agde, c. 53.—(19) Council of Orleans, can. 15.—(20) Can. 11.—(21) Jerome on 1 Cor. xi. ; Chrysostomus, Hom. 27 in 1 Cor. ; August. Ep. 54.—(22) Can. 28.—(23) August, Conf. vi. 2; Ep. 22.— (24) Conc. Quinisext. can. 74.—(25) Chrys. in 1 Cor. Hom. 27 ; in Matt. Hom. 31.—(26) This change was effected in Constantinople in 490 (see above, note 15), and at the same time in Gaul ; comp. Synod of Orleans (511), can. 14, 15. In the cathedral church the bishop received a half, in other churches a third.—(27) Chrysostomus, Hom. 50 in Matt.—(28) Hieronym. Ep. 34 ad Nepotianum.—(29) Augustinus, p. 355.—(30) Salvian, de avaritia, ii. 48, ii. 4.—The clergy, moreover, were not legally bound to leave their property to the Church.—(31) De avaritia, iv. 133.—(32) De avaritia, i. 29.—(33) De avaritia, iii. 101.—(34) De avaritia, iii. 80: Cessit sanguini fides et vicerunt devationem religionis jura pietatis.—(35) Zschimmer (Salvian, Halle 1875) has endeavoured to explain and justify Salvian's urgency for wills by the hypothesis, that he was striving against a reform of social relations upon an ascetic basis, a Christian communism. Such a hypothesis is neither well founded nor needed. Salvian only expresses in strong terms what, as we shall afterwards more particularly see, was implicitly held during the whole period.—(36) Chrysostomus, Hom. 64 in Matt. ; Hieronym. Comm. in Ezech. c. 45, 46; August. p. 219.—(37) Synod of Antioch in Encæniis, can. 24 ; vi. Carthag. can. 5 ; Cod. can. eccl. Afric. c. 33. The Romish Synod under Symmachus, 502, in Hefele, ii. 616 ; Synod of Agde, can. 7, 33, 51 ; Epaon, can. 12-17. —(38) Antioch, can. 25; Agde, can. 48.—(39) Agde, can. 33 ; Orleans, can. 22.—(40) Council of Chalcedon, can. 26.—(41) Comp. Richter, Gesch. d. weström. Reiches, p. 339.—(42) xxvii. 3, 14, 15.—(43) Ambrosius, Ep. 18.—(44) Palladius, Vit. Chrys. c. 5.—(45) Augustinus, p. 356, § 13.— (46) Socrates, viii. 26.—(47) Conc. iv. Carthag. can. 51 ; Council in Encæniis, can. 25 ; Carthag. iv. can. 15 ; Con. Apost. 39.—(48) Council of Agde, can. 7.—(49) Ambrosius, de off. ii. 28.—(50) August. Ep. 50.— (51) Gregory very specially promoted the division ; comp. Epp. iii. 11, iv. 42, vi. 49, xi. 29, 51.—(52) Joann. Diac. Vita Gregor. vi. 29.—(53) Very characteristic is in this connection the narrative found in Sozomen, vii. 27, of Bishop Epiphanius of Cyprus, who gave so abundantly out of the Church treasury, that his steward had often to remonstrate with him. Here the steward only is the medium. There is not a word of deacons. —(54) Conc. Chalc. can. xi.: "Περὶ τοῦ μὴ δεῖν τὰς λεγομένας πρεσβύτιδας ἤτοι προκαθημένας ἐν ἐκκλησίᾳ καθίστασθαι." The canon is very differently understood. Many think of deaconesses or upper deaconesses (Hefele).

But it is impossible that the object of the canon was the abolition of the institution of deaconesses, which lasted for centuries longer. Others speak of presbyteresses, but there never were such. πρισβύτιδις are not πρισβυτέριδις or πρισβύτεροι γυναῖκες. These existed only in the sects (comp. Epiph. Hær. 69). πρισβῦτις is simply an aged woman (comp. Tert. 21; Const. Apost. ii. 57, iii. 5), and denotes the aged widows, who in the church presided over the women (Epiph. 79, 4). The canon means nothing else but the entire abolition of the ancient institution of widows in the Eastern Church. —(55) Basilius, ep. 199, c. 24 ; Chrysost. on 1 Tim. v. 9. Comp. Dieckhoff's above-named work, p. 399, notes 54 and 60. —(56) In Ambrosius, de viduis, c. 2, 5, much is indeed said of the good works of widows, but nowhere anything about their official position in the Church. On Augustine comp. Dieckhoff, p. 400, note 59. Can. 12 ad Conc. Carthag. iv. still speaks of widows and sanctimoniales (virgins living a monastic life) assisting at baptism. But this canon may be of older date than Augustine, the so-called canons of Carth. iv. being only a collection of canons of various councils. Besides, even in Augustine we see that the sanctimoniales were beginning to supplant the widows.—(57) Conc. Araus. (447), i. c. 26 ; Conc. Epaon. (507), c. 21 ; Orleans, ii. (513), can. 18: "Placuit ut nulli postmodum feminae diaconalis benedictio pro conditionis hujus fragilitate credatur."—(58) Sozom. viii. 23.— (59) Balsamon, Resp. ad Marci patriarchæ Alex. interrogationem 35. The "inquinatio menstruorum" is stated as a reason for deaconesses no longer having "gradum ad altare."—(60) In the Pontificale Jacobitarum it is said : " Potestatem intra altare nullam habet diaconissa quoniam et quando ordinatur in ecclesia tantum stat." So too in the resolutiones canonicæ of Jacobus Edessenus : Ordinatur non in nomine altaris sed ecclesiæ. They were allowed to administer the communion to children up to the age of five. They could not minister at the altar, but might place the incense, though not utter the prayer aloud in so doing. They washed the sacred vessels and read the Gospel in monasteries for females. Comp. Assemani Bibl. or. iii. P. 2, p. 847 sqq.—(61) Conc. Trull. can. 16.—(62) Ep. 292.—(63) De offic. ii. 10.—(64) De Nabuthe, c. 8. —(65) Ad Hebr. Hom. 11.—(66) Or. xix.—(67) Joannes Diaconus Vita Gregor. ii. 26, 28.—(68) Cod. Just. lib. ii. tit. 25.—(69) Nov. Tit. ix. c. 4, 5.

CHAPTER III.

(1) Chrysost. S. de eleemosynis, Opp. iii. 248.—(2) Augustinus, S. 62, 12. —(3) Chrysost. Hom. 88 in Matt. —(4) Gregorius Nazianz. de pauperibus amandis. — (5) Chrysost. Hom. 85 in Matt.—(6) Augustinus, S. 355, 5.—(7) Compare the fine passage in Chrysostom. Hom. 88 in

Matt., where Chrysostom says that they would all give willingly to the Lord if He came to beg in person, but that we ought to see Him in the poor, who supplicate us.—(8) Augustin. S. 83, 2.—(9) Augustin. S. 123, 5. —(10) Augustin. S. 9, 19.—(11) Chrysostomus, Hom. iii. 1, on penance. —(12) Chrysostomus, Id. Hom. vii. 6.—(13) Leo the Great, 6th Collection Sermon.—(14) Id. 9th Sermon.—(15) Ambrosius, Sermo de eleemosynis, c. 30, 31.—(16) Ambrosius, de Elia et jejunis, c. 20.—(17) Augustin. S. 42, 1; S. 210, 12; S. 206, 2; S. 83, 2.—(18) Gregor. M. Evang. 1 Hom. 5.—(19) Salvianus, de avaritia, ii. 64, 65.—(20) August. Enchiridion, xvi. 70.—(21) August. de fide et opp. c. 26.—(22) Augustin. S. 9, 17-19; S. 56, 11, 12.—(23) Ambrosius, Sermo de eleemosynis, 30, 31. —(24) Gregor. M. Moralia xiii. ; Evang. ii. Hom. 34; 1 Hom. 20.—(25) Cæsarius of Arelate in the Pseudo-Augustinian Sermons, S. 142; in Augustine also the three weeks of fasting, praying, and almsgiving stand together as the three chief, S. 9, 11.—(26) Leo the Great, 8th Collection Sermon.—(27) Id. 11th Sermon.—(28) Augustin. Enchir. xvi. 72.; Id. S. 42, 1, he distinguishes duo genera of alms "erogando et remittendo, erogando quod habes bonum, remittendo quod pateris malum." We find here the root of the distinction—quite general in the Middle Ages— between eleemosynas corporales and spirituales.—(29) Ambrosius, de pœnit. ii. 9.—(30) Augustin. de civ. dei, xxi. 27.—(31) Gregorii M. cura past. 21. —(32) Leo the Great, Collection Sermon 6.—(33) Augustin. S. 172.— 34) Augustin. Enchirid. xxvi. 110.—(35) Comp. also Chrysost. Hom. 27 in 1 Cor. ; Hom. 31 in Matt. ; Hom. 29 in Act. Apost.—(36) Orelli, 4432: "Si quis post nostram pausationem hoc sarcofagum aperire voluerit inferat ecclesiæ Salon argenti libras quinquaginta." Examples of heathen graves, Or. 4428, 4549.—(37) Examples in Le Blant, inscript. chrét. de la Gaule, 207. Si quis hunc sepulcrum violaverit partem habeat cum Juda traditorem—habeat partem cum Gezi—cum Juda gemitus experietur inops —habeat anathema ad cccxviii. Pat (the Council of Nicæa) ; also in Angel. Maio Scriptorum vet. nova collectio v. 216, 217.—(38) Chrysostomus, Hom. 29 in acta: "Ἔθος ὁ δεῖνα ἔχει ποιεῖν τὴν ἀνάμνησιν τῆς μητρὸς ἢ τῆς γυναῖκος ἢ τοῦ παιδίου.—(39) Gregor. M. dialog. iv. 39.—(40) Id. iv. 57.—(41) Id. iv. 55. (42) Comp. my "Studies for a History of Christian Charity in the Middle Ages," in the Zeitschrift für kirchliche Geschichte, iv. 1, p. 73.— (43) Augustin. p. 104 (Cæsarius, 8).—(44) Salvian, de avaritia, i. 29. Augustin. Enchirid. xxvi. 110.—(45) Gregor. M. Mor. xiii. 21; Epp. vii. 25.—(46) Comp. Rothe, Lectures on Ch. Hist. ii. 33. Rentu, Augustinische Studien. Zeitsch. für K. Gesch. iv. i. p. 33.—(47) Comp. Ratzinger's above-named work, p. 112; Chatel's above-named work, p. 203 sqq.—(48) In the homily on Luke xii. 18, Opp. ii. 49 sqq.— (49) Ambrosius, de Nabuthe, lib. c. 1.—(50) Hieronym. Ep. ad. Hedibium. —(51) Ambrosius on Luke viii. 13.—(52) Hom. ad pop. Antioch. Hom. 2.

(53) Augustin. S. 50.—(54) Chrysost. in Matt. Hom. 90.—Hieronym. Ep. ad Hedib.—(55) Enarrat. in Ps. cxxxi. 5, 6 : "Abstineamus ergo nos, fratres, a possessione rei privatæ aut ab amore si non possumus a possessione."—(56) S. 61, c. xi. 12.—(57) De off. i. 28 : "Natura igitur jus commune generavit, usurpatio jus fecit privatum."—(58) Chrysostomus, Hom. xi. in Acta Apost.—(59) August. S. 219 ; in Ps. cxlvii. ; S. 249.— (60) Hieronym. Ep. 150.—(61) Comp. above, Book i. chap. 3, note 4.— (62) De Nabuthe, lib. c. 12.—(63) The impossibility of carrying it out is proved by the fact, that the ethic of the Middle Ages wore itself out at this separation.—(64) De off. i. 9.—(65) De off. i. 32 sqq.; ii. 15.—(66) Basil, to adduce but one example, had but one tunic and one cloak, and slept on the earth : Gregor. Naz. Or. 43, c. 61.—(67) Comp. on Macrina : Greg. Nyss. de vita Macrin. Opp. ii. 177 ; on Olympias ; Böhringer, Chrysostom and Olympias ; on Nonna ; Ullmann, Gregory Nazianzen. — (68) The chief sources are the letters of Jerome, which, as being well known, I omit quoting particularly.—(69) Hieronym. Ep. 27, ad Eustochium.— (70) Hieronym. Ep. 26, ad Pammachium.—(71) De Rossi Inscr. christian. 62.—(72) Corp. Inscr. v. 2, 6286.—(73) Le Blant, Inscr. 386.—(74) Id. 407, 450.—(75) Id. 17.—(76) Id. 425—(77) Id. 426.—(78) Id. 451.— (79) Id. 218.—(80) Id. 516.—(81) It is of special interest to ascertain when the formula, "pro redemtione," or "pro remedio animæ," afterwards so current, first appeared. Chatel, in his above-named work, appeals for its occurrence at this time to Maio Call. script. vet. v. p. 216, but the inscriptions there found are of more modern date. The one dated inscription given in Le Blant, Inscr. 374, is the only certain one, and this, as at least the oldest inscription yet discovered, well deserves a place here. It is twofold. On the one side is :—

        Hic requiescit
        In pace bonæ
        Memoriæ Arenberga
        qui vixit annos xxviii
        Obiit in pace viii.
        Kalendas Maias
        Avieno viro cla
        rissimo consolo.

On the other :—

        Hic reliquit
        leberto puero
        nomine Mannone
        pro redemtionem
        animæ suæ.

With due regard to the corrupt Latin often occurring in inscriptions, the words can only mean, that Arenberga gave freedom to a slave named Manno, "pro redemtione animæ suæ." Avienus appears in the consular Fasti

450, 501, 502. Even adopting the last date, the inscription is the oldest I know of, in which the formula occurs. It is also found in Paulinus of Nola, who, Ep. xiii., congratulates Pammachius for having cared, by means of alms, for the salvation of Paulina's soul. "Pro salute" occurs more frequently. I have, however, been able to find no inscriptions in which almsgiving is mentioned "pro salute animæ," but only the building of churches and such acts. In Corp. Inscr. v. 1583-1616 are found a number of inscriptions relating to the restoration of the church of St. Euphemia in Aquileia, undertaken in 515. It is frequently said of the contributors, that they did thus "Pro salute sua et omnium sanctorum." Willmanus seems to regard as Christian an inscription from Africa. Corp. Inscr. viii. 8629 : "Fl. Innocentius num (mum) pro salute sua suorumque omnium tesselavit." I regard it, however, as doubtful. The formula "pro salute" is also heathen, and therefore first borrowed by Christians; comp. e.g. Orelli 1214, where some one dedicates an altar to Jupiter O. M. "pro salute sua suorumque." Here too the leaning of the Christian custom on the heathen is visible. In the Corp. Inscr. Græc. 8616 an inscription occurs, according to which a certain Elias has built a martyrium of St. Theodore, "ὑπὲρ ἀφέσεως ἁμαρτιῶν." It is of the year 417, and comes from Syria.

CHAPTER IV.

(1) Comp. Häser, Geschichte der Krankenpflege, p. 3 sqq.—(2) So e.g. Moreau, Christophe, Histoire de la misère, ii. 236. Comp. Ratzinger's above-named work, p. 93. Chatel's, p. 264.—(3) Morin, Histoire critique de la pauvreté in the Mem. de l'Acad. des inscr. iv. 305. Comp. Chatel's above-named work, p. 265.—(4) Ratzinger, who advocates this view (p. 25), quotes only one passage in Sozom. vi. 13 (p. 86, note 1), for the existence of such special rooms for strangers in the bishop's residence, but "τὸ ἐπισκόπικον καταγώγιον" there denotes the bishop's dwelling itself, and there is not a word of a "diversorium" for strangers. Can. 12 of the so-called Conc. Carthag. iv. also proves nothing.—(5) In Pontus, e.g., as Epiphanius (adv. Hær. 56) mentions, the ξενοδοχεῖον is called πτωχοτροφεῖον. In Conc. Chalcedon, c. 8, too, they are called πτωχεῖα.—(6) St. Zotikus, who had already departed from Rome for the new Rome on the Bosphorus, is said to have founded there a lobotrophium, which Constantine restored (comp. Du Cange, Fam. Byz. p. 165). This is the only example of a xenodochium under Constantine. The information, however, is very doubtful. According to Du Cange, it is derived from later sources. It is also suspicious to find, that the first institution of the kind should have been quite a special one destined for the maimed and for cripples. The

spurious canon 70 of Nicæa also shows that there was a tendency in later times to remove institutions of the kind to the earliest possible date. The Apostolical Constitutions know as yet of no xenodochia, neither do Eusebius and Lactantius.—(7) Sozom. v. 16.—(8) Gregor. Naz. Or. 30, in laudem Basilii.—(9) Basilius, Ep. 143.—(10) Sozom. iii. 16.—(11) Chrysostomus, Hom. 66 in Matth.—(12) Palladii Vit. Chrys. c. 5.—(13) Comp. the Acts of the Council, 11 Session, Hefele, ii. 471.—(14) Conc. Chalcedon, c. 8.—(15) Muratori, Script. Ital. Medii ævi, iii. p. 575.—(16) Hieronym. ad Oceanum—ad Pammachium.—(17) The passage is remarkable. Exposit. in Ev. Joann. tr. xcvii. c. 16, "et xenodochia et monasteria postea sunt appellata novis nominibus, res tamen et ipsæ et ante nomina sua erant." On the xenodochium of Leporius, S. 356, 10.—(18) Anastas. pp. 82, 107, 114.—(19) Can. 13-15.—(20) Gregorii M. Ep. viii. 14; x. 11; iii. 24.—(21) Du Cange, Constantinopolis Christiana, iii. 163 sqq.—(22) Baronius, Ann. eccl. ad a. 610.—(23) Procopius, de ædificiis Justin. 1, 2, 9, 11.—(24) Theodoret, Hist. Relig. c. 21.—(25) Comp. in Palladius, Hist. Laus. The history of St. Piterum. Weingarten (Ursprung des Mönchthums Zeitschr. für K.-Gesch.) here passes an error. He thinks the statement "οὕτω γὰρ ἐκεῖ καλοῦσι τοὺς πάσχοντας depends upon the words ἐν τῷ μαγειρίῳ ἐστίν," so that "she is in the kitchen" is an expression currently applied to the insane. It simply depends on the preceding "μίαν ἔχομεν σαλήν."—(26) Chrysostomus, Hom. 66 in Matth.—(27) Baronius, Ann. ad 610.—(28) Histor. Laus. c. 6.—(29) Compare on the legal condition of institutions, Jacobson's article "Wohlthätigkeitsanstalten," in Herzog's Real-Enc. xviii. 234 sqq.—(30) Comp. Gregory's letter, quoted note 20 above.—(31) Corp. Inscr. viii. 1, 839.—(32) Comp. Rückert, Culturgeschichte des deutschen Volkes, ii. 345.—(33) Gregor. Nazianz. Or. 30.— (34) De Vogüe, La Syrie centrale, Paris 1877, pp. 128, 138. The inscription on the pandocheion in Deir Sem'an is as follows : † X M Γ (Christus Michael Gabriel) 'Εγίνιτε τοῦτο τὸ πανδοχεῖον ἐν μηνὶ Πανεμου β' τοῦ ζκφ' ἔτους Χριστὶ βοήθι.—(35) παρατιμπτοντις, comp. Gregor. Nyss. Or. 30.—(36) Theodoret, Hist. Eccl. v. 18.—(37) Socrates, iv. 23 ; Palladius, Hist. Laus. c. 140.—(38) Hist. Laus. περὶ Παινσιου καὶ Ἡσαίου.—(39) Paulinus, Nol. Ep. ad Severum.—(40) Gregor. M. Ep. iii. 24.—(41) Gregor. M. Ep. xi. 10.

CHAPTER V.

(1) Salvian, de gubernatione Dei, vi. 173.—(2) Conc. Laodicea, can. 36. —De Rossi, Inscr. christ. 172 ; Hieronym. in Matt. 23 ; Chrysost. ad pop. Antioch. Hom. xix.—(3) Chrysost. Hom. in Annam. iv. 3.—Hom. 6 in Genes. Hom. 7 in Lazarum. Comp. Cod. can. eccl. Afric. 61.-- (4) Theodoret, Ep. 147.—(5) Chrys. Hom. 36 in Cor.—(6) Salvian, de

gubernat. Dei, iv.—(7) Id. vii. 24 : " Populus Romanus moritur et ridet."
—(8) Hom. 30 in act. ap. Comp. also Neander, Chrysostomus, ii. 107.—
(9) Aristoteles, Nicom. Eth. x. 7, 6-8.—(10) Ambrosius, de off. i. 11.—
(11) Hieronym. Ep. ad Pammachium.—(12) Gregor. Nazianz. Ep. 8, 9.
—(13) Augustinus, Confess. viii. 6.—(14) Neander, Chrysost. 1, 90 sqq.—
(15) Hieronym. Ep. ad Rusticum.—(16) Cassian, de Instit. Cœnob. x. 23.
—(17) Comp. generally Harnack's excellent lecture.—(18) Basil's Ascetic
Instructions, iii. 1.—(19) Basil's Greater Rule, c. 37.—(20) Id. c. 41.—
(21) Id. c. 38.—(22) Hist. Lausiac. c. 39. Theodoret, Hist. Relig. c. 10.
—(23) Chrysost. in Matth. Hom. 8.—(24) Theodoret, Hist. Relig. c. 10.—
(25) Sulpicius Severus, Dial. ii. 8.—(26) Id. i. 25.—(27) Augustinus, de
op. monach. c. 35.—(28) Id. c. 33.—(29) Regul. S. Benedicti, c. 48.—
(30) Id. c. 39, 40.—(31) Basil's Abridged Rule, 302.—(32) Sozomen, i. 11.
—(33) Socrat. iv. 23.—(34) Cassian, Instit. Cœnob. x. 22.—(35) August.
de moril. eccl. cathol. i. 31.—(36) Theodoret, Hist. Relig. c. 22.—(37)
Basil's Greater Rule, 15, 38, 53. Chrysost. adv. opp. vit. Monast. iii.
12 sqq.—(38) Regula S. Benedicti, c. 4.—(39) Id. c. 46, 53.—(41) Gregor.
M. Dial. ii. 28 ; iv. 22.

CHAPTER VI.

(1) Ambrosius, de offic. ii. 29.—(2) Conc. Elib. (305 or 306), can. 56.—
(3) Council of Arles, can. 7.—(4) Basilius, Ep. 61.—(5) Synesii Epp.
57, 58, 72.—(6) Theodoret, H. E. iv. 6.—(7) Comp. on Sanctuary
Bingham's Antiquities, iii. 353 sqq., and the article "Sanctuary" in
Herzog's Real-Enc. — (8) Gregor. Nazianz. Or. de laude Basilii. —
(9) Augustin. Ep. 268.—(10) Council of Orleans, 511, can. 1.—(11) Comp.
Neander, Kirch. Gesch. i. 490.—(12) Council of Agde (506), can. 7.—
(13) Id. can. 7.—(14) Can. 32.—(15) Gregor. M. Ep. ix. 102.—(16)
Council of Agde, can. 56.—(17) Council of Orleans (538), can. 26 ; Leo
M. Ep. iii. 1.—(18) Conc. Chalcedon, can. 4.—(19) Council of Orleans
(541), can. 24.—(20) Gregor. M. Ep. v. 12.—(21) *E.g.* Neander, Kirch.
Gesch. ii. 52.—(22) So *e.g.* Ratzinger in his above-named work, p. 91.
—(23) Hom. xxix. in Genes.—(24) August. Enarr. in Ps. cxxiv. 7.—(25)
Chrysost. Hom. 29 in Genes.; 22 in Ep. ad Ephes.—(26) Augustin. de
civitat. Dei, xix. 15.—(27) Id. xix. 16.—(28) Chrysost. Hom. 15 in Ep.
ad Eph.—(29) Augustin. de civitat. Dei, xix. 16.—(30) Augustin. de
sermone Dom. in monte, i. 59.—(31) Council of Epaon (517), can. 34.—
(32) Council of Orleans (511), can. 3.—(33) Council of Epaon (517), can.
39.—(34) Basilius, Ep. 73.—(35) Chrysost. Hom. 40 in 1 Cor.—(36)
Augustin. S. 355 and 356. Hist. Lausiac. c. 19.—(37) Le Blant, Inscript.
374, 379.—(38) Neander, Kirch. Gesch. ii. 53.—(39) Comp. Hefele, Con-

ciliengesch. i. 755.—(40) Theodor. Cantuar. capit. eccl. c. 16. "Graecorum monachi servos non habent, Romani habent." Comp. Wasserschleben Bussordnungen der abendländischen Kirche, p. 146.—(41) Council of Agde, can. 29. Council of Orleans, can. 7.—(42) Can. 27.—(43) Euseb. Vit. Const. iv. 27.—(44) Can. 13.—(45) Council of Orleans (541), can. 30. Council of Macon, can. 16.—(46) Gregor. M. Ep. iii. 9 ; v. 31 ; vii. 35. Comp. on slavery generally, Overbeck, Studien zur Gesch. der alten Kirche, i. 1875, p. 158 sqq.—(47) Theodoret, Ep. 23.—(48) Examples in Augustin. Ep. 241. Gregor. M. Ep. i. 44.—(49) Chrysost. Hom. 61 in Matth.—(50) Comp. note 47 above.— (51) Ep. i. 51.—(52) Ep. i. 36.—(53) An example in Gregor. M. Ep. v. 12.—(54) Basilius, Ep. 85, compare also 36, 37, 76, 83, 84, 110, etc.—(55) Theodoret, Ep. 43.—(56) Gregor. M. Ep. v. 12.—(57) Gregor. Nyss. Ep. canon 6.—(58) Basilius, contra feneratores.—Chrysostom, Hom. 5 in Matth.—(59) Ambrosius, de Tobia, c. 5, 6. —(60) Id. c. 8.—(61) Id. c. 14.—(62) Conc. Elib. can. 20 ; Laodicea, can. 5 ; Carthag. iii. can. 16 ; Hippo (393), can. 22, etc.—(63) Augustinus contra Faustu, xix. 25 ; Hieronymus in Ezech. vi. 18.—(64) Augustin. Ep. 268.—(65) Gregor. M. Ep. i. 44.—(66) Gregor. M. Ep. v. 8.— (67) Comp. the work of Ambrosius, de Nabuthe, which is especially directed against such tyranny.—(68) Ambrosius, de off. ii. 29. Augustinus, Ep. 252.—(69) Baron. Ann. ad a. 401, v. 142. Neander's abovenamed work, ii. 115.—(70) August. S. 171.—(71) Ep. 252-255.—(72) Synod of Vaison (442), can. 9 and 10. Also the second Synod of Arles and the Synod of Agde.—Augustinus, Ep. 98. "Aliquando etiam quos crudeliter parentes exposuerunt nutriendos a quibuslibet, nonnumquam a sacris virginibus colliguntur et ab iis offeruntur ad baptismum."—73) Can. 17.—(74) Cod. Theod. xv. 8, de lenonib. i. 1, 2.—(75) Ambros. de off. ii. 15. It is striking that both Salvian and Augustine approve of and defend houses of ill-fame. Salvian says : " Minoris quippe esse criminis etiam lupanar puto ; meretrices enim, quae illic sunt, foedus connubiale non norunt. Ac per hoc non maculant quod ignorant." Augustin thinks that there must be a drain, so that the whole house may not be infected.—(76) Cod. Theod. ix. 3, de custod. reor. i. 7.—(77) Can. 20.— (78) Ambrosius, de off. ii. 15.—(79) Gregor. M. Epp. iii. 17 ; v. 34 ; vi. 13, 23, 35 ; vii. 23.—(80) Gregor. M. Epp. iii. 17.—(81) Theodoret, Hist. Rel. c. 10. On the price of prisoners comp. also Le Blant, Inscript. ii. 287.— (82) Hieronym. Ep. 125 ad Rusticum.—(83) Ambrosius, de off. ii. 28.— (84) Gregor. M. Epp. ii. 46.—(85) Le Blant, Inscr. 543.—(86) Socrat. H. E. vii. 21.—(87) Theodoret, Ep. 70.—(88) Theodoret, Epp. 33 sqq.— (89) Comp. especially Rückert's excellent work, Culturgesch. der Deutschen.

INDEX.

ABBOT in a Xenodochium, 338.
Acacius of Amida, 392.
Agapæ, 75, 89 sq., 144, 181 sqq., 253.
Agde, Synod of, 265.
Alimentations, 18 sqq.
Alms, 4, 30, 34, 36, 45 sqq., 52 sqq., 66 sqq., 84 sqq., 121 sqq., 142 sqq., 211.
Alms as sacrifices, 149.
Alms sin-atoning, 211 sqq., 279 sqq., 294.
Ambrose, 228, 263 sqq., 270 sq., 280, 284, 297, 299, 302, 303, 305, 364, 383, 384, 388. 390.
Amulets, 342.
Anchorets, 349.
Annona, 11 sqq.
Antioch, Council of, 265.
Antoninus Pius, 15, 18.
Antony, St., Life of, 349.
Apocrypha, 52, 213.
Apostolic legends, 135.
Arca, 22, 27.
Arcani disciplina, 172.
Aristotle, 33 sqq., 345.
Arles, Synod of, 362.
Arsacius, 326.
Asceticism, 127, 350.
Assurance of salvation, 294.
Astrology, 342.
Athanasius, 363.
Athenagoras, 202.
Athens, 9 sq.
Auguries, 342.
Augustine, 264, 275, 277, 278, 286, 288, 294, 299, 301, 328, 347, 372, 373, 380, 383.

BANQUETS, heathen, 24, 32.
Baptism, 212, 284.
Barnabas, epistle of, 122, 126, 211.
Basil, 275, 296, 352, 353, 381.
Basilias, the, 327.
Begging, 4, 33, 201, 243, 249, 271.
Benedict of Nursia, 355, 357, 359.
Bishop, the, as ruler of the relief of the poor, 161 sqq., 246 sq., 256 sq.
Bishop, the, the manager of church property, 260 sqq., 306.
Blesilla, 310.
Blind, the care of, 330.
Brephotrophia, 330, 380.
Bureaucracy, the, under Constantine, 221, 235.
Burial funds, 23.
Burial of the dead, 24 sq., 189, 289 sqq.

CÆSAREA, Synod of, 248.
Cæsarius of Arelate, 287.
Calling. See Vocation.
Candidus, 391.
Capitalism, 104, 110.
Carthage, Synod of, 176.
Cassian, 358.
Celibacy, 207, 319.
Chalcedon, Council of, 261, 328.
Chrysostom, 264, 254, 259, 274, 276, 279 sq., 297, 298, 300, 302, 354, 363, 372, 373, 374, 380.
Children, education of, in monasteries, 359, 386.
Church, the, the reliever of the poor, 56 sq., 88, 137 sqq., 141 sqq., 160 sqq., 246 sqq.

422 INDEX.

Church arca, the, 27, 142.
Church, the, and charity, 57, 70 sq., 397.
Church, attendance at, 254, 378.
Church discipline, 179, 205, 207, 283.
Church penance, 213.
Church prayers, 144, 147.
Church property, 260 sqq.
Cicero, 303.
Clement of Alexandria, 121, 129 sqq., 150, 169, 182, 208.
Clement of Rome, 147, 210, 211.
Clement, book of, 157, 164, 172.
Clement, epistle of, 214.
Clergy, the, mode of life of, 136.
Clientela, 17.
Collections, 87, 94, 153 sqq., 201.
Collegia, 21 sqq., 141 sqq., 290.
Colonia, 240, 379.
Colonies, 16.
Community of goods, 73 sqq., 127, 296 sq., 300.
Congiaria, 13.
Constantine, 203, 219 sqq., 385.
Constitutions, the Apostolic, 135, 139, 142, 157 sq., 162, 169, 172, 196, 214.
Copiates, 335.
Corban, 143.
Corn, distribution of.
Cyprian, 120, 123, 142, 150, 152, 153, 156, 161, 187 sq., 207 sq., 213 sq., 288.
Cyril of Alexandria, 361.

DAMASUS, 261.
Deaconesses, 70, 79 sqq., 165 sqq., 248, 276 sq.
Deacons, 74 sqq., 144, 160 sqq., 248, 266 sqq.
Defensores, 261, 332.
Departed, masses for the, 287, 291, 396.
Diocletian, 385.
Distributions at graves, 25, 289.

ELIGIUS, 322.
Elvira, Synod of, 195, 362.
Emancipation of slaves, 190 sq., 367.

Endowments, 24 sqq., 42, 125, 290, 396.
Ephraem, 327.
Epiphanius, 172, 310.
Episcopal jurisdiction, 365.
Episcopal intercession, 384.
Epitaphs, 24, 289, 320.
Essenes, 126.
Ethic, ancient, 32, 304 sqq., 341, 345 sq.
Ethic, Christian, 304 sqq., 341, 396.
Ethic, double, 206 sqq., 344 sq.
Eudaimonism, 32, 304.
Eudoxia, 384.
Eustochium, 311.
Exemption of a hospital, 338.
Expiations of the heathen, 30.
Exsuperius, 390.
Eustathius, 376.

FABIOLA, 310, 312.
Fasting, 154 sq., 205, 285, 350, 358.
Financial ruin, 118.
Flavian of Antioch, 363.
Foundlings, 186, 385.
Free trade, 109, 239.
Furia, 310.

GANGRA, Synod of, 297, 298, 376.
Gazophylacium, 149, 245.
Generosity, 34 sq.
Germans, the, 222, 231, 393.
Gifts to the Church, 255 sqq.
Gladiatorial games, 342.
Gnostics, 126.
Good works, 283, 293.
Goths, 388, 393.
Gratian, 331.
Gregory the Great, 266, 285, 286, 287, 291, 294, 332, 368, 370, 379 sq., 382, 389.
Gregory Nazianzen, 275, 278, 300, 347, 371.
Gregory of Nyssa, 307, 382.

HERMAS, 121, 127, 128, 154.
Hippolytus, Canons of, 157, 173.
Honorius, 380.
Hospitality, 91 sq., 123, 198 sqq. 325 sqq.

INDEX. 423

Hospitals, 14, 312, 323 sqq., 395.
Hospitia. See Xenodochia.
Humanity of the heathen, 19 sq., 41.

IGNATIAN Epistles, 169.
Institutionalism, 324 sqq., 397.
Intercession, 151, 185.
Interest, reception of, 383.
Interments, 24, 189.
Irenæus, 148, 149, 156.
Isidor of Pelusium, 375.

JAMES, St., 87.
Jerome, 256, 302, 310 sqq., 328, 347, 352.
Jerusalem, Church of, 73 sqq.
Jews, the, slave dealers, 378 sq.
John, St., 87.
John the Almoner, 262, 330.
Judaism, Post-exilian, 51 sq., 213.
Julian, 271, 326.
Justin Martyr, 142, 149.

NATIONAL Church, idea of, 206 sqq.
Natural products, delivery of, 114, 238.
Neocæsarea, Council of, 163.
Nicea, Council of, 173.
Nonna, 307.

OBLATIONS, 142 sqq., 254.
—— for the dead, 150 sq., 287 sq.
Old Testament, 48 sqq.
—— in the Church, 143, 156 sqq., 213, 259, 268.
Olympias, 307 sq.
Ordination, 267, 369.
Origen, 152, 155, 157, 207.
Orleans, First Synod of, 363, 378.
—— Second Synod of, 267, 323, 379, 386.
Orosius, 230.
Orthodoxism, 342 sq.

PALLADIUS, 336, 349.
Pammachius, 311 sq.
Parabolani, 335 sq.
Pastophorium, 149.
Paul, St., 82 sq.
Paula, 310 sq., 316.

Paulina, 311, 316.
Paulinus of Nola, 313 sq., 317, 318, 389.
Pelagius II., 328.
Perfection, Christian, 207, 299, 320, 344.
Persecutions and charity, 124, 195 sqq.
Pity in the ancient world, 37.
Placilla, 336.
Plato, 32 sq.
Poor, houses for the, 326 sqq.
Poor, the amount of means for the relief of, 158, 261, 330.
Poor, relief of the, 5, 9, 30, 39, 44 sqq., 105, 125 sq., 141 sqq., 177, 178 sqq., 246 sqq., 274 sqq., 323 sqq., 358 sqq.
Poverty, estimation of, 126, 146 sq., 208, 296.
Poverty, extent of, 99 sqq., 233 sqq., 248 sqq.
Poverty, voluntary, 200, 298.
Prayer, 152, 213, 285.
Presbyters, 76 sq., 160, 170.
Prisoners, 190, 195, 357 sqq.
Private benevolence, 85 sq., 124, 138 sq.
Proletariat in Rome, 99.
Prostitution, 357.
Provincial towns, 15, 100, 238.
Purgatory, 291 sqq.

RECLUSES, 350.
Reformation, 398.
Repasts, Christian. See Agapae.
Repentance, 205.
Rome, 10 sqq., 21, 99 sqq.

SALVIAN, 229, 257 sq., 281 sq., 294, 343, 345, 393.
Sanctuary, the Church's right of, 365.
Sardica, Synod of, 384.
Satisfaction by good works, 285.
Seneca, 35, 111.
Seven, the, 75 sqq.
Sick, the care of, 186 sqq., 311.
Sins, forgiveness of, 211 sqq., 282 sqq.

Sins, mortal, 205, 213, 283 sq.
Sins, venial, 284, 291 sqq.
State and Church, 224 sqq.
Stips, 22, 30, 31 sq., 136 sqq.
Stoicism, 35 sqq., 58, 346.
Strangers, care of, 91 sq., 323 sqq.
Sub-deacons, 163.
Symmachus, Pope, 328.
Symmachus, Prefect, 263.
Synesius of Ptolemais, 363.

TALMUD, 54.
Taxation, 100, 105, 113 sq., 234 sqq., 381.
Tertullian, 23, 27, 127 sq., 132, 142, 150, 181 sq.
Testamentary bequests to the Church, 258, 331.
Thalassius, 330.
Theodoret, 380, 381, 392.
Theodosius I., 271, 364.
Theodosius II., 335, 361, 386, 391.
Thomas Aquinas, 396.
Tithes, 46, 122, 148, 156 sq., 259.
Toledo, Synod of, 386.
Tours, Synod of, 260.
Tribute, reception of, 383.

Trulla, Council of, 253, 269.

UNIVERSALISM, 38 sq., 41, 49, 59, 67.
Usury, 48, 111, 242, 381 sqq.

VALENS, 223, 388.
Valentinian I., 256, 386.
Valentinian II., 271.
Vandals, 388, 392.
Victor, Pope, 137.
Vigilantius, 319 sq.
Vocation, 83 sq., 136, 317, 319, 397.
Vows of the heathen, 30.

WEALTH, greatness of, 104, 241.
Wealth, estimation of, 127 sqq., 146 sq., 208 sq.
Widows, care of, 45, 90 sq., 184 sq., 323, 361, 384 sq.
Widows, houses for, 184.
Widows, institution of, 80 sq., 165 sqq., 184, 267.
Worship, connection between, and charity, 30 sqq., 145, 394.

XENODOCHIA, 267, 323 sqq.

www.ingramcontent.com/pod-product-compliance
Lightning Source LLC
Chambersburg PA
CBHW022105290426
44112CB00008B/558